Note for Librarians: A cataloguing record for this book is available from Library
and Archives Canada at www.collectionscanada.ca/amicus/index-e.html

Printed in Victoria, BC, Canada.

ISBN: 978-1-4251-2069-6

*We at Trafford believe that it is the responsibility of us all, as both individuals
and corporations, to make choices that are environmentally and socially sound.
You, in turn, are supporting this responsible conduct each time you purchase a
Trafford book, or make use of our publishing services. To find out how you are
helping, please visit www.trafford.com/responsiblepublishing.html*

*Our mission is to efficiently provide the world's finest, most comprehensive
book publishing service, enabling every author to experience success.
To find out how to publish your book, your way, and have it available
worldwide, visit us online at www.trafford.com/10510*

www.trafford.com

North America & international
toll-free: 1 888 232 4444 (USA & Canada)
phone: 250 383 6864 ♦ fax: 250 383 6804
email: info@trafford.com

The United Kingdom & Europe
phone: +44 (0)1865 722 113 ♦ local rate: 0845 230 9601
facsimile: +44 (0)1865 722 868 ♦ email: info.uk@trafford.com

10 9 8 7 6 5 4 3 2 1

Dedication

For my wife, Sylvia, and daughters, Jocelyn and Monique; and grandson, Cameron for all their support and patience during the writing and production of this book.

A special dedication goes to my father, Louis P. Cote for all his support and encouragement through the years.

Acknowledgements

I owe special thanks for all the help and encouragement in writing this book to help those individuals achieve a better understanding of criminal justice. It is a noble profession.

I owe and like to offer a special thanks and gratitude for Brauni Joleen Cudjo, a criminal justice graduate student for her dedication and tireless effort in helping to edit this book. The following is what she wrote about the book:

> "Editing this book may not have initiated my life-long learning choice of becoming an undergraduate or obtaining a Bachelor of Science in Criminal Justice Administration at the University of Phoenix nor continuing on in their Master of Science/Administration of Justice and Security program. On the contrary, what this editing experience definitely did was not only validated but also richly enhanced and reinforced my education and future management career goals; enriched my purpose in life to include: defending and enforcing integrity, sharper ethical decision-making skills and professionalism. The author's methodology takes managing for success to newer and greater moral heights and could receive universal acceptance of global marketing high performance management."

I would like to thank my daughter, Monique Cote for the wonderful creation of the cover for this book. She is a wonderful graphic artist. Her ideas in developing this cover are preciously treasured.

I would like to offer a special thanks to my friend in Florence, Arizona Raul Manjarres who during my tenure as police chief in Florence help offer support and guidance through difficult times. He helped my family and me after Hurricane Katrina. You cannot ask for a better friend.

I would also like to think my friends and colleagues at the University of Phoenix for their support. The University of Phoenix of Phoenix is a great institution and I consider it an honor to teach and develop courses for them.

I would also like to thank the following reviewers: Chief Bob Ingulli, Florence, Arizona; Captain Robert Birdsall, Apache Junction, AZ; Ken Savoie, Delgado Community College, New Orleans, LA; and Steve Isham, University of Phoenix, Phoenix, AZ. Their comments were truly appreciated.

Lastly, I would like to thank my friends and family while I was embarking upon this endeavor. Their guidance and support are deeply cherished.

Disclaimer

The intent of this book was to illustrate examples through my life experiences while working in four police departments. The intent was not to embarrass, offend, defame or ridicule anyone by mentioning names or not mentioning a name in particular scenarios. The focus was on a particular situation as it affected my police department or to illustrate an example how some people can be counter productive in an organization.

Table of Contents

Preface

Perseverance, imagination and hard work will accomplish things beyond your wildest dreams. Believe in yourself and your expectations will be realized. Never give up.

There is information out there somewhere that gives some details about the process involved for individuals who want to be a supervisor, middle or upper management or police chief. Where do you find this information when you need it? You can ask others who were in involved in the police chief process or simply ask a police chief. Gathering this information is certainly not easy. What happens after that? Even though it is a tremendous challenge, many are ill prepared, lack the experience and have no clue what to expect. Some are doomed to fail and often it is not the person's fault. A newly hired Police chief may be caught up in political turmoil from the very beginning and not realize it until it is too late. I wanted to write a book on the realities of police management from a practitioner's point of view. There are no theories here but actually practices.

I have a diverse background in law enforcement totally 30 years of service, of which the last 11 years has been Police chief in three communities in three different States. First, I want to give you an overview of my background. I started my career with the Bristol Police Department, Bristol, Connecticut and rose through the ranks and attained the rank of Captain. In 1988, I became the Chief of Police in Somersworth, New Hampshire and stayed for seven years. The seacoast area is a beautiful, picturesque area.

Next in 1995, I moved to Florence, Arizona, a small community and the home of the Arizona State Prison. Senior Citizens (snowbirds) from all over the United States spend the winter there. My stay lasted two years and not by my choice. The town fathers did not want to renew my two-year contract. Even after all the accolades about the job, I was doing I fell victim to the political environment. I was let go without cause. You can say that I was fired, let go or they did not renew my contract. The result was my being without a job for the first time in over 27 years in law enforcement. What did I do to disserve this disgrace? In retrospect, there was nothing I could have done to avoid the inevitable. There were circumstances beyond my control. You can do everything right and still have problems. I will go into detail about the political environment so that the reader will have a better understanding and have better insight in dealing with these problems or issues.

Being without a job, I decided to apply for Chief of Police positions in parts of the country I was interested in. I finally accepted a Police chief position in Fort

Lupton, Colorado. Fort Lupton is located about 25 miles northeast of Denver and a short distance from the mountains. The scenic mountain area was a wonderful place to visit anytime during the year. What they say in the travel brochures about Colorado is all true. I stayed in Fort Lupton just over two years. Why the short stay? In a short period, I accomplished the objectives and goals that I set out to do and I needed at this point to move to the east coast to be closer to my family.

The purpose of this book is to help others to achieve their goals, whether it is a promotion in their own organization or aspiration to be a Police chief in some community. Some organizations may want to use this book for management training. Other professionals may want to have some insight into the inner workings of a police department and the political dynamics involved. There will be pitfalls and I will help you to avoid them. This book will provide the details to be a successful Police Executive in a law enforcement agency or simply to be a better manager of a division or supervisor. You might have detected that I did not specify small, medium or large agency. You can be successful in any law enforcement agency. Once you get there, how do you stay?

I will walk you through the process from developing a cover letter, resume, interview process, offer of employment and much more. How can you prepare for an interview process? There are many different types of interviews but with certain information, you can be very well prepared. It is important to know what to do if you should be offered a police chief job or a management position. Just because you are offered a police chief position that does not mean it is the job for you. Even though the competition is tough, you still can be selective. I will discuss the different ways to beat out the competition and even as simple as a promotion. I will speak of the move, transition and some of the first things you should do once you get to your destination. What happens if you get fired? I have been there. There is life after being terminated. Learn how to overcome these problems.

I will go into detail about my experiences. You will learn first hand about my career, some of the pitfalls and what I did to overcome them. Often times, I heard about and read about accounts of individuals who were frustrated at the process. Sometimes it is a long road but there is a brass ring at the end of the tunnel. I want to pass along my experiences to you so that you can succeed. Law enforcement is a wonderful profession and it can only get better with true professionals. Having information readily available to use as a guide can only help you to improve and thoroughly understand the organization. I wish that I had this information when I first started.

The book is divided mainly into two parts; the first dealing with my experiences so that the reader can get an insight into what is involved through my eyes and the second dealing with specific aspects of the police department. I think that it is important to find out what other individuals had gone through to get an appreciation of the dynamics and complexity of police operations. Many textbooks generally do not discuss any of these issues. Many of these textbooks are a rehash of older principals and concepts. It is not necessary bad if they still work. What I look for is not only new ideas but also something from a practical approach or just "common sense." What is it truly like to be a police chief? Each chapter deals specifically about an aspect of the police organization from a contemporary point of view. This book can be used simply as a refresher for the Police Executive or Manager or just as a textbook in an advanced management college course. It is my sincere belief that this book can be very useful for both.

Chapter 1
The Beginning

In order to provide someone with insight into my philosophy of supervision and management, I must first discuss my career so that you can get some insight into what I am discussing. I will take the reader for a journey, a magnificent ride during my 30 years in law enforcement. Through these insights the reader will begin to understand what is involved climbing the career ladder. I will pass on what I sincerely believe are the necessary elements to be a successful police executive or manager. Can everyone be a police chief? The answer to that question is simply no. One has to be very careful about the "Peter Principal" – reaching the level of incompetence. You have to realize that many officers just want to be a front line police officer and there is nothing wrong with it. Sometimes, when I look back and reflect, I ask myself did I make the right decision? Many officers in every level of the organization aspire to be promoted to a higher level.

Many individuals have the desire, experience and education to lead a law enforcement organization. Some find it very difficult and a traumatic ordeal especially on the family. It is not an easy thing to accomplish. However, I will provide some insight, a "guiding light" if you will to make it possible to achieve your goals. I will provide numerous tips and suggestions, like a checklist to be one-step in front of the competition. Paying close attention to detail will give you knowledge based upon my experience.

It is a goal for many officers to one day to be promoted to a higher rank. In the beginning all I wanted to be was a police officer and to do good job. This was how it was with me. Gradually, over time I wanted to be good enough to become a sergeant. I believe fate and luck had something to do with it. It started when I became eligible to take the test for sergeant. I was with the Bristol Police Department, Bristol, Connecticut for five years and I thought it would be neat to take the big test. At that time back in 1975, the test was passed on 70% passing grade and seniority. Other words, all one had to do was pass and have seniority. It did not matter what you scored. There were no oral boards or any other mechanism to evaluate performance. You could have gotten 100% and if someone else had seniority, you were out of luck. Old lady luck was with me that day. Another officer and I passed the test and everyone else flunked. Guess what? I was promoted to sergeant.

Prepared?

Was I prepared to be a sergeant? No! The department after about a year sent me to Babson College to attend the New England Institute of Law Enforcement Management. It was a very good school that lasted three weeks but it was truly inadequate to prepare me for the day-to-day operations of a police department. Learning about theories was good for some but for me I wanted much more. What I was looking for was how to be a good supervisor using training and experience as a guide. Theories will not help you. However, I made many friends who provided me some direction and insight into what I was doing. Networking is an important part of the process. I learned that other supervisors were in a similar situation. We actually learned from each other's experiences. I knew that if I wanted to succeed I would have to do help myself to succeed. This is a key element for success.

Fortunately, I worked the graveyard shift for four years leading a squad of officers. Taking this low profile on the night shift was the place to stay out of trouble. New sergeants were low on the seniority list so the third shift is where everyone goes. I decided to do something about my inadequacy. I had received my associate degree in science from Tunxis Community College, Farmington, Connecticut in 1976. I continued my education at Western Connecticut State College in Danbury, Connecticut. I knew that education was another key to success. Above all, I had the awesome responsibility as a leader so it was important to me to be a success. Eventually, I received my bachelor in science degree in criminal justice administration and later a masters of science in criminal justice administration from the University of New Haven.

Develop Confidence

I learned from my education and on the job. I observed the good sergeants and lieutenants and paid attention to how they operated. I asked many questions and eventually the principals of supervision began to make sense. I had confidence in myself to make a decision. Everyone kept telling me that it is just "common sense". It is more than common sense. You have to know what you are doing. Sure, I have made mistakes, but I learned from them. Guess what! I paid attention to others who made mistakes and was able to avoid the pitfalls. There are so many that you could be up to your "neck in alligators" and not realize it until it is too late. There will be many surprises but by talking the right approach, you can minimize your risk.

You cannot worry about failing. If you think about it too long, you will. By thinking where you are and where you want to go is helpful in the planning process.

I stand by my old formula for success, using the five P's – Prior Planning Prevents Poor Performance.

The Bristol Police Department was a good leaning environment for me. I had many mentors but the one who stands out the most in my mind is Lieutenant Carl Suchodolski (retired), a Patrol Commander and Lieutenant Buzz Barton (deceased), the Detective Division Commander. I learned some practical aspect of management from them. They took the time to teach and coach these important concepts. Coaching is an important part of the management learning experience. If I did not ask questions, I would just observe and learn. I am curious by nature and if I received an answer to a question then I would need to know why?

In 1980, I took a test for lieutenant and was fortunate enough to pass it. During the time from 1980 to 1985, I was assigned to different divisions. I was the commander of the Detective Division, Traffic and Planning Division, and Training and Planning Division. There was a time when I was the shift commander. Ultimately, I was responsible for the entire city in the absence of the captain and chief. That was a scary thought. This experience helped prepare me for my ultimate goal as Chief of Police.

During this time, I truly learned about supervision and management. From 1981 to 1985 I drove about 60 miles three times a week to West Haven, Connecticut to attend the University of New Haven. I finally completed my graduate work and was awarded a Masters of Science degree in Criminal Justice Management. I was only one of two individuals in the department who had a master's degree. Having a Master's degree would unlock many of the doors or a least get an opportunity to be invited to an interview. The degree is not everything, but it sure helps. I have known many individuals who had a degree and were smart but did not have any practical knowledge to be successful.

In 1985, I was promoted to Captain. I thought to myself what a wonderful opportunity, but I found myself relegated to night duty. Most of my personnel assigned to me were on days and the boss worked nights. Imagine the boss was never around. It did not make any sense. I was the Commander of the Support Services Bureau responsible for Communications, Traffic, Court Liaison, Records, Citizen Complaints and Internal Affairs and duty chief on the second shift (3 pm – 11 pm, Tuesday through Saturday). The Police Commissioners thought in their infinite wisdom that it would be better to have a captain work nights and Saturday. Here common sense went out the window. The other captain was assigned as Commander of Operations working the day shift.

Organizationally, it would have been better to assign the Operations Captain to nights and weekends for better continuity of the command structure. The unity of command principle was violated all the time. What I am saying is that the organization could have been much better and I will leave it as that. I stayed at this position for three years and rather enjoyed it. I did the best that I could consider the circumstances at the time. At this point, there was much more to learn about management. I thought that I knew a great deal but in reality, it was not nearly enough.

Sometimes, we look to others for guidance and as a mentor. Chief John Roche (retired) of the Plainville Police Department, Plainville, Connecticut gave me a great deal of insight. He was a long tenured Police chief who was chief for many years and well respected not only in the community but law enforcement circles as well. I remember his words very well. "Throw out the management books and use good old common sense." What he was saying was that you have to look beyond what is written in the management textbooks. A police chief who governs his or her actions by what is written in the textbooks is in for a rude awakening. Textbooks are used as a base of knowledge or guide. Each situation or problems as they come up may not be addressed in any textbook. Common sense seems to be a recurring theme. What troubles me about it is what is it? Knowledge combined with practical experience seems to be the prevailing thought. One has to acquire experience first as a police chief and you have to get hired by some community to get the experience. It seems to me that it is a paradox.   As we go further along, the reader will be able to get a better understanding of what it means.

I worked for Police Chief John F. Oliver who is now happily retired in Florida. Matter of fact, I enjoyed working for him and learned a great deal about what management is all about. He probably knew best how to play the political game and I paid attention. I considered him the master political artist. He was police chief in Bristol for 10 years. There were some trying times but he weathered the storm each time. He was friendly with everyone including the police commissioners and police union. Getting along with a union was a feat in itself but he did it. I will go into more detail about the unions later. You have to know how to play the game smart; otherwise, you will be the odd person out. I do not care how smart you are, if someone or a group wants to get rid of a police chief chances are good they will succeed.

Sometimes I wonder how someone can be so lucky and obtain their first police chief position after their first try. I realized that there were other possibilities. Sometimes it was just plain luck. Other times it is being at the right place at the right time. There is no explanation for it. It just happens. Last, the political situation is very prevalent at the time. We will discuss the politics in the decision-making process and I will devote an entire chapter to it.

Applying For a Police Chief's Position

The process for application and submission of a resume is a very time consuming process. There are individuals who have been applying for police chief positions all over the country and never had an opportunity to be offered the job. There are others who have been police chief multiple times, like me. We are commonly referred to as "carpet baggers." Why is it that one cannot find a job and for others it is a little easier? The reality is that they will never achieve their goal. There will be others who will be asked to resign, get fired or in some way find themselves terminated.

Like many others, it took me a long time to be offered a police chief position. It took a great deal of patience, perseverance and understanding from my family. I was persistent in this ordeal. I never gave up. I was eventually offered a Police chief position in the City of Somersworth, New Hampshire. Somersworth is a small city of about 11 thousand people. The city borders Maine and is considered part of the seacoast. This community has some light industry, commercial establishments but is mainly residential. By this time, I had participated in several other interviews for police chief so this particular one was not very stressful. It was a standard type of interview, a question and answering sessions lasting about 45 minutes.

I did not realize it but there were spies lurking about. It seems that some local officers wanted to know who the competition was. They had someone on the look out for any out of state vehicles. All they had to do was get a listing on the plate to see who owned the vehicle. The scheme went awry because my wife dropped me off near the building and drove off to spend some time shopping nearby. They never found out who the mystery person was from out of state until they hired me. I could not believe that someone could resort to that type of tactic. I did not make a big deal about it and rather dismissed it for the time being but I registered it in the back of my mind. This so-called insignificant attempt to find out about the competition would prepare me for the little surprises that would come up. There will always be surprises.

Being Prepared Is Smart

I always learned to be prepared prior to going to an interview. It is important to find out what were the circumstances for the prior chief's departure. It helps to find out what the City is looking for in a chief. It would not be too smart to walk into a powder keg and not have a chance to succeed. What is the real reason? Other words what is the agenda of the City Manager or town fathers. The former chief, believe it or not, was secretary of the Somersworth Police Association and was in charge of the Coke machine. It was alleged that he misappropriated funds from the Coke machine for his own personal use. I was amazed that a police chief could be caught up in a scandal of this magnitude. Whether it is true or not, I do not know and did not want to know. The city manager handled it and the matter was concluded. The former chief was terminated from his position. It is best not to get involved in these past incidents, speak of, or take sides.

His trusted subordinates who were friends made the complaint. One of these subordinates was vying for my position and the same one who had spies near the interview site. I think the picture was getting a little clearer. The moral to the story about the Coke machine is do not personally handle any money whatsoever. Handling money could get you into trouble.

I accepted the position and eagerly began my duties. I will never forget when I opened my desk drawer I found an antique pistol. I asked the Acting Chief, a Sergeant about the ownership of the gun and he did not know. I told him to enter the firearm into evidence. I always did wonder if the gun was purposely left in the drawer as a test to see what I would do. I was wondering if I was being set up? I did not want to be paranoid about it but it struck me odd that it was there and they did not tell me about it. I also realized that the acting chief was a sergeant and not a lieutenant. I guess the City Manager had a good reason to pass over ranking officers.

My former city manager was a good boss to work for. I enjoyed working for him very much even though he did not last long. He resigned his position and reapplied for it. It seems that he wanted to withdraw his letter of resignation and the City Council refused to let him. The politics behind the scenes were very strong. Because I was new, I was not privy to this type of information. It was interesting that they let him go though the interview process for his job. Sometimes I cannot understand the rationale of a town or city council.

Surprise, Surprise

Going into this position, I thought I was fully prepared and was very knowledgeable about what I was getting myself into. You have to be prepared for the unexpected. After a few days as police chief, the city manager called me to his office and wanted me to take care of a little problem. No big deal, I could handle anything. He wanted me to take care of the four mummified babies that were in an old trunk in the evidence room. I sat there in shock. I thought that he was kidding me but it was for real. I said, "Are you kidding me?"

It seems that a resident during the early 1980's opened an old trunk that she was keeping for someone who had passed away long ago. She opened it and to her horror found four mummified babies wrapped in old newspapers at the bottom. Nothing ever developed from the investigation. Eventually the mummified babies were kept in the trunk in the evidence room and forgotten. No one knew what to do with the babies. It seems that an autopsy could never prove the babies were alive.

I went into the evidence room myself to see first hand. The trunk was very old perhaps early 1900's and yes indeed still wrapped in newspaper were the babies. The papers were dated early 1950's. What a mystery! By this time the media was asking questions. There is a lesson to be learned here. Be prepared for the unexpected. You never know what may be in store for you and it may never come out of the interview process or the newspapers. There always seems to be a hidden agenda. The city manager wanted me to find a way to deal with this problem.

First thing I did was to call the State Attorney General office. The Assistant States Attorney guided me properly and after about a week the police department received authorization to bury the babies. With the assistance of a local funeral home we were able to properly bury the babies at the local cemetery and the funeral director even donated a small headstone. The local media was asking me questions about the investigation. I confidently told the reporter that there was nothing new and the babies were finally being put to rest. If the babies were never alive at birth, then there could not be a homicide. This was the official closure to the investigation. This task should have been performed long ago prior to my arrival. In the end, I was proud that I did the right thing and took steps to resolve this dilemma for the community.

Learn From Wisdom

Somersworth was a wonderful learning experience. There were many other situations occurring during my seven years that I will discuss in later chapters. Before I move on, I would first like to speak of one old sergeant who retired about six months after I was hired. His name was Roger Witham, a dear friend who passed away a few years ago. He was probably from the old school of policing but he was a likeable individual. He was a loyal and a dedicated police officer and was the epitome of community policing. Quite often we would have some candid conversations and he would say to me, "I know what you are doing." "My son goes to college and he is studying management." I would just smile and walk away. Yes, there was a method to my madness. I did not just wing it. I had a methodical plan that I was putting in place to bring this agency up to professional standards.

At that time the department did not have a good reputation and it was considered a "dumping ground" for police chiefs. Prior to my arrival every police chief either resigned or fired since the early 1970's. If I had known all the facts, I probably would not have accepted the position. However, I do like a challenge. Matter of fact, no one lasted longer than five years. I was determined to make it last longer than five years and I did. I served with distinction for seven years.

During that time, I became involved with the New Hampshire Association of Chiefs of Police and eventually served on the Board of Directors. I became associated with some of the finest people whom I had ever known. **Networking** is in my opinion an integral part of being a police chief. Some chiefs for whatever reason refuse to get involved and as such miss a great deal of information and as important provide input into an organization. I learned much from many chiefs who had been chiefs for a long time. There was a reason for longevity and it will make sense to the reader. The average tenure nation wide is about three years for a police chief. During my time, I saw many chiefs come and go just in my vicinity and some lasted for only a short time. The record I think is about a month. Imagine being fired after just being on the job for a short time. This person must have made a huge mistake or got one of the town fathers very upset. Sometimes it does not take much and it is a reality check.

There are courses on police chief survival and I attended them as well as many others. I did get some insight but I think perhaps some of these courses fell short of expectations. The reason is simple. There simply is not enough time to cover everything and all situations. Perhaps, some of these situations never occurred yet. I believe that some chiefs self-destruct while others have no control over the situation.

Do Not Overstay Your Welcome

It was time to move on for several reasons. I believe that one can overstay his welcome especially for an outsider. I accomplished as much as I could for the department given the restraint regarding the budget. It was getting to a point that I was operating on a bare bones budget, which affected morale and productivity. It was time to try for another department. I decided to target the west and mid-west area of the United States.

In 1995, I interviewed for a police chief position in Florence, Arizona. I was offered the position and after considerable thought accepted the position. Knowing what I know now it was a big mistake and in hindsight should have turned it down. Some political factors should have been considered very carefully. The Town of Florence, an old, historic community is situated between Phoenix and Tucson. Just as a point of trivia, "Murphy's Law" starting James Garner and Sally Fields was filmed there. I loved the idea about bring professionalism to policing to this small community. Here is the interesting part. The best way to describe it is that there was political chaos. The Town Council was undergoing a council recall. Four members were being challenged. The town manager fired the former police chief, who was still very influential in the community, and is the mayor today. Just picture this. The former police chief was like a lunatic yelling and cursing at the town manager. The town manager had no alternative but to fire him. This person was simply out of control. The town manager did what he thought well. It turned out to be an unpopular decision. **You can do the right thing and still lose.**

Expect the Unexpected

About three months later the special election occurred and the four members of the town council were ousted. I could not believe it. The first order of business when the new members of the Town Council took over was to fire the town manager. In a display of the truest professional that I have ever known, he calmly gathered his paperwork, stood up and thanked the Town Council for the opportunity to serve. He then left the council chambers. At this point, everyone was in the state of shock especially me. I was now the person on the "chopping block" who had been recommended to be the police chief by the former Town Manager and former Town Council.

Shortly thereafter, the mayor called a staff meeting to reassure everyone that their position was not in jeopardy. Sure says the lion calling the sheep into the lion's den for slaughter. The mayor sounded convincing but I did not know what to believe.

When I was hired, I negotiated a two- year employment contract with a six months severance clause. The council knew this and probably decided to keep me around for a while. In reality they needed me to restore order and rebuild the police department. The department was in complete disarray. The police department existed but there were no programs in place, no policy and procedures and many basic fundamentals of management were violated or ignored.   The police department was there in name only. My task was to develop this organization into a respected, professional police department.   I tried to make the best of a bad situation.

Even though I reported to the town manager, the Town Council appointed me. It was as if I did not have a boss. I was responsible to the Town Council. In the manager and council form of government it should not have happened. The town manager would assume no responsibility and it would definitely hurt later on.

I stayed with the Town of Florence exactly two years to the day. Without any warning or prior notification, the Town Council voted not to renew my contract. I was simply devastated. I was without a job. It must have been a well-kept secret. I had no idea that my job was in jeopardy or they were dissatisfied with my performance. To the contrary, the Town Council gave me rave reviews regarding my performance and had given me a substantial increase in pay after my performance review. The town manager relegated the performance review to the Town Council. No one had anything bad to say about my performance. I kept asking myself the same question, why? I am sure there are many other chiefs who met similar fate.

During my discussion in the other chapters, I will talk more about the problems that existed. Sometimes there are circumstances beyond the Chief's control. You have to tell yourself, "It is not your fault." Many external factors played a part in my departure.

After the Council voted, I gathered up my papers, got up and left. I was in a state of shock. I could not bring myself to say anything. I felt ashamed and humiliated. I felt that I had failed. Sometimes ones mind can be your own worst enemy. I am sure many others who had suffered a similar fate simply faded away and were never heard from again. I could have given up and pursued another line of work.

Do Not Give Up

Guess what? I decided that they were not going to beat me. I decided to apply for another police chief's position. Many questions raced through my mind. Who was going to hire an old washed up former chief. There is life after losing your job. You do not die or vanish unless you choose to do so. I have seen too many former chiefs quit and I was not going to be one of them. The moral to the story is **do not quit.** If you take the right steps, you can get hired again. I will discuss these steps. There are exceptions such as unethical types of behavior and misconduct. These individuals need not apply because they will never get hired again as a police chief. There are certainly ways to get you fired. By out right stupidity, it is the worst way.

Florence was a lesson well learned. However, there were many positive points and I think we can say that about any community. I do have to say one thing about the Town Council members. They treated me very well, believe it or not, during my tenure. They supported many of the changes and programs that I had put into place. My impact upon the police department and community still remains today. There were many external factors that played into the political hands. I made many friends and I was truly sad to leave the community. There was no way that I was going to live in a community and have everyone say they feel sorry for me or there goes the former chief. The community was appalled by the action of the town council. Even though the community was in shock, the silent majority remained silent. If the people do not agree with the actions of the Town Council why did they not do something about it? I believe that the people did not want to go through another recall and the fact remained that I was an outsider. The Town Council's action was law and there was not anything I could do about it.

Setting the Record Straight

Sometimes it is best to not look behind but in this case it was hard. I know that I probably should not have but in this situation I got out my pen and wrote a letter to the editor of the local newspaper to let the citizens know the circumstances for my sudden departure. Everything was done in secret and I wanted the truth be known. The citizens only knew that the Town Council voted not to renew the police chief's two-year contract and the circumstances were a personnel matter. Any time you read in the newspapers about a dismissal of a police chief, the town fathers usually refuse to discuss it. The cloak of secrecy that a town or city government uses for an excuse is called a "personnel matter" This seems to be a recurring theme by government officials. Why hide from the truth? Granted, there are many individuals who deserve to be fired and would not want the truth printed in any of the newspapers. My reputation was on the line and I wanted to set the record straight. I spoke of the meeting in executive session about the trumped up accusations and outright lies. I guess that the council members wanted to believe the lies from others. It will take a complete analysis of the situation to completely understand the dynamics of politics. This present council did not appoint me so they had no ownership. It seems that they perceived me as tainted because the former Town Council hired me. You would think that a rational person might want to get the facts right first before rushing to judgment. After thinking about it now, it is somewhat humorous how it all went down.

All the work that we a team had accomplished went down the drain. The Town Council in their rush to hire a police chief selected a cousin of one of the council members who had been out of law enforcement for 18 years and had recently retired from the Arizona Department of Corrections. What an idiotic move and the people did not say anything. Where was the silent majority? All the good personnel either resigned or terminated within the first year. It takes a good three to five years to rebuild a functional police department.

Lawsuits

One indicator whether a chief is effective or not in how the department is managed is the **number of lawsuits**. It is not a sole indicator but if there are many outstanding lawsuits such as excessive use of force or sexual discrimination then it should be a wake up call. There has to be some underlying reasons and the council should be paying closer attention.

If an aspiring police chief wants to succeed in a community, the Town of Florence is a glowing example of what could happen. Florence is just one community but similar situations happen in other towns or cities as well. You can **learn from your own mistakes, but also learn from others** as well. If you make the same mistake twice and make the same mistake as other, then you may suffer a similar fate. You will get what you deserve.

Forget It and Move On

You probably thought by now that I initiated a lawsuit. No, I did not. My reasoning is simple. They abided by my contract and paid me severance pay. They just terminated me Without Cause, which means that they did not have to have a reason. No one in their right mind would hire me if I had an active lawsuit against the town. I decided to put it behind me and move on with my life. Another lesson learned. We must **try to forget and move on**. You cannot dwell on the past. I would like to make it clear that I am no longer bitter, and at the same time have no regrets. I truly felt sorry for them. Sometimes it is hard to forget. In the end it is their loss and some else's gain.

I was not sure that I was going to get hired again, but I began to apply for police chief position with vigor. I began to get calls for interviews. Thinking to myself, I knew that it probably would be an uphill battle to land a job. Within six months, I had two offers for a police chief position. One was in Fort Lupton, Colorado and the other was in Montevideo, Minnesota. Both communities had good and bad points. Obviously, Minnesota would have been in a colder climate. After much thought, I decided to accept the police chief position in Fort Lupton, Colorado. Fort Lupton is a small community of about 6,500 people situated about 25 miles northeast of Denver and near the Rocky Mountains. What a beautiful place. This community was growing and they were in the process of building an 18-hole public golf course. It seemed to me an ideal place to work.

Another Fine Mess

It looked like I was being pigeonholed as a hired gun to clean up a department. This was my third police department. Was it going to be like Florence? The circumstances were very similar except this time the City Council was already recalled and the new Mayor and Council Members were in place. The previous council had fired the police chief but the new council let him resign and gave him some going away money to keep the matter from going to court.

The former chief was with the department for about 12 years. Originally, he was with the Brighton Police Department, a community about 10 miles south of Fort

Lupton and left the state to accept a police chief position in a small community. He came back to the State of Colorado to take over the Fort Lupton Police Department. He was not what one might consider a carpetbagger. He was local and had lived in the area for a long time. I wondered why he fell into disfavor after a long tenure?

It seems some of his personnel decided to make a complaint against him for sexual harassment, favoritism and problems in hiring practices. It seems his problems started after the former City Administrator terminated from his position. The former chief was close to him and things got worse after the interim city administrator took over. Apparently, there was a concerted effort to get rid of him. I believe my theory about **staying too long in one place** is coming true again. One can get too complacent; too trusting and letting down your guard are the key ingredients in this particular case for failure. Some of his own personnel were out to get him. This seems to be a **common theme** in each of my previous departments. By the time that he realized what was happening, it was too late. The prior chief was history. I did not want to make a mistake and dwell on the past. I did not know the former chief and was not interested in his demise. When I took over the department, it was a new beginning. We needed to focus in on the future and move forward.

I was led to believe that the department was dysfunctional, but in reality it was not that bad. It needed some fine-tuning. That was the perception from the City Council, other city staff, community and even some police officers. I knew that the department suffered from a poor public relations image. A poor public image and bad media coverage could spell doom. I knew that the department badly needed leadership. There were too many factions splitting the department and it did not help matters with the way the department was organized. There were three sergeants, each in charge of a shift and each reported directly to the chief. Each sergeant pretty much did their own thing according to the way they wanted to do it. Goals and objectives of the department were not a priority, only for each individual sergeant and did not enter into the picture at this point. It was unfortunate because the department had excellent, dedicated personnel. They just need a focal point and I was going to provide it.

Introductions to Staff

As usual there were going to be many surprises that Management 101 did not prepare me for. You would think that after three college degrees including a Master's of Science in Criminal Justice Management they would have prepared me better to tackle these unique problems. My first priority was to acquaint myself with my personnel. They never saw me before and I was coming in from out of state. They were probably as nervous as I was. I conducted a department meeting to introduce myself and to reduce any anxieties about the direction the department was going to take. I did the same thing in my previous departments and it worked out very well. Having a meeting **sets the tone** for things to come. It was a good move on my part. My priority was to get to know the personnel, learn about the department and the community as quickly as I could. The points being, you have to **hit the ground running**.

A chief cannot sit back in his chair and expect everything to happen. It does not matter whether a chief is from a small, medium or large agency. The **shoe leather needs to hit the pavement** as a former chief use to say. Chiefs need to **manage by walking around**. I delved into the job with earnest. I needed to quickly get the department back on track and move forward. There were too many external factors affecting the department's progress.

Another Surprise

Sometimes, there was a surprise. The shock of my life occurred when my investigator called me from home and wanted to have a meeting with me. I thought that he was having some type of marriage problem. He said that I would probably want to have my lieutenant in the meeting and have it tape-recorded. All kinds of thoughts went through my head but I waited for the two o'clock meeting. I observed the officer walking into the building with another person whom I learned was his preacher. He sat down at my conference table and he calmly informed me that he had been stealing cocaine from the evidence room and using on and off the premises for the past three months. I rather sat there in shock for a minute. He related that he felt guilty about it and wanted to get it off his chest. He knew that his career as a law enforcement officer was finished. It took a great deal of courage for him to come into my office and confess and I admired him for it. He would have been the last person in the world I could have thought to be addicted from drugs and we were his supply. Matter of fact, it could have been a long time before anyone found out if ever that he was taking drugs from the evidence room. This person was responsible for the property and evidence room. The drugs were taken from court cases already disposed of and were in a pile to be destroyed. Thankfully, none of the other court cases were compromised. Perhaps, we would have never found out what he was doing. Another lesson was learned here. Always have someone **audit the money and drugs**. Do not trust any one person for this task. It could lead to disaster for the police chief later on.

I was presented with a new problem and I had to deal with it. I placed the detective on suspension and immediately initiated an internal investigation. I also had the Weld County Sheriffs Office conduct a separate criminal investigation. It was not too long before the results came back. Even though everyone knew the outcome, we had to conduct an independent investigation even with the admission.

Ultimately, the detective was terminated from his employment with the City of Fort Lupton and he was criminally charged as well.

There Is No Perfect Department

Actually, with my prior experience as a police chief did not have too many problems. There would be discipline problems and some personnel turnover but that is to be expected. Because we were so close to the Denver Metro Departments, we were like a training ground. Sometimes it was frustrating but it was to be expected. You have to keep in mind that there is **no perfect police department.** As such, things will go wrong from time to time.

My tenure with the Fort Lupton Police Department lasted just over two years. After 30 years in law enforcement I decided to retire. It was time to consider family first and we chose to live in North Carolina. It is closer to Connecticut where my father still lives. The City Administrator, Mayor and Council Members were all disappointed that I decided to leave. It was a good feeling to know that he appreciated my work and that I will be missed. Fort Lupton was good to me. It was a **good match** for the community. For one reason or another town fathers always brings up at the interview process the need to match the person to the community. It sounds good but sometimes I do not think they even know what they want. How could anyone determine this after a 45 minute interview? There are many factors to consider why someone is chosen over another during the interview process or whatever he or she decides to call it. We will talk more about this later.

After everything considered it was time to move on. I had accomplished many things beyond my wildest comprehension.   I probably could have stayed another couple of years but not more. I believe that one can overstay their welcome. Even long tenured police chiefs can get into difficulty. Figuring out how long a police chief should stay is difficult because it depends upon many external and internal factors. The point is the chief should be aware enough to recognize these issues and problems and take action before the ax falls. Many police chiefs, including myself are caught completely by surprise but keep in mind there are always some telltale signs.

Chapter 2
The Process

Assuming one has the experience and education, there has to be some logical starting point in the process. Generally, someone should have at least 7 to 10 years in law enforcement and should be at the rank of lieutenant or higher. The advertisement will list the minimum qualifications for the position and they usually have listed a bachelor degree in criminal justice or a related field. There are some that even lists a master's degree in criminal justice or related field. Sometimes they list the master's degree as preferred and list a preference for the FBI National Academy. The bottom line is if you do not possess the minimum qualifications listed in the advertisement **you need not apply.** The important consideration is how do you get from the big pile to the short stack of applications for further consideration? The process is quite involved considering municipalities will usually in some cases start with one hundred or more applications and most will meet the minimum qualifications. Just making the first cut is quite a feat.

What communities are looking for is a similar match. Other words, your chances are better if your community that you work in is close in size to the community that you are applying. If you were already working in a community of 12 thousand people it would make not sense to apply for a chief's position in a large metropolitan area. Chances are you will not make the first cut even if you have a great deal of experience as a police chief executive. The odds will improve tremendously if you are more selective and stay with the size department you have experience.

The Competition

Depending upon the size and location of the community, you can expect 50 to 100 or more individuals submitting their resumes for the position. To make matters worse, these individuals probably have just as much experience as you do and possess similar credentials or better. Much of the competition will already be existing police chiefs and high-ranking officers, such as captains and deputy chiefs. The competition will be fierce. Usually one or two persons from the department that you will be applying for will be vying for the same job. However, it is possible to obtain your goal and beat out the competition if you are **determined and persistent** enough. You need to develop a **mind set** that you can do it and not worry about the competition because you will be going up against individuals who have been chief of police multiple times and are comfortable with the process. You have to be **confident**.

If you still want to continue, you can read on and pay particular attention to the detail.   The information presented will provide you with enough information to be better prepared. Sometimes you can "blow" it the first time, simply because you did not know what to expect. Let us face it there are no two interviews alike. What separates one who succeed and one who does not? Sometimes it is luck or politics but more often then not; it is someone who is better prepared. You can increase the odds to get invited to the interview process by being more knowledgeable and better prepared. Keep in mind that the town fathers have an underlying agenda. It is important to try to find out or have a good idea so that you will be better prepared for the interview.

Thinking On Your Feet

I still remember my first interview. It seemed my "heart was in my throat." We all go through this type of reaction because of fear of the unknown. It is a natural reaction to stress so being nervous is good. However, keep in mind the more you do it the better and more confident you will be for the next interview. You just need to develop confidence so that stress is controlled. You are probably more worried about doing well and not able to thing clearly. I know all about it. Once we get the fear of the unknown out of the way, we can do a much better job controlling the stress and are able to think "on your feet" better.

The first step in this process is to decide where you want to go. If you are interested in your own state then your selection and opportunities are definitely limited. If you are interested in another state, then you have to investigate the certification process for that state. Anything is possible. It all depends upon how badly you want the job. If you do not care which part of the United States that you are interested in then you will increase your opportunities to be invited to an interview. It would be better if you targeted certain parts of the country rather than apply to anything and everything all across the United States. The goal is to get invited to an interview and the more you are invited to an interview the better odds you will have to be hired. I approach interviews with the same intensity and you will find that there are many similarities with each.

Once you decided where you want to apply, then you are ready to begin. First, you have to make sure that your family supports what you are doing. Even though it may be your career this change in location will affect your entire family especially teenagers.

Include Your Family in Planning Your Career

Even though my family was supportive, when I finally accepted a police chief position in Somersworth, New Hampshire the reality set in. We would have to sell our home in Bristol, Connecticut and move to New Hampshire. Little did I realize that my youngest daughter would now become a senior at a strange high school? She was not very happy about the prospect of moving and leaving all her friends behind. If I had to do it all over again, I would definitely include my children in the discussions and the ramifications. I probably would have given the decision more thought. It is very important to include your family in this important decision.

The Cover Letter and Resume

Once you have decided where you want to go now you can send your cover letter and resume. First, it is every important to provide all the information requested in the advertisement. If you leave anything out you may be rejected. Sometimes they want you to include additional information such as your transcripts from your college and credit checks. It seems kind of unnecessary to request all this information when they will have 50 or more applicants. It is a great deal of information to sift through, but it is their community. Sometimes you cannot understand their rationale. If you want to apply for the position, you will have to follow their instructions. If you think about it, it is a quick and easy way to eliminate someone who is not interested. No one wants to waste their time.

The cover letter is extremely important. It may be the difference between you getting invited to an interview over someone else. The object is to get selected in the initial screening and make the short list. What should be included in the cover letter? The cover letter should only be two or three paragraphs and no more and limited to only one page. It is an opportunity to **sell you**. You have to give them a reason to hire you. Write about your accomplishments that are in line with contemporary law enforcement. Other words, if they are looking for an individual versed in Community Policing, then write some specifics about what you had done. Even better, if you helped design a new trend setting program this would be a great opportunity to highlight your achievement. This is where you have to be specific and make sure you address what they are asking for in the advertisement. The cover letter should stand out from all the rest. There has to be something in it to grab their attention for them to put your resume into the short stack. Most of the time the screener is just quickly looking at the highlights so quality and not quantity is the order of business.

You probably have heard it all before. It is extremely important that your cover letter is free from spelling errors and is grammatically correct. Chances are that you will not get a second look if there are glaring errors. I know. When I reviewed cover letters and resumes, I usually did not read any further if the cover letter was full of mistakes. Why should I take this person seriously if he or she is not careful enough to take the time to construct a nice cover letter? You have to be considerate of the reader. Another fatal error that most people make is **not proof reading**. Let a friend or spouse and others give your cover letter a critical look. Do not be too sensitive. You need their honest opinion this time. No one likes to have their egos hurt. As you are reading it ask yourself this question. What is in the cover letter that may attract a prospective employer? Put yourself in the place of the reviewer. Cover letters should be under continuous revision. Using a standard cover letter like a "boiler plate" will not get you far unless you continuously update it.

The resume is another piece of vital information about you. There are many resume services out there and there are many good examples on the Internet. Generally, it is best to only have one or two pages, as most experts would say. My resume use to be four pages long and it seems to work for me. This is an opportunity to demonstrate your work experience. I know that it works because I had been invited to many interviews. There are many good examples on the internet.

When I first started to get serious about becoming a police chief, I utilized a resume service. This person helped with my cover letter and resume. You will pay some money but it will be worth it. Sometimes you will be surprised. It took a couple of months but before long, I had many interviews. There were a few I had to turn down because I could not physically be in two places at once. Sometimes you will have to wait and other times the phone will keep ringing. It is a crazy business. You will get calls even after you had accepted a position. The critical thing that I have to say about municipalities and the process is that it is slow and cumbersome. Municipalities should understand that their town or city is not the only a person had applied for a position. Many good candidates withdraw simply because they had a better offer from another community.

There will be times when you will become frustrated, as many others have already experienced. It is a waiting game, and you have to be patient. Remember one thing; the city fathers are usually not in a hurry. Chances are they are taking their time especially if they have confidence in their interim chief of police. In many cases, they are watching and evaluating their interim police chief. Sometimes, the interim person gets the position.

A good cover letter and resume will open some doors for you. Therefore, I cannot stress enough, be articulate and careful when you are drafting them. Keep track of where you sent your resume. It is somewhat embarrassing to send it to the same place twice. It is like telling them you are not careful and you are flooding the United States with resumes. Sometimes you will get a reply after they receive it and other times you will not. Many times, they will not inform you if you did not make the cut. If you do not get a telephone interview or an invitation to a personal interview, review your cover letter and resume. At this point, you may consider revising it to give it a fresh look. If you do a good job with your cover letter and resume, the interviews will come.

In my opinion, I think that it is rude for someone not to give an acknowledgment one way or the other. It has happened to me countless times but do not take it personal. If they sent out a letter or packet to hundred or more applicant, it will cost them some money. I guess it is easy to ignore the rejects. Remember do not take it personal. You will get many more rejections than invitations to interviews.

You are probably wondering how do they select an individual to go to an interview? How often wondered about it too. Generally, a community will have a screening committee review all the resumes. Sometimes there are over a hundred so the process can be quite consuming especially if they are trying to narrow the field down to the final five. I have been involved in the process myself so it works this way. The resumes are screened initially to see if they meet minimum requirements. The ones that do not will simply be discarded. There will be some resumes that meet minimum requirements and those that exceed the requirements. Now, the field is reduced to about 40 or 50 for the first cut. Next, the selection committee will review each resume to see if it meets the criteria what they are looking for. You can see the importance of the cover letter especially if it outlines the accomplishments of a particular candidate.

The selection becomes very difficult with the top 20 or so. At this point, each individual probably has outstanding credentials. The community may either conduct a telephone interview to attempt to narrow the field or simply make additional cuts. Sometimes I wonder how they make the final cut with very little information. The telephone interview is a good way to get a feel for the applicant and is cost effective. You never know what they are going to ask but you can still be prepared for some basic questions. The more probing questions would still come from the interview panel if you make it that far. The telephone interview is still difficult because you cannot see them and they cannot see you. Essentially, they are trying to determine if your responses, which would indicate your philosophy, would be compatible with theirs. They are looking for someone who will do good things for their community. Somehow, you have to convey this message. I try to come across that I will be able to help them with their problem. At the same time you try not to appear to be overly confident. Sometimes it is difficult when you keep asking yourself this question, "What do they know about law enforcement?" Maybe they know nothing and they are just trying to feel their way along in the process. The larger communities will hire a consultant to help them along and the smaller communities will "fly by the seat of their pants." The message that you need to convey is that you are the expert and you can help them with their problem. You can say it in a humble way without being overly confident.

"Do Not Count Your Chickens Before They Are Hatched"

I remember one of my competitors for the police chief position in Colorado thought he was so good that he had the job. He was even shopping for homes in the area and was telling the mayor all about it. He probably would have been offered the job and perhaps done a good job but he make **a fatal error. He bragged about what he could do.** There are times when you have to be humble.   Be careful of what you say and to whom you say it to. It might mean the difference of a job offer or no job offer. The powers to be probably were a little intimidated by him.

I have been invited to interviews where I was interviewed on video and the tape was forwarded to the municipality. Still another interview was the closed circuit TV conducted live. I had gone to Kinko's in Mesa, Arizona for the live transmission to Minnesota. I must have done very well because I was invited to go to Minnesota for a follow up interview where I was subsequently offered the police chief position. The interview felt a little weird because of a five-second delay. I declined the police chief job because of reasons that I will not go into right now but later in another chapter.   There were some potential ethical problems and other issues about the community that would have made it more difficult to succeed. In simple terms, I was not going to be a "hatchet man" or a union breaker for anyone. Just because you are offered a position, it does not mean you should accept it right away. Take some time to think about it and discuss it with your family.

The Interview

The interviews will come but you have to decide what it is worth to you to get there. The right thing for a community to do is to pay for the transportation (air fare), car rental and hotel accommodations. If a community is serious about you, they will pay the costs. Sometimes, you have to pay your own way. Generally, if the field is narrowed to five, there will probably be two from out of state, one from the department, and the remaining from in state. Ask the person inviting you to the interview if your travel expenses will be paid, and if not all what will they pay exactly. Do not be shy about asking. It is business at this point. Apparently, they see something in you that they like and they want you to get there. What upsets the interview process is when a potential candidate cancels at the last minute. If two candidates cancel then you can see what may happen. The interview panel will only interview three candidates that will increase your odds for being selected.

The trend for communities is to get out of it as cheaply as possible and they may not offer to pay expenses except for the hotel accommodations. This holds true in the smaller communities. You will have to decide if it is worth the expense to get to your destination. I have done it both ways. I paid for some and others have paid my expenses. It all depends on how bad you want to be a police chief. If you paid your expenses, it would be a legitimate job hunt expenditure that you can claim on your income taxes.

Now that you passed one hurdle, it is time to discuss the interview process and how to prepare. It is possible to be completely prepared for the interview. In order to be prepared you have to **find out something about the community**. This is definitely a strategy. Do not make the mistake and take the interview too lightly because you are the greatest law enforcement officer that ever came along. First, you have to find out why they need you. There are always some underlying reasons that with a "little leg work" you can find out. You do not want to be surprised at the interview. Second, you will have to do some research about the community and learn as much as you can. Third, you will have to interview some citizens to get some insight.

Let us discuss the underlying reasons first. It is important to know what happened to their chief. It is vital to know if he or she was fired, forced to resign, retired, resigned under mysterious circumstances or there was some scandal. It is important to know because it will help you to be better prepared. Perhaps after you find out some information, you may not want to continue in the process. If the police chief was fired or there was a scandal you can easily find out about it in the local newspapers. All you have to do is go to their local library and begin searching the back issues of the newspaper sometimes there will be a vertical file about the police department. All you have to do is ask for it. Now with the Internet you probably can find out much about the community and police department line without ever leaving your home.

In Fort Lupton, Colorado, the police chief was termination but later allowed to resign. He got into difficulty over hiring practices and sexual discrimination. I do not know if the allegations were true but the perception from the city leaders and community was that it was the chief's fault. The fact of life is that the responsibility, right or wrong, lies with the police chief. The former chief appeared on the surface to run a good department but there were some organizational and morale problems. The problems were fixable from what I could see. The community had already terminated their city administrator and now they were terminating their police chief.

The police department, city administration and community were in turmoil. The reality is that many communities, like Fort Lupton are in turmoil and they are looking for leadership to help them out of this predicament as quickly as possible. Some communities are more in a hurry to hire a police chief than others. Even though there were many problems, I was confident that I could succeed with Fort

Lupton. It was easy because I had the support of the city administrator, mayor and all the council members. Matter of fact, they informed me more than once that it was my department and to run it the way I saw fit. Basically, I was told I could do anything I wanted within reason of course to straighten out the department. There were some implied hints from one or two council members regarding some alleged corrupt employees and some might need to be fired. I did not say anything other than, I will find out for myself. In my experience if there is a former police officer on the city council or police commission they tend to think they know more than you do. Just remember, do not get intimidated. Keep telling yourself you are the expert they hired.

You can use this information to your advantage. There will no doubt be some questions regarding this problem. You should be prepared to tell them how you are going to put the department back on track and move forward. The city leaders are looking for a philosophy similar to their own. Other words in more simplistic terms, they want to know if they can work with this individual. They certainly do not want to hire someone that will make their situation worse. I was asked a question one time how I would be able to get along with the individual who was vying for the police chief's position and did not get it. I diplomatically discussed having coffee with the individual and would speak of ways to work together towards common goals, which would be to make the department the best it could be. The wrong thing to say is "it is my way or the highway." Maybe it may be the result but you do not want to say it in this manner. It is better to get cooperation from the individual in the beginning even though he or she may be bitter about losing the position to an outsider.

My Way or the Highway

I actually had a person be insubordinate towards me in front of others at a social function. Keeping in mind that there is always a time and place for something like this, I called this person into my office the next workday. Behind closed doors, I set this person straight. In so many words I told him that this type of behavior would not be tolerated especially from a ranking officer.   He was the person who did not get the police chief position. I had to let him know that in so many words, "it is my way, or the highway." Sometimes you have to tell the person in strong language that if he did not like it he could resign. I wanted him to know if he was on the "Train." It is funny some time later; I observed a framed cartoon of a train on his office wall. I guess our conversation must have sunk into his head. After that, we had a good understanding and working relationship that lasted seven years. The police chief has the authority but one has to remain strong and from time to time assert him or herself. Perhaps, it was just another test to see what kind of person I would be. He certainly found out in a hurry.

All the information that you can glean regarding the police chief's departure will be relevant to the interview process. In each of my communities and those where I was not selected I did my research. I was always curious about how the police chief failed. I certainly did not want to relive history and make the same mistakes. Remember, you can learn from your mistakes, but you can **learn from others** as well. It is not being nosey, but being smart.

The interview committee is always impressed with someone who had gone the extra mile to find out about his or her community. **A little bit of knowledge is better than none.** There may be some underlying reasons in selecting a particular individual. The more you can find out the better for you.

There may be a perception of a police Gestapo image, an occupying force, excessive use of force, or the unfair treatment of minorities in the community just to name a few examples. Some people will complain no matter what. You cannot please everyone. The reality is that it may be just a bad public relations problem and nothing specific. If you were aware of some of these issues, it will help you to formulate a plan in advance of the interview. This information will put you one-step ahead of the others. The most important thing to remember is be armed with knowledge and be confident going into the interview process. It sure helps to keep the stress level down.

I always found it usual to talk to citizens about the perception of the police department and sometimes you will be surprised with the responses. Back in Fort Lupton when I was preparing for the interview, I found myself in a crime-ridden neighborhood and these individuals were surprised that I was interested enough to ask questions. This person candidly said that he really did not have a problem with the police department except with certain officers. I found out later that this person was a convicted felon and had been in prison. He gave a decent evaluation of the department. I interviewed other citizens and was able to get a great deal of insight. I even interviewed the coordinator of the city owned museum just about an hour before my scheduled interview. This person gave valuable information about the city, the staff and police department employees. She did not say anything derogatory about anyone. It was a fruitful discussion. This information was not only useful in formulating a plan for the interview process but helped get the police department back on track.

One piece of information I did not know and found out later was a question about their communication center. The interview panel wanted to know what ways I could improve the center. I politely told the panel that I did not have an opportunity to tour the police department and would be more than happy to assess the dispatch center if given the opportunity. Rather than guess, I candidly told them

I did not visit the Dispatch Center prior to the interview. **A fatal error would be to guess** and make it up as you go along. If you do not know something, just be truthful. The interview panel will have more respect for you and it could be a deciding factor. **Be honest** with the panel and I cannot stress it enough.

It is not only important about what you say, but how you look and present yourself. I have observed many individuals go to interviews as if it was a casual affair. If you are serious about the position and have already invested much time and effort, be particular about your wardrobe. Remember you are going for a police executive position so you have to play the part. You have to look and act like a real police chief. Kindly leave your police tie clips and police type shoes at home. Anything that uniform police wears leave at home. It is just a pet peeve of mine. The appropriate attire for the occasion would be business, usually a navy blue or grey suit with matching tie. Remember to polish your shoes. There is nothing worse than wearing a nice looking suit and spoil it with old, dirty shoes. The serious candidate should not wear a sports jacket and slacks. A nice suit is more appropriate for the interview. If you do not own a suit then I would recommend that you invest in several. I am one not to discriminate. Many women have gone on to be police chiefs. Ladies should be appropriately dressed in business attire as well.

Sometimes questions arise about the color of the suit. I heard from one candidate who went out and bought a "power suit" prior to the interview. This person did not get the job. The power suit is a traditional navy blue suit with a white shirt. Does one candidate have an edge over another because of the color of the suit? My opinion is that it does not matter as long as the suit is cleaned and pressed and looks good on the individual. What matters most is what kind of image does this person project? You have to remember that their police chief will be representing the community and this person should project a good appearance.

I remember one individual in Fort Lupton who was being interviewed by me for a promotional advancement to the rank of corporal. I shocked to see him showing up for an important interview in a tee shirt and shorts. It should be no surprise that he did not get the job.

Now, you should be ready for the interview process and very well prepared. At this point we will only discuss the interview panel. There are many ways to assess a candidate and the most common and traditional is the interview panel. The interview panel will usually have three to five evaluators, some of whom may be police chiefs and community members. Having community members on the interview panel is a great idea. The interview will last about 45 minutes to an hour and each panel member may ask two or three questions.

What kind of questions might you expect and how should you approach it. First, when asked a question, just answer it and then keep quiet. If you did not answer it sufficiently, they will follow up with additional questions. It is just that simple. One problem for a candidate is talking too much. It is hard but sometimes you have to know when to keep your much shut. Either a candidate does not say much or he or she talks too much. You have to find your comfort zone. Some candidates that I have interviewed are so nervous you have to drag the answer out of them. Saying too little can certainly hurt as well. The candidate must be able to articulate an answer with substance and clarity and know when to stop.

Another common mistake of a candidate is not answering the question. Going off on a tangent is a big mistake. Listen to the question very carefully. When you feel like you had answered it sufficiently, you should know when to stop. Make sure you have good eye contact and smile as if you are having a good time. You want to appear to be relaxed before the panel. It is your opportunity to shine so have a good time. I know that it is easier said than done.

The Interview Questions

What kind of questions could an interview committee ask? If you had done your homework you would have gathered much information about the police department and the community. It is possible to find out before the interview what qualities they are looking for in a candidate. The following are some possible questions:

- What are your strengths? What are your weaknesses?
- What is leadership? What are your qualities?
- What is your management style?
- What is Community Policing and how would you implement it?
- What crime prevention programs have you put in place?
- Have you worked with budgets before?
- Have you sought supplemental funding through grants?
- Have you ever fired anyone?
- What is diversity?
- What is your view on racial profiling?
- What can be done about Juvenile Crime in your community?

The questions asked by the interview committee are not extremely difficult. They are asking these questions to find out about the philosophy of the person.

However, if you did your research and you know the duties of the police chief it is possible to anticipate almost every question. There is a reason for each question. Sometimes these questions surround an issue regarding the chief's departure. They want to see how you would handle the so-called hypothetical situation. They also want to see if they will be able to work with the individual given the limited resources in a community. The key point to get across is being able to promote and implement programs and staying within the budget. If I had a big pot of money, I would be able to implement any type of program that the council wanted.

Other Side Issues

I recall in Fort Lupton, Colorado the council was more interested in code enforcement than anything else. Believe it or not, the council would bring to my attention violations of the city code, such as trashcans left in front of their home too long, dogs running at large and snow left on the sidewalk over 24 hours. I could go on an on but you get the picture. I knew that code enforcement was a priority so I made sure that the job got done. I certainly did not want to tell them that it was not real police work. Sometimes a city council has pet peeves and after a while, you will figure it out. I made sure that my code enforcement officer handled the complaints, patrolled to spot violations and followed up. It took some time but we were able to control the situation so that we could concentrate on other important issues.

I bring up this issue because it is possible to find out before hand some of the underlying issues. There are always some underlying issues and it may have resulted from the prior police chief's deficiencies. However, I would like to mention a word of warning. It would not be appropriate when you are being asked a question regarding the police chief's mistakes or problems to dwell on the issue. There would be no quicker way to turn off an interview panel. Just think about it. If you were well prepared, the interview process would be a snap.

Some of the common themes that keep coming up are Community Policing and Crime Prevention programs. When I first started as a Police Chief the concept of Community Policing was not even mentioned by the town or city managers and Councils. The concept was still fairly new and no one knew what it means. You can expect a Community Policing type question, not only the definition but also some of the programs. Everyone thinks and breathes Community Policing. Later on in another chapter I will discuss Community Policing and crime prevention programs and give some good example of some cost effective programs. Some of the programs I had implemented in my former communities were successful.

There are other types of interviews. Some communities may opt to select a modified assessment center or a full assessment center. They are more expensive because of the materials and time involved. Assessment centers could take as long as two days. There are pros and cons but essentially, they assess the candidate's ability to perform the job as police chief. They involve both written and oral exercises. The assessment centers can learn more about an individual over one or two days than the traditional question and answer type of interview. It is an exercise in futility especially since there are current police chiefs that are going through the exercise with everyone else. Those police chiefs should be able to do the job. Sometimes the assessors are not even police chiefs. In my opinion, this type of interview process is overly expensive for the police chief position. Communities would be better served in devoting more time and resources in the background investigation phase. In this way they will find out about the candidate.

Generally, the standard question and answer type of interview will be the most predominate and one that you should expect but there may be variations. There may be other types of interviews, such as interviews with the public, department heads and personnel but in the end, they are all the same. They may have you go through several stages of interviews to get the community involved. It seems that in keeping with the community policing concept, communities are involving everyone in the process. I think that it is a good idea. The candidate may have to spend two or three days being interviewed. In the end, someone asks a question and you will have to provide an answer. On the positive side, the more time they can get to see you the better they will get to know you as a person. This seems to be a popular thing to do. However, it still will be the city or town manager's decision. As stated before with a little preparation and knowledge about the community, you can be prepared.

The Offer

If you are so fortunate enough, the city or town manager of the community will call you up and offer the position to you. This is the time to negotiate because your position from a negotiation standpoint is strong. Just think after much thought and deliberation the city or town will now commit and make you a job offer. They want you so make your best pitch. Take your time and put down on paper all the benefits that you are looking for. It does not hurt to ask. If you do not ask, then you will not receive. Even during the interviews stages while traveling from one community to another you can still think about it. When the time comes do not jump at their first offer. If your requests are reasonable, they will negotiate with you. Remember, they are now anxious to fill the position and your bargaining position is very strong. For example, when I was offered a police chief job in New Hampshire the city manager offered me the following:

- Specified Salary
- Fully paid moving expenses including packing and
  setting up

- Closing Cost on my new Home
- Paid apartment for six months
- Same fringe benefits as the other Department Heads

When I analyzed the offer, it was more than fair. It did not include a severance clause because a police chief in New Hampshire could only be dismissed with clause. The police chief was included in the department head associate so I was really protected. The city manager outlined the offer in a letter of understanding. This amounted to a contract and some are more detailed than others are. In any event, whatever document you may come up with their city or town attorney will review it. In the end, you have to be comfortable with it.

There are some communities that can dismiss a chief without cause. They can do it and not have any reason. I know, because it happened to me in Florence, Arizona. Many states are a right to work state. I signed a two-year contract that included a six months severance clause with full benefits. I figured if I do my job as I did in New Hampshire, they would be pleased with my performance. I was not worried about the "Without Cause" section of the contract. I was protected, so I thought. Besides, I thought that I was invincible since I had just completed seven years in New Hampshire. The thought never crossed my mind about failing. The City of Somersworth presented me with a nice plaque for my years of accomplishments. We will explore the dynamics of politics later so that my experiences could help someone else. I certainly would not want to have someone else placed in a similar situation as I had found myself in.

In March 1995, I had signed a two-year contract with the Town of Florence, Arizona. Everything went according to plan, I had rebuilt the department and put community policing in place. I was the President of the Pinal County Law Enforcement Association and elected to the Rotary Club Board of Directors. Everything was going well, so I thought, and I did not consider the hidden agenda of the Town Council. The Town Council gave rave reviews regarding my performance during my performance evaluation during July 1996. They gave a nice raise. Why should I be worried? When my contract came up for renewal in March 1997 it was pay back time for the previous council. This current council had no ownership in me because the previous council hired me. The council voted not to renew my contract and suddenly without warning, I was without a job. They had no problem in paying me my severance pay it was no big deal. Just as a point of information, I filed for and received unemployment compensation. Even though I would be collecting my severance pay, the Town of Florence was still liability for unemployment compensation.

I think that it is important about it because what happened to me has happened to others and will happen again. It happens all the time. A police chief in North

Carolina returned home after a long day and found an envelope from the city manager taped to his door. In it was his letter of dismissal. What a shock after serving 13 years as the head of the department. The city manager had been only there for three months. When the media started to ask questions, the city manager said, you guessed it, "It is a personnel matter." I am sure there was more to the story.

I think that the damaged can be minimized if the potential job offer had some type of provision for protection. Having a severance clause in the contract is helpful. Ideally, it would be better to negotiate a contract for three years or longer. It takes that long to establish programs and see the results. If they want to get rid of you, they will do it no matter what. The new police chief has much more to lose if he or she suddenly found himself or herself without a job. The police chief has to protect his or her reputation, so a dismissal without cause needs to be clear in your contract. It seems like it is happening all over the country at a frightening rate, and as often a town or city managers. It happens to city or town managers all the time. Essentially, they are fired for doing their job. Sometimes a conflict may result from one or two council members and all it would take is a simple majority by the council to terminate a city manager. In some cases, it is just that easy to dismiss a police chief.

To Buy a Home or Not?

Buying a home or renting a home is a difficult decision. You never know what might happen. My last city administrator that I worked for in Fort Lupton, Colorado had it right. He found a home and rented it. The Town Fathers usually want their management team, especially the police chief and city manager to reside in the city and I can understand it. The town fathers were kind upset because he decided to rent a home and not buy it. I think that he was being smart. Who says that you have to buy a home? You can always buy a home when the time comes when you are more comfortable with the position. Considering the track record of police chiefs and city managers why would a person want to invest in a home if there is no job security? You have to make sure your family is protected. Remember, this a business arrangement that could be short or long term and only time can tell.

You are going to hear some talk about you not making a commitment to establish roots in a community. The town fathers might even ask you directly. You can always tell them diplomatically that you are searching for the right home to buy or you are thinking about building a home. It is an important decision to make. Maybe you will buy a home in the future. Telling them it is none of their business is the wrong thing to say. You have to be smart and protect yourself. If you do not, no one else will. If I had to do it all over again, I would definitely find a rental home in the beginning.

At the very least, make sure that you have a good contract that protects you. You can be sure the town or city will protect their arrangement with their police chief. It is hopeful that the stay with the community will be a long and prosperous one. Many chiefs have a long career while others are short lived. In many cases, it is just politics, pure and simple.

Chapter 3
Political Gamesmanship

I thought at this point we could get right to the important aspect. What I am about to impart in this chapter was gained through by my personal experiences, experience of others, success and failures and knowledge of the political system. I believe that you have to learn to live within the political system and if you do not then you will find yourself on the outside looking in. Just remember one thing, you can be replaced very quickly and many police chiefs all over the country found themselves in that situation. It does not matter how intelligent you are and what you have done through out your career, it is **how well you play the game**. If you do not succeed in the political gamesmanship then you will have a short-lived career as a police chief.

Know What You Are Getting Yourself Into

You do not realize the political implications when you are rising through the chain of command. Middle management, lower level management, front line supervision and the rank and file are generally insulated. The person who takes the brunt of abuse by politicians would be the police chief. In my former communities where I was police chief, I made an effort to shield my personnel from the politics. I was not trying to put a muzzle on my personnel. I did not want to place my personnel in an uncomfortable situation and not get the facts right. I believe that if I am going to be held accountable, then the political body needs to hear from me to get the facts right. It is an unpleasant fact that some of your personnel will play politics. They will go behind your back whether you like it or not and speak directly to the police commissioner, selectman, or council member whatever the government entity happens to be. You will not believe how the truth can be twisted and suddenly you are on the defensive trying to explain the half-truths or lies. Whom do you think the politician will believe? Of course, the person carrying the "mail" to the politician usually will have the impact. What can you do as the police executive? More often than not, you are at the mercy of the politician. This politician now has an inside information from the department. There are ways to deal with this problem. I have known some police chiefs who were very savvy at playing politics. Better yet, I worked for one who was a master at the game.

Know the Players

The American Heritage Dictionary defines politics as the activities or affairs of a government, politician, or political party. It is a broad definition but it essentially means every person who holds some type of position or is involved in some way in city government could be considered a politician. A person may not be on the town or city council but may serve on one of the many committees such as the Finance Committee and have considerable amount of power. This person may have more power than a city councilmember. I can think of several individuals as well as you can who have this type of magical power and believe me this person knows it and uses it to his or her advantage. One such individual served as Chairman of the Finance Committee for many years in Bristol, Connecticut. Even though the council members would have their vote on the city budget, this Finance Director helped shaped the budget and was very influential on which programs were approved or not. He was a very well respected member of the community. He never served as a city council member, but in my opinion carried more weight. He was not a person to get angry. You have to know who the **players** are and who carries the most influence. The real players are not necessarily the council members. You have to find out who are influential in your community and use this information to your advantage.

Each community has their influential person either on the council, committee or community. It would behoove the police chief to find out who these individuals are and what kind of agenda they may have. My former police chief in Bristol, Connecticut told me to be especially nice to the finance director. The answer was obvious. This person had considerable amount of power because he or she had control of the purse strings of the city. Finance Directors can make life miserable for the police chief or anyone else. I always admired the way my former police chief conducted business. He was like the conductor in a large symphony playing beautiful music. I considered him the master craftsman at the political arena.

The Ego

I would always ask myself this question when I was going up through the ranks. Why do we have to kiss up to the politicians? What do they know about law enforcement? The point is they may think they may have the answers. I had to bite my tongue many times and not say what I wanted to say. They may know very little about law enforcement, but what matters the most is the political power base. I learned very quickly after see many chiefs come and go. They failed in my opinion because of a huge ego. Their way was the right way. Just ask them. I have heard it from others. The famous quote you often hear is "No one will tell me what to do because it is my department."   It may be fine but there are other individuals who may have more power than you do.

It is sad to think that someone would lose his or her job because of politics. I have seen it repeatedly. I have had many friends who failed because of politics. They knew how to run a police department and were very capable but got a failing grade when it came to politics. They suddenly found themselves on the outside looking in. Perhaps, much insight can be gained through my experience with three departments. The reader will be able to see how I had handled these situations.

Be Nice and Respectful

Before I discuss each community, I want to mention police commissioners. They are a body usually elected by the people and they provide oversight over the police department. The police commissioners directly supervise the police chief. Whether you work for police commissioners, city or town manager, or City or Town Councils, you have to learn to work within the system and above all else learn how to get along with your bosses. You can hope that someone else may be voted in but do not count on it. My best advice is to be **nice to everyone, be respectful and do not talk about anyone** even if their assessment is correct. It looks like you are kissing up again but I say no; it is being smart. When you put everything together, you are using the political body, whether it is the police commissioners, City, or Town Council to help you to do your job. It is just that simple. You need to get them on your side so that you can be an effective police chief.

City of Somersworth, New Hampshire

The City of Somersworth, New Hampshire was my first police chief position beginning in 1988. This was my first real experience being introduced to politics. If you recall, I came from Bristol, Connecticut and even though I was a captain, I was still sheltered from politics. It was a unique learning experience for me even though Somersworth had a reputation for being a "dumping ground for police chiefs" Just hearing that from respected members of the law enforcement community made me have second thoughts. I asked myself this question many times and began to second-guess myself. What was I doing here? When I had accepted the position, no other police chief had last longer than five years during the previous 20 years. The reputation of the police department was not good and I knew that I had a challenge and an opportunity to shape the police department.

Political Dynamics behind the Scene

During the first two years I worked directly for a city manager who did not want me to attend council meetings unless he specifically wanted me there. He also did not want me to speak to any council members about their concerns unless he knew about it. I thought at first that he was being paranoid. He needed to know the council members concerns regarding the police department so that he could be able to respond. He did not want to get blindsided at a meeting. It seemed reasonable because he was responsible to the City Council. Everything was going fine until he suddenly resigned but then changed his mind. The council refused to rescind his letter of resignation, but allowed him to interview for his position. You figure that one out. Apparently, there was more going on behind the scenes that I realized. There are always some political dynamics that goes on behind the scenes. Sometimes it is too late to do anything about it when the politicians are having their secret meeting. You might ask, "Are there secret meetings?" Legally, if three or more council members are discussing an issue, they are required to publish the meeting 24 hours in advance of the meeting. The official meetings are posted but what about the unofficial. The reality is that there many informal meetings going on behind the scenes whether it is by telephone or at the local coffee shop. This goes on all the time. Much of the dealings and support are garnered at the unofficial meetings.

Get To Know the Council Members

Generally, I was pretty much insolated from the council but I made it a point to get to know each one of them including the mayor. Mayor Jim McLin was an excellent mayor and good friend. The City of Somersworth was a good place to work but the politics were still strange to me.

There were a few times I was worried about my job. We had received information that the former mayor and currently a State Representative had planted an ease-dropping device in the telephone panel in the cellar of his estranged wife. This particular person was popular in the community. It seemed that he was listening to his ex-wife's telephone conversation and had no right to be on the premises without permission. I initiated an investigation and had one of my new officers positioned in the cellar to await the return of the ex-mayor. Neither captain knew what was going on because they were friends. I am not trying to imply that either one would have tipped him off but I figured that the less people who knew about the investigation the better off we were. As luck would have it, the former mayor fell for the bait and was immediately arrested inside the cellar. The media made big headlines out of the story. This event turned into front page news.

Keep Everyone Informed

I made sure that the City Manager, Mayor and council members were aware of the arrest of the former mayor. I wanted them to know before they read about it in the paper or heard it on radio. The **key is to keep everyone informed**. No one liked surprises. Everyone knows that **Justice is blind**. It does not distinguish between the wealthy, middle class or poor people. Even then, some people figure the law does not apply to them and many politicians believe it. I was relieved to find out that the council members were in agreement with our police action. I still wonder what would have happened if the opposite were true. I probably would not have been there long. The important thing is not to worry about doing your duty. Do the right thing.

The Laws Is Not For Everyone?

Another example occurred in Bristol, Connecticut years ago. I was in charge of the Detective Division and one of my detectives reported that gambling was taking place at a carnival. Gambling is considered a victimless crime but it was still against the law. I instructed my detective to make the arrest and confiscate the gambling devices. It should have been cut and dry but I was a little surprised to catch some political disagreement from the captain. The impression I got was that we were wrong to make the arrest. It seems that the owner of the carnival was very influential in Bristol politics. Word got back to the police chief and captain that he was not very happy about his man arrested for illegal gambling. Even though the arrest was righteous, I began to learn that it was perfectly acceptable to arrest certain people and not others. Ethically, it is not right. It sends a bad message to the community. Some people are untouchable while others are fair game. The law has to be enforced equally, not selectively.

I made up my mind years ago there are no special class of people when it becomes necessary to enforce the law. In my mind, the law applies to everyone. It is not fair that there is a special class of citizen in our society. I never regretted making the decision to arrest the individual at the carnival. I was relieved to find that Somersworth was going to be different from Bristol. I mean it in a positive sense. You have to know what **your community wants.**

Know Your Boss

I was gaining confidence as time went on in Somersworth. I made sure that I did not overstep my bound when it came to dealing with the city council members. The City Manager still wanted to know what was going on but allowed me to operate more freely. I always remembered that he was the person who was the boss. **Other chiefs should remember that they have a boss**. The Unity of Command concept being responsible to one person also applies to the chief. I made sure that I did not circumvent the city managers authority. It is my opinion that the primary reason for dismissal of police chiefs is not for incompetence but mainly doing an end run around the manager and challenging his or her authority. This will certainly spell disaster to the police chief. He may as well start updating his or her resume and starting looking for another job.

Treat All Council Members the Same

You can still be friends with the Mayor and stay neutral when it comes around re-election time. I did not campaign for him but I gave him my support. Perhaps, it may have been a different situation if he had lost the election, but he is still the Mayor. One has to be careful when you align yourself with a political faction. It may come back to haunt you. From my experience one has be **proceed very carefully** and **treat all council members the same**. Showing any favoritism to any one person may spell doom for the police chief in the future especially if his or her favorite elected official loses the election.

I felt it was time for me to move to another community. I had accomplished the goals and objectives and it was time to move on. Sometimes a person can stay too long. I will talk more about this later. The Somersworth Police Department had come a long way and I was pleased with the results. My next stop was Florence, Arizona.

Florence, Arizona

The Town of Florence gave me a lesson in politics that I will never forget. Usually when a community hires a new police chief there is a match. Other words, there is a chemistry between the police chief, town manager and Town Council. The chemistry occurred in the beginning with Bill Galletley, the Town Manager, and the mayor and town council members. However, there was a recall election for the mayor and three council members. It seems that some of the town's people were very unhappy about the dismissal of the former police chief. He was a local homeboy. Now the town manager dismissed the police chief with the approval of the town council. The police chief was being difficult and was doing everything to circumvent the authority of the town manager. Someone had to go, either the police chief or the town manager.

The town manager was new to the community having been there for only about six months. The town manager in his mind did the right thing by firing the Police

Chief. Picture this scenario. The former chief was standing in the middle of the street challenging the town manager to come into the street to meet him. Sounds like to me another shoot out at the Okay Corral would have taken place, just like Tombstone in the old West. I had to remember we were in the West. Obviously, the town manager did not go into the street to meet the former police chief. It was not too long after that when he fired the police chief. What a volatile situation and who knows what could have happened. The former police chief help orchestrate a recall election. It seemed strange to me but if you were unhappy with your current council members all one had to do was get a certain percentage of signatures from the voters in the community and petition for a new election. About two months after I took over as police chief, the recall election took place and to my surprise as well as the town manager, the recall committee won the election. Before I knew it, we had a new mayor and three council members.

In order to dismiss a town manager there needs to be a simple majority. I could do the math. This was a seven-member council and there were now four new members. Their main platform was to get rid of the town manager who had the audacity to fire their friend. Every one knew that the reputation of the former police chief but no one wanted to see him lose his job. His brand of law enforcement was different from the ordinary. There was no such thing as contemporary law enforcement. There was a different brand of justice; it all depended upon who you were and whom you knew. This situation resembled justice out of the Old West.

I was hired to professionalize the police department and bring it back into contemporary policing standards. This department had regressed so far that the Arizona Police Officer Standards and Training was considering decertifying the department because of substandard training. I certainly had a challenge in front of me.

Politics

I will never forget when the Town Council officially met and their first order of business was to dismiss the town manager. Even though it was inevitable and everyone knew it was coming, we were all in a state of shock. Even that evening when the council was going to take a vote, the town manager knew it was coming. He had already packed up his office. This town manager had hired professional people in key positions to implement many new programs. There was no doubt he had done a great deal in the community even though he was only there for a short time. Many of his ideas and programs are still carried out today. They showed their appreciation by firing him. I have to say that was a low point in my live. How could any political body do something stupid like that? It was the local influence of politics and cronyism was live and well. It was going to be a major educational experience for me regarding my career.

I decided to go into detail about Florence because of the uniqueness of the political environment. I think that it is best to discuss it to help prepare others for the harsh reality of politics. You never know what is going to happen. Politics can be unfair especially when I saw the caliber of person who was fired. Fortunately, for my former town manager he later became the city manager of Clinton, Oklahoma. Everything was going well for him and I was happy for him.

Be Wary of the Lamb going Into the Lion's Den

The Mayor called a staff meeting to reassure staff that everything was going to be all right and no one was in jeopardy of losing his or her position. I said to myself, "sure." The Town Council did not interfere in what I was trying to do. They needed me to resurrect the department. I knew that I had a contract and they knew it too. It was always in the back of my mind whether they were going to renew my contract. I realized that it was their friend, the former police chief who was fired and I never forgot it, not even for a second.

The former police chief was a thorn in my side. **One sure way to fail is to please everyone**. I set out to do my job the best way I knew how. Little did I realize that I would have to utilize all my experiences and more as a police chief and did not realize what was in store for me?

Expect the Unexpected

My first contact with the former police chief was not a good one. I received a call about midnight regarding a confrontation of the former chief with one of my officers. The dispatcher requested my presence at the police department. Not knowing what to expect as I was walking through the police lobby he said to me, "I want to talk to you." I told him that I had to speak to my officers first to find out what was going on. My officer related to me the following. He operated radar on Main Street and stopped the former police chief's son for speeding. The officer wrote a speeding ticket to the violator. I did not see anything out of the ordinary and it appeared that the officer took the appropriate action.

When the son spoke to his father about the traffic ticket, he went ballistic. The former Chief sought out and found the officer running radar in the vicinity. He immediately initiated a confrontation with the officer that amounted to disturbing the peace and interfering with the duties of the officer. I asked the officer what he would have done if it were someone else and not the former chief. He replied by saying, "I would have made the arrest." I told him that the answer was obvious. If the former chief was so out of line, then an arrest was warranted in this particular situation. The officer issued the former Chief a summons to court for Disorderly Conduct, Threatening and Interfering with Governmental Operations.

After analyzing this situation, I figured we had no other recourse. I knew that the former police chief was not going away. In his mind, it was still his police department and I was an obstacle in his way. I knew that the decision was not going to be popular with the council members. They did not say anything, but I knew it was on their mind. In retrospect, I would not have changed a thing. If I had decided to overlook this situation, I would have undermined the authority in my personnel and more importantly, my ethical values of law enforcement. Anything less would have compromised my values. It was a decision that I would not regret but I knew there would be more to come. I did what I thought best considering all the facts.

The former police chief's case went to our local District Court. It was a "hot potato"; no one wanted to handle it. The judge and prosecutor cited a conflict of interest. A special prosecutor and judge were brought in to handle this particular case. In the end, the former chief was found guilty of all charges and received probation and a small fine. It was a joke because he did no probation at all. There was no supervised probation.

There were other confrontations with the former police chief. He was arrested several more times and again he was found guilty in court. I guess it would be fair to say that we were never going to be friends. The people in the community were neither sympathetic nor supportive. It should have been a clue about the community. It appeared to me that the community did not care one way or the other. The silent majority remained silent.

A Few People Hold the Power

In this small community in Arizona, no one cared if there was any change at all. A hand full of people controlled town politics. No one wanted to get involved even if they did not think it was right. This was evident during the recall election when only a small number of voters turned out for the election. You would think that more people would have had a stake in the issues. This was a type of politics that I was not accustomed to and it was scary. The Town Council had the power and they could do anything they wanted.

It was difficult trying to make sense out of this mess. In the meantime, valuable staff was leaving the Town. All the professional individuals who the former town manager hired were now gone. I was the only one left. If I had enough sense, I would have started to look for another position.   No, I decided to stay to professionalize the police department.

Watch Out For the Lion

Knowing what I know now, I read the Town Council wrong. I sincerely believed that they liked me and wanted me to stay. The council members kept telling me that I was doing an excellent job with the police department and to keep up the good work. I let down my guard and believed them.

If you recall, I had signed a two-year contract with the Town and it was up for council consideration.   Apparently, someone realized my contract had to have council action and at the last minute, it was on the Council Agenda.   I was not suspicious because the day before the Mayor was in my office and I asked her if something was going on. She told me there was nothing going on and we had a very good meeting.   The same week another council meeting told me that she appreciated the job I was doing. There was no need for me to worry or so I thought.

I will never forget what happened. At the Council meeting, the Mayor called for an executive session and invited me to discuss my contract. It was like a lamb being led into the lion's den for slaughter. One after another the Council members took their turn citing their concerns regarding my leadership and morale in the department. The Town Attorney and Town Manager basically sat there and said nothing. Any Town Manager with integrity would have come to the rescue of their police chief. I felt that I was being "hung out to dry." I viewed it more like a kangaroo court. I responded to their questions but they were hearing me. It was now payback time. The "handwriting was on the wall." Apparently, one of my sergeants had aspirations on becoming a police chief and was conveying information to the Mayor, which was simply not true. I remember the Mayor asking me, "Why did you not fire your Lieutenant like we told you to?" I told them that I could not in good conscience fire him because he did nothing wrong. Matter of fact, he was doing a great job for me. As we were going through this silly exercise, I knew that my fate was sealed. I knew that they were not going to renew my employment contract with the town. A short time later, they went out of executive session and went into public session. When they went into public session, they swore in a new council member. One had resigned and they were now filling the position. I did not know the new council member at all. The council voted and it was unanimous not to renew my contract. The new council member whom I did not know voted. The council member who stated that I was doing an excellent job just the week before voted not to renew my contract. Apparently, there were some political debts that had to be paid. There must have been a great deal of discussion among them after hours because I was fooled as well as others.

Telltale Signs

The Town of Florence taught me a lesson in politics that I will never ever forget. There is always a moral to the story. Try to watch out for **telltale signs** that something may be wrong. If someone approaches you about a potential problem, you should pay attention to it. Often times **the ego of the police chief might get in the way**. You might tell yourself, "I am the greatest law enforcement officer ever." It may be true but any police chief is expendable. The reality is that anyone can be replaced at any time. I certainly found out in a hurry. Before you realize what is happening it may be too late to do damage control. If there is a **rumor** out in the community try to get to the bottom of it as soon as possible. Rumors can fester and before you know it will get out of control and everyone will believe it. The rumors could be false but your enemies will want to believe it. The small faction out to get the police chief usually exist in every community. Why give this group ammunition? Do not want to give them any more help. Above all, it is best to maintain your high level of ethics and integrity.

Trust

Another issue that I have been alluding to is trust. There has to be mutual commitment and trust on both sides. Trust has to be established right front the very beginning. If I had to do it all over again and knowing about the ineffective and lack of leadership of the Town Manager, I would have had **more rapport** with each council member. I would have asked for more input and direction from the Town Council utilizing the executive sessions.

Another way to head off the inevitable is to align you with a **trusted peer**. Whatever you are going through you have to remember, "You are not the first, and you will not be the last." Sometimes, more often than not, a friend may be able to give you free advice. You can take it for what it is worth, but it may be enough to get you out of this predicament. We often forget as a police chief that we are not alone. Many others have experienced problems especially in the political arena.

Ask questions about the **rumor** to the town manager and if he or she is not aware of it ask permission to talk to the council members individually to see if they are upset about something. If the Mayor had told me the truth at our meeting prior to the council meeting, I would have spoken to each council member individually and privately. Maybe I could have done damage control.

Do Not Ignore the Signals

I guess after thinking about it there were some signals but I chose to ignore them. Perhaps I could have prevented what was going to happen. I found myself in a situation beyond my control. Here I was now unemployed. The sergeant, who had given information to the mayor, was made Interim Chief of Police. The Lieutenant was not even considered and it was no surprise, because they wanted me to fire him.

The sergeant who was interim police chief did not get the job. I guess they discovered that he was not telling the truth and he was the heart of the problem. I should not have been surprised but my permanent replacement was a local person who had retired from the Department of Corrections and had been out of law enforcement for 18 years. This is the best part. He was a cousin of one of the council members. Cronyism was live and well in the Town of Florence. As this time, the department had gone through a tremendous turnover and the department was embroiled in discrimination and lawsuits. I guess what goes around comes around. From a professional point of view it bothers me that in a short time the police department regressed even further from when I first took it over. It was difficult but I knew that I had to forget it and move on with my life. Just remember you cannot save the world.

Other police chiefs who find themselves in this situation should follow my advice. You probably have heard this saying, "You may win the battle but you will lose the war." The rationale is simple. If the politicians want to get rid of you there is nothing you can do about it but start looking. You may appeal to the court if you are not an at will employee. Some states have an appeal process for police chiefs but let us face it; the powers to be will eventually find a way to get rid of you.

Now many police chief who had found himself or herself in a similar situation simply fades away from law enforcement. It is possible that given the circumstances I was not going to be run out of law enforcement. I felt it was a low point but I could resurrect my career. While I was collecting my severance pay, I was applying for police chief positions. I made up my mind that they were not going to beat me. At the same time, I wondered how other communities would look at my situation?

I personally know other police chiefs that were terminated some appropriately and some as a victim of politics. I have known some very talented individuals who chose not to enter the political game again. It was too bad because law enforcement could have benefited a great deal if they had chosen to continue. I was determined to become police chief again. I had much more to offer to law enforcement and it was not time for me to go.

Much to my amazement there was still interest in my abilities as a police chief. I was getting invitations from towns and cities all across the country. I was offered a police chief position in Montevideo, Minnesota and Fort Lupton, Colorado. I was amazed and at the same time humbled. I finally accepted the position in Fort Lupton, Colorado after much thought and deliberation. It would turn out that move to Fort Lupton was an excellent match and one of my best decisions to further my career.

Fort Lupton, Colorado

I began my duties as Police Chief in Fort Lupton, Colorado on August 27, 1997. It took five months but I found myself working at the job that I love so much. You should never say, "Never." I told myself that I would never work in another community that had recalled the council. The situation was entirely different. The prior police chief had been terminated by the previous City Council and now the new council was in place.

Who Is The Boss?

This City Council was different from most. When I began my duties as their new police chief, there was an interim city administrator. The mayor and council members had more hands on control than other communities I have seen. Other words, the City Administrator was in name only, the real authority lay with the Mayor. He was the real boss of the municipality. It was **his way or the highway**. It would behoove any new police chief to **learn quickly about city government**. They are all different. It is important to find out the real power base.

I knew that I did not have to compete against the former police chief. He was now out of the picture and he had moved out of the community. The situation was very different from my previous community of Florence, Arizona. The City Council wanted me to keep them informed about the progress of the police department. I had no problem with their request. I always wanted someone to know what we were doing.

Mutual Trust

One point I want to make clear. Some police department, which remain nameless run a secret organization. No one knows what is going on. You probably know some organizations that still exist today. I discovered that the more people in the community knew how the police department operated the more people accepted its department. Other words, there has to be a **mutual trust.** When the community does not trust the police, it is the telltale sign of problems. Fort Lupton had this mystic of secrecy and there was a poor image of the department. The perception was that the community did not trust the police.   There were hints and even suggestions from influential community members regarding corruption. It was a formable task but I had to win back the trust of the community.

I wanted to establish a rapport with the mayor and council members. I made it a point to get to know each person on a personal basis. I wanted to reassure them that I needed their help as much as they needed mine. They wanted me to attend each council meeting, which amounted to two workshops and two regular sessions. It required a great deal of time but I thought it was necessary.   From the very beginning, I wrote a monthly report outlining all the programs and major accomplishments. It is important to **keep the channels of communication open** at all times. It was so successful that they wanted me on the council agenda ever month usually at the end of the meeting when staff would present some information. Now, I would like to point out not every Town or City Council will do this. Often times there are answer and questions at the end of the Council Meeting. I was very careful not to dominate the discussions, because it was their meeting. I wanted to present major accomplishments and other important information. Each workshop and council meeting was televised on the local community access cable network. I knew that even though the Council Meetings and Workshops were not well attended, there was a fair number of the community who watched the meetings on their television.   It was an opportunity to use the media to highlight the department. I will talk more in detail about the media in another chapter.

Mayor Ron Jones became a good friend of mine. We had a mutual respect for one another and in many ways we were alike. I was impressed with his demeanor and style even after the first interview. Their interview was the traditional type of interview but with one exception. The mayor, interim city administrator and some council members were seated directly behind me. They observed the entire process. They heard each question and listened to each of my answers. Now, I am sure the way it was done it would have been intimidating to some, but it was not for me. Matter of fact, I asked a question about the recall that caught some of the panel members by surprise.   They were pleased that I knew something about their community. They referred the question to the Mayor who later brought me into a conference room after the interview to discuss my concern regarding the recall. The Mayor and I had an informal discussion but it was an informal continuation of the interview process. The Mayor appeared to be honest and forthright. I think that it began an understanding and liking for one another. The interview panel liked another candidate from a large city better, but guess who got the job? The Mayor convinced everyone else that I was the best candidate for the job.

Try To Get Along

This example demonstrated to me how politics works. I became even more interested in the dynamics of politics. It does not matter how smart you are as I found out in Florence, but how well you can get along with the powers to be. Some police chiefs find out the hard way and never learn.

There was never a time during my two years in Fort Lupton where I found my job might have been in jeopardy. The Mayor and City Council Members told me in the beginning that they supported me and they would do whatever it takes to straighten out the department. Their endorsement was very refreshing.

Know When to Challenge

There were a couple of times when I may have pushed the envelope a little further. I took a chance but I knew that I had the support. There was one time early on when a council member was critical of a budget request. She related during the meeting that her uncle, a police lieutenant with a metro department in the Denver area gave his opinion regarding an issue. I said diplomatically that I was their police chief and local expert. If they wanted to find out about something, all they had to do was give me the courtesy to respond to the question first. I did not want to imply that the police lieutenant did not know anything, but he did not have any details about the issue and circumstances. It was a chance that I took in front of the council and it was televised to the community. My tactic worked because the next day she called me to apologize. Matter of fact, she later reversed her stance on the issue. It was a big chance to take but the issue was too much to ignore. I wanted to **get the facts right** because a council vote on any budget items would affect the operations of the police department and ultimately service to the community. Sometimes you have to do what you must as a police chief. Taking a **calculated risk** is good in some cases.

One other situation that comes to mind could have had a reverse affect. One of the council members was a retired police sergeant from Greeley, Colorado about 25 miles north of Fort Lupton. If you recall, sometimes it could be advantageous to have a former police officer on the city council, but other times it could be a hindrance. If I had my druthers, I would not like to have a former police officer on any city or town council or Police Commission. It is an opinion, because during my experience I observed more damage than not. These former police officers in their now in an important position as a council member tend to believe they know more about police work and are now experts in knowing how to run a police department.

It was during a council workshop that this former police officer did not agree with the budget request for a new police vehicle. I could see that he was having an impact with the other council members. Because he was a former police officer, they were starting to accept his reasoning. Now there were some other dynamics going on here, which must be explained further so you can get a better understanding. The Mayor and this person were beginning to have disagreements about everything and it was puzzling because they were what I thought friends. I thought I was a friend of the council member. I found out that a friend of his was very critical of the Mayor and was thinking of making a run for Mayor in the future. It was apparent to me he was now aligning himself with his friend for whatever reason. It is still a mystery to me. He knew that the Mayor and I were friends and it was an opportunity to criticize my budget requests.

Get the Negative Person on Your Side

Now, for the good part! The police department had a police committee made up of members of the community. When I first took over the department there was no active police committee. I actively recruited members of the community and got them appointed by the city council. The council liaison was the former police officer. He never attended very many meetings, just a few in the beginning. I enlisted the help of the police committee and chamber of commerce to help me with my budget request. At the next council meeting there were four or five people who spoke regarding this issue and urged the council to support my request. When it came time for the vote, it was unanimous. The former police officer council member to my surprise voted in the affirmative too. After the council meeting he pulled me to the side and said, "You orchestrated the while thing." I shrugged my shoulders and smiled. I told him apparently the community members felt strongly about this issue too.

Keep in mind that you do not want to embarrass anyone, especially a council member. It is always a good idea to **give them an out to save face**. This way everyone wins.

It was not too long after that when I found out that this council member resigned from the city council. Apparently, he was bitter over the ongoing feud with the Mayor. It was too bad because he was a good person at heart. Sometimes you wonder why a person changes, but it is still politics. Some people play the game better than others do.

Create Your Own Style

Even though I was successful in dealing with the City Council in the manner that I described, I have to throw out a caveat. Just because it was successful for me, it may not be successful for someone else. Sometimes these tactics can blow up in someone's face. I had taken a calculated risk, but it was a risk I was willing to take to further the cause of the police department. Besides, I knew that I had the support of the Mayor and other council members. The moral of the story is to understand your council members and **know what you can get away with**. Sometimes you have to take a risk but the percentage may be heavily weighted on your side so it is worth the risk. Any Chief **worth his salt must take a risk** from time to time. The police chief's primary responsibility is public safety for the community. Remember one thing. Do not get caught up in the political gamesmanship. If you get caught on the wrong side, it could be devastating to your career. **Maintain the appearance of neutrality**, which is the best advice I can give. Politicians always like to align themselves with the police chief in many cases, because the police chief in his or her own right has a certain amount of political power.

All and all Fort Lupton was a good opportunity for me to grow professionally. We were able to accomplish many things and it was the result of the direct support from my personnel and City Council. They were saddened to hear that I was going to retire and move to the east coast to be closer to family. It was an experience that I will never forget. The political situation was good for me.

It made me wonder how I can be accepted by a political body in one community and not another. To me it was strange. My management style was the same for both communities. Sometimes you can never figure it out, so why try. All you can do is be yourself and not worry about the political ramifications. Everything will fall into place.

Chapter 4
Management Styles

One question that always comes up during the interview process is what is your management style? This question is always problematic to me. I was always wondering if I was answering their question fully. You can pick up any management text and you can read all about the different styles and types of leaders of a manager. You can also pick up another book and read something completely different. However, there is one problem. There is not one style that fits me, which is why I have a problem with it. I am sure others vying for management positions have been perplexed by this very issue. I am sure the interviewers do not know what they are really looking for. It seems like a good question to as though. One retired police chief told me once, "Throw the book out and use good, old common sense."

What is a good management style for a police chief to use? Why does one style work in one community and not another? There have been many instances of police chiefs succeeding or failing because of their management style or lack of a particular style. I do not know anyone who intentionally decided to fail. We hear a great deal about autocratic, democratic or lazy-fare in the early days of management. Other buzzwords have surfaced to try to define or coin a particular type of management style better such as participative management. It sounds nice but what is it? Textbooks are full of different management styles.

I know one thing for sure. There is no best one style suited for the police chief. It really depends upon the individual and what he or she feels comfortable with a particular style. One style may work best in a particular situation while another is better suited for another. My style of management is a combination of different styles acquired during many years of experience as a police chief. It is difficult to name one but if I had to name one, it would be more participatory than anything else.

The "Ivory Tower"

It is difficult to put a label on any one type of management style because no two people are alike. I spent much of my time early during my police chief career trying to learn more about management styles and what works best. One person, a wise retired police chief and the director of the police academy from New Hampshire gave me some good pointers. You can manage best by **"walking around."** He also said, "The chief must get him or herself out of the "ivory tower" and **put the shoe leather to the pavement**." These were profound statements by a successful police chief. For those of you who do not know what the "Ivory Tower" is let me explain it further. It is the chief's office. Some police chiefs enter into their office in the morning, and leave in the evening except for lunch. This person disappears in his office, and is usually not seen unless there is a problem. He or She is doing police chief's work. I am sure that you may know of someone who fits this category. This type of person is in the office for so long the people in the community do not know who he is and have not seen him. The chief needs to get out of his office to meet people.

Matter of fact, the chief that I replace in Fort Lupton did not venture into the community much. He was chief for 12 years and I would have thought he would have been highly visible. There was more than one person in the business community that did not know the police chief and never saw him. I thought it was pretty sad to think someone who had worked in the community for so long did not spend more time talking to the business people and citizens. There is just so much more to the job than occupying an office.

Perhaps, I can describe management styles by what I have done in three different departments. My style in three departments was similar yet different. For the interviewer's benefit I was always "participative management" but maybe one should coin a different term?

Establish Your Own Style, Be Yourself

If someone had asked me about what my management style in Somersworth, New Hampshire, I am not so sure if I could have answered the question properly. My answer probably would have been the standard book type response. What I found out was that the **books tell you one thing but in actual practice, it is entirely different**. The theories and discussions about management style in texts are nice but it is only the perspective of the authors. The police chiefs have to be comfortable with their **own style** and not worry about emulating someone else. It is that simple.

When I first went to Somersworth, I thought that I was prepared to be a police chief. At the time, I had 18 years experience in law enforcement and had risen through the ranks rapidly. Being a captain in a medium size police agency and having a master's degree in criminal justice management surely made me qualified to be a police chief or so I thought. You never know what to expect until you finally get the brass ring, a police chiefs position. My own management style evolved after years of experience, trial and error and good fortune on my side or otherwise known as luck. I think perhaps timing and luck has a great deal to do with being successful.

Somersworth was a good department. There are problems to contend with in any department and it is usually in disarray when a police chief has been dismissed. One has to remember there are no perfect organizations because people are human and they make mistakes. The police chief is a person who has the leadership and ability to hold things together, or "glue" if you will. I like to use the orchestra as an analogy to illustrate my point. When the conductor is at the peak of his or her performance, the orchestra plays beautiful music. All the musicians are in sync and in harmony. When someone is not playing well then the orchestra will not sound right to the listener, there is a break down of the unit.

The same could be held true of the coach and basketball players. The coach can be the best and most intelligent in the world but fail miserably in a losing season. What matters is getting the players motivated and playing well as a team in order to win games.   The same can be said of the police chief.   As the leader of the department, it is his or her role to motivate the employees to be the best they can be. You have to convince them to want to do a good job for the chief and the community. When these employees are motivated to do a good job then the goals of the organization are achievable.   Unfortunately, many employees in police departments are just looking at it like a job and to earn a paycheck. The challenge for the police chief is to continually motivate personnel to want to do the job.

Establish Confidence and Trust

My job as the police chief was to bring the organization back into sync and in harmony. In order for any leader to be effective, he or she must have confidence in their personnel and vice versa. Being a leader is a two way street. A person may officially be placed in a leadership position because of a promotion, but the real test lay with their personnel. Ultimately, the subordinates or employees must want to follow their leader. You must give them a reason to have confidence and trust in you before they will follow. Just because you are now the "boss," you do not have to remind them. It may be a difficult concept to grasp at first. Many employees will take a wait and see attitude. It is only human nature. Just remember, what you were thinking when you were a lowly police officer way back when and a new chief arrived to take over a department. Everyone was suspicious at first, because you do not know him or her. The trust and confidence that you will build occurs over time. You can threaten or try to intimidate a person but eventually the leader will be doomed to fail.

Being new and an outsider or sometimes commonly referred to as the "carpetbagger," I knew that I had a long road ahead of me to win over my personnel. Just because I was their police chief did not mean they were going to instantly follow me.   It was a situation where we had to grow together as a department if we were going to accomplish anything as a department. The "Honey

Moon" period can be short or as long as six or more months. It is a feeling out process for each side, the community and City Council.   What develops is a wait and see attitude. They want to what this person is truly like. The feeling is that they are going to wait to try to figure this person out before anyone makes up his or her mind.

I did not take this wait and see attitude as an insult. They did not know me. The fear of the unknown is just human nature. No one wants to have a new person come into an organization and upset the so-called "apple cart." No one knew my capabilities or me.   Sometimes people are afraid of change.   Change in an organization is good as long as it is done carefully. The police chief will be tested at some point, and I was tested early on as well.

Being Tested

The person did not get the job in Somersworth tested me. **Do not be intimidated by anyone.** If you recall, he was the person who had spies out there trying to figure out the competition.   There were many hints and innuendos about how certain department members managed to remove the former police chief? I am glad that he talked spoke it because I knew I had to be very careful.   This particular person, a lieutenant decided to try to embarrass me at a reception for a new officer who graduated from the New Hampshire Police Academy. He was upset that I did not want to go to dinner at the department's expense right after the graduation exercise. In my mind, I could not justify the expense. He said, "The former chief use to do it all the time." He had the audacity to say that I was "cheap" in front of family, friends and other police officers. I did not say a word. Actually, I was surprised at first, but I figured it was going to be a test. I knew that I had to do something; otherwise, I would lose all credibility as a police chief. If I did not do anything, I may have just as well packed my bags and move out.

The following morning I called the lieutenant into my office to discuss the incident. What it amounted to was a flagrant insubordination in front of others. I decided to issue him a written reprimand for his conduct. He was at first shocked and visibly angry with me. He said, "You will have to talk with my lawyer." I told him "you know what you can do with your lawyer and if you did not like it you can put your badge and gun on my desk and get out."   At this point he was truly flustered and was at a loss for words. He realized that the attempt at intimidation failed. Perhaps I was at the end of my "honeymoon" period. You can say this is certainly not participatory management style.

What a way to begin my police chief career. I was having a confrontation with one of my senior ranking officers. After he had left my office, he came back a short time later and apologized for his behavior. I accepted his apology and told him that

I would review his written reprimand in six months and if there were no problems I would remove it from his personnel file. Let me tell you that my confrontation with the lieutenant went through the department like wild fire and everyone was on their best behavior at least for a while. I certainly asserted myself in a hurry and it was not by choice. I knew that I was going to be tested and I found out it was sooner then later. Actually, we had a good working relationship after this incident. Sometimes you have to do what you have to do. Perhaps, it was a test to see what I was going to do. He found out in a hurry.

Management Staff

Normally, I try to work with the present staff even if one or more have some deficiencies. My philosophy is that no one is perfect. Some chiefs bring in their own management staff and in a way it is good. You can rely on the person who you have selected for a management position to get the job done. The private sector does it all the time and most of these large corporations are successful. If chiefs could pick their own management staff then I believe the success rate would be higher.

If someone is weak in an area then it is my job to teach him or her. You would think that if someone went to the FBI National Academy this person would be a gold mine for ideas and implementation of programs. This program is considered the best in the country for developing police executives. Actually, I always wanted to attend the FBI National Academy but remained on the list in Bristol, Connecticut. My focus after that was to develop my personnel to be the best that they could be. The lieutenant that I spoke about attended this very program and what a disappointment. I wondered what kind of program did they taught? I knew that I had my work cut out for me.

Managing By the Seat of Your Pants

I think in the beginning **I was managing by the "seat of my pants."** I was trying to figure out ways to fit in the organization and be effective. Some police chiefs are very much into this mode of management. It seems that many times he or she is always reacting to some incident or situation. You probably heard this old cliché that 20 percent of the personnel cause eighty percent of the problems. This is so true. The chief is embroiled in personnel issues that take away from the planning process. We will talk more about unions and disciplinary matters in other chapters.

I knew that if I wanted to succeed in Somersworth, New Hampshire or anywhere else I had to be decisive and involve my personnel in the management of the department. The whole key regarding a management style depends upon the particular situation at any one time. The police chief **has to be flexible** so that he or she can change their style when the opportunity calls for it. It sounds like a tall order but it is not so complicated. I utilize the following management principle to guide. I called it the **"5 P's of Management – Prior Planning Prevents Poor Performance."** The concept is not too hard to grasp. Whether you are from a small, medium or large law enforcement agency you have to plan for the future – immediate and long-term. Many police chief fail because they are too preoccupied with personnel and union matters. They fail to see the "forest through the trees" or the big picture. They are one issue at a time orientated and it could easily lead to disaster.

I wanted to involve my personnel in a team effort even though the ultimate responsibility was mine. I wanted to change the focus of the department, look to the future and not dwell on the past. One problem that I could see was that some department members were still preoccupied with the ghost of the former chief. It is very easy to get caught up with the former chief's problems and eventual departure. You have to make a concerted effort to stay away from these issues. What happened in the past should stay in the past. The issue should be to concentrate on the present and plan for the future.

In the very beginning, I conducted weekly staff meetings and department wide staff meetings. It was important to involve everyone in the new direction of the department with the emphasis on improving services to the community. The department through the eyes of the community appeared to be a huge problem and dysfunctional. There was very little respect for the department and I wanted to change it. The department was stagnated in its own self-serving culture.

Back in 1988, other police departments were getting involved in the Community Policing concept. At the time, it was fairly new but I thought it was a good direction for the police department. Slowly but surely, I began to change the way we were doing business as well as upgrading the badly needed equipment for my officers. We discussed these changes in staff meetings. I did not want to scare them away by making changes too quickly. Slowly I began to implement changes in the department. Human nature is such that no one wants to break his or her routine. People are scared of change. I think that it is important for a police chief to time these moves and not move too fast. Personally, my approach is to prepare my personnel for change before the change takes place.

The police chief has to be **decisive and take control** when the situation calls for it. Some times the chief has to say **no**, and that should be your final answer. The chief has the ultimate responsibility for the department and he or she will be held accountable. You cannot be democratic all the time and take a vote on everything. It is proper to get other views and opinions on a management issue, but the police chief must have the final say. I have had to be the bad person and say no because it was in the best interest of the department. You have to remember one thing **you**

cannot please everyone, so why worry about it? There will always be someone or some people who will never agree with you no matter what you do, so do what is best for the department. I always maintained my interest was in the department and community and not what was in it for me.

There are times when the police chief has to challenge tradition. A few personnel dwelled on the past and were self-serving. The attitude was what was in it for me? I needed to effect change and slowly change the traditions. One thing for sure, I was not going to take over the Coke machine. For the last 10 years or so the police chiefs always took care of and were responsibility for the Coke machine. The money was supposed to go to the police association to help the children in the community. It appeared some of the money was allegedly diverted. This is truly a common sense issue. The police chief should not **handle any money**. It could be an integrity issue but why put you in a situation to be criticized. I have seen too many police chiefs fired because of mishandling funds.

Changing Attitudes

I think that I was effective in changing attitudes. We have gone through many changes including a complete rewrite of the Policy and Procedures Manual and reorganization of the department. You guessed it. The lieutenant was not a happy with the change. He was always resistant to change and I was not surprised. Matter of fact, I expected it. Do not be surprised if there is resistance in the changes you are making to improve the organization. I reassigned the lieutenant from Patrol Commander to Support Services Commander. He called himself the "Janitor" because he was responsible for the building maintenance. I guess some people will not get with the program and be on "the train" no matter what you do. You have to be prepared to act accordingly.

Just thinking about Somersworth I established myself in giving the department direction. There were a few times when I tried to give "you know who" a chance and listen to his advice. Well, I found myself in hot water every time. Against my better judgment I listened to him and in hindsight I should have given these problems more thought. The moral to the story is **nice guys finish last.** The police chief needs to make the best possible decision with good information at the time. If you do not have good information and the person who is giving advice appears to be "winging it," the best advice I can give is to **defer the decision until such time you have better information**. It makes good sense to me. Just think if I had fallen into the trap and had taken this person's advice all the time, I would not have lasted very long in Somersworth. It would have been a very short career. When you lose confidence in a person, what do you do about it? You have to do something or it will come back to haunt you.

This brings up another point. How do you deal with someone who may be incompetent to do the job? Sooner or later, the police chief will have to deal with this issue. My best advice is to approach it very carefully. Others might say just fire the person, but this person is not in the hot seat. This might be fine for some, but there could be political repercussions if this person is a long time resident of the community. If you take action and you are not careful even though you may be right, you will ultimately find yourself without a job. This individual was born and raised in Somersworth and many of his friends and relatives were still there. The smart thing to do is to try to work with the individual to make him or her succeed. If this is not possible then eventually there will be an opportunity for the chief to take action. Terminating employees were always my last resort. I never terminated someone just for the sake of getting rid of a person. I always had empathy for the employee because he or she is supporting a family and whatever action the chief takes the family is affected too.

Being Flexible

After leaving Somersworth, I began my new position as Police Chief in Florence, Arizona. Did I do everything the same as I did in Somersworth? The answer is no. During the seven years, I grew into the position. I made my mistakes but learned from them. I was a different but a confident person in Florence. My management style was **flexible** and had evolved to deal with contemporary law enforcement, community issues, and political environment and personnel issues. I could adjust my style to fit the situation. I believed that I had the flexibility and ability to handle a new challenge and what a challenge it was going to be.

Nothing could have prepared me for what was in store for me in Florence. I viewed it as repairing a disaster. After the police chief was terminated, the Town Manager appointed a Patrolman as the Interim Chief. He had bypassed two other sergeants. The department was being run on a day-to-day basis without any thought for planning and program development. Why I took this position, I will never know? Maybe, I enjoyed the challenge. In the end, there were too many obstacles to overcome including and more important, the prevailing political environment at the time. The political environment had changed shortly after my arrival. I was thinking that if they recognized my ability then perhaps I have a chance to succeed. I do not know what I was thinking but it seemed logical to me at the time.

I knew it was going to be a great deal of work and more so when I asked an officer, "where are the General Orders." He said that there were General Orders but they were all drafts. I asked him if there was a use of force policy and he said, "We just follow the state statutes." I knew we were in trouble so I began to write the high liability General Orders. The Town Attorney and Town Manager reviewed and approved each high liability General Order and then I issued them to the police personnel.

Because there was no management staff, my management style had to be more **controlling**. All the sergeants had left the department, which left me in a precarious situation. I did not have the time or luxury to get advice from my personnel. I guess in some instances I was more direct in reestablishing contemporary management practices. However, I made a point to have department meetings to discuss our situation and potential changes. I strongly feel that it is important to keep your personnel up to date on any changes or potential changes.

Unanticipated Problems

There were many issues that I seemed to have had to tackle all at once. I not only had to hire more officers to replace the ones who left but had to promote staff to fill the vacant supervisory positions. With the approval of the Town Manager and former Town Council, I promoted the former Interim Police Chief to Lieutenant. The recall council later used this issue against me two years later. They kept bring up why I promoted this person without a test? They just did not like him because he replaced the former police chief. He was like a traitor in their eyes. Even though this person was competent and had management experience in the private sector, I should have opened up this promotional opportunity to department members and sworn police officer from outside the department who met the promotional criteria. This was a missed opportunity to have a competitive promotional process to fill the position. I could have gone through the charade and have a promotional process and hire the person I wanted anyway. I felt that I had the right person and therefore made the decision to promote him. I guess if he got promoted regardless of the process, there still would have been criticism by others. Nevertheless, I did it and if I had to do it all over again I would have **done it differently**. However, I wrote a procedure for promotions and used it for the sergeant's promotional process. The procedure was effective and it quieted the critics for the time being. Little did I realize the initial promotion to lieutenant struck a sore spot with some folks. They looked at the lieutenant as if he was some sort of traitor to the former police chief. However, what people failed to consider that the former police chief's actions leading to his dismissal were unavoidable.

Another problem that I did not anticipate was dealing with the former police chief. This person lived in the community and he was not going away unlike my predecessor in Somersworth, New Hampshire. If you think that a situation can get worse, it can. Who would have thought the former chief would be a factor. Usually former chiefs accept their fate and move on, but not this guy. He was not going anywhere. The former police chief was good at intimidating my personnel. Some actually believed that he was coming back to the department and I was just there for a short time. There were two more occasions when we had to arrest the former police chief. He was just plain hardheaded and stubborn. He was not a bad person. I see good in everyone. Sometimes there is just a matter of disagreement. He was still protesting on how he was fired unfairly and wanted his job back. Every time when he got into trouble, it was because of his son. The father believed that his son could do no wrong and he was taking it out on the police department. Each times our Town Attorney and Judge would cite a conflict of interest and defer to an out of town prosecutor and justice. I suppose they were right, but in reality, they did not want to deal with the former police chief. It is not a fun process, but the police chief has a duty to do what is ethically right.

The community appeared to accept me very well and did not have any problems with the decisions that I had been making. Matter of fact, they welcomed the changes. There was one type of tradition that I wanted to immediately change. Some people in the community were treated differently from others. Other words, it was the good "O'boy's network" was live and well. It was acceptable to arrest some people but others were considered untouchable. I wanted to treat everyone the same regardless of money, power, race or political influence. It was a welcomed change to the general community but not to the political elite. **Be fair to everyone.**

Establish Teamwork

I wanted to incorporate teamwork so that my personnel would feel that they have contributed to the organization. Generally, people in any organization whether it is the police or private sector want to feel needed. I think that I was successful in establishing teamwork. On the downside, I can see a problem. If the personnel are allowed to become so strong that they could easily undermine what the chief is trying to accomplish.

I strongly believe that even though the police chief's style of management is always changing depending upon the circumstances, the teamwork style is by far the most effective in getting things done in an organization. If you can unleash the creativity of your personnel, the job of the police chief is much easier. It is important for a person to express his or her opinions and ideas. I like to unleash each individual's creativity. One successful city manager told me, **"If you want to be successful, surround yourself with good people."** It makes sense to me.

The City of Fort Lupton, Colorado was a good place to work even though the City had turnover and morale problems. I believe that it had a great deal to do with the former City Council, recall Council and the aftermath. The City Government was in turmoil. Even though there were innuendos about firing certain individuals, I wanted to see first hand what the problems were before I took any action. I knew one thing for sure; if I had acted too quickly, it would have been a short-lived experience for me. The most important thing on my agenda was to win the trust of my personnel. I certainly could not do that if I outright fired people. **Win the trust of your personnel and everything will fall into place.**

Rumor and More Rumors

What were hurting the organization were rumors. If you recall, I mentioned the rumor mill could hurt any organization. The first thing I did was to call a department meeting to introduce myself, and discuss a plan of action to get the department back on track. Many of the personnel were taking a wait and see attitude. I wanted to reassure them regardless what they heard that I did not come here to terminate certain individuals. I also wanted them to know that they could ask me about any rumors. It is important to get the facts out and let the truth known. I certainly did not want to repeat the same mistakes in Florence, Arizona. The mayor and town council chose to believe the rumors instead of asking me. It was truly unfortunate for them. I even reminded them about the rumor mill. I instituted an **"open door policy"** for my personnel. It is important to maintain the chain of command but what is equally important is to allow a mechanism for anyone to talk with the police chief.

I have heard it before and it has happened to me. The new City Administrator in Fort Lupton, Colorado told his department heads that if they wanted to talk with him they would have to make an appointment with his secretary. He introduced his secretary as the "Bosset." Talk about killing morale in a hurry, this was it. He wondered why no one wanted to speak to him. He quickly changed his mind and allowed an open door. It is just common sense. You have to allow your personnel to have access to you. Many police chiefs limit accessibility and it has to hurt their effectiveness.

Some People Intentionally Create Problems

I am more comfortable with my style by having an open door policy. This way I get to know my personnel better especially in a smaller agency. On the positive side by establishing a rapport with your personnel, you will have a heads up on any potential problem. If there is a potential problem, then you will be able to deal with it before it gets to be a big problem. Some chiefs suffered because they found out about problems too late. I believe that some people intentionally cause problems when the organization seems to be running good. Why would someone want to cause trouble? Sometimes it is a mystery. Some people, I believe, have it in their nature to cause trouble for the organization. Some people manifest having problems when there are actually no problems at all. I would wager that you already know some personnel who fit into this category.

Make Your Personnel Feel Important

I did manage to win the trust and support of my personnel. It did not come overnight but it does take work. We developed a good working relationship. The teamwork concept worked better in this situation. Matter of fact, we were able to get the police department back on track quicker because of the support I received from my personnel. The Mayor and City Council were very pleased with the progress of the police department and the many programs that had been implemented. One thing that I always did was reinforce all the time what we had accomplished together. It is important to tell your personnel when they are doing a good job. People wanted to feel wanted in an organization and I made them **feel important and wanted**.

In order to make my personnel feel more important I introduced the Employee of the Quarter and a medal and commendation program. There will be more on this in another chapter. If someone did a particularly good job, many times I went out of my way to compliment the individual. Saying something nice to a person is important. These things that you do will help establish your relationships and set the stage for better things to come. It is important for your personnel to know that you care about them as a person. What is one complaint that we often hear? "The chief does not care about me."

Management styles vary according to the situation. The police chief has to have an **adaptable style of management** to deal effectively with contemporary management. There is not one size that fits all. What may work in one organization may not work in another. It all depends upon the effectiveness of the police chief. As the situation changes the police chief must do so as well and adapt.

Chapter 5
Media Relations

Many police chiefs look at the media as the enemy. In my opinion, the media can be your friend. The media can help or hurt the police chief and often it is how one approaches media relations. I will discuss the positives and the negatives so that you will have a better understanding of the dynamics involved. The media has a job to do too, just like the police chief. They will report the news one way or the other. I would rather have them report accurate news and hear it from me rather than having them chase down every rumor. I have learned to deal with the media and it developed into a mutual trust with one another. I look at it from a pragmatic point of view. I like to use the media and have them help me to do my job.

In Bristol, Connecticut, I never had to deal with the media other than a few words at an accident or crime scene. The word was out not to talk to the media. I was always telling them you have to talk with the lieutenant or captain. I always put the monkey on someone else's back and that was how we were taught. Police officers were always told to watch what was said because the media will always misquote you. They were considered the enemy. Even to this day, many police officers view the media in this fashion. I never had to present an official prepared department press release other than some crime news until I was appointed police chief. There were police officers that intentionally lied to the media when they called to ask what was going on when there was actually a major crime the police were investigating. Hey, they are going to find out anyway so you may as well be truthful. I wanted to change the way we did business with the media.

Tell the Truth

When I became the police chief in Somersworth, New Hampshire, I had to learn very quickly on how to deal with the media. My first exposure was a story about the four mummified babies stored in the evidence room. Who would have thought I would have to discuss mummified babies. You can take media relation courses and they are helpful to a certain extent but nothing prepares you for the real thing. When the media found out that we still had the mummified babies in our evidence room I knew that I was going to be bombarded with many questions. Why the babies were still there and why were they not buried? Heck, I would ask that question myself. It just did not make any sense to me. There were good questions and I had asked my staff the same thing. I think the truth of the matter was that they were forgotten about and just left there in the evidence room. The main investigator for the case left the department. This certainly raised a great deal of community interest not only in Somersworth but also all over the state. I think that I passed my first test. I did not duck any questions and I was truthful in my response.

One fatal error that you should never commit is intentionally lying to the media. Telling a lie will certainly hurt a police chief's career. One thing for sure, if you get caught in a lie the media will never ever forget. Matter of fact, they will go out of their way to try and catch you in a lie again. Why risk losing your credibility? If you do not have the information do not make up a story. Actually, the media conducted a good interview and they were satisfied with the information that I provided. If I did not know something, I would say so or I could not provide the information because it may hurt the investigation.

The reporter covering the story was the initial reporter who had covered the story years ago. He knew more about it than I did because he was thinking about writing a book about it. I had contacted the State Attorney General's Office and they provided me with some guidance. After a few weeks, we were finally able to put the babies to rest in the local cemetery with the help of a local funeral director. He generously donated a small coffin and secured a plot in the cemetery. With people helping in the community, the job is easier. We were able to put this matter to rest forever. After the babies were buried, there were no other inquiries from anywhere. I do not know if the reporter had ever finished the book but it would certainly make an interesting mystery novel. Where did the babies come from? It was rumored that a political figure in Somersworth fathered the babies. The babies were born during the early 1950's and they were aborted to probably conceal the truth. The babies had been wrapped in old newspapers. Many people still wonder about it even to this day. The mystery continues.

Getting Caught In a Lie Spells Doom

After the initial inquiry for a story, the reporter will write his or her story and that is usually the end of it. Sometimes the reporter will smell a deception and will dig further to write more stories to find out the truth. Somehow, they can smell a lie. Once they caught you in a lie you are done. They believe the public has a right to know and will stop at nothing. Sometimes the enemy is within our minds. Sometimes we are our own worst enemy. I have seen it so many times where the police chief gets into trouble with the media. Many times the police chief blames the reporter for everything. You cannot blame the reporter for doing their job. Guess who gives the reporter the information for their story? The police chief is the culprit. Often the reporter has contacts within the department. Many of them obtain their stories this way. One lie leads to another lie and before you know it, you fell into the trap. When the police chief makes a mistake or does something unethical, immoral or illegal, he or she should accept responsibility.

There has been countless number of situations where media inquires are inevitable. How much information should I release? If I release too much could it hurt my investigation? I approach it in this manner but first my philosophy. Many police chiefs and sheriffs have a designated media person. It is considered a good practice for medium and large police department to have a spokesperson for serious crimes and other matters that arouse the curiosity of the public. At some point, the media will want to hear directly from the police chief or sheriff. Police chiefs and sheriffs should not continually duck the interview. There are times when the media wishes to hear directly from the chief. I usually gave information about a major incident or crime without going into too much detail. **Any information that would jeopardize an investigation should not be given out.** I like to make their job easier and use a common sense approach. Generally, they are very satisfied especially if everyone is cooperating.

Incidents Off-duty

Incidents off duty can affect the police chief negatively or positively in the eyes of the media. It is tough enough for a police chief to stay out of the media limelight for incidents involving personnel but when something happens to the chief as in my case it can go either way. It is a police chief's worst nightmare to personally get involved in an incident that could ultimately lead to media frenzy. However, I was able to survive it because I used a little common sense.

It my sound a little far fetched but you never know what might happen. One Sunday morning after Church services my wife and I decided to go to the supermarket to pick up a few groceries in our neighboring city, Dover. As I was driving through the parking lot, I could see an individual standing at the edge of the parking lot. It looked like he was attempting to cross and stopped and let my vehicle pass by. As I was driving past, he started to shout obscenities at me saying I was trying to run him over. It was kind of absurd because I was only traveling at about 20 mph. If I had to do it all over again, I would never have stopped, but in this case, I did. This person just charged right up against my driver's door and continued his barrage of expletives directed at me. As I was trying to explain to him and at the same time, I opened my door and managed to get out of my vehicle. No sooner had I done this the individual suckered punched me and hit me right square in the eye drawing blood. I told my wife to go into the store and call the police.

In the meantime, I thought for a split second to punch him back but one thing stopped me. What immediately flashed before me was a deluge of media inquires as to how I got involved in fisticuffs with a citizen. It would not look good for a police chief to be involved in a street fight no matter what the circumstances, self defense or otherwise. Instead, I took out my badge, identified myself as a police chief from Somersworth, and told him to stay right there to wait for the Dover

Police. By this time, he did not want to have any more to do with me and decided to leave. I followed him to the front of the supermarket where we were involved in a tug of war. Every time he turned away to leave I grabbed his sleeve of his shirt to hold him there. It probably looked comical in the eyes of the onlookers. Out of the corner of my eye, I observed the Dover Police responding to the incident. When the officer approached me, I told him this individual assaulted me. After they questioned us separately and inspected our hands for cuts and bruises, they arrested the individual for assault. Because I did not strike the individual, there were no cuts on my hands but when they inspected the individual's hands; his knuckle on his right hand was cut. They arrested him and took him away in handcuffs.

I was sure glad that I did not fight the individual. I could see the headlines, "Somersworth Police Chief involved in fight." The headlines instead read, "Somersworth Police Chief Assaulted." It would not have looked very favorably for me if I had fought back and possibly would have arrested for assault too. A little common sense goes a long way. After I got home, I made a phone call to the City Manager to let him know what happened so that he could inform the mayor and council members. Some people asked why I did not hit the individual back and I certainly could have in self-defense. After he hit me he backed away from me. There was no need to hit him back. I figured it would be best to let the law take care of him and in the end; it was the smart move to make. I had to use considerable restraint. If you are involved in an incident, you need to **inform the city manager, mayor and council members.**

The police chief not only has to worry about the positive news but the negative ones as well. Sometimes you can be right and still lose. The incident in the parking lot could have been a media nightmare and an embarrassment to the City of Somersworth but because I showed considerable restraint the incident was caste in a positive light for me. This time I was the victim. Like, I said if I had to do it all over again I would never have stopped. You never know what may happen. A seemly innocent incident can suddenly get out of control very quickly. In this particular incident, I managed to survive. Police chiefs have gotten into situations and found themselves without a job. As a police chief, you have to be aware of your off duty activities. As a side note, this individual was found guilty in Dover District Court for assault and paid a fine. Oh, on the day of the incident it was his birthday. I guess he had a bad day overall.

Do Not Remind the Media of All Their Mistakes

I have seen too many police chiefs and upper management fight with the media. The winners are guess who? The media wins every time. They have the last say on the written word. What is written in the newspaper certainly does not look favorable to the police chief. One thing for sure I did not want to get into any arguments with the reporter. If I did not particularly like a story and the facts were not right, I would just mention it to him or her during a discussion. Sometimes they would print a retraction and other times it was just left, like the way it was. The retractions are usually buried deep in the papers and very few people read them anyway so this is why I do not make a big deal about it. Unless it is a major gaff then I usually will not say much about it. I can live with mistakes because everyone makes them including reporters. I do not remind them of it every time they make a mistake. How many times have your personnel approach you to say that the reporter messed up the news article? I usually tell them that I will mention the mistake to the reporter. Why continually remind the reporter every time they make a mistake? You have to know when to cut your losses and **keep your mouth shut.**

Invite the Reporter to Your Office

Every time there is a new reporter, I make it a point to invite the person into my office to introduce myself and to put the reporter at ease. Many times in a small community, their first job after college is at a local community newspaper covering town news. They generally want to learn their craft quickly so that they could move on to bigger and better things. I tell them up front that I will help them to do their job. If there is a news-breaking event, we will call them first. I maintain that we should take care of our local media first. Often times there are news worthy events that attracts State and National coverage. Sometimes when they converge on you for a press interview, make sure that your local reporter does not get left out. **Take care of your local media.** It is easy to see the pecking order of the media. The little guy tends to be pushed to the side and is left out. If you take care of your local reporter, he or she will remember it and treat you more favorably in the future. I always make sure they have access to the same information and have the opportunity to ask questions during a press conference.

My experiences with the media have been good. I can think of only a few times when the news was not reported accurately. It is going to happen so there is no reason to get upset about it. Most of the time, it was an honest mistake. When my personnel tell me that the press release was messed up, I tell them I will take care of it and talk with the reporter. Most of the time I may mention it to the reporter, but I do not intend to make it a big deal.

In Somersworth every time we started a new program, purchased a new piece of equipment, purchased a police cruiser I called the reporter to ask if he or she would like to write a story or take a picture. Most of the time, they are always looking for a human-interest story. I provided them material for a story. Take for example, when we switched to a new striping scheme for our marked police cruisers in Fort Lupton and Florence, I called up the reporter and asked if he wanted to take some pictures. It did not take long for him to beat a path to the police department. Some would say why bother. The reporters are looking for stories to write all the time. Instead of them researching rumors, I give something positive for them to write about and believe me it works. It seemed after a while the community was reading positive things about the police department all the time. Every now and then, my picture as well as my personnel would be in the paper. It was not like I was trying to get my picture taken all the time but it was positive news. I wanted the community to read good things about the department. It was important to build confidence and have trust in their police department. During the preceding years, there was too much focus on the negative.

I try to remind the public that the police department is their department and there should not be any secrecy. We certainly do not want to give the impression that the police are an occupying force. How many times have we heard this? How often do we read about positive programs in a police department? It is not very often. How often do we hear about the negatives from the public? We hear about it all the time. My point is to keep the public informed on what we are doing. I like to use the media to help highlight the police department and at the same time, they are getting their article for the week.

My personnel were trying to figure out what I was doing. In my mind, the answer was obvious. It was time to rebuild the tarnished image of the police department and the media was going to help me. In each of my departments, I used the media to improve the image of the police department. Some of the police department that I had known and some that I took over were a public relations nightmare. I take a positive approach to this challenge by saying, "I can turn this program around." In each case I was successful.

Chief's Corner

In Florence, Arizona I continued the public relations approach and brought it to a new level. This time I added articles about the police department and appeared on the local cable television network. I had a featured "Crime & Prevention" column. Each week I wrote an article for the local newspaper. The articles focused on crime prevention, programs and different things happening in our community. I tried to inject some humor in trying to make a point. One article featured the theft of golf clubs from a golf cart in the winter visitor's residential area. One day I drove around to see how many golf bags were left in plain sight for anyone to walk away with them. The article's main focus was crime prevention to show how easily senior citizens can be victimized. The following is an article written by me as it appeared in the Town of Florence's local newspaper, The Florence Reminder:

Where Are the Golf Clubs?

During the last few weeks, we have been experiencing a rash of thefts lately including golf clubs. Several sets of golf clubs were stolen from the Caliene and Florence Gardens area. The golf clubs were left out in the open in the golf cart and apparently someone driving by decided to stop and help themselves. It was easy pickings. No one called the police to report anything unusual. Just for fun, I drove around Caliente and Florence Gardens and counted seven sets of golf clubs out in the open. It would have only taken seconds to stop and load them into a vehicle even in broad daylight. There is a lesson to be learned. Even though the crime rate is low in that area occasionally, some thief will decide to try their luck. Property of any value should be kept under lock and key.

In the downtown area we have been experiencing a rash of thefts of three wheelers. The thieves are driving them around the area but we do not get any calls. If you notice a three-wheeler being driven on our streets without any plates, give us a call. We will check it out.

People have to get involved and watch out for their neighbors. If someone observes any suspicious activity, you should try to obtain the license number of the vehicle, description of the vehicle and occupants. We will respond and check them out to see what they are doing in the area. It may be nothing but then again, it may be a major break in a case. Sometimes people are reluctant to give their name and address when calling the police. That is okay, you can remain anonymous. We would rather get some information rather than no information at all.

Some of our citizens are calling the police to report suspicious activity and that is good. It is a good start and I commend those individuals who are not afraid to get involved. We need to get more people involved.

As the summer season is upon us, traditionally our crime rate will rise. Now is the time to be ever vigilant. We need to obtain more information on criminal and drug activity in our community. Call or write a note about what is going on. Watch over your neighbor.

The articles were an instant hit with the community. With each article, I tried to convey a message to the citizens. Florence has a large senior citizen winter visitor population and many of them looked forward to reading the articles each week. It was more work for me, but I had fun doing it and at the same time I was promoting the police department in a positive sense.

The people responded to the articles. Not once did anyone have anything bad to say about the articles or disagreed with the content. It was my way to communicate to the people using the media. The mayor and council members thought that it was a great idea. If you recall, the town was in political turmoil before and after the recall and there were a great deal of adverse publicity regarding the circumstances behind the police chief being fired. Everything was is disarray including the police department. I had to do something to rebuild my personnel's esteem and to have the community regain its confidence in the police department. Virtually everything previously written about the police department was bad. Now the articles were positive.

I brought communication to a new level with the medium of cable television. I was invited several times for programming to be broadcasted to all the cable subscribers in the Florence area. The talk shows were a success. Most of the topical areas were about our new programs, such as the Triad – Seniors and Law Officers Working Together and Crime Prevention. Again, people had positive things to say about the police department. Some departments actually use the local cable television stations and some have a weekly or monthly program about crime prevention or other topics of interest. Overall, police departments do not take advantage of this great opportunity to say positive things about the department.

Even though the Town of Florence is located in the desert between Phoenix and Tucson, it seemed that the media was always present in the area. Florence probably is considered the prison capital of the world. There is the Arizona State Prison Complex, Correctional Corporation of America, INS, and the County Jail. Every time there was an escape, it would generate news. The Arizona State Prison housed the most dangerous prisoners under one roof in Arizona including death row. If there was an escape or an execution the news media would flock to Florence. There were a few times when I had to give press conferences in front of three or four television camera.

I was answering questions about an escape from the Correctional Corporation of America before the television cameras when a reporter asked me questions about our relationship with a private prison. What does that have to do with an escape? I knew they were fishing for a bigger story. The truth of the matter was that our relationship with the private prison was good. They wanted to know if the private prisons were inferior to the state prison and if they may pose a safety risk to the public safety of the community. Unbelievably, the residents do feel safe in the community with the number of prisons there. Besides, if there was an escape the goal of the escaping inmate was to get out of the community as quickly as possible and it was usually in a stolen vehicle. Considering the size of the prison population there were very few escapes. The state prison was a part of Florence since the early 1900's so it was not a major concern. I was impressed with the operation of the private prison. It seemed that they could provide the same service and do it better with fewer personnel. They had the latest state of the art security system. How could anyone escape? It was because of their latest building phase, adding more units, and a mental lapse by several correctional officers. After I briefly answered their questions, they did not pursue this line of questioning any longer.

Be Able To Think On Your Feet

The police chief has to be able to think on his or her feet and try not to be intimidated by the overwhelming response of the media. One pointer that you should always remember even if there is a great deal of pressure is to do a press conference soon as possible. **You need not do it on their terms**. I never give a press conference until I am ready on my terms. **I am in control of the time, place and content**. If someone asks you to do an interview right away, you can simply explain that you are not ready and need time. You just tell them that you are still gathering the facts about the incident and you will be ready shortly. Keep in mind that it is their deadline, not yours. Your mission is to get the facts from your staff but you want to make sure it is right. Nothing is more embarrassing than to give out the wrong facts. How many times have we seen someone make blunders on national television? **Do it right the first time**.

My media relation skills were fine-tuned even further in Arizona. There is always something to learn and when an opportunity occurred to attend media relation courses I jumped at the chance. There is something you can always pick up and besides it is important to hear about other chief's experiences. We certainly can learn from one another especially the mistakes. This is an area where new and seasoned police chiefs have to proficient. Saying too much and not knowing about sound bits can easily get a police chief into difficulty and some embarrassing moments. When a major media network is in town they are interested in getting their story ready for the evening news and sometimes it is a live broadcast. They are not worrying about you being nervous or not or if it is your first time. If you are ready for the interview at the time of the broadcast then so be it. If you need more time, then just say so. They will have to do their broadcast without your interview.

Use Humor When Appropriate

Most of the time, the media will call your office first to schedule an interview. I schedule it when it is convenient for me but I am also mindful of their deadlines. I simply explain that I would be more than happy to grant an interview when I had all the facts. It is a reasonable response and they usually do not question it. Actually, I have fun when I do an interview. Sometimes you get a little nervous at first but it is only natural. I will try to inject some humor, not to be funny but to relax me. After a minute or two I feel calm and relaxed. The more that you do it the better you get at it. There will be times when you have to do a more formal press conference in front of many cameras that will be broadcast nationwide. We already know of several cases that attracted nationwide attention for a long time. They were the OJ Simpson trail, JonBenet Ramsey murder, and the Columbine High School massacre. What a nightmare for the law enforcement agencies to give a press conference every day about the case. How many times have we heard the negatives about the police agency? We hear about it too often.

Be Prepared

We can minimize our mistakes by being better prepared. It is a scary thought that could turn into a public relations disaster for the agency. I do not have to give you any more examples. All you have to do is pick up a local paper and read about a major event. The reality is that these types of incidents can occur at any time and at any place anywhere in the country. A police chief of a small police agency could suddenly find himself or herself on national television.

You can ask yourself how I can be better prepared. Here are **some tips** to be better prepared:

- Be aware that any incident could suddenly generate **national attention**
- Make certain that you are briefed on **all the facts.** It is embarrassing to find out later that you gave out inaccurate facts.
- Designate only **one** person to give the press release and news conference. Make sure your designee gives out only authorized information.
- **Be prepared** to address the media. They will want to hear from the police chief or sheriff.
- Dictate the **time and place** of the interview or press conference
- Have a **prepared statement.** It makes the job much easier. Winging it at this level is not a good idea.
- If you **answer questions**, try to find out what the questions are. You are preparing yourself against being surprised.
- **Limited the question and answer period** if you decide to have one
- Having too many press conferences about a case could be a fatal error. Too many police chief and sheriffs have fallen into this trap.

- **Do not misrepresent the facts. Be candid and truthful.** If you do not know the answer or you are not sure, say so. You are not looking stupid you are being smart.
- **Be professional** in the way you look and act

These are just some suggestions that I had developed over time from actual practice or observing others who were in the hot seat. Some police chiefs approach it as excruciating pain. Remember that people look up to the police chief or sheriff for leadership in a trying situation. If you think about it, the community is looking to you for answers. The police chief must appear to be in control of the situation. Now is the time to step up and make your community proud.

Say Something!

I understand that in some communities someone other than the police chief may give the press conference. It could be the district attorney or the FBI's spokesperson. Let me say this. Even though there may be several jurisdictions involved in an investigation, if it was my community, I would definitely say something at some point. You ask why put yourself in a precarious position? Why not take the easy way out? The people are looking for their police chief or sheriff to step up and take charge of the situation. They want to hear from the police chief or sheriff. People talk negatively when they do not see or hear from the top person in-charge.

You never know what type of story generates national news coverage. Here is a case in point. While I was in Fort Lupton, Colorado, we had a bank robbery. Normally this would only generate local or state coverage at the most. It just so happened that a 70 year old female decided to put a plastic bag over her head with two holes cut out for her eyes and walked into the bank to get some money. She implied that she had a gun but at the time, no one took her very seriously. One of the tellers locked the outer doors so she could not make her escape and someone else called the police. It was lucky for them she did not have any weapons.

When the police officer arrived on scene he found the female bank robber trapped inside the bank. He was surprised to find out that he had in his custody a senior citizen. It is a bit unusual to have someone commit a crime like this but it happens every so often. After she was brought to the police department for booking, I looked in and saw a small, frail old woman. Further investigation revealed that our bank was her second bank robbery. She had robbed a bank in Brighton, about 8 miles from Fort Lupton a few days previous and made off with about $6,000. It seems she was trying to support her invalid husband at home. Most of the money if not all was recovered from both bank robberies.

Nation-wide Interest

This case generated nation-wide interest. The television stations were calling for interviews. I knew that this was an unusual case and it would perk some interest around the country. It even made some good humor on the late night talk shows. It is not every day when a senior citizen decides to rob a bank. I was prepared for the barrage of media inquiries and requests to do interviews. This media flurry of requests lasted for several days. As a side note when this person's case was finally disposed of in court it generated very little publicity. It is sad to think no one cared about the disposition. As it turned out, she received probation and no prison time. She turned over the money from the Brighton bank robbery to the authorities and was very cooperative in the investigation. I agreed with the sentence. It would have served no purpose at all for her to go to prison. As far as I was concerned justice was served. Incidentally, her husband passed away a few years later.

Practice Makes Perfect

There were many times when I had to step up and give an interview to either a reporter or a television stations. After awhile I was quite comfortable with either format. Who is to say my way is the best? If you consider all the positives versus the negatives, the positives far outweigh the negatives. I believe my approach to the way I handled the media worked for me and it could work for you as well. Granted, there are those who are not as comfortable talking to the media. My suggestion is that if you want to have a better chance to succeed then you will make the most of establishing good media relations. In order to be good, you have to work hard at it. Remember the saying, practice makes perfect is very true. Generally, law enforcement is not accustomed or trained to deal with the media. You have to find a way to improve.

My way to practice was quite simple. I volunteered to go on the local cable television talk shows to discuss our programs. It was not only an opportunity to highlight our department but to get comfortable being in front of the television camera. The more I did it the more confident I became with the format. After a while, I became more relaxed and was able to think and give answers to questions while under pressure.

Networking

Sometimes we forget about contacting other chiefs. Networking, if you recall is important. If you have a friend, who happen to be a police chief you can help each other by seeking out his or her advice. More often than not you will get some excellent input on how they deal with the media on an individual basis and press conferences.   There were many times when I called a friend to get his advice especially if the situation was something unusual.   It was good to just discuss a situation even if the decision had already been made.   I give credit to my many friends in New Hampshire who gave me timely advice.   I do not know another police chief who wants to see another fail.   I found that the New Hampshire Association of Chiefs of Police was an excellent opportunity to network.   This was without doubt a fine organization.   There are many other fine police chief organizations around the country.   The point is to get involved.   Generally, police chief do not network enough.   There will be more on this later in other chapters to illustrate more examples.

Media Relations Courses

If you have an opportunity to attend a media relation's course, you should take the opportunity to do so.   You will get some valuable training.   If the trainers are actually media types, ask some pointed, candid questions about what they are actually looking for.   Unfortunately, there are only a few courses on media relations that are offered.   Periodically, the International Association of Chiefs of Police offers this type of training.   I might add that the training they provide is excellent if you can find one in your area.

Sometimes the best teacher is through trial and error.   Everyone makes some mistakes, but you can learn from them.   If you are willing to learn, remain calm and patient everything will come together.   It will not be long before you will find that after a little experience you will become a veteran in media relations.

As I stated earlier, I like to use the media in promoting police programs.   I will be giving some specific examples on how this is done in the chapter dealing with police programs.   You can use the media to your advantage and consider them your friend, not the enemy.

Chapter 6
Communication

It is critical that police chiefs and executives are able to communicate orally and in written manner. I say this because if leaders cannot communicate effectively, then he or she is in deep trouble. They will experience a short-lived career. It is not because leaders do not know how to talk, but mainly **because of their attitudes**. There are those who think that they are the greatest police chief or manager that ever walked the face of the earth. Maybe they are great, but you still have to communicate effectively with people. There are some police chiefs and managers who think that they are so important that they are god-like. Perhaps you know someone like this. A person can get knocked out of the "Ivory Tower" before they realized what happened. We read about the individuals who are super smart but somehow they forget to **use good old common sense**. Common sense seems to be a recurring theme. Sometimes the smartest or the brightest do not succeed.

If you read about a police chief or executive fired after a short time or even after a lengthy stay, I will bet the problem is communication. Matter of fact, I will save you the guesswork; it is without a doubt the reason why a police chief is terminated. There may be some other reasons too but communication is always at the top of the list of reasons. Somehow the communication becomes distorted or misunderstood. Sometimes there is no communication at all. We read about the barriers of communications and you probably have a good idea what they are, but we must put aside these barriers. The barriers of communication must be caste aside in order for a person to succeed in communication. Each person must work hard at communication skills to fine tune them and put aside their prejudices. If there are any weaknesses then a concerted effort must be undertaken to correct these deficiencies. **Learn your communication weaknesses.**

I will discuss improving communication to various groups. You will be able to get an insight into the process and learn some tricks of the trade in how to improve yourself. One caveat that I would like to throw in at this time as some food for thought; you have done everything possible to try to improve communication and it may appear it is a one-way effort. If you are communicating with the city or town manager, or the City or Town Council then you may want to think about updating your resume and looking elsewhere for work. It may be that they have already made up their mind to sever the relationship.

Personnel

Keep in mind that you have to talk to people at all levels. The most important group of people who you have to convince to sell your philosophy to is your own personnel in your department. This is where communication starts first and communication can make or break, depending upon how you **set the tone**.

Department Meeting

When I started working with a department, one of the first things that I did was to set up a department-wide meeting as soon as possible. By this time everyone was probably on edge anyway because they did not know who the chief is. There is fear of the unknown and it is just human nature to have some fear about what is going to happen. Is the new chief going to be a hatchet man for the city manager or city council? What type of person is he or she? Are there going to be a long list of changes? These are just a few of many questions that flows though ones perceptual framework. Keep in mind that sometimes it is difficult to change ones thinking or perception after people have settled into a routine for a long time. If the police chief or leader have been fired or resigned then there will be some uncertainties about what is in store for the staff and their future.

The purpose of the meeting was mainly an introduction so the personnel can get to know me as a person. It is helpful if you can set the tone early and relax the recruits by having some refreshments available for them. Try to have some finger foods or pastry and some soft drinks helps to place them into relaxed moods so employees will not be so uneasy. Let us face it, everyone likes to eat. Having some refreshments helps to break the ice. It is a minor cost item out of your budget or even out of your very own pocket. I want them to get to know me and understand what I am all about. I can understand if some are apprehensive about a new person, but if the personnel take the stance of "we will wait and see" then I have accomplished what I had set out to do.

Attend Roll Calls

Some police chiefs and managers are reluctant to set up a department meeting because of the size of their department and the amount of overtime they would have to pay out. One alternative is to speak to your personnel in groups by visiting the roll calls on each shift. It may be time consuming but it will pay off in the future. I can remember when our new Police Chief John Oliver in Bristol Connecticut visited our roll call on the second shift or swing shift. I was impressed that he took the time to talk with us for a while. Some things just stick in your mind and the chief's visit was a positive thing to do. Case in point: It is important for the "rank and file" to know who the police chief or leader is. You have to work on the small things first.

One might ask what should be said during the first department-wide meeting. My purpose first is to get the personnel to know me as a person. I then explain that I will not be making wholesale changes for the sake of making charges. I explain that I will be assessing the department and will be looking for input from personnel before any final decisions are made. I further explain that if there are changes to be made, I will explain why the change is necessary and when, where and how the change must take place. The personnel know that changes in the department are inevitable especially if the chief or manager was forced out one way or another.

Open-Door Policy

The political powers may want some positive changes, which is why they hired a new police chief or manager in the first place. In a general sense, the personnel know changes are coming so newly hired leaders do not have to remind them of it. Last, I encourage the staff to ask questions. Now employees may be a little reluctant to ask a question, so you might encourage them to write their question on a piece of paper without their name. In this way, you might solicit some good questions and have a good discussion. The meeting usually lasted about one hour, which was long enough. I usually end it by discussing my **"Open-Door" policy**. I encourage police chiefs and leaders to have an open-door policy. I invite those who have a special problem or concern to talk to me about it. It is not intended to by-pass the supervisors. I strongly believe that the supervisor should try to help first if possible. My intent is not to shut anyone out if someone wanted to discuss a matter with me. Matter of fact, unless I was in conference with a command level officer, my office door was always open. I mean, it was physically open. I was never too busy to meet with any of my personnel. One barrier is the door. I wanted to make my personnel feel at ease and that they were welcomed into my office. Sometimes police chiefs and managers give the impression that the only reason a person is invited into the office is to "get chewed out" for something or to be disciplined. Often it is not a good experience, so you can see why there is a little anxiety when a person is called to the office.

Rumors

Rumors, rumors and more **rumors will kill an organization** quicker than anything I know. People thrive on rumors. Some may even think a rumor is funny at someone else's expense. Every time someone discusses a rumor or you hear of one, you must take immediate steps to find out the facts and then disseminate the truth. Someone in your organization will intentionally start rumors to see where it goes. If these rumors are not dealt within a quick and orderly fashion then rumors can fester and get out of control. When rumors reach the Town or City Council members, you as a leader, have reason for concern. The members may choose to believe these rumors. This was the case in Florence, Arizona, which led to my contract not being renewed. You ask yourself, is it not the reasonable thing to do is to ask the police chief or manager? A reasonable person just may and again you are dealing with a Town or City Council. They may not want to know the truth. They may have already made up their minds and they do not want anything else to cloud their judgment. This seems to happen often.

The Best Way to Kill A Rumor is With Facts

How can one combat the rumors and the untruths that are circulating the department or community? There are precise ways that you can deal with the problem of rumors. I simply tell the person I will get the facts and let everyone know. Sometimes it maybe just a simple matter to just give the facts if you know what the facts are to the person and the problem is solved. It maybe more complicated than this, especially if the rumors have circulated outside the department and other people like the city or town managers are asking questions. I cannot count how many times the manager has asked me about rumors and some were simply outrageous.

There are different ways to do dispel rumors. It could be as simple as publishing a **Rumor Mill Bulletin**. I have seen some that were very humorous, but to the point. I have not personally published a rumor mill bulletin but they can be quite effective if used appropriately and at the right time. Simply said, you cannot generate a bulletin every time you hear a rumor. You will go crazy putting out little fires. Selectively used, rumor mill bulletins can be quite effective. I like the direct contact better as opposed to putting it down on paper. I like dealing with these rumors head-on.

Weekly Staff Meetings

Having weekly staff meeting with my command staff is a way to take communication to another level. I invite other interested personnel into my staff meeting. These meetings are called **open staff meetings.** This way, staff members can see first hand how brainstorming sessions can lead to a planning process. Besides, what is there to hide? Many times rumor originates from staff meetings. Next, I have my secretary take minutes of the meeting and post it where all can see. I have told my personnel if there were any questions all they would have to do is ask. Sometimes we get so busy, we tend to delay the weekly staff meetings and they suddenly get hard-pressed to occur once a month instead. It is a mistake to keep delaying open staff meetings though. It is important to keep the communication on going at all levels of the department. Sometimes the rank and file will bring up important issues that I had not thought about.

I always make time for the staff meeting and the next trick is to find a good time for everyone to attend. I scheduled them in the morning and late afternoons and during different days of the week. I find, for me, - the Monday morning staff meeting, first thing in the morning, works well - but in the end, it depends upon your daily work schedule that would dictate a good time. Generally, I like to find out what kinds of problems and serious crime we had over the weekend. This way I could brief the town or city manager on anything he or she should know. Remember, communication is the key!

Newsletter

What I try to do on a monthly basis is write a department newsletter. It works on all levels, small, medium or large departments. It may be time consuming but it will be worth the effort. I try to include everything that the department was working on. It is a good opportunity to address the positives the department is doing, including the direction the department is headed and other interesting tidbits of information. You see, everyone wants to know what is going on. If they do not know, then they will make it up and very soon you will be trying to dispel another rumor. If you keep your personnel informed then you have accomplished half the communication battle.

Managing By Walking Around

I heard a wise old police chief tell me the best way to manage is by walking around. If you think about it for a minute, it makes perfect sense. Too many police chiefs and managers hide in their office, commonly known as the **"Ivory Tower,"** and stay for a long time. I know administrative work is important but it is equally important to be seen. The only way you are going to find out anything is by walking around. I call it **managing by walking around.** Managing by walking around allows you to see firsthand what is going on in your department and it truly assist in opening up the lines of communication. I like to get a heads up on what is going on. Besides, I am ultimately responsible for the effective management of the police department. I always made it a point to walk around and talk with personnel especially around roll call time. Why not spend some time with your officers at roll call? It shows that you are interested in what the workforce are doing.

Being new to the community, it is not unusual for a police chief to ride with his or her officers. Ride-a-longs serves two purposes. You can personally get to know each officer and they can get to know you plus at the same time, you can find out more about the community. Many times these officers will discuss some real problematic issues off the record with you. Supervisors generally hate it when the boss rides with his or her subordinates. The intent is not to undermine the sergeant but to get more insight in the department. It is a fact that supervisors, middle and upper management do not tell you everything. They only tell you what they want you to hear. I like to find out the complete picture, which is why I ride with the officers occasionally. I find the police officers on their beat will know best about what is going on in the community and they may have some good ideas of how best to approach problems facing the different communities. Listening to them to find out what is going on is good practice.

City or Town Manager

It is understood that you have to get a long with the boss. It is much easier when the city or town manager had the task in hiring his or her police chief. Generally, a rapport is established most of the time and one need not worry very much. Their management styles are more compatible. It gets more complicated when a new manager takes over and the police chief is already in place. I believe it does make a difference whether the manager hires a police chief or not. How can one avoid being a casualty? I have seen too many police chiefs resign or all of a suddenly fired shortly after the arrival of new town managers. What changes the dynamics? Does this signal or resemble a sign or threat of a power struggle?

As I had stated earlier, a police chief was fired in a small community in North Carolina after the city manager took over after three months. What happened to warrant this action? The police chief was commended for doing a good job for 13 years and more recently, had been commended for doing good work. In an instant, he found himself without a job. Was it a communication problem, or a power struggle? I believe it is both and perhaps some external factors were thrown into the mix as well. People in the community had asked questions about his dismissal, and so far, the only official comment from the city manager was that he could not comment on that removal from office because it was a personnel matter.

I believe in telling someone to his or her face if they are not performing up to standards and to take measures to correct their deficiencies. It must have been a shock for the police chief to come home to find his termination letter taped to his door. In my view, it is a poor way to communicate to someone and a poor way to handle this situation. At the same time, it sends a message to the rest of the city staff regarding the manager's style. This may have been a shock but there must have been some telltale signs for the manager to take this action. There had to be a communication problem and someone has to go. Dismissals of police chiefs happen all the time all over the country. Just remember, the city or town manager's job is at stake and given the choice, the police chief will go first.

I use to think that town or city manager getting fired was just the way of life and another order of business for the council. I thought managers were more expendable. Now, currently police chiefs are expendable too. There seems to be no loyalty to the police chief in their position. Gone are those days where a police chief has been with the same department for 20 years. These examples are few and far between.

What can the police chief do to improve communication? It is easier said than done, especially when a new town or city manager takes over the reigns of the city. I can offer specific ways to improve the lines of communication that will improve your odds for success. Sometimes there is going to be a personality conflict between the police chief and the manager and little can be done about it.

Playing the Game

The police chief must know how to **"play the game."** Some may say it is kissing up to the manager and some refuse to take the first step. If this is the attitude, then you can rest assured that the police chief's career will be short lived. There has to be an open line of communication and there needs to be direct access to the manager. What I always do when a new manager comes on board is to have a meeting to establish the groundwork for a good relationship. I like to find out what he or she wants from his police chief. I like to find out when he or she wants to be notified about a problem, major crime or unusual incident and to what degree. Now, I am not saying to call the manager for every little thing. I certainly do not want to be the bearer of bad news all the time. On the positive side, I like to tell the manager about some outstanding work.

One time when a new city administrator came on board in Fort Lupton, Colorado, he stated that he had an open-door policy, but his secretary had to set up an appointment to schedule some time. What he created was communication barrier. He meant well though, because he was a busy person. After he was surprised a few times with some major incidents, he and I had a nice discussion about accessibility. I simply pointed out to him that I needed access without going through his secretary all the time. Now, of course, you have to use some common sense when the boss is busy and involved in a meeting. I only interrupted him only when it was necessary. After that, we had a very good relationship. All it takes is some diplomacy and some candid discussions.

Make Yourself Available

Playing games with the manager and not keeping him or her informed will certainly land the police chief in hot water at some point. Purposely avoiding the manager will cause further problems, especially if you have not seen or spoken to him in days. Something has to give. I always make it a point that if I am in my office and the manager wants to see me; I make myself immediately available. If he or she wants information, I make it a priority to get the information to him as soon as possible. I do not want to have a problem fester any longer than necessary.

When people are complaining to the council members and to the manager about the police department all the time, the chief will soon undoubtedly be told. If the manager continually have to devote much of his or her time to problems of the police department that takes away from other city business, then believe that he will do something about it. You have to remember that town or city council members and the mayor are always calling the manager or visiting him or her in person to discuss problems. Guess where they get the information? They get much of their information from city employees. This should come at not surprise. There are individuals who are chronic complainers and will never change. It is a fact of life. I found through experience that much of the information given to the council members or mayor is not very accurate. There was numerous times I had been called into the manager's office to respond to questions and found myself full of laugher because those questions were so ridiculous!!! Somewhere along the line, a rumor was started and now the council members and mayor heard about it and they want some answers.

As time goes on and after the manager, council members and mayor develop confidence in the new police chief, mutual trust and respect will develop. They will rely more on your judgment and pay less attention to rumors. What happens when the city council members or mayor changes after the election? The city manager of Somersworth, New Hampshire did a very smart thing. He had the foresight to have an **orientation for new council members** after each election. He would invite each department head at a specified time to come to his office to discuss the police department. This way, the new council member would get to know their police chief and learn something about how the police department operates. After the session was over, I would always invite the council member to the police department for a tour and a ride-a- long with a police officer if he or she desired one. I found that this practice was an excellent management tool.

Playing the game is more of knowing how to treat a city or town manager, council member or mayor in a positive way. It makes sense to do everything possible to help them succeed at their job and at the same time solidifying your position even more. All too often, the police chief or leader decides to get cute and think he or she is more politically powerful than the city manager. Besides what does he or she know about the police department? Perhaps, he or she knows very little, which is why you were hired to run the police department or organization in the first place. The point is that there has to be cooperation in order to coexist. If there is a breakdown in trust, it is inevitable but the police chief or executive will have to go.

Police Commission/Committee

There are some departments that utilize the police commission concept. My first community, Bristol, Connecticut was one of them. My last community, Fort Lupton, Colorado had a police committee that was mainly advisory. Instead of reporting directly to the town or city manager, the police chief reports to the police commission. Some communities have strong police commissions and can hire and fire the police chief. It is not necessarily bad but I prefer to report directly to one person, the town or city manager.

Open Communication

My former Police Chief John Oliver in Bristol, Connecticut was a master politician in dealing with the police commissioners. He simply kept the commissioners informed and talked to them all the time. I thought it was a smart thing to do and just by observing him, I learned a great deal and it helped me later on as police chief. I thought that sometimes he gave them too much information. Apparently, it worked very well because he served with distinction for 10 years until he retired in 1998.

The commissioners are usually very influential in the community and have some allegiance to the mayor, which is why they were appointed to the position in the first place. Other words, a political debt was being repaid. The commissioner had at some point contributed to the mayor's political campaign and now he or she was being rewarded. Some police commissioners are elected to their position. The concept is still the same when you are dealing with commissioners instead of a city manager. You still have to have open dialogue with them. As a new chief or executive, you have to ask government or top officials what they want and the direction they want the department or organization to go. Remember, you will need their guidance and support. It is always good to get endorsement when developing goals and objectives so that you give the appearance you are willing to work collectively with them. These same individuals are the ones who will evaluate you, give you a raise and decide your fate. The commissioner or top executives hold the power and sometimes it is a power trip for some individuals. Because the commissioners or chief executives are the bosses, you have to follow their direction even if they know very little or nothing about law enforcement or the organization. This is the reality of being a police chief or senior manager. Some commissioners or top executives know very little, so it would behoove the chief or manager to educate them.

I had a friend who learned the hard way about police commissioners. After a long search for a police chief position, he took a position not too far from Bristol, Connecticut. The job started out well, but he eventually began to receive criticism from the police union and later the police commissioners. I will discuss police unions in greater detail in another chapter. I think that a union member from that department wanted to find out about their new chief so they called his former department. This individual was not very popular with the police union and I do not think they did him any favors. They probably badmouthed him, which is not unusual for a union member to do, especially if the union member does not like the person. I remember when I was a finalist in a city in Ohio, one of their union members called my department in New Hampshire asking questions about me. Of course, it was a little embarrassing because my personnel did not know that I was interviewing for another position. I had to explain myself by saying I was just testing the waters and besides I was not going to brag about it. Anyway, do not be surprised if a union member calls your department making inquires. Eventually, someone will find out about those interviews. You should expect it so be prepared to have a response. Besides, it is not unreasonable to improve one's career and your personnel will understand. However, it was a little awkward for me though.

You Cannot Fight City Hall

My friend in Connecticut could not overcome these problems. Eventually, some of these individuals had the ear of the police commissioners. It is just a matter of time before something happen. If commissioners keep hearing the same old complaints, eventually they will believe the complaints to be true. Ultimately, my friend was terminated from his position. He tried to fight it but you know the old saying "you cannot fight city hall." Even though police chiefs have good protection against termination without cause in Connecticut, it is very difficult to win a case against the city unless you are independently wealthy. The city has deep pockets and if a case goes long enough, most of the time, the city will prevail. Unfortunately, my friend did not prevail. If the city wants you gone, the city will find cause to terminate you. If the cases last long enough, eventually, the city will pounce on your mistakes and develop just cause.

Police Committees Are Excellent

I found dealing with Police Committee members especially gratifying for me. Even though these committee members did not have any powers but only an advisory capacity to the city council, it was a good experience. Members knew what their roles were and did not overstep their bounds. We had open communication and an excellent rapport. The committees I had the honor to work with provided a great deal of insight about local communities and were very helpful in providing guidance in helping me to formulate programs. They supported our police programs. I would encourage other communities to follow suit. During our meetings, we had good discussions and when the time came, these particular committees supported me when issues came up in front of the city council.

In one particular case, the committee helped me get approval for capital outlay, namely a police vehicle that was sorely needed. Several council members did not think that the car was necessary at the time, one of whom was a former police officer who should have known better. You have to replace the police vehicles on a timely basis before they totally fall apart. Everyone knows the longer you keep a vehicle, the higher the maintenance costs will be. The committee members came to my rescue and spoke before the city council requesting them to purchase a police vehicle.

Town/City Council Members

Dealing with a town or city council is at times very tricky, especially if they are coming and going all the time around election time. First, you need to find out what is your role with the town or city council. Your roles change, depending upon the desires of the managers. Some managers will not want you to be at the council meeting unless you are asked to attend. Others will request your presence for each council workshop and meeting as a resource person to help the manager answer technical questions about the police department or the organization in which you represent.

Some chiefs and managers simply do not like attending council meetings. I, however, find these meeting to be very beneficial for several reasons. First, I get a change to observe the dynamics in city government. I like to visualize the "big picture" and know what is going on so that I will be able to respond better in answering their questions during the meeting or at a later date. Secondly, there will be many questions. There will be questions before the council meeting, during the official portion of the council meeting and after the meeting as well. I also have an opportunity to talk to citizens about any potential police problem or even suggestions. Council meetings provide an excellent opportunity for police chief and managers alike, to communicate to council members and citizens.

Council Report

In Florence, Arizona, I was required to attend every workshop and meeting. I looked forward to the meetings. We discussed problems and potential problems. I provided members in the meetings written reports on the previous month's activities and mentioned the highlights. Even though this council did not renew my contract, I kept the council informed and they complimented me many times on the format and information. I kept them appraised on the direction of the department and any new developments and they liked the results. I have to admit, the council supported me while I was police chief.

In Fort Lupton, Colorado, I was again required to attend every workshop and council meeting. In addition, I provided a monthly report highlighting the police department activities to council members. The report was a good forum to mention the department's accomplishments and new programs. It was an instant success. This city council had a place for the police chief on the agenda under staff reports after the city clerk give the city council a report.

I simply could not find a better way to keep the channels of communication open than by attending city council meetings. It is true that some council meetings will last a long time but is it a waste of your time? On the contrary, it will be one of the best moves that you could make. It is not only an opportunity to answer questions but also a chance for council to get to know you as a person. After council members get to know you, they will not feel intimidated when calling you up to discuss a problem. Some managers are paranoid about this, but if it is a police problem, I would like to hear first hand about it from the person whether he or she is a council member or not. I simply tell the city or town manager a council member called and we discussed a police problem. They are usually satisfied with the answer but you may want to establish the parameters first. Establishing a rapport with your council members and mayor can certainly establish a longer longevity for the police chief or executive and a better chance to succeed.

Department Heads/City Staff

The police chief and top officials must remember that he or she is part of the management team for the city. There must be ongoing rapport and cooperation with other city departments including their staff. Sometimes police chiefs and managers get caught up in the power struggle between departments. I look at it as a win-win situation. If you can provide assistance to departments and staff when they need it, then the dividends will pay off later.

Sometimes there is an ongoing struggle with the fire department. Now we know that the fire department gets everything that they want. Just look at the expensive fire trucks that are parked in the fire station. It can get very competitive between departments especially when competing for tax dollars around budget time. Life is much easier if everyone can get a long. I do not mind the Fire Chief getting a new ladder or pumper truck. The police chief or executive will get a turn.

Public Safety Dispatch Center

I know police and fire departments that do not get a long. There is a conflict, usually a power struggle or ego-trip between the two chiefs. The fire department and police departments were completely separate in Bristol, Connecticut. Even to the extent of having a separate dispatch center for each. However, times have changed. Now, there is a combined dispatch or Public Safety Dispatch Center. It was a long struggle but it was a good move for the city. It is very expensive for one, never mind two dispatch centers to staff it - 24 hours around the clock 7 days a week - and pay for expensive equipment. The city has been trying to correct this problem for years but it is difficult to deal with the unions. If they give up the dispatch center then they would want something in return. The municipality saved considerable taxpayer's dollars to consolidate the dispatch centers into one Public Safety Dispatch Center.

After I became chief, I made it a point to be very cooperative with all departments especially the fire department. In my point of view, I believed that I had an excellent relationship with the fire departments in the three communities where I had become police chief. The fire chief in Somersworth, New Hampshire and I had a special relationship and friendship. We were very comfortable in working on different programs such as developing the emergency management plan for the city. I was chairperson of the Traffic Safety Committee and he was part of it. We interacted on a daily basis. If there was a dispatch problem, we worked together to sort it out. The police dispatched the fire department. He included me in on some of his activities. In my mind, it is easier working together than against on another. Incidentally, in each community I was given the responsibility of the Public Safety Dispatch center.

Other Law Enforcement Agencies

The police chief and managers need to interact with other law enforcement agencies. All too often, the chief or executives just works within his or her domain and forgets about the other agencies. It is hard to believe but there are police chiefs and top executives who do not participate in any organizations. Some associations are better than others are, but in my mind, there is no better way to interact with your peers than the state's police chief association. In my experience, I found that police chiefs were eager to help one another out. Here is a case in point: When I was in Fort Lupton, Colorado, I attended a meeting with other chiefs in the City of Denver. I met David Michaud, the former police chief of Denver. After a few minutes of conversation, he mentioned that if I had ever needed his assistance from the Denver Police Department just to let him know. He even told me that he offered the assistance of his homicide detectives to assist Boulder Police Department in the murder investigation of JonBenet Ramsey but the Boulder Police Chief declined his offer. In hindsight, maybe the Boulder Police Chief should have taken him up on his offer. To me, it was a no brainer. The Denver Police investigates homicides all the time and Boulder not very often. It is too bad that Boulder did not take him up on his offer. Maybe the case would have been solved. Here, more than 10 years later, there is no solution to that crime in sight.

The Lone Ranger

During the Police Chief Association meetings in New Hampshire I found myself engaged in numerous conversations with other police chief about problems they had experienced ranging from personnel to union problems. The common denominator, so it seems, is police unions. Unions give the chief fits and I will go into detail about unions later. Some chiefs deal with police unions better than others. They know how to play the game. Talking to peers about problems helps to deal with your mental health. First, you are not in this profession alone. Unbelievably I found that many police chiefs have similar problems, some are a little different in magnitude.

If more police chiefs networked more often, they would see that they are not in this dilemma alone. Some are alone because they chose to be alone. I call them the "the Lone Ranger." If some of these chiefs did talk to one another more often then perhaps they would not have been forced into resignation or firing. The police chief who ran into difficulty, first with the police union, and later with the police commissioners, was "the Lone Ranger." He lasted almost three years but it was a rocky road. He was doomed to fail and it was magnified even more because he kept it to himself. Just think, maybe the result would have been different if someone was able to get to him early on. I know the problem. Police chiefs or top executives do not want to admit that they are weak in any way; their egos get in the way. Sometimes you have to be humble and ask for help when the time comes. Do you know of anyone in this particular situation? When you read about a chief's or top executive dismissal in the newspaper, do you say it is too bad? The point is that your position is never secure; the same thing could happen to you. All it would take is one or two negative incidents that are magnified by the media. Now, there is a great deal of pressure on the chief or senior executive to respond. How do you handle the situation?

In the instances of police chiefs, some meet more often at their County Police Chiefs Association meetings. Some county associations are more active than others but the result are the same; you get to network with your peers and work together on the County level. It is equally as effective. In Florence, Arizona, I was the Chairperson of the Pinal County Law Enforcement Association for two years. It was a very good experience because we had many accomplishments and generally the most improved law enforcement in the county. One of the proudest moments was helping to arrange for a sculpture to be made consisting of a municipal police officer, county law enforcement and the State Department of Police Safety or DPS, as they are called.   We had our unveiling at the Peace Officer Memorial Day in recognition for peace officers who had lost their lives through the years.

The Public

I like to dispel the impression that the police department is an occupying force or a secretive organization.   Everyone views the police as unavoidable in his or her community.   My philosophy is that if the public knew more about the police department then there would be greater acceptance and assistance.   It makes sense to me to involve the community in their police department.   I use the word "their" for a specific purpose.   I always tell them it is their department and it is a privilege to run it.   The idea is to have the public respect, trust and confidence in their police department.   I know that it is a tall order and very difficult to do at times but it is necessary to work with the public.

When you read about police chief getting into difficulty, many times, more often than not, it has to do with a respect, trust or confidence issue.   The integrity of the department is at stake at all times and one event can caste a shadow of doubt upon the police department and create a public relations nightmare.   We have read about accounts dealing with large police departments such as the Los Angles Police Department and New York City Police Department, but often times questions about the integrity of the department is being directed to the smaller police agencies. Police chiefs and top executive have to be ready to deal with these issues.   There was a time when the public believed the police chief when he or she explained the incident in question but not any more.   More questions are being asked and the police chief is even held more accountable.   Even former President Clinton committed perjury when he was questioned about an affair with Monica Lewinsky. Law enforcement agencies are not immune from scrutiny.   Who would have doubted the integrity of the Federal Bureau of Investigation?   Over the past few years, they have had their share of problems.   There is no doubt because of miscues with investigations; the public lost some confidence even though the FBI is still an excellent organization.   The point is there is a perception of mistrust with law enforcement agencies. Distrust takes a great deal of hard work to overcome.

There needs to be improved communication with the public.   The more open law enforcement agencies can be without jeopardizing law enforcement investigations the better it will be.   Just look at some of the news broadcasting stations and talk show programs after a major crime occurred involving a prominent political figure. They discuss every possible angle including key suspects with attorneys for hours, days and even weeks. They will also be quick to point out all the mistakes made by law enforcement. Law enforcement blunders are something to consider.

Newspaper Articles

I always found it particularly useful to write a newspaper article, called "Crime & Prevention" or whatever you wish to call it. Some call it the Chief's Corner. The important thing is that the public is informed on different issues. I wrote an article once a week for almost a year for the Florence Reminder in Florence, Arizona. I wrote articles ranging from crime prevention issues to more humorous articles such as leaving golf clubs in your golf cart. In all, I wrote about 50 articles, and eventually put them on the police department's website. I knew that people liked the articles because they told me all the time. It was a good medium in conveying a message to the public about new or existing programs.

Someone may say, "I do not have time to write articles for the newspaper." It may be very true but you can be selective and pick your own writing schedule, whether it is once a week or once a month. Sometimes the citizen may write a letter to the editor asking questions or just making a response. Again, you can go in all kinds of directions and you can moreover be selective. It is fun to do and the public appreciates it. When I went to Fort Lupton, Colorado, I wrote a letter to the editor periodically.

Civic Organizations

Civic organizations represent a microcosm of the community. In each community, I joined in a least one and participated with the group. In Somersworth, New Hampshire and Florence, Arizona, I was a member of the Rotary Club. Eventually, I was elected to the Board of Directors. In Fort Lupton, Colorado, the city was a member of the Chamber of Commerce and I participated in their meetings on a weekly basis. I was elected by the group to be on their Board of Directors. It was quite an honor.

Regularly, especially in the beginning, I was asked to speak to different groups. I enjoyed speaking to these groups and discussing the police department. I would seize every opportunity to highlight our department. There are chiefs who do not speak to the public at all except on rare occasions. After a chief or executive has been around for a while, he or she might want to be in contact with the leaders of civic groups and ask about giving them a presentation. Sometimes police chiefs and managers wait too long to ask. Usually civil organizations are always looking for someone to be on their program. Be more assertive and get yourself on their agenda. It will be an excellent move on your part.

Surveys or Questionnaires

Not that I was paranoid, but if I had not heard from the public, regardless if the news were good or bad, I start to wonder if I am doing the right things. Even though I considered myself very good at public relations, I wondered if there was anything else I could do to improve the department. I look for ways to improve the department all the time and occasionally I used a questionnaire to gauge how the department was doing. It takes a great deal of work, but in the long run, it was worth the effort. They say, if you get back 20 % of the questionnaires, you are doing good. Just think what you do with surveys when you get them at home. I cannot tell you nor count how many surveys I threw into the wastepaper basket. I just did not want to take the time to complete them.

The approach with police questionnaires has to be different. It has to be designed in such a manner to elicit a quick response. A one-page questionnaire works the best. Even at the police department, if a questionnaire came cross my desk and it is more than two pages -- forget it. Those surveys also ended up in the wastepaper basket. You can use Police Explorer Scouts to help with distributing them. The results are useful because you can use it as a barometer to see how your department is viewed in the public's eyes.

Telephone Surveys

One project that I had a college intern do was randomly call citizens who had requested a call for service. I particularly did not care who they called. I wanted the survey to be as unbiased as possible. I was interested in whether or not citizens were generally pleased with the officer's efforts and if he or she was courteous. The intern even called people who had been issued citations for motor vehicle violations and arrested on minor criminal charges. I am always interested to see if all people are being treated properly and fairly. If they are not, then it is up to the chief to do something about it.

Sometimes, I was amazed at the results. The results spoke very well and positive about the department. I always made it a point to compliment my officers on a job well done. The reason I wanted to do this was to head off any potential problems. It was simply not a tool to get an officer into trouble. It was mainly for my purpose to gauge how well the public perceived us. If there were any problems, then I had to figure out ways to correct them. In some cases, it may have been the approach or demeanor of the officer or just a training issue. If you can find out about potential problems early enough then you can do something about them before they become big problems.

Proactive Approach

Too many times, police chiefs wait until something goes bad before he or she responds. I always like to take a **proactive approach**. It is critical that the chief maintains the pulse of the community. I like to keep the public informed and as I had explained earlier, there are different approaches. The main point is, do something about it before it is late. Many chiefs have found themselves in this predicament and this is unfortunate.

Public Forums

One area that is not used very much is the public forum or a town hall meeting. It is a question and answer type forum and a good opportunity to address problems in specific areas of the community. I have used this forum on different occasions in my previous communities. Some were well attended and others were not and it depended up the subject matter and the interest and how well advertised. If the citizens in an area of the city were interested in a crime wave in their area then they will come out in droves. If the Police Chief is there at the forum then he or she can reduce a great deal of anxieties about a situation. I find that this format can work very well

Police Department's Web Page

The last area that I want to discuss is the police department's web page. I had a web page for my last two departments. I found them to be an excellent public relations tool. It can be as sophisticated that you want it to be. You would be surprised to find out the number of people who surf the World Wide Web these days. Many people surf the web on this vast information highway. The potential is limitless and police departments need to tap this resource more. Law enforcement agencies are taking advantage of this opportunity and have an excellent website.

The web page is an opportunity to highlight your department and to provide information to the public, especially in the crime prevention area. The more that you can describe the operations of your department, the more informed citizens would become.

Here is one example of good public relations where we were able to help someone in Fort Lupton. One citizen who I later found out to be handicap, e-mailed me about a traffic problem in his neighborhood. We were able to help him with his problem. We probably would not have known about the problem if the department did not have a webpage. Apparently, this individual was more comfortable in using his computer rather then the telephone. Technology has come a long way in providing better service to the public.

In summary, communication is the key in running a police organization whether it is a small, medium or large police department. There are many tools at the disposal of the police chief and managers and ultimately it is up to him or her to gauge the pulse of the community to initiate a response to perceived problems. Ideally, the more that you can communicate orally and in written form, the better chance you will succeed. Only time will tell.

Chapter 7
Running a Police Department: A Balancing Act

Now you are the new chief or executive and what do I do? When a police chief or manager goes to a new department, it can be scary. The people do not know you and you do not know them. I remember my first time when I became police chief in Somersworth, New Hampshire. I was brought into the council chambers for the swearing in ceremony. My wife and I along with several of my closest friends from Bristol, Connecticut were there for the occasion. I looked around and saw a whole gallery of strangers from the police department. I remember that I was nervous about it. Thoughts kept racing through my mind. I said to myself, "Am I doing the right thing?" There were many questions still unresolved in my mind. What am I going to do next? Here I am the police expert from out of town that will do good things for the community. I was wondering if I was over my head.

When you are with a police department as long as I had been in Bristol, Connecticut you get zoned into a comfort level. You are familiar with your surroundings and you know everyone in the department. You feel comfortable with your managing style. Now, you are in a completely different environment. It was a culture shock going from a department of about 100 employees in a community of about 60,000 to a city of about 12,000 people with 26 full time employees in the police department in a different state. The building in Bristol, Connecticut was at the time a new police/court complex with parking garage having been built around 1978. The building in Somersworth, New Hampshire had undergone several changes throughout the years. It was a historic building having been built around 1930's. It was originally an apartment building and a store front on the first level and now a police department. It was a culture shock to be in an old building, which certainly could have used more renovations and better yet, a new building. Plans are now underway for a new police department building. This building was not originally built for a police department. I wanted to be a police chief. I must have been crazy to want the job. The police officers did good police work in New Hampshire. In reality, some of the most professional departments are in New Hampshire and this is a fact.

I should mention that I beat out the inside candidate for the position. It seems everyone wanted the other guy but guess what? The position was offered to me. You have to keep in mind your in-house competition may still be bitter about being passed over for the chief's position and eventually you will have to face lingering tensions or resentment. The conflict may not rise for a few weeks or even months, but I will guarantee you one thing that he or she will be mulling over their defeat every day. It is just something to consider right now but there will be a time when you will have to be assertive and make peace with the person before the problem festers and may get out of control. I can assure you that there are many situations you are familiar with already and may experienced what I have mentioned. How do you effectively deal with a disgruntled employee in a management position? Sometimes you will have to make tough choices and sometimes, making those choices is not going to easy. Maybe the sheriff has it right when elected into office. Essentially, the top management staff is fired and he brings in his own management staff. It makes a great deal of sense to me. Loyalty is more important in an organization if you want to get things done in predisposed or predefined situations. More often than not, you do not have the luxury of selecting your management staff in the beginning. You inherit the one from the previous administration and you try to make do with what you have already in place. I will discuss dealing more effectively with personnel in another chapter.

Coming in from another state, I knew that the job would not be easy. I knew that I would have to earn the trust and respect from my personnel. One of the command staff officers referred to chiefs that were brought into the department as "carpetbaggers." I did not take offense when he referred to other chiefs in the state as carpetbaggers. I knew that he was also referring to me. I did not take offense and besides, I was the outsider. I expected the comments. This particular officer was involved in the State's Police Association. Each month, he would write a column called the "Blue Graffiti" for the police association monthly magazine and would select a humorous topic of interest. I have to say his articles were very well written. One particular month, he wrote an article on how to become a police chief. He warned me about it and said, "Do not take offense." I appreciated his letting me know. At the time, he made reference to a number of outsiders that were hired and many, like me, were brought in from out of state to run the department. He suggested that if a person was interested in a chief's position in his department then he should leave and reapply for the police chief position. He was making a point that many quality candidates had been passed over. He was right and I would agree with him, to a certain extent, on this point. However, there was a motive to this madness. Then again, I was not the one making the decision.

The town fathers were looking for someone with new and fresh ideas. Many times a town or city manager will bring in someone new that he feels comfortable working with and to break away from the cycle of the **"Good O'boy"** network. It seemed everyone was a friend with one another. It is nice to have friends, but if your friendship with colleagues runs too deep, it may cloud your judgment causing biases in your decisions or hinder performing your duties. Most likely, the town or city manager will go outside the community looking for a police chief especially if there were many problems in the department. They do this under the guise of getting someone with some fresh and new ideas. Putting someone in charge, owing no favors to anyone and being loyal to the city manager is the key ingredient. Often the inside candidates may have some skeletons in their closet that many people know about. If you think that some personnel would try to blackmail the chief, you are right. Some individuals would stop at nothing to advance their own agenda. The chances for an outside candidate to get the job over the inside candidate are usually better.

Changes Need To Be Made Gradually

Obviously, I was brought in to make some changes in the police department and not maintain the status quo. Being new, I realized being apprehensive was just human nature. I conveyed the message to my personnel that changes would be gradual. Changes for the sake of change would not be implemented but only where needed. I have a philosophy that I would tell them. **"Rome was not built in a day."** No matter how simple or complex the task, it would behoove the police executive to take his or her time in assessing the department to make some necessary changes.

Even though the city manager briefed me about the police department, I still had to undertake the task of assessing the department. My first order of business on my first day was to sign some purchase orders that my secretary gave me. I am glad she knew what she was doing because at that point I did not. She was funny and a sweet woman and she helped me a great deal. Believe me; a good secretary is worth her weight in gold. She told me that I was the fifth chief she had worked for and had notches on her belt to prove it. She was kidding of course, or was she? I read an editorial in the local newspaper that Somersworth was a "dumping ground for police chiefs." Every police chief since 1970 was fired for one reason or another. It was a scary thought but what had I gotten myself into. This situation and many other similar situations happen all over the country. I guess every department has their "cloak of mystery" behind it. A new chief going into a police department for the first time has to have what is called a "thick skin" and be aware of the hidden messages people are saying. It may not be personal but people will criticize the police department. What they say may be true. The more that you pay attention to their comments and innuendos the more prepared you will be to deal with the current and future problems in the department. They are giving you helpful hints so you can do something about the problems. Changing the prevailing culture of the police department was a monumental task.

Review Personnel Files

One of the first tasks that I had undertaken in the department and my other departments as wells was to review the personnel files of all my personnel and the General Orders or SOPs (Standard Operating Procedure). I wanted to get to know my personnel and by reading personnel files, you can learn a great deal of information about individuals. In particular, I was interested in the commendations, evaluations and disciplinary record. I wanted to learn about the disciplinary problems. Eventually I would find out but it was nice to know something about him or her, good or bad. In the meantime, I had numerous meetings with my management staff. I wanted them to tell me what they thought was wrong with the department and the best way to fix it. Some of their input was very good and it gave me a great deal of insight in planning.

Involve Your Personnel

I believe the best way to make any changes is to have your personnel involved in the process so that they will share a sense of ownership. If your personnel have a hand in the development process of change, then the implementation process to change is much easier. The changes for success were greatly improved. I can cite a good example. At the time the police bicycle concept was still new to law enforcement especially in New Hampshire and I wanted to have a bike patrol on special occasions. They did not know it yet but it would be the beginning of our Community Policing effort. The patrol officers were not too keen on the idea so I established a committee made up of a sergeant and several police officers to check the feasibility of having a bike patrol. Their task was to check other communities that have a bike patrol, verify the type of bikes, equipment and uniforms and then suggest some guidelines for a General Order. They did a magnificent job in researching bike patrol, equipment and made suggestions for the General Order. They even found a local business to donate a police bike. I could not have asked for any better result. Based upon their recommendation the bike patrol was implemented on a part time basis as part of our new Community Policing effort. I will talk more about this later. The bike patrol was an instant success. It was a success because I had involved my personnel in the planning stages. They liked and bought into the idea.

Reviewing General Orders: A Necessary Evil

I reviewed all the General Orders and found that many were outdated and had to be replaced. Many orders had to be added as I went along. Any new police chief has to first review the high liability General Orders, such as Use of Deadly and Non-deadly Force, Arrest, Search and Seizure, High Speed Pursuit and so forth. Any area where a lawsuit can be generated should be reviewed, revised and finally reviewed by the city attorney.

Some chiefs and managers take this area too lightly and here is a case in point. The police chief who replaced me in Florence, Arizona never revised or added to the General Orders. I only cite this example because I know about it but it is a common problem with many police departments. Matter of fact, my signature was still on the last page of every General Order. I always ended them by writing, "By Order Of" and signed my name. How could it be by my order when I was no longer there? A police chief going to court on this issue would look somewhat silly. I had a General Order on promotions and he decided to promote an individual without following the order. He probably never read any of them anyway. The employees submitted a grievance stating that the chief did not follow the procedure as outlined in the order. Of course, they were right. The town manager reversed the chief and made him bring the orders up to date. By this time he had been there for almost two years. The only changes he made were to retype the last page and that was the signature page. It was an honor to consider my work so highly. The point is that writing General Orders is hard work and a never-ending process of reviewing, revising and writing new ones in keeping up with contemporary law enforcement. It is a **necessary evil** that needs to be done on an ongoing basis.

If you do not agree with a General Order, either revise it or rescind it as soon as possible. You have to practice what you preach and the policy manual is the bible for your personnel to follow. If you are going to hold them accountable then these orders should be what you want to have in place. You have to make sure that these orders are in line with your own philosophy. You can avoid a great deal of trouble this way.

There are some departments that do not have General Orders. I would like to think these are rare. There will be some departments unbelievably where you will find very few or no General Orders, such was the case when I first arrived in Florence, Arizona. When I asked for the General Order manual I was given a small notebook with some proposed General Orders, and some still had another department's names on it. Police Departments are notoriously known for borrowing orders from another department and adopting them. Besides, why reinvent the wheel if another department's order could fit a particular situation. I borrowed many other departments' orders but I always changed them. It is all right as long as it conforms to how your department operates and I would be willing to bet there needs to be some changes. At least take out the other department's name. Obviously, the previous chief saw no need for any orders. Everything was by word of mouth. Word of mouth is nice, but what if the chief is not around then what? I asked the firearms instructor in Florence about the Use of Force policy and he replied, "We follow the state statute." I knew at this moment that I had my work cut out for me in this small western town. Apparently, they "winged it" and made it up as it best suited them. The department was in an early 20th century mentality. Does this seem familiar to you?

When I first arrived in Fort Lupton, Colorado, I reviewed the General Orders and found them to be in good order but many were outdated. The department had been State Accredited and the five-year renewal was due in about a year. The books had been published into a small, loose-leaf notebook. This notebook type was too small and cumbersome to make changes and updates. I began the task of revising them on an 8 ½ by 11-inch paper for incorporation into a larger notebook. It made the task much easier and later revisions and new General Orders were printed and placed into the notebook. Each employee was required to maintain a General Order Policy Manual. I took it one-step further, each person was required to sign off on a page that he or she read and understood the General Order and it had to be also signed by their Supervisor. The Supervisor was also required to explain the order to their squad. The sign off sheet was put into the file as part of the accreditation documentation. However, on a practical side, I wanted my personnel to understand the orders. I did not want the officers to just put the papers into their locker and forget about it as they did in my old department in Bristol, Connecticut. I knew that they read them because many times I had to revise them again based upon some good suggestions from my personnel. I was quite pleased that I was getting input from them and it did not bother me at all to make the changes.

One thing I always did with General Orders was to staff them. Other words, I posted a draft on the bulletin board.   I posted the draft to give some time for my management staff to review them and I posted a copy for the personnel to review and comment. Sometimes I would get some suggestions and other times nothing at all. Maybe they were getting tired of looking at all the drafts. I would let it stay on the bulletin board for about a week and finalize it for later adoption. Often I would delegate the writing to some of the orders to my management staff. Whatever the case might be, **always involve your personnel** in reviewing, rewriting and writing new General Orders. It made good common sense and sound management practice.

Murphy's Law: The Unexpected Problems

If this was a perfect world and if there was no crime then there would be no problems. It is like Murphy's Law. If something can go wrong, it will. This holds true especially in police departments. There was always a monkey wrench thrown into the works. I try not to get too upset when problems crop up because of employee carelessness or stupidity. These little surprises will come up every once in a while.

Everything was going just fine until my top management staff in Somersworth, New Hampshire came into my office and asked if they could speak to me about a problem. They said that there was an incompetent sergeant who they wanted me to get rid off, namely fired. I said, "Okay, what did he do?" I had already inspected this sergeant's personnel file and did not see anything derogatory. It seems the city had a long-standing contractual agreement with the police union that disciplinary matters would be removed from the file after one year if there were no repeat offenses. What a sweet deal the union had with the city. The two captains related an incident that occurred the previous year when he allegedly assaulted a prisoner in the booking room. At the time, they admitted giving him a break by only recommending a short suspension. The sergeant was disciplined for assaulting a prisoner and served his suspension. Incidentally, these days most officers would be fired and arrested for assault. I knew that I would have some more surprises as time went on. I told them I would have no problem in firing someone if it was warranted. What they presented me with was a disciplinary matter that had already been handled. I told them the next time there was a problem with him to write it up and I would evaluate it. I certainly was not going to get rid of someone because they wanted me to. I think I handled the matter very diplomatically. However, I knew the captains were disappointed with my response.

Another incident came to mind involving the same sergeant. It seems that he had been subordinate with one of the captains and that was the motivation for bring this matter to my attention. The incident in question occurred before my arrival and it had nothing to do with me. The city manager neglected to tell me that there was this incident that had been lingering for a couple of months and the matter concluded. I simply spoke to the interim chief, a police sergeant and asked him about it and if he had any recommendations. After a lengthy discussion, he thought and I agreed this incident would warrant no more than a written reprimand. You see, this incident went on too long. I gave the sergeant a written reprimand and it did not make this particular captain very happy. This disciplinary matter should have been addressed long before my arrival. Disciplines should be carried out as soon as possible. Sometimes a police chief or manager will procrastinate too long. If there is a problem, leaders must deal with it fairly and quickly. Delaying the execution of any discipline only hurts the overall morale. In reality, the officer's captain should have dealt with the problem himself instead of directing it to the police chief. Apparently, the captains were trying to pressure me and put me on the spot to see what I was going to do. Maybe it was another test to see if I had a "backbone" and to see what I was made of. Anyway the little scheme did not work. I figured out what they were up to. It is funny when I think about it now. When both captains wanted to talk with me about a matter then I knew something was up. I was prepared for a surprise. I always keep it in mind to do the right thing.

Integrity and ethics is a big part of being a police chief or executive. It is a reoccurring theme.

I had already discuss this incident previously and it had to do with mummified babies wrapped in old newspapers from the early 1950's in an old turn of the century, seaman type trunk that was now in the evidence room. Speak of an unexpected problem, what a surprise. The evidence room reminded me of a dungeon in an old castle. I use to get that damp, eerie feeling every time I had gone into the evidence room. The City Manager told me about the four mummified babies that were in the evidence room and he wanted me to find a way to remove them. The two captains knew about the case and told me about a former lieutenant who worked on the case in the middle 1980's and could not go anywhere with it. They simply could not prove the babies were alive at birth. They said that the babies were still in the evidence room and I asked to look. Apparently, after the former lieutenant left the department, the case never went anywhere. It turned into a cold case for sure. It was difficult for me to believe anyone could forget about human remains that were locked away in the evidence room.

The captain and I went into the cellar and into the evidence room so I could see first-hand for myself. Yes indeed, the old trunk was opened and lying in the bottom were four bundles wrapped in newspapers. It was a sight to behold. Wrapped in old newspapers like a piece of meat were the babies. It was true. How could a police department hold little corpses as evidence? It did not take me long, but I made it a priority to get the babies buried. This was another surprise that should have been dealt with a long time ago. No, they had to wait for me.

It seems there were surprises at every department. Here is another case in point. One evening near midnight, I got a call from dispatch that the former police chief was in the police lobby and wanted to speak to me. I found out that one of my officers gave a speeding ticket to his son and he was very upset about it. Come to find out, this former police chief initiated a problem with my officer near the location where his son had been stopped. He approached the officer, opened his cruiser door and began to yell at him, asking, "How dare you give a ticket to my son? Why this was nothing but police harassment. Here he was yelling at the officer in public. No doubt, the officer was intimidated by the former chief's bizarre behavior.

Even though there was a police sergeant on duty at the time, I thought it would be best if I see first hand what was going on. When I arrived, I observed the former police chief and his wife in the police lobby and as I approached, he said in a sarcastic way, "I want to talk to you." I politely stated that he and I would converse but I had to speak to my officers first. After spending a few minutes talking to the officer and sergeant I realized this incident should never have gone this far. The officers needed some direction as to what course of action they would have taken. I simply asked the following question, "What course of action would you take if it involved anyone else in a similar situation?" The officer replied that he would have arrested him. I told the sergeant and officer the course of action was obvious; just issue the citation to the former police chief. They issued him a citation for disorderly conduct and interfering with governmental operations. To make a long story short, when the case finally went to court and after they brought in a special prosecutor, the formal chief was found guilty for these offenses and given probation.

Now, supporting the officers when this action was taken certainly did not put me in high esteem with the former police chief. Matter of fact, it probably hurt me in the long run because my two-year contract was not renewed by the Town Council. I truly believe that my support of officers had something to do with it. After that incident, officers continued to have confrontations with the formal chief and the current council members were also friends of the ex-chief. I kept them informed with these developments but I knew deep down, they still liked him even though he was getting into trouble. If I had to do it all over again, I would not have changed a thing; I have no regrets. It was a choice I had to make. A police chief and managers have to **demonstrate support for his or her personnel** when they are right. In this particular case even though the decision had not be popular with the town council members, I would not have handled it any differently. You see the police chief has to take a stand and support his personnel when it is necessary. In this case, I had to do something and my only best option was to have the officers initiate criminal action against the former police chief. I was not thrilled about seeing a former chief get a summons to court but leaders have to do the right thing even if it may jeopardize your job. Doing nothing was not an option.

I have to mention another big surprise that happened to me in Florence, Arizona. Everything was going along well for a few weeks without any problems until I received a call from dispatch about 4:00 a.m. The dispatch said that she had some bad news for me. She said one of my new officers was arrest for driving under the influence of intoxicating liquors in Phoenix and was being booked. The Phoenix Police did give him a break and let him sleep in a nearby motel instead of going to jail. Well that was nice. The dispatcher also said that was not all, though. I said, "There was more?" It seems the reason he was picked up in the first place was because he was stopped on Van Buren Drive in downtown Phoenix. He had a prostitute in the vehicle with him. I thought to myself, how stupid can someone be? Everyone knows where the "hookers" hang out. Even I knew that and I was not from Arizona. The officer had some domestic problems with his girlfriend in Mesa and he decided to do a little more drinking.

The officer was on probation only for a few months after being hired. I gave him the opportunity to resign in the best interests of the department and he took me up on my offer. He knew that he had made a big mistake and even his peers gave him a hard time. I can forgive a little mistake but this person truly made a big mistake. He was "up to his neck in alligators and he got swallowed up." I liked him but sometimes you have to take action that you do not like. This is all part of being a police chief or even a mid-level manager. Later on, this person still maintained a good relationship with me. There were no hard feelings between us.

In Fort Lupton, Colorado, I had a surprise worth mentioning. My investigator called me up one day and asked to speak to my lieutenant and me. It was his day off and I wondered what the problem could be. Many thoughts went through my mind thinking he may have gotten into trouble as a result of a domestic disturbance. He and another person, whom later I found out was a pastor of the church the officer attended, arrived at the designated time. He confessed to taking cocaine from old drug cases and using on and off the premises. I was almost in a state of shock. Who would have thought that a clean-cut guy would have been taking cocaine? Being chief in my third department would have prepared me for anything but this one was a complete surprise. I guess you may never know what may happen while you are police chief or even a manager for that matter. You always have to **be prepared for the unexpected**.

The Looking Glass

You may know as well as I do that the police department and its employees are under the magnifying glass all the time. The media seems to think that they need to know about every little problem within the walls of the police department. Metaphorically speaking, a police department is more like a fish bowl and the police officers are the fish. If you think this is bad, just think about how the police chief or boss is perceived in the eyes of the employees. The employees have the looking glass and there are many eyes looking at the actions of the police chief or manager. There will be many times when leaders' actions will be questioned, good or bad, and second-guessed many times.

Good feeling or not, it is an unpleasant fact with police chiefs and/or leaders. You not only have to worry about the public, city or town manager or city council, you also have to worry about your personnel. It is difficult, if not impossible, to keep everyone happy. If your personnel do not agree with the chiefs or managers actions, then other pressures build by way of a "vote of no confidence" initiated by the police union or by the personnel themselves. This certainly can get any chief or administrator's attention especially if the media got wind of it. I have come close to it but managed to dodge the bullet and will speak more on this later.

Just keep in mind, whatever you do, will be scrutinized by everyone. My best advice is to not worry about it and go about your everyday business. If you do not worry about it then everything will fall into its proper place if what you do is in the best interest of the department and city or organization. Sometimes there are unexpected events or situations that can be an unexpected surprise for the police chief or manager even with years of experience. It is just part of the job and you have to live with it. I guess that is why I liked the job of being a chief so much. It was a challenge everyday and I never know what to expect. You can try to anticipate but believe me, you cannot anticipate everything.

Setting Priorities

Because of the uniqueness of the position, everyday is a new experience. You may start one priority and have other set plans for the day; nevertheless something would happen to change your priorities for not only the day but for the entire week. I cannot tell you how many times it has happened to me, other chiefs and leaders. You have to expect that your set schedule is only good until another priority takes precedent.

Such was the case during what I thought was a routine day in Somersworth, New Hampshire. I got through most of the day as scheduled, until I got a call from a manager at the General Electric Plant on Main Street. One of their workers had been in the process of removing leaves from their canal when much to his surprise he discovered a body floating in the water. It is somewhat unusual to find a body floating in the canal in the middle of the afternoon. The managers of the plant wanted the situation handled low-keyed. The Investigations Captain and I went to the location and found the body. At that point, I notified dispatch to notify the fire department, the corner's office, County Attorney and the Attorney General's office. Anytime there is a suspicious death these agencies must be notified. We did not know at that time if we had a homicide on our hands or not. As it turned out, the body turned out to be a missing person who was reported missing a few days previous. After an investigation, it turned out that he apparently slipped into the water and drown. There were no signs or evidence of foul play.

As you can see, changing priorities can be an almost daily occurrence. I think that a police chief or manager can quickly get into trouble if he or she has what I call **"tunnel vision."**   I know individuals who can only handle one task at a time and get flustered when something else comes up. The idea is not to become flustered; it is part of the job. Usually these individuals do not last long as chief or the person in charge. A police chief or leader has to be able to juggle priorities and be able to **handle multiple tasks at the same time**. As other issues come up, these matters are added to the equation. It will be just another task to juggle. You have to be able to see the big picture. Seeing the big picture is very important.

One example that I want to point out to illustrate my point even further involved my personal secretary in Somersworth, New Hampshire. One day I was working at my desk and it was a typical busy day. I was working on multiple tasks as usual and at the time, I was working on an important report for the city manager. Actually I did not want to be disturbed so my chain of thought would not be broken. My secretary came into my office and wanted to speak to me. I knew that it was important to her because she was visibly upset. The last thing that I wanted to say to her was, "Not right now, I am too busy." It would have been the wrong thing to say. I did the prudent thing like any other police chief or executive would, I stopped what I was doing and for the next hour or so I listened to her discuss a personal problem she had at home. Apparently, she needed to talk to someone and I was there. I recognized the importance of her message and I immediately changed priorities to accommodate her. Everything worked out for the best. I helped her with her problem and I finished my report so it was a win – win situation all the way around.

An officer friend of mine living in Connecticut got himself into difficulty with the police union and eventually with police commissioners. Generally, there are those who are a one task at a time-orientated person but as chief or manager, you have to deal with many issues. On a positive note, this officer did a superb job on each task and was very bright. Sometimes people get into a mind set about **"seeing the trees through the forest."** It is an old saying and it is true. I believe this officer got into trouble because he failed to recognize and take action on other issues that came up that interfered with his task at hand. Of course, there were individuals who were trying to undermine him. It was a difficult situation that could happen to anyone. By not changing priorities when called for, may cause the problem to intensify. Now, when you are dealing with a police union or personnel issues, as leaders, one cannot forget about problems or put them off.

Learning how to excel in setting priorities and juggling tasks comes with a conscious effort to do well and experience. I made my share of mistakes but I learned from them. I think we can do a better job if improvements are made in establishing priorities and learning how to adjust. When you are dealing with people, especially in a labor-intensive environment such as police departments, then your priorities will keep changing. This is a natural fact, and certainly comes with the territory.

Setting the Example

One important quality that a police chief or manager should have is to set the example for others to follow. What we are discussing is a type of leader who **leads by example**. This is all part of leadership. Just because someone is the police chief or manager does not mean he or she is a leader. All we have at that point is a person in charge of the department. It is true that people will follow a person if a person is threatened with fear of punishment. This type of negative leadership can only go so far and this type of leader is doomed to eventually fail. Just think of the possibilities if the chief's or manager's personnel want to follow him or her because of this leadership style. Positive leadership, however, the followers simply follow because they want to. This is exactly the type of leader who I wanted to be and hoped that I had become.

There are many great leaders who evolved over the centuries. The one who comes foremost in my mind is General George S. Patton commander of the 5th

Army during World War II. His men followed him everywhere into battle and some to their death. Matter of fact, many of the old veterans still speak of him and hold him in high reverence. The General had that great ability to be a great leader and had the charisma so that his men would follow him into battle. What a great feeling to be able to do just that.

The police chief or manager, if he or she is to be effective, must practice what he or she preaches. Leaders must set the example for others to follow. You can be in another community and still get recognized. My wife and I were on vacation one time in another state when we bumped into people we knew. It happened all the time. We could not go anywhere without being seen and recognized. There are more people out there that know you than you know of them. Let me further explain this one. The police chiefs are in a high profile position. Many people can recognize their police chief even if the chief had not been introduced to the person. Let us fact it, the police chief is a high profile person.

You have probably heard that the two B's do not mix: "broads and booze." It will be a deadly combination or even by itself just as lethal. I cannot tell you how many times it has happened to friends of mine who were police chiefs. You probably know of many examples yourself. The result was them being terminated or forced to resign. What kind of message are you signaling to your personnel or the public, for that matter when they know you are engaged in these types of extracurricular activities? Sooner or later, it will catch up with you. All levels of the department are affected if behavior like this is tolerated.

A good friend of mine who happened to be a police chief in a small community in New Hampshire for 29 years got himself into trouble. You would think that someone who was in this position for a long time would be untouchable. No, this was not the mentality to have. It seems this police chief was involved in helping a woman through some marital difficulties and he allegedly got romantically involved. Of course, he denied his romantic involvement. The town's selectman got involved because a Judge of the Superior Court questioned the motivations of the police chief in applying for an arrest warrant for the husband for domestic violence. Apparently, the Judge questioned the chief's motive, which led to a red flag being raised.

In fact, the chief was trying to obtain a high bond and to begin deportation hearings for the husband. What do you think about this sweet deal? All he felt he had to do was to get rid of the husband and he would have this woman to himself. The problem was that he was married and the selectman did not buy into this scheme either. If you cannot fool the Judge, the Selectman, and the Community, how can this chief possibly believe he could fool his department personnel? The obvious answer is that he cannot. The Selectman placed the police chief on a one-week suspension and put him on administrative leave with pay until they could sort it out. After several months of legal maneuvering, the chief submitted his letter of resignation. What a way to end a long and distinguished career, almost 30 years, only to leave in shame. Unfortunately, many chiefs and other top executives end their careers in shame because of stupidity involving women, drinking and even gambling and who knows what else. Let me add further that this also happens to other police department employees, managers and police officers.

Even when the Town of Florence, Arizona tried to find a reason to get rid of me, they could not find one. The reason was simple, I did not fool around with women and I did not drink. It is somewhat difficult to find dirt on an individual that merely goes home to his family after work. You see, when I was in Bristol, Connecticut I **never got into the habit of drinking with fellow officers** after the shift. Many would go to the bars and clubs and drink until it closed. I just went home to my family after work.

Integrity and Trust

The police chief and manager have to present an image of integrity and trust. If police officers or staff does not have anyone to look up to then there will be a problem. I had already given many examples on integrity and it truly works both ways for the officers, managers, and chiefs. I always have a high regard for the Law Enforcement Officers Code of Ethics. The Code of Ethics was always at the beginning of my policy manual for all to read and absorb. I had a framed copy hanging on my wall. I was very serious about these codes of ethics.

Anyone who has a desire to become a manager, police chief especially must make sure that his or her personal life is in order. I hate to see anyone tarnish the principles of the office. As I see many police chiefs were terminated because of their questionable lifestyle; it is difficult to undo the "Tarnished Badge" image. It is complicated enough to maintain a positive image in the community and even harder when there are integrity and trust issues with police personnel or any labor force. It becomes more compounded when the police chief or manager has integrity and trust issues as well. Sometimes there is no alternative but to terminate the police chief or manager.

Such was the case in my three former departments. In each case, the police chief was outright fired. When I went to Somersworth, New Hampshire, the police chief was fired because he allegedly stole money from the coke machine that was in the break room. Yes, you heard right. Who would be stupid enough to steal money from the Somersworth Police Association? The former chief was the secretary for the police association and he collected money from the coke machine and handled the account. It seems the coke machine never made any money and some of his personnel were starting to question the chief. It was a reasonable question. What happened to the money? After he turned a deaf ear to his personnel, they decided to complain to the City Manager. An investigation led to the chief being suspended and finally terminated. The chief still had the audacity to say the coke machine never made any money. It was a common sense issue when you get right down to it. The machine had to make money. They made 100% profit every time they sold one can of soda. The City Manager figured that a conservative estimate put the profits of about $2,000 in the former chief's pocket. The officers did the math too. The numbers did not add up, which is why these officers made a complaint in the first place.

Imagine it is silly and embarrassing to lose your job over some cans of coke. The former chief thought he could trust his so-called high-ranking friends. In retrospect, does the police chief have any friends in the department that he or she can trust? This is a good question to answer. This was another example of a distinguished career gone down the drain. This should serve as a lesson to all. Do not handle any money especially from vending machines. It is another common mistake made by police chiefs. I do not know why but I will bet there are still many chiefs out there who handle money.

I look at it in this regard; it is like giving an opportunity to the disgruntled employees to get the chief. Give them the opportunity and they will take it. When I was in Somersworth, there was a constant reminder of the coke machine caper. One of my captains had numerous coke memorabilia displayed in his office. I think he was giving me a signal, a constant reminder of his trophies on the wall. Perhaps, he was telling me that I was going to be next. They took the right action against the former police chief but why continually boast about it. Essentially, I was glad that he reminded me. If he thought that I was going to trust him, he had another thing coming. I was not going to do anything stupid to get myself fired. I was going to tread very carefully and make calculated moves.

Another issue that was not even mentioned and I thought about often was winning the community over again. I knew it would be a monumental task for me. After all the adverse publicity about the department for months, the image of the police department was not only tarnished but in the bottom of the pit. I had to find ways to resurrect the department and to improve its image. I knew that I would not get much help because some of my personnel were still gloating over their triumph over the former police chief demise. I was determined not to be another notch in my secretary's belt.

Setting the Tone for Excellence

I always operate from this premise. I cannot dwell on the past. I can only **take care of the present and work for tomorrow**. It was difficult because of what had transpired in the past. I had to work hard to bring the Somersworth Police Department up to contemporary standards. Come to think about it, there were similar problems found in each department I have worked in. After a department has been hurt it takes a great deal of hard work to build the department back up again.

There will be ups and downs, **a balancing act** to insure everything is going the way it should. Believe me there will be many opportunities. Again, setting the example is very important. I believe that if my personnel see me excelling at what I do then they will get excited. **Enthusiasm breed's enthusiasm and it is contagious**. Over time, I saw many good things happening. Generally, everyone was pleased with the direction the department was going in.

As the new police chief, I knew that some of my personnel were deficient in some management areas, so I set about the task to teach them. Actually, I enjoyed my role as a teacher. In the year 1988, computers were still new. There were no computers in the department yet and the dispatch center was a mess. I brought my own personal computer into the police department to begin writing General Orders and other administrative tasks. The staff was amazed at my wide range of expertise in all areas so I was able to establish instant credibility. Establishing **credibility** is an important focal point for a chief or executive. Because I had achieved this important point, the officers were more willing to be involved in a number of projects.

One area that we made tremendous improvements was the dispatch center. Working together as a **team,** we were able to create a new dispatch center with computerized law enforcement software. Matter of fact, we were the showcase for other departments. In the meantime, whatever we accomplished, I made sure the community knew what we were doing. I wanted the community to sense a feeling of renewed commitment and pride. In fact, the task was made easier because the City Manager, Mayor and City Council were very supportive and helped with some capital outlay equipment.

If It Looks Like a Dump

We set about improving the work areas. We improved the looks of the department instead of having it look like what I call a dump. Some of my colleagues and I did a management study of a police department in a small community in New Hampshire. One of the major recommendations we made was to clean up the department. You would have thought that the former chief would have taken care of it long ago but he just kept making up excuses. If you want to look professional, you have to act professional. I have seen the inside of many police departments and the impressions some displayed were horrible.   At the very least, several departments walls can use a coat of paint. Small amounts of paint will do a world of wonders. When I was in Fort Lupton, Colorado my wife and I spent countless hours repainting the walls in the police department and the building was only 15 years old. We had it looking good too. It was a good example for others to see because we actually were able to get some volunteers to help. After we completed the project, we heard many favorable comments including some from city council members.

I believe that if the building looks like a dump then the employees will treat it like a dump. The employees need to buy into keeping the department presentable for the public at all times. Even though the building was old, we kept it neat and clean. It was now a sense of pride for the police officers. This concept carried over to the police vehicles.   I insisted that the vehicles were kept mechanically maintained, neat and clean. You know that some of the officers leave their cans, bottles and paper bags in the vehicle. I do not know why it is so difficult to remove trash. After a while, the vehicles could look like a garbage trunk. The appearance was unprofessional.   I told the supervisors to inspect the police vehicles for cleanliness.

Sometimes you can gauge the morale of the employees in how they treat their equipment, vehicles and building. If the employees do not have pride then it will certainly show. When I interviewed for numerous communities for the police chief position I always checked out their quality of the police vehicles and building. You can tell a great deal in a short time if the police department personnel have pride.

Delegating Responsibility

I have seen too many police chiefs take on too many tasks. It is physically impossible to do everything him or herself and I assure you, there have been many chiefs as well as managers who tried. I have seen many chiefs and executives work long hours to try to get jobs done all by themselves. However, his or her personnel are going home and the chief or manager is working longer and harder. I think something is wrong with this scene. My former Town Manager in Florence, Arizona had it right. He said, "You surround yourself with good people and let them do their jobs." His philosophy was right on. Why work harder when you can work smarter? The key is getting the job done through others.

I realized a long time ago that I could not do all the tasks by myself.   There simply is not enough time in the day. What is the answer? The answer is simple; you **delegate some responsibilities** to your subordinates and hold them accountable. Believe me, your subordinates will realize they are part of the team and will appreciate it. Police chiefs and executives have to balance everything to make sure everything is running smoothly like some fine-tuned and well-oiled machine.

The most important part of delegation is the follow-up by the police chief or manager.   If you do not follow-up and your subordinates continually miss deadlines, then shame on you. Sometimes police chiefs and leaders are so busy that they forget about the project and do not remind their personnel when the projects are due. I like to use a tickler file to help remind me to check on their work. What happens if you do not check periodically? Your personnel will think that the project will have a lower priority and will not be very concerned about it. Remember that is the impression you will give if you do not check. They will think the project is no longer important.

Human nature is such that personnel will often display more of a lazy-fare attitude if the chief or manager does not show an interest in what they are doing. I tend not to give my management staff busy work that I do not want to do. Some examples are questionnaires that crossed my desk on a daily basis. They are a pain to take the time to fill out. It seemed everyone was doing a survey. My intent was to give them more meaningful projects that would improve the operations of the police department. It was just that simple. In addition, I encouraged my management staff to delegate a piece of the project so that other employees would have some input. You accomplish more through teamwork. I know individuals are very possessive about their assigned project but if you can involve others then the quality of work is even better. I always say, "More heads are better than one."

Your Department Running Smoothly?

How many times have you wondered if your department was running too smoothly? You have not heard any criticism or problems for two or three weeks or even a few months and you think everything is just great. No one is bringing any problems to your attention. Perhaps, at this point you should pay more attention and watch out. It is not being paranoid. It is being cautious and more aware that there could be some problems lurking about. It would be more appropriate for the police chief or manager to ask a few questions to find out what is going on.

Sometimes there is always a lesson to be learned from life's experiences such as the previously mentioned lesson learned in Florence, Arizona. There has to be some tell tail signs that something is wrong in the organization. It is like a lull before the storm. A police chief or executive should be able to gauge the climate of the police department or organization and ask more questions. It is a never-ending battle to insure problems are kept to a minimum or controlled. I believe if a police chief or manager kept more of a **pulse on his or her department** then he or she is better prepared in dealing with these issues.

Perhaps, if I had paid more attention to some of the clues left by my personnel, I would have had a chance to prepare by myself better in dealing with the council on that fateful night of doom. As I recall this particular police officer told me to watch my back with a certain sergeant. After all, I just had a council member tell me I was doing a great job and had meetings with the mayor who never gave me the impression that I was in trouble with the council. I told that officer the sergeant was doing a good job and it was hard for me to believe what he was telling me. In hindsight, I should have heeded his warning and asked more questions. I let down my guard. As it turned out, he was right. After the Town Council voted not to renew my two-year contract, their next order of business was to appoint an interim chief. Guess who they appointed? They appointed the sergeant that the police officer warned me about.

It was a lesson learned. I should have started asking questions and even confront the sergeant. Oh well, you live and learn. As I went about my journey to the next department destination, I decided I would make sure I would not repeat these mistakes. I made a pact within myself that I would pay more attention and ask a great deal of questions.

You see, you never know if one of your management staff will do anything to get your job and will stop at nothing to get it. Such was the case in Florence but the little scheme of the sergeant did not work. Apparently, the Town Council saw there were problems with this individual and they appointed someone else, a cousin of one of the council members. It was an interesting selection. The cousin, I might add, was out of law enforcement for 18 years. Other highly qualified individuals were not selected. I am not surprised about politics anymore.

In 2005, we moved back to Florence, Arizona after evacuating from Louisiana after Hurricane Katrina struck the area. While living in Florence again, the former mayor wanted to speak to me. After all these years, she apologized for the action the town council initiated against me in 1997. She and the other council members discovered that I had been telling them the truth all along. I appreciated her apology and respect her for saying some kind words after all these years. However, I was not bitter. You have to try and forget and move on with your life.

Yes, there will be many challenges in running a police department. The police chief has to be up to the challenge. It seems that everyday something was new, whether it was a personnel issue or a major incident in the community. The more that the police chief can balances these issues the better chance he will have to succeed.

Chapter 8
Dealing Effectively With Police Personnel

Dealing with police personnel can be a roller coaster ride and what a ride it can be. I have a simple philosophy that I would like to relate: **Treat people the way you would like to be treated**. It just makes good sense. Dealing with police personnel can be so difficult at times but also rewarding. There will be times when police officers or staff members will come into your office and want to talk. The police chief or leader may be busy, but if you preach an open door philosophy, it will be in your best interest to listen. Being a good listener is half the battle. Over the years, I have seen many chiefs and managers come and go. In one year in New Hampshire, there were new police chiefs in every community that bordered our community. Of course, I asked the question, "When will I be next?" I must have done something right because I stayed in Somersworth, New Hampshire for seven years and perhaps even longer had I decided to stay on. The choice was for me to leave on my terms.

Some chiefs and managers have different styles in managing people and most of it comes with experience. True leaders say experience is the best teacher and it comes with time. It sad to say, some chiefs, captains, lieutenants and sergeants will never learn to be effective leadership skills. It is not what you know but the attitude that managers conveys. One lieutenant used a special technique to deal with his personnel. He had a unique embroidered towel, "The Crying Towel" hanging on the wall behind his desk. What kind of message did he send? Just thinking about this towel would make you laugh. He did not get very many individuals to come to him with problems unless you were one of his friends. He just did not want to talk to people about problems. He sent the message loud and clear, "Don't bother me." Guess what? His staff never would confide with him either. It was too bad because he missed opportunities to help his personnel. It is the nature of our business to deal with people problems, not only in the community but in the department as well. Everyone has their share of problems and even more so when you deal with people problems all the time.

Making and Keeping Promises

When I first became a police sergeant, I quickly learned that I was responsible for others. I did not come on too strong and did not give them the impression that it was "my way or the highway." I wanted to be a good sergeant so I listened to their problems or complaints and watched other sergeants in how they approached supervision. At each level of the organization, the supervisor has to learn to listen. It is not just giving them lip service and then doing nothing. It will mean much more and have a lasting impression if you put your words into motion and do something about it. Remember; **do not make promises that you cannot deliver**. Your personnel will have a long memory and will not let you forget the false promises. Many supervisors make a common pitfall error including police chiefs when they cannot deliver a promise. It ruins the credibility of the person and the lack of confidence worsens as time goes on.

It is fair to say that the root of most chiefs and managers problems lie with their personnel. I believe the key to success in running a department is your personnel. The personnel under your command can make or break you or the organization. I would rather have my personnel help me and the organization. I never convey the impression that I am better than they are. This is another pitfall many chiefs and managers make. Many leaders think that they are the greatest police chief or manager that ever came along and if they convey this type of attitude, they will surely be doomed to fail. You see everyone knows that you are the leader so why keep reminding him or her of it. Some chiefs or managers become humbled in a hurry and others find it is too late. If that is the case then you may as well update your resume and move on or find another line of work.

When I first went into the community, I wanted to win my personnel over first and that is why I involved them in everything. You see, the concept is simple: if you can get your personnel to like you then they will be more apt to want to improve the department or organization. Now I am not saying you have to win a popularity contest. Of course, you do not but it helps if they like you as a person first. It takes a great deal of time and effort in trying to convince some staff members they are an integral part of the organization. If a police department or other organization have many problems and the perception of the department or organization by the community is poor then it will take more convincing. Once the staff buys into what the chief or manager is trying to do then they will be more willing to follow. Sometimes this is not an easy road to travel on.

In each of three communities I was employed in as chief, I spent time talking first at the department meeting, weekly staff meeting and meeting with individuals on an individual basis. The key is to keep talking. Eventually you will develop a very good rapport with your personnel. Some chiefs and managers will say, "It is all well and good, but I don't have the time." I say make the time; it is in your best interest. If you can occasionally ride with your personnel on patrol or plainly praise them, it will show them you have an interest in what they are doing. It is one of the best management ideas that I had. Sometimes it has been awhile since a chief, captain or lieutenant has been on patrol or even openly praised the staff member. It will be an eye opening experience for you. You will observe things that you have not been exposed to in a long time.

When I was in Fort Lupton, Colorado, I would periodically ride on patrol or drive around in the community to see what was going on at night. Many times my officers were surprised to see me backing them up on a motor vehicle stop. Well some chiefs would say I am a big-time chief in a large metropolitan area and do not have the time. I will tell you that the police chief from Denver before he retired routinely backed up his officers at night. He found the time. Just think about it for a minute. If you look at it from the officer's point of view what a good feeling to know that the police chief cared enough to show up as a back up on a motor vehicle stop. After awhile the officers would talk freely and even offer suggestions on how to improve the department by recommending certain equipment and suggesting programs or candidly discussing problems in the department.

I did not care who comes up with a good idea. It did not matter to me. The police chief cannot come up with all the ideas and sometimes it would be questionable if they would work. Often it is better if the officers came up with the ideas because they knew what was going on and if it would work on the street. It made a great deal of sense because they work the streets every day. I would not hesitate to give credit for an idea if it improved the operations of the department. What a concept! The police chief should use the ideas of personnel to help implement programs.

In Fort Lupton, Colorado there was a major problem with drugs in our community, like many other communities. It seemed someone was always tipping off the bad guys. It was an unusual problem and it was thought someone inside the department was the source. Who would stoop so low as to tip off a drug dealer? I guess when it comes to money anything could happen. I got together with some of my key personnel who wanted to make a difference in getting drugs off the street. These officers want to become involved in a special drug operations unit in addition to their regular patrol duties. They outlined an operational plan that made sense and I approved it. The plan worked because these officers were able to make an impact in the drug trafficking in and around the community. The community and town fathers were starting to take notice. We made many arrests and seized a great deal of drugs in the time that I was there. To my knowledge, we were able to eliminate much of the information going out to the drug dealers. I do not know if anyone inside the department was involved with the drug dealers but no information was getting out either. I had my suspicions but could not prove anything. Maybe they were afraid to get caught. By utilizing the plan of a few officers who wanted to do something about drugs in the community, we were able to make an impact. The sky is the limit with a little cooperation.

Another problem we had in Fort Lupton was a reputed gang problem. Certain young people were coming into the community and harassing our residents. People would get hurt and rarely was anyone arrested. The problem was the police would arrive after the fact, interview the victims, interview witnesses, and gather evidence. This was where they fell short because of the resulting inaction. The officers did not make very many arrests. The community was criticizing the actions of the officers and the officers themselves were complaining. The real reason the officers took no action was due to the criticism of the former chief in how they performed their duties. When they made an arrest, someone was always complaining so the officers took the easy way out. They made no arrests at all. Other words, there was very little or no support by the police chief. I met with the officers to determine how to resolve this problem in our community. We could not allow any gang types to come into our community at will and terrorize our citizens. We need to protect our community. The officers stated that they needed the support of the chief to back them up when there was an arrest. I told them as long as they made a good arrest then I would support them. I would take the heat if someone complained. It was like a changed police force. The officers were making motor vehicle and criminal arrests like there was not tomorrow. Some citizens said it was police harassment. No, I said it was "zero tolerance;" We were taking back our community. The people who were complaining were the bad guys. Of course, they would complain. They did not have their way any longer.

The "want-to-be" gang bangers apparently received the message after a number of them got arrested for various crimes. It seemed the gang problem was solved. The intimidation methods no longer seem to exist. Our patrol strategy worked as a result of the police officer initiatives and my support. The key point to remember is to **get your personnel involved and to show them you care**. The reason so many individuals want to be police officers in the first place is to help people and to make a difference. Just think way back when you were a new police officer. You wanted to conquer the world but were let down when you did not receive the support. It was like a kick in the chest. It helps to get support from the chief or manager. It is only common sense.

My philosophy did not change. It was the same for each department. In order to be effective with my personnel I needed to involve them and be part of the overall plan. Another example to illustrate my point was in Florence, Arizona. By the time I had taken over the department, it was pretty much in shambles. It took a rebuilding process. I meet with my personnel not only in the department, but in also riding along on patrol with them. I wanted to get a feel on how they felt about the problems and how they could be resolved. Matter of fact, I also spent a great deal of time talking to citizens about problems in the community. You see, no one wants to work for a loser organization. Everyone wants to feel pride and a sense of accomplishment in an organization. I gave them just what they were looking for. I involved them in helping to resolve policing problems in the community. Essentially what we were doing was simply called Community Policing.

One noticeable problem was a traffic problem. It seems that in this sleepy little western town motorist like to cruise up and down Main Street. As these motor vehicles and motorcyclists were cruising down Main Street, they would just make a U-turn in the middle of the intersection. This was going on as long as anyone could remember until I came along. I asked my personnel about it and they came up with some suggestions but the consensus was that something had to be done because it became a dangerous traffic problem for motorist and pedestrians. The solution was simple for this problem. With approval from the Town Council, no U-turn signs were installed at every intersection and it worked. The signs were very effective even to this day 10 years later. Most of the signs are still there.

Keeping Them Happy Is a Trick

Morale in an organization could be good one day and down in the dumps the next day. How can a chief or manager accurately gauge morale in his or her organization? At times, it is difficult and there are no easy solutions in helping your personnel to be happy. It could be anything that can damage morale; a rumor, a broken promise or even the perception the employee is getting the shaft. Some employees' morale will be high at times and some others will be low. Maybe the employees' low morale is the result of problems at home. It is more like a balancing act to keep the morale of the department upbeat. It is a great deal of hard work to make it happen. The chief has to be able to recognize some of these problems and take action or it will get worse. Low morale is contagious and it will only get worse if nothing is done to prevent it.

One issue that comes up all the time is low pay and poor equipment. You should realize that money is not a real motivating factor in making someone happy. You can keep throwing money at people and their happiness will be short-lived and forgotten. In any event, in each department that I worked in I set about the task to increase their pay. I was successful in convincing the town fathers that a pay raise was needed to keep personnel. It seemed like small departments were a stepping-stone to a higher paid department. We would train the staff and after a year or two they would leave. I promised my personnel that I would try to get them a well-deserved pay raise that would at least bring them up close in pay scale with other departments. The plan worked because the Town and City Councils approved pay raises. Even after the pay raises were given, the morale level at some point would drop. It was like the pay raises were expected and my personnel soon forgot about my efforts. At least they remembered my efforts for a while even though it was short-lived. I made them a promise and I delivered.

Another issue that affects morale is poor or no equipment. I wanted the personnel to have the best equipment and besides the police vehicles were like mobile offices. My theory was simple; if the employees were happy with their equipment then their performance would improve. In my mind, it is important to be able to have access to the tools to do the job more effectively.

My personnel were simply amazed at the amount of equipment that I had approved in the budget. The Town and City Councils wanted to see improvements in the department and I told them what was needed. I have to say, every council supported requests for new equipment. If I needed something, I demonstrated a need and asked for it during the budget process. Somehow the city always approved my capital requests. The idea is to be reasonable with your requests for capital purchases when asking and to develop a plan to accomplish it. The strategy would be to make these improvements over a few years. Usually, everything that I had asked for in my proposed budget was approved. Equally amazing was the expression on my officer's faces every time that I had our budget approved. Apparently, the chief in the past never bothered to ask. Even in poor economic times, the police chief's or manager's responsibility are to insure the public safety of the community and organizational success. He or she still needs to ask for the tools for the officers or staff to do their jobs efficiently. **If you do not ask, then you shall not receive.** In a short time, I managed to obtain badly needed equipment to replace the outdated ones.

Another way, I was able to obtain funding through State and Federal Grants. There are many grant opportunities. Police chiefs and other leaders should apply for grants to obtain personnel, equipment and funding for specific programs. Although there are some cost sharing and reporting requirements, generally City Managers and City Councils are supportive. The more creative that you can be in obtaining funding for department the better you will look in the eyes of the town fathers. Now, there is the new Federal Homeland Security Department. There is grant opportunities to collaborate with the fire departments to obtain new equipment to fight terrorism.

Another issue that comes up is the personal problems of the officers and it could be an explosive one. What happens at home, affects what happens at work or so they say. There could be no doubt about the truth of this statement. You cannot save everyone. Here is a case in point: While I was in Fort Lupton, Colorado I received a call from one of my officers that he got arrested as a result of a domestic dispute with his live-in girlfriend in Thornton, a community about 25 mile away and was being booked for assault. He said that he would be going to the county jail and he expected to be bailed out. It was another surprise and I never had any inkling that this person was having difficulty. There was no sign that his quality of work had gone down. I made a few phone calls and found out the real truth about the incident. The officer got into an argument with his girlfriend and threatened her with his department issued firearm. To make matters worse, there were other people at the apartment witnessing these events. He, at one point, went into the bedroom and put the barrel of the firearm in his mouth as if he was going to commit suicide. His brother who happened to be there at the apartment got involved and managed to talk him out of shooting himself. In the meantime, some one called the police and law enforcement waited in force outside the apartment. The police managed to get my officer out of the apartment at gunpoint without incident and without anyone getting hurt. Thankfully, the incident ended peacefully. The officer spent a few days in the county jail before being released on bail.

Wait, the problem gets worse. This officer called my lieutenant at home and told him that he was at a local motel in Fort Lupton and he was going to shoot himself. The lieutenant called dispatch to send police to the motel immediately and this was when I was called. By the time the officers got there, and it was only a minute or two, the officer shot himself in the mouth with a .22 caliber pistol. The bullet went into his mouth and out his left cheek. It was only a superficial wound and he would live to see another day.   The officer was put on administrative leave for psychological evaluation until everything could be sorted out but this officer eventually resigned. By just looking at the officer, you could not tell something was bothering him.

The Mask

Sometimes there are no tell tails signs. Matter of fact, the officer never told any of his coworkers that he had any problems. He masked the problem. On the surface, the officer appeared to be a competent and articulate person. On the inside, he was a mess. It was a shame we did not pick up on it earlier. Perhaps, we could have done something about it. I regret somehow not being able to recognize the problem. Some of his family members were quick to blame the department for not responding to his problems. I guess someone have to be blamed. However, you have to know about the problem first before action can be taken. Many people, especially cops, hide their emotions in their inner self. They do not want anyone to see a crack in their psyche. They do not want anyone to see anything is wrong in their life. Generally, police officers do not want to appear weak. They are a super cop or so they think.

The indicators are there. It is up to someone to come forward and say, "My friend needs help." I would have done anything to help him out. A department can have the best program in place in dealing with personal issues, but the person has to take the first step. My favorite expression is that I do not have a "crystal ball." In order to deal effectively with a problem I would need first to know about it. I regret we were not able to see some of the warning signs before it were too late.

The Problem Employee

Because you are dealing with people, there will be someone who is always complaining about something or trying to beat the system. This is just human nature once more. Some employees will take the path of least resistance in working hard to try to get out of work. This is another way of saying lazy. You probably know many individuals in your own department or organization. These are the same individuals who have the nerve to ask you for favors, such as getting a better shift, getting out of work for a doctor's appointment when it could have been scheduled some other time and days off when the manpower is needed. If you do not give them their way, they are quick to complain. Who wants to listen to a bunch of whiners and complainers anyway?

It is fine when a chief or leader goes to the interview and effectively answers all the questions like so many such as:

- What is diversity?
- What is your leadership style
- What can you do to effectively deal with the Juvenile Problem in your community?
- How can you effectively implement Community Policing?

There should be more questions about how to deal effectively with personnel. Someone may have all the answers to the questions. What good is it if you cannot get your personnel to follow you? However, it can be accomplished, while still keeping your   management philosophy in place.

A chief or manager will have to spend most of time resolving problems with five percent of the employees. This is a fact. Most employees will go with the flow but no matter what you do, the 5%'ers will still complain. A few bad apples can spoil the rest of the barrel if you do not do something about it. Knowing that I cannot please everyone, I do my best to resolve problems. Police chiefs and leaders are in the people business and it is not just the people in the community but in your own department as well.

Some Unique Issues

Here are some examples of some department related problems that I had to deal with. When I was in Somersworth, New Hampshire, my secretary came into my office and wanted to speak to me about another issue. She went into this lengthy story about how she was "grand fathered" into the police retirement system. At the time, when she was first hired they did not have a retirement system for civilian employees. What she wanted me to do was retire and have the city rehire her the next day. I said to myself, "You have got to be kidding." It appeared to be an ethical issue. She said that she had called the State Retirement System and posed the question to them and they did not have a problem with it. I told her I would check it out and true enough what she had told me was accurate. Unbelievably, they did not have a problem with her retiring and being hired by the same city again. I figured that I would never get her request passed by the City Manager but I told her I could not make any promises and would try. After briefing the City Manager on this issue and after a lengthy discussion, he finally decided that if the State Retirement System allowed it then it was all right with him. My secretary wrote a letter outlining exacting what she was planning to do and the State wrote back approving the retirement. On the day she retired, she was rehired by the city again. She did not miss a beat. It was truly amazing to me that the system would allow it. I still think it is an ethical issue. The retirement and rehire was approved. It was a unique situation.

If I had told her no, there would by no question than I would have lost her as an effective employee. Sometimes it does not take much to turn a good employee into a negative one. Apparently, she had already done her homework before she had come to me with her request. Now, the next problem dealt with the same issue but with another employee. My dispatcher was another long-term employee almost just as long as my secretary. I realized it would open the floodgates for the other employees. This female dispatcher found out that my secretary retired and was rehired by the city again. There is no doubt that my secretary spoke to her about it. You cannot do for one and not do for another, but I had known another employee would probably be affected by my decision. It was not long before she came to my office wanting to speak to me. After listening to the issue I told her when the time comes, she would have to write a letter to the State Retirement Board outlining exactly what she wanted. I did not want anyone to think that the State Retirement Board was being flimflammed. Even though I was concerned about an ethical issue, the state approved the dispatcher's request as well. In the end, everyone was happy with the outcome.

If you make exceptions for one employee then you have to realize that you set a precedent for the rest of the employees. It makes sense that other employees will soon find out so you have to be prepared to be of service for the others. Actually, to be fair, whatever I did for an employee, I made sure that I treated the others the same way. This is where chiefs and managers get into trouble with other employees. Do not think for a minute that secrets are kept. No way will this happen. If you show favoritism to one or a few, it will haunt you later on. I always strive to be fair and to treat everyone the same. This practice has always worked for me.

Another issue arose with another employee in Fort Lupton, Colorado. One of my police officers wanted to take a trip in the fall to Africa and needed to take four weeks off. This officer had the time coming to him so the time was not an issue. He had given me at the time about six months in advance. Generally, the practice was to allow only two weeks at a time unless there were special circumstances. One sergeant was against it because we were short on manpower. Who is not short on manpower these days? One argument you may hear is that others would come forward to ask for a lengthy vacation. It is true, but I would also do the same for someone else if they had special circumstances. I approved the time off because it was the right thing to do. He had given plenty of advance warning and he needed the approval to plan for his expensive hunting expedition to Africa. I figured the department should be able to accommodate this officer's request if it was reasonable. In this case, I did not have a problem with it.

Just think what may have happened if I had said no and it was within my right? He probably would have been another disgruntled employee and would have looked else where for employment. As it turned out, he was a happy "camper." He was a very productive employee and did a good job day in and day out. After he got back from his safari trip, he continued to do a good job. He showed all his pictures he took on the trip and they were wonderful. I jokingly said one day, "I would have gone in your place." Some of my friends who were already police chiefs no doubt would have denied the request. I did not regret the decision for a minute. We managed to cover the shifts.

There is a method to my madness. There would be times when this employee would be asked to do special tasks and he would be asked to cover other shifts when we were in a pinch. You know something? There was never a problem. He would volunteer to take a shift and never complained. Everything works out for the best in the end. The morale of the story is **look out for your employees** and good things will happen.

The "Naysayer"

What is a "naysayer?" In the simplest of terms it is the negative employee. If you have a negative person in command of personnel then you are in for some frustration. I had one such person on my staff in Somersworth, New Hampshire. This person was you know who? He was the captain in charge of patrol and dispatch. No matter what I tried to do and how I tried to prepare him for change, this person was the epitome of a pessimist. Every time that I pitched a new idea or reworked existing programs I could see it in his face, the agony he portrayed. He was one of those individuals who was use to the old ways and was very reluctant to change. He was the same individual who had gone to the FBI's three-month management school for police chiefs and command officers and graduated. He did not change his old ways and did not want to try anything innovative. What do you do with individuals like this? Let me tell you now, an employee's resistance to change is very difficult to overcome.

There was no doubt that if I wanted to succeed, this individual had to change his ways. There were some frustrating times ahead for me. To make a long story short, there were some glimmers of success but it did not last for long. The patrol division settled into a lazy fare attitude and I had to do something. With the approval of the City Manager, I had reorganized the department. I made the other captain, the Operations Commander in charge of the detective and patrol division. I moved the problematic Captain to Support Services in charge of Dispatch Operations, Cruiser Maintenance and Building Management under my watchful eye. It was the only place I could put him where he could not do anymore damage. The move was just short of termination. Now, the morale of this individual went even lower. He called himself "the janitor." Oh well, some times you cannot teach an old dog, new tricks.

After I left the department, the other captain became police chief. He had been a personal friend with the Support Services Captain and now he put him in charge of the Detective Division under his watchful eye of course. A few years later, he called me seeking my advice as to what to do with his friend. It seems and I was not surprised that the employees under the direction of the Detective Captain were now complaining to the chief. This particular person was not carrying his share of the load. He was sitting back and doing nothing. I knew what the problem was right away. I hate to say it but he identified with the Peter's Principle long ago. He had reached his level of incompetence and was continuing to hurt the department. Some people cannot grow at all and he was one. I suppose it was not his fault if that was what he was capable of doing. I told the chief that if I had still been at the department I would have eventually moved to terminate him. Apparently, what I said must have made sense because it was not too long before the Detective Captain submitted his retirement papers. The fallout resulted in a strained and probably non-existent friendship. Sometimes leaders have to make the choice for the good of the department or organization.

Turning the Negative Person Around

Leaders can try your best to work with individuals to make assist them in becoming productive employees but no matter what, some individuals still revert to their old habits. How can you turn the negative person around? I truly believe that you can turn most negative people into a positive, productive employee but it will take work. Sometimes no matter what you do, however, some employees will not change no matter what you do.

I like to turn these issues around when employees are saying negative things about police operations or programs and get suggestions from them. Some people like to complain all the time. Who knows, maybe it is just in their nature. Instead of them being part of the problem, if I can manage it, I have them become part of the solution. It makes perfectly good sense to me. Even with the negative captain, there were times when I did turn him around. I just got him directly involved in different programs. He did not want to be labeled as a failure, so he tried harder to accomplish the task.

I found the easiest way to turn the negative person around was to directly involve him or her in programs. Often, I tried to find out what programs they were interested in and when I could, I got the person involved in it.

On The Train

Which is more important task or morale? The obvious answer is they are both important. You need your personnel to accomplish the task. You can threaten them to do the task and it will work for a while but something has to give. If the morale is good and everyone is working together then the task will take care of itself. I call it being "on the train." The trick is trying to get everyone working together to stay on the train.

I like to use the following analogy. It is like sailing a ship. If you try sailing a big sailboat by yourself, you may become shipwrecked. Using your personnel to accomplish given tasks and working together as a unit on the sailboat helps to get to your destination.

You need to find a balance for the task and morale. I worked hard to bring this balance to fruition. Making your personnel believe in themselves and have them believe in the teamwork concept is the key. I like to make it fun and have the employees share in the glory of the accomplishments. There is nothing that will turn off an employee more then having the chief or manager take all the credit. **Sharing the credit is the key.** I always make it a point to recognize my employees for a job well done whether it is in public, to the media or before a City Council meeting. Putting employees first goes a long way. The personnel in the department want the chief or executives to care about them. Whether I am on the local cable television network or quoting in the newspaper, I always find a way to recognize my employees.

The **little victories lead to big victories**. The accumulative effect will show the desired effect. You see, people in the community will talk and eventually all the good things you and the department or organization are doing will filter to the council members. The city, town council or political leaders' wants to see results and improvements in the police department or organization and at the same time they do not want to hear about any problems from their constituents.

More recently, I read about the hiring process for interviewing prospective chiefs that had taken place in the City of Raleigh, North Carolina. The City Manager was doing it right for a change. The City Manager had the candidates go through a series of interviews before different groups of people, one of which was the rank and file of the police department. The rank and file officers had an opportunity to listen to questions asked of the candidate and to hear their responses. They were also given the opportunity to rank the candidates in how they responded. In my view, it was an excellent process and a smart move by the City Manager. You have to be careful so that the process does not turn into a popularity contest. In the end, the City Manager will make a selection and this process give him more information to make a decision. This was one of the most comprehensive processes that I have seen and I have been personally involved in quite a few. I hope that the decision that was made was in the best interests of the department and city. There were four candidates, an inside candidate and three from outside the State.

Finding Some Morale Builders

If you recall, money is not a real motivating factor. There needs to be something else to recognize the employee. I like to motivate employees by using different incentives. Keep in mind that whatever you decide to do, you have to be sincere. It will go against leaders if the staff thinks their chief or manager is trying to show off at their expense.

One favorite is the employee of the month program. I like to recognize employees for doing a good job. Anyone can recommend an employee for the award. All one have to do is write a memo outlining their reasons.   Many departments do it and there are different ways to go about it. I usually give them a certificate and their own parking space for a month. In addition, I treat them for lunch at my expense at a restaurant of their choice. Everyone knows that the lunch is not coming out of the budget. I think that it means more to them this way. To me, it is another opportunity to get to know my personnel even better. I also recognized the employees at the monthly City Council meetings.

Another program that I put together was a police medal awards and commendation program. There are different commendations and awards that my personnel can be recognized for. Everyone wants to hear about doing the good job and I make it a point to recognize them. When I was in Somersworth, New Hampshire, an officer approached me to tell me about catching a person in the act of committing a burglary. He said that no one mentioned anything to him and it was the first I heard of it. I told the officer that I would look into this matter. I asked the

Captain about it and sure enough he was aware of it but had done nothing about it. I suggested to the Captain that it would be nice to write a letter of commendation and forward it to my attention. I reminded my supervisors to watch out for the good jobs and write up a commendation if they fit.   There is nothing worse to an employee than doing a good job like catching a criminal in the act of a burglary or other praiseworthy deeds and not receiving positive recognition about it from anyone, only acknowledgment of mistakes. I think everyone can relate to this. It is even worse when someone else does almost the exact same thing and gets recognized for a good job. Everyone has probably experienced something like this over the course of his or her career. We need to recognize officers and other staff members for good police work and/or job well done more often. I always made it a point to tell the person they did a good job when I saw the officer. Most of the time, I would go out of my way to find the officer.

There are other ways to recognize employees for outstanding performance. It is not hard to come up with ways to recognize employees. It is left up to one's imagination. When it is appropriate, why not reward the person with a day off with pay.   More police departments do it and I think the employee appreciates this gesture more than just getting a piece of paper or certificate. It is like hearing the famous comment, "Show me the money."

Some departments wait until their annual awards banquet. I guess it works but I like to recognize the employee as soon as possible. Over time, people forget about the good deed that happened months ago. People have short memories. I tried the banquet or dinner route before and what worked best for me was the recognition of the employee as soon as possible and often recognition of the officer before council meetings.   At the council meeting, I made a presentation of police medals or commendations and spoke of commendable deeds. I believe this appreciation technique works very well. Whatever you do, the employees will appreciate your efforts. At least try to do something constructive.

I have seen police department have a physical fitness room and acquired a great deal of conditioning equipment. A fitness room is fine for those who work out but not everyone wants to hang around before or after work to exercise. I have tried it and it only benefits a few. You would probably be better for the City to offer a partial or full membership at a local health club.

One program that I thought about was developing something along the lines of **"Getting caught doing it right.**" Supervisors are quick to blame employees for making mistakes but what about recognition for doing it right. The more that we can give the employee a pat on the back the better off we will be. Too many chiefs and managers are stressing out over the task and not worrying about recognizing the employee when the opportunity presents itself.

There are many different ways to recognize employees and many departments have implemented programs. The sky is the limit for innovative approaches. Why not have employees sit on a committee to discuss ways to improve morale? This is just another practical approach.

Some Problem Areas

There are some problem areas for a police chief or manager to consider. Sometimes police chiefs and mangers are their own worse enemy. Take for example, a police chief approving a seminar request for a police major, keeping in mind the cost for the registration, transportation and hotel expenses. Generally, this would be no problem if the monies were in the budget. However, it is a questionable expense when the approval was given even though the police major was going to retire in a week. The City Manager responded in the paper saying that it was a legitimate expense because the employee will still be doing some consulting work after retirement. This did not make any sense at all. You can fool some people some of the times but not all the time. People in the community will be asking questions. The appearance is that the employee was given a vacation at taxpayer's expense. What is the chief thinking of? Why put yourself in a situation like this. This certainly presents an ethical dilemma. Trying to be a nice person all the time, could just get you more in trouble. Doing the right thing is the smart way in doing business.

It is a never-ending game trying to correct some of these problem areas. As long as the police chief or manager is aware of it, he or she can try to do something about it. One area that presents a problem is what to do with an employee who is not working up to standards or the probationary employee having a difficult time with field training or obeying rules and regulations. The easy way out is to terminate the employee and be done with it.

Back in Fort Lupton, Colorado, I took a different approach. We were having police officers experience a difficult time completing field training. It is an expensive proposition getting them to this point and even more expensive repeat the hiring process again. In Colorado, a police department need not sponsor a person. A person could go to a community college, enroll in a police certification program, and complete the required number of training hours. Once a person is certified then he or she can apply to any police department. On the surface, it is a good program because police departments had not had to spend any money up to this point. All the department has to do is advertise for certified individuals. The problem begins when months and months go by without being hired by a department. When the person finally lands a police job the person may have forgotten much of what was taught at the community college's law enforcement program. The expectations are much higher on an individual after the person is hired and police departments are too quick to give up on the person. Before I left the department in Colorado, I was making it a practice to extend the field training to give the individual more time to refresh their knowledge to succeed. It is a known fact that individuals learn at a different rate so why not apply it to those who are in field training. It is incumbent upon the police chief and manager to insure every possibility for a person to succeed and not be afraid to be creative.

Real Trouble Ahead

If you are not very careful, the following areas can be a real mess and threat to your career:

- Harassment
- Discrimination
- Sexual Harassment
- Sex Discrimination
- Sexual Favors

Do not dig yourself a hole that you cannot get out of. If the police chief or manager is aware of sexual harassment problems or if someone makes a complaint he or she must act immediately and not ignore the problem. Where police chiefs and leaders go wrong occurs when they ignore these problems and do not take it very seriously. These matters can easily escalate out of control and end up with the chief or executives named in a lawsuit.

Perhaps it was just luck but more realistically, I was aware of the stigma of a sexual harassment and discrimination complaint. In each community in Florence, Arizona and Fort Lupton, Colorado, each chief before me was named in a complaint. The complaint seems like it goes on and on while it finds it way through the court system. Of course, the media will be following the complaint and periodically write articles about it. It is negative news that undermines the effectiveness of the police department and it can erode the partnership with the community. Many of these issues can be avoided.

The sexual harassment complaint was just an aftermath from the fallout after the police chief's dismissal in Florence. First the complaint was entered as an EEOC, Equal Employment Opportunity Commission complaint, and was first investigated by one of their caseworkers. Many times these complaints end up in a lawsuit. While I was there, I did not have any complaints registered against me due to my trying always to be careful. I treated all my employees with respect and always conducted myself in a professional manner. This is the key. I cannot say the same thing for the chief who replaced me in Florence. He had a series of complaints registered against him by several female employees and it did not take long. They did not think that the chief treated them very fairly. When you involve yourself in the "Good O'boy" system, I guarantee there will be problems. I believe these series of complaints helped to expedite his departure. The town council members were tired of hearing complaints.

The police chief who I replaced in Fort Lupton had a hiring discrimination complaint lodged against him by a prospective female candidate, a former employee. It seems that he had promised a police vacancy position to the candidate and had reputedly made some disparaging remarks to other employees. When another person filled the vacancy, she asked him why she was not selected as promised. The chief at the time told her she did not pass the background investigation. The broken promise led to a lawsuit after which the city paid a sizeable sum of money in an out of court settlement and female candidate was given an opportunity to work for the city. The City offered her a court clerk position, the only position available at the time and she accepted. This fiasco ultimately led to the police chief's termination, so apparently there was some merit to her complaint. I asked myself the question of "How could people be so stupid?"

Another complaint was ongoing while I was police chief of Fort Lupton and it just concluded after I had left the department. A Hispanic Police Officer filed a discrimination lawsuit because he thought he was denied a promotion because of his race. This individual was very straightforward with me and told me the complaint had nothing to do with me. At one point, he even applied for a corporal's position and had gone to the interviews but ultimately he was not selected. His attorney added his denial of a recent promotion as part of their complaint. It was sad to say that this individual never applied himself or did anything to help his cause, which was the primary reason for being passed over for promotion this time. It had nothing to do with his race and it had all to do with his lack of ability and application of effort. Eventually his lawsuit was dismissed by the court because there was no substance to it.

I personally think that this individual was looking at the city's deep pockets for an out of court settlement as previously noted, with the female candidate for police officer. The female candidate and Hispanic Police Officer were friends and spoke a great deal about the settlement. The Hispanic officer thought the city would be becoming intimidated again but this did not happen. The insurance carrier wanted to have an out of court settlement but the City Council told the city administrator, "no way." I applauded the City Council for taking a stand. More City Councils should do likewise that would send a message to those thinking about initiating frivolous complaints.

I am reminded of an incident that occurred in the Sheriff's Department in North Carolina. One of the command staff had a habit of groping female employees. It seems he liked to put his hands on females whether they approved of it or not. Some made complaints and others did not. In this particular instance, a Major inappropriately touched a contract female legal advisor of the department. This Major was in-charge of the Investigation Division and was also a personal friend of the sheriff. One female employee mentioned an inappropriate touching incident on her to the sheriff while they were working out at the department's physical fitness facility. The sheriff just blew off her comment and she eventually filed a sexual harassment complaint. Some of the other female employees came forward to also make a complaint. While this was going on, there was adverse publicity that ultimately led to the Major's resignation from the department. The sheriff eventually terminated the contract employee and she filed a sexual harassment lawsuit. In my mind, there is cause for suspicion when a whistle blower is fired. There is protection but because she was a contract employee, it did not apply to her or so the sheriff stated at this point. It would have been interesting to find out what happened with the lawsuit.

This was a pitfall that could have been easily avoided. These incidents take place all the time all over the country. I could go on and on citing more examples but you get the general idea. Some sheriffs and police chiefs did not heed the warnings of others who found themselves in similar predicament. Believe me, I was paying attention.

My best advice to leaders is if there is a complaint to do something. Do not put it off because it just causes the situation to get worse. Notify the City Manager or upper management and immediately inform him or her about a complaint. The City Manager or top executives may want to look into this matter and you as a leader, will get some direction. If the complaint is investigated promptly and some disposition made, then you will be looked at in a more favorable light in the eyes of the media and more important the community and within the organization itself.

How to Avoid the Pitfalls

You may ask yourself how someone can be so stupid to get involved in a sexual harassment or discrimination complaint. The truth is many can be avoided, while others will initiate a complaint to try making some money. Some of the complaints will be bogus. Some, if not most sheriffs, chiefs or upper management will put on their best defensive in fighting complaints.

There are definitely some steps that could be taken to avoid these complaints and if you think about it, they are common sense. Somehow some chiefs and leaders lose the sense of reasoning. Some feel they are bigger and more important than anyone. Several convey this type of attitude. How dare they try to fire the police chief or person in charge? If you have this type of attitude, it is just a recipe for failure. Here are some suggestions:

- Do not put yourself in a position to be compromised.
- Be respectful of everyone.
- Treat everyone alike.
- Counseling or disciplining a female should be witnessed.
- Document and record problem areas.
- Keep your **hands off** employees even in jest.
- If someone brings a complaint to your attention, initiate an investigation.
- Do not wait or pass it off as a minor complaint—it will escalate.
- Be professional at all times.

What happens if someone makes a complaint against you? You could be in big trouble and just the implication alone will put you on an uphill battle of trying to save your job. It is not the end of the world. Here are some suggestions:

- Notify the City or Town Manager and City Attorney about the complaint. At this point, they probably will have already known about it.
- Find out the specifics of the complaint, document and find witnesses on your behalf.
- Cooperate completely with the City Manager and/or Investigators.
- Do not say too much to the media.
- Only release what is necessary and no more.
- Refer any official response to the city manager or city attorney.
- Do not retaliate against the employee.
- Be professional.
- Accept the results with dignity.

These are just some suggestions and there are probably more, but most of all, it is just common sense.

Some Positive Approaches

Why wait for a complaint to happen? A police chief or executive should be able to take some of the following proactive approaches to avoid this problem:

1. Do what is right for your employees.

2. Take care of your employees.
3. Taking care of the employees also takes care of the task because they are interrelated.
4. Looking out for your employees and being professional at all times with them. These actions could also increase your longevity.

I am reminded of another story, which took place when I was interviewing for a police chief's position in a city in Minnesota. The City Manager apparently wanted someone to straighten out police employees. I had visited the community and on the surface, it appeared to be very nice. This position came up after the Town Council did not renew my contract in Florence, Arizona. After being offered the position, I thought long and hard and decided to decline at the last minute. My rationale was simple. I just did not want to be put into a position to fail. The City Manager gave me a tour of the City but left out the most important part. I asked him to see the police department, and he replied, "Oh, there is nothing to see right now." Apparently, for some reason he did not want me to see the police department. The next morning I went to a local restaurant and found one of the police officers and we had a nice conversation with him. Apparently, the city had already gone through the process of hiring a police chief several times and every time the position was offered to a candidate, it was declined. After investigating a little further, I could see the reason.

The City Manager was very candid about what he was looking for. He was having trouble with some union rabble-rousers and he needed someone to straighten resolve this conflict. It is the wrong way to approach the job and the City Manager and I would have clashed. When a City Manager selects a police chief it should be a good match, not only for the City Manager but also more for the community. I certainly did not want to approach the position as a "union buster."

I do not mind a challenge but I look for an opportunity to succeed. It is not in my nature to be the "hatchet man" for anyone. If I were going to succeed, I would need my personnel to help me accomplish the goals of the organization. I cannot first go into any organization and begin from a negative approach. The idea is to win over the personnel, not antagonize them. Reluctantly, I declined the offer because it was not right for me. Anyone going for the position of Police Chief should keep the "match" in mind. It has to be a good match or it will not work. It is also nice to have a job but it will be one of short duration.

In order to be successful in running a police department or any other organization, you also have to be successful in dealing with your personnel. Your personnel are the key and do not ever forget this. Recognizing your personnel in a positive way will help solidify relationships and guide the department and organization to be the best it can be. The community and other stakeholders will recognize your hard work.

Chapter 9
Recruitment and Selection Process

The recruitment and selection without a doubt is one of the most important functions of a police department. The idea is to be able to recruit and select the best candidates or the cream of the crop. The problem area that comes up all the time is how to retain personnel after you hire them. This is without doubt one of the most challenging features of any police department. Many police department are very good at this function while others could improve. However, I think we can all agree that trying to keep good qualified candidates is an on-going challenge for most organizations. This area is so important that I will try to provide you with some insight with the hope of trying to retain good officers or workforce.

The quest for qualified police officers and staff is so competitive that some departments and organizations will resort to a practice called "stealing." They steal from one another all the time. It is an accepted practice. Recruiting police officers or other personnel from other departments or organizations is ethical and fair game because it saves time and money if you can hire someone already trained. Usually a department or company will advertise for a police officer or staff member and if someone is already certified applies for the position he or she may be selected. I can say that I hate to lose good personnel but at the same time I cannot blame a person for trying to better oneself. Police officers are using police departments as a stepping-stone to jump to a larger, better-paid department that could offer more promotional opportunities and lateral advancement in specialized functions.

Years ago I can relate that when a person was hired by a department there was a certain amount of loyalty and they tend to stay a long time until retirement in most instances. Now the trend is for a person to jump two or more times to another department. There seems to be loyalty for the all mighty dollar. Many departments are always in the training mode because as soon as their vacancies are filled someone else decides to leave the department. It is no doubt a very frustrating experience and a never-ending process for the police chief or manager. It is a very costly proposition for a municipality to recruit, select and train police officers. Once you hire quality personnel you have to try to figure out how to keep them. As soon as a police department waives an instant $5,000 or more increase in someone's face, a person may more than likely jump at it. This offer is almost too enticing to pass up. In a way, you cannot blame them. How can a small department compete with the larger ones? It is difficult but it can be done. You have to **give employees a reason to stay**.

First, I will go into greater detail and discuss the problems associated with recruitment and selection citing some of my experiences as police chief in three former police departments. I will also discuss the steps I took to stem the exodus from these departments. I was moderately successful and there are definitely some ways that it can be approached. Did I stop the exodus completely and the answer was no. I still lost some officers but other departments lose many more. The smaller, low paying departments are vulnerable to the medium and larger, higher paid police departments. On the other hand, if a problem employee or union rabble-rouser wanted to jump to another department I would not lose any sleep over it. However, these individuals seem to be weeded out right away. Imagine that! When you want them to leave, you cannot get rid of them.

Problems, Problems

I have seen recruitment and selection change through the years. It has gone from what ever the police chief wanted to do to a more coordinated effort through the human resources departments of a municipality or county government. The later is the way to go. There are too many problems associated with the hiring process that normally ends with a lawsuit. Why involve yourself in a lawsuit? If your community advertises equal employment opportunity then that is exactly what you have to do. The idea is to have a fair process for everyone and I am in full agreement.

Too many police and sheriff departments as in other organizations still adhere to the "Good O'boy" system. The numbers are getting less because departments are being forced to do it the right way. Hiring friends and relatives will certainly find a chief or sheriff in hot water before too long. If you decide to hire a friend, he or she must go through the process. Some people will go out of their way to criticize the police chief or sheriff. Why give them the opportunity?

I told my staff in each department that we were going to have a set procedure for hiring beginning with the advertisement. Some chiefs or managers will only hire certified officers and other personnel and not necessarily recruit them through advertisement. I make everyone go through the same process including the written, agility and oral board examinations. I just did not want to play games with the hiring process. I knew that the chiefs before me did it his way without having to follow any specific guidelines. The goal was to get a good candidate to fill the position. My philosophy is not to get just any warm body off the street to fill a position. I wanted someone who was qualified to be a police officer with the hopes of retaining this individual for a long time.

I established guidelines for the hiring process that was approved by the City Manager in each city. The guidelines were reasonable and fair to the individual.

After the selection phase was completed, a hiring list was created that was good for one year. At first, the list was good for two years, but after awhile the list became quickly exhausted after a number of candidates was rejected after the background investigation phase. I amended the process to one year. This seemed to work better.

Sometimes there will be a controversial hiring. I hired the Mayor's son in Somersworth, New Hampshire after completion of the testing process. I know what you are thinking. I must have been crazy. A council member and some of his friends were accusing me of favoritism and playing politics. Actually, the decision was easy because the Mayor's son went through an extremely competitive process and scored number one after the written test and oral examinations had been completed. I would have discriminated against him if I had by-passed him because his father was the Mayor. The council member told me to let the other department take him. At the time, I discussed this situation and the implication with the City Manager and obtained his approval. I hired him and never once regretted the decision even though I was criticized for it. Why let another department take your top-notch candidate.

I knew there would be some political fallout and true enough there was publicity in the local newspaper and an official complaint to the New Hampshire State Police regarding favoritism and the hiring process. I knew the storm was coming so I got my "ducks" all in order. I was ready for the investigation. When the investigator arrived to conduct the investigation, I told him that I would cooperate fully and he could have access to any of my records. He had access to the tests, test results and oral board questions and results. At the time, we used a test developed by a testing consultant specializing in police examinations. The investigator was very satisfied with all the documentation. The investigator had no problem with the hiring process and selection at all. There was no criticism regarding this particular individual.

The moral of the story occurs when you go through a hiring process make sure that you document everything in case there is a complaint or eventual lawsuit. I had been questioned about my hiring practices but no one was ever successful with their complaint. The council member who had made the complaint was quiet for a while and eventually became an ex-council member. A police chief or manager has to expect complaints and at the same time you have to be smart and use common sense. In the past, police chiefs and some managers use to get away with some questionable hiring practices but now more are being called on it. You cannot do whatever you want anymore and your may try to talk you into skipping a step or two. Be wary, because eventually you just might get burnt. **Do it right the first time** and you will not have anything to worry about.

Where police chiefs get into trouble is the lateral entry; the police officer from another agency wants to go to your agency. There are some problems that need to be resolved but the first is the pay issue. Generally, they will ask for more money than what it normally calls for in the salary pay scale for starting and it becomes more complicated when there is a police union looking over your shoulder. You just cannot start someone on a pay scale at step four and hire another person at step three and both officers are already certified. An inequity has to be addressed. There should be an established procedure with the city as to where the certified officers will start on the pay scale and it should be based upon years of experience. This way, everyone hired will be treated the same way depending upon the person's level of experience. The key is hiring a certified officer after going through a process. Circumventing the process will only lead to legal trouble. A police chief or manager may be tempted to hire a certified officer or personnel from another department without putting him or her through the standard hiring process. There is no doubt you will save money from advertising the position, and the testing process.

When I was in New Hampshire, I hired two certified officers from a nearby department. I had them go through the hiring process and eventually hired both of them. Each officer did not last more than a year with my department. One officer broke his hiring agreement with the nearby department but they knew up front that we were going to hire him. He stayed for a while and left my department to become a police chief in a small community. He was the only full time police officer. I guess it was a good move for him and a bad move for me to hire him in the first place. The other officer had problems with following orders. He did not heed the warnings about driving too fast with his emergency lights and siren on. He became involved in several accidents with the police cruiser and I eventually terminated him. He was still on probation so the termination was easy. Guess what? He had the same problems with his former agency. They were probably thrilled that he decided to leave their department.

In hindsight, we should have done a better job in screening these lateral entry candidates. I listened to the patrol captain who was enthusiastic about hiring these individuals. He was "stealing" the officers from the nearby department who incidentally were paid more than our department. This should have been a tip to us that something was wrong. Because they wanted to leave their department so badly, we should have done a better job with the background investigation. Apparently, there were problems with both individuals and we did not recognize them. It was a lesson learned. With a little more effort we would have found the real reason they wanted to leave. Yes, we saved some money in the beginning but then we had to spend more to begin the hiring process all over again.

My advice to police chiefs and top managers considering lateral entry hiring is simple and realistic. The transferees could be a good addition to the department but it is imperative that a thorough background investigation be completed before any hiring decision is made. Why get someone else's bad baggage? If someone causes trouble in his or her department, chances are that he or she will have the same type of behavior in their new department. Do not let anyone tell you differently. My next piece of advice is being wary of a command level officer or personnel pushing hard for a particular candidate. Check out the candidate thoroughly before making a rash hiring decision. Too often, I had relied on my patrol captain for his input and each time I got burnt. After a while, you lose faith in the person's judgment. The police chief or executive has to accept responsibility and the buck stopped at the top. After being burnt a few times I became very careful. Each department must make a serious commitment to the hiring process and nothing should be taken for granted.

I had one little problem in Florence, Arizona with lateral entry officers that I want to discuss. After I was in Florence a short time, I was approached by two Deputy Sheriffs from Penal County who at one time worked for the Florence Police Department under the former Police Chief. These individuals were former employees who left the agency. They inquired whether I would hire them back at the department. I told them I would not hire them because they left once and if I could not make them happy then they would leave again. They were not very happy. It did not take them long to spread negative untrue statements about me to the other Deputy Sheriffs. In retrospect, I probably should have said that they could reapply for a position in the event there was a vacancy but they would have to go through the hiring process again like everyone else. This would have been a more suitable response to handle the situation. If these officers were serious, they would have gone through the hiring process and who knows what might have happened.

After I left the department, the police chief who replaced me hired both of the Deputy Sheriffs. Since then one had already left the department and the other is still with the department. It appears 10 years later that he is doing a good job for the current chief. Sometimes a person needs to prove him or herself to do the job.

During my seven years with the New Hampshire police department, I thought overall we were successful with our hiring practices for sworn police officers and dispatchers. We were able to retain many for several years and some did manage to jump from our department to a better paying department. We were successful because we adopted a professional approach.

Instead of putting together our own entrance examination for entry-level police officers, I contracted with a testing consultant who specialized in police examinations. The department had used an old I.Q. type test prior to my arrival and in my opinion it was outdated and unreliable. I wanted a more job related test.

Matter of fact, our cost was very little because if a person wanted to take a test for police officer, he or she had to pay a testing fee of about $20. The cost to the department was a small administration fee. They would grade the test and numerically rank the candidate from the highest to the lowest score. Those candidates who passed the test would go on to the oral board phase. The process was extremely fair and the results were never contested. The candidate was allowed to check his or her test after first conferring with the consultant. Most of the time, the consultant coordinated the oral board examinations. I was extremely proud of our process. Most of the time, we truly did select the best-qualified candidate for the position.

Background investigations are extremely important and some departments actually take shortcuts. I found that some departments or organizations perform limited background investigations while other does extensive ones. The criminal record does not provide the complete picture of a candidate. Everything in a person's background is important. When we discuss the law enforcement code of ethics, we are speaking of individuals who will represent the department well and not be a big embarrassment. The saying is true "a few bad apples will spoil the rest of the barrel." When a few police officers embarrass their department people tend to remember the bad things. They tend to generalize and say all the police are corrupt and it is very difficult to turn around a bad public image. Here is an example of a police agency. New Orleans Police Department is a nationally accredited law enforcement agency yet they maintain a corrupt image. It is not fair to say all officers are corrupt. Only a small minority has tarnished the symbol of the badge. Most are honest and hard working, yet they carry this stigma. People view them as still being a corrupt force. **It is difficult to change a tainted image**.

If police chiefs and managers concentrated more on the background investigations, they would be able to uncover some of this problem area. I rejected a candidate who had scored second overall on the testing but his driving record was horrendous. In a span of three years he was convicted of speeding 10 times. Sure, I am going to give him a cruiser so he can speed some more. No, it would have been the wrong thing to do. He wanted to know why I rejected him and I did not have any problem telling him.

Still other problems may surface during the background phase. I had a very good candidate for a position in Fort Lupton, Colorado. This person had gone to the community college to be certified as a police officer and he was at a point that he was going to be hired if he had successful completed his background investigation. Everything looked good except for one little problem. He failed to disclose a motor vehicle violation in a metro city in the Denver area. When we checked with the city, we were surprised to find that the police had responded to a number of complaints to his apartment for domestic violence. A "red flag" was raised. We confronted him with this issue and he said that the police were not there for a domestic violence but for a noise complaint. We asked him why he did not divulge the motor vehicle violation and he said that he forgot. Ordinarily forgetting to mention a motor vehicle violation in a community is not a big deal but it appeared to us he was trying to cover up something. I sent my sergeant to the community to continue the background investigation including checking with the neighbors and speaking to the police officers. The police officers that had responded to the original complaint verified that it was domestic violence. We checked with the neighbors and the person's spouse and they verified it was domestic violence. It was apparent that the candidate not only failed to disclose information but also was untruthful to the investigator. At this point, I just withdrew my offer of employment and rejected him. He was a little disappointed but it served as a good lesson for him. If he had been truthful in the beginning, I probably would have hired him.

You never know what may be uncovered during a background investigation. Sometimes these little problems escalate into bigger problems later on with these individuals. I have seen it time after time with police chiefs. I know chiefs are anxious to fill vacant police positions as soon as possible especially if they have been covering the position with overtime. Overtime will certainly do a number on your budget. However, the prudent thing to do is to take your time and do it right the first time. Uncovering these problems in the beginning will certainly save a great deal of grief and aggravation in the long-run. I made my share of mistakes with background investigations and I learned quickly.

The Community College

Another area that could be a problem is a candidate from a community college's Basic Law Enforcement Training program. Many states have these types of programs and they seem to work very well. I am not criticizing these programs but there are a few points that I would like for you to think about. Community college typically will only do a limited background investigation that would include a criminal and motor vehicle history check. This background is only limited and rightly so but there may be some other problems in the candidate's background that may come up later. The colleges do not have the time or personnel to conduct a thorough background investigation when a police department will do one anyway. Some police chiefs are surprised as I was when there were problems with a person's background. The agility-conditioning program is not as comprehensive as some other police academies in some other states. The physical conditioning of some of the candidates that I have seen is questionable.

Police departments have to understand that these individuals are paying tuition to become certified in the hopes of a department later hiring them. It is a win-win proposition for the individual and the police department. The person lands a police job and the department hires a certified officer. In some States police departments have to hire the individual first before sending him or her to the police academy. The police department ends up paying the tuition and salary. It is very costly to hire individuals for many departments and you can see why police chiefs get upset when someone leaves the department only after a short time. You would think there would be a certain amount of loyalty to the hiring agency but there is not. However, most individuals tell their ex-leader that they appreciate the opportunity to be employed at a police agency.

Many individuals truly want to be a police officer and even after completing the requirements at a community college, they are still unable to find a police job. The same holds true for business management students after they graduate. For law enforcement, the reason is simple. The candidate cannot pass the background investigation. There are individuals who graduate from the program but many months go by before an offer of employment is made. This type of individual will have a more difficult time with the field-training program because of a lack of retention of the material. After not being exposed to the material for a long time, an individual will retain less and less. I actually experienced this problem in Colorado. One female police employee had competed the certification program a year earlier could not grasp the field-training program.

I believe that there is a need for providing a refresher program before undertaking field training. Field training must be tailored to the individual in law enforcement and at times, other unrelated fields as well. Some individuals learn more quickly than others do and some need more time. I see no problem in giving an individual more time. The goal is to get the individual to function adequately as a police officer or leader. After I left the department in Fort Lupton, Colorado, the female probationary employee was terminated because she did not successfully complete field training. I believe they should have worked with her more and given her more time. I think it is in the police chief or manager's best interest and for the department or organization to help new hires succeed.

The problem could have been avoided if the Community Colleges helped place some of these individuals with police departments and other agencies even if it was on a voluntary basis. There need to be some amount of internship with a department so that he or she could understand better and apply what was learned in class. This will help to fill the void from the time he or she graduates from a program to the time hired by a police agency or firm. At the same time, the police department or organization would be able to observe the candidate and eventually hire him or her. The successful rate for completion of the field-training program would be increased. Other disciplines have extensively used internship programs. Why not law enforcement.

Community colleges do an excellent job in providing a service to the community. The candidate can complete the Basic Law Enforcement Training and/or management program and earn college credit at the same time. The candidate bears the cost of the tuition and books and the police agency or firm does not have to pay to send someone to the police academy or intensive administrative training. In my mind, it is a great deal. The only problem that I have is that most organizations do not work enough with the individual to help him or her to succeed.

Residency Requirement

Some departments actually have a residency requirement. There are some who actually requires their officers to live within the community within a certain time-frame upon being hired. There are still others who have a mileage requirement such as 15 miles from the city or town line. There are departments that have a response time requirement such as 30 minutes and there are some with no requirements.

The only requirement for residency in any of my departments was Florence, Arizona and the officers had to live within a 15-mile limit from the town. It was a requirement established by the Town Council long before I got there. Their rationale was that they wanted their officers to be able to respond to emergencies. The community next to Florence was Coolidge and they required all their officers to live in the community. Perhaps, the policy has changed by now. I can understand why they wanted their police chief to live in the community, but I could not fathom residency requirement for all officers? The town fathers just made recruitment more difficult. Keeping in mind that the Town of Florence was a rural community out in the desert, many police officers do not like to live in the community they work in and I can understand their rationale. In Fort Lupton, Colorado, the officers had a 30-minute response time. Most of my officers lived within a 25 mile radius from the police department. To be honest with you, I never bothered to time them. Actually, my concern was for them to be on time when reporting for duty.

My thought is why require a residency requirement, mileage restrictions and response time requirement? As long as officers arrive at work on time, then I am happy. I do not care where they live. They could live in "Tin-Buck-Two" for all I care. I had one officer who was commuting 50 miles every day from Fort Collins, Colorado while arranging to find a place to live. This officer was always on time for work. I cannot ask anything more than that. Some of the town fathers will argue we would like the officers to live in the community so they could respond to emergencies. Another fable rationale openly given was because police officers are being paid with tax dollars, officers should spend their money in their community. Unbelievably, I had some council members tell me this. These individuals are living in a dream world. How can you tell someone where to spend their money? I do not agree with this philosophy. It is an excellent idea to have your off duty personnel respond in the event of emergencies but the surrounding departments and sheriff departments will respond if asked. There are mutual aid agreements for these special situations. I never had any problems with other departments responding to our requests for assistance.

Having a residency requirement and other restrictions will limit your pool of candidates. I have had candidates withdraw because of the residency requirement and observed the same with neighboring departments. It is a real problem. It is difficult enough to find qualified candidates and even more difficult when there are residency requirements. My best advice is not to have any restrictions at all. I believe that police officers or any staff member should live within a reasonable driving distance from their department or organization. Some communities are so outrageously pricey that some people would not be able to find and afford a reasonable rent or home.

If your department or organization happens to have a residency requirement, so be it. You have to live with it. Now, sometimes police officers will play games. Sometimes police officers are amazing. Some will try to beat the system. I knew one police chief in Colorado who had a problem with one of his officers. All his officers have to live within their community. This particular officer decided to maintain a ghost apartment. He allegedly shared an apartment with some of his friends and kept a few articles of clothing there. He actually lived in Thornton about 50 miles away. The chief did an investigation and brought him up on charges. This individual had been previously warned and he knew the requirements. The chief eventually terminated his employment. I do not agree with residency requirements but if it is a condition of employment then you have to live by it. The police officer in question should not have accepted the position if he did not intend to live in the community. No, he tried to be clever and got caught. Some people think they can out smart the police chief or management and beat the system.

Hiring Pools

Some departments are involved in a testing pool. This is where a number of departments or businesses are involved with a testing consultant to give one test. Departments or organizations will draw from a pool of candidates. Overall, the department or agency could save money from advertising and paying the cost of the test themselves. Those departments or agencies involved in the process would share the cost. The successful candidates would be on a list whereby police departments or agencies would draw from the list as vacancies occur.

On the surface, this may seem the way to go for departments or industries on a shoestring budget. However, the better candidates, the cream of the crop will be siphoned off to the larger, higher paying departments or organizations. Actually, I cannot blame them but why should a small department or company pay for a process where the better candidate will go to the larger agency anyway? I always decided to have only our department involved in the hiring process. I had been approached in New Hampshire and Colorado to be involved in the candidate pool concept but each time I declined. However, there are positives. The department or company could save money and always have a pool of candidates to select from. The concept is interesting and worthwhile to pursue to see if it could benefit the department or organization.

I would suggest that if a department or organization wanted to pursue the hiring pool concept and try it, some details should be worked out first. If I were to do it, I would have an understanding with the consultant that the individual would first declare which department or organization they are testing for so another department or agency would not "steal" him or her away. The cost should be dependent upon the individuals testing for a particular department or agency only. It would not be fair for a department to share the cost equally if only five individuals are testing for the department while the other 95 individuals are testing for the higher paid agencies. The details could be worked out as long as it is fair for everyone concerned.

I Want You

Recruitment is so competitive now that large agencies that typically did not advertise out of state are doing so now. It is a continuing challenge to find qualified candidates. These agencies are looking for certified officers from other agencies. How can you compete with them? Actually, many police departments all over the country are having trouble filling their vacancies as a result of new positions and attrition. Police Departments all across the country asked for federal Cops grants in the 1990s to add more officers to their department. It is not a bad deal when the federal government will pay three-quarters of the officer's salary over three years. The problem now is those police departments are having a difficult time finding qualified police candidates. Employment is so good in other fields and higher paying too that the vast majority of quality personnel are not going into law enforcement. As a result police department as well as other organizations are advertising in-state and out-of-state to attract the certified police officers and highly skilled managers.

Many veteran officers and managers are leaving for the better paying position. The dilemma for the department and many organizations is losing the veteran officers and experienced managers are that police agencies and other organizations alike are filling their ranks with lesser-qualified candidates. The problem that I see is those police departments are filling its ranks with rookie officers. The threat of a lawsuit for false arrest, improper search and seizure, and improper use of force is even more apparent now then ever before. I believe police departments are more vulnerable now. Just look around you and determine the average tenure of police officers. You will find - unless you are fortunate - most do not have very much experience at all. This especially holds true in small departments. If you are relying upon rookies to make critical decisions then you could be in trouble.

One problem that I have with other departments trying to recruit your personnel is an ethical issue. If the recruitment is professional then that is the nature of the business. If the Sheriff or Police Chief go out of their way to "steal" your personnel by targeting certain ones then I take issue with it. It is just a pet peeve of mine because it has happened to me a number of times. It just annoys me to no end after countless numbers of dollars have been spent training the individual just to have this person leave. It is like saying "Thanks for the training Chief—see you later."

Incentives

A Police Chief, Sheriff and managers similarly have to be creative if they plan to attract and keep qualify police employees and personnel. The private sector has been doing it for years and some in the public sector are doing it now. During tough times, why not give someone a hiring bonus. This may be just the lure to have a candidate commit to your department or agency. I know it is more difficult in unionized departments because of the labor agreement but it can be done. The City Council or CEO can do anything they want and it could be a good tool to attract quality candidates. I have seen anywhere from $500 to $1,000 signing bonus providing that police candidates pass their background, and physical. Some departments and agencies suggest completing field training or internship should be included too. There is merit to the argument. Why pay someone who fails to complete the field training or internship programs. In my opinion, they should get the bonus after they had started work. Most individuals should pass their field training or internship anyway. It would be a good faith gesture by the police chief or top manager and it shows confidence in the person. There is merit to both side of the argument.

The pay issue is always present. The City Council or top executives should review employees pay plan every three years to make sure they are in line with other departments or organizations comparable in size. If the pay plan is comparable to other departments or organizations or slightly higher, this in itself is an incentive.

The main incentive is the benefit package and how it will benefit the individual and his or her family. However, there should be more to entice the individual to want to work in the municipality. I have a few suggestions that could work.   In addition to the number of holidays a person could take off and you already realize it is difficult to take a holiday off when you are scheduled for a shift; the person could take his or her birthday off.

Another possibility is a take-home car plan. More departments or agencies are going to the take-home car plan such as what we did in Florence, Arizona. The idea is to have more cars visible during the day and the officer would be able to respond in the event of an emergency. The officers were encouraged to use the cars off duty but only in the community. A person would not have to worry about the wear and tear of his or her own personal vehicle, insurance and gasoline so instantly there is a savings. This idea seems to be popular with the officers but there has to be a check and balance to insure the take-home cars are not being abused. I had one officer in Florence who did not maintain the take-home car vehicle and he did not keep it clean. It looked like a garbage truck with the empty bottles and coffee cups on the floor of the vehicle. This particular officer had to find another way to work because I made him park his take-home car at the police department for a couple of weeks. He decided to play the game and keep his car clean.

Having a Christmas bonus around the Holiday is a good idea. In Somersworth, New Hampshire, the city issued longevity checks just before Christmas. Most communities do not have longevity bonuses but Somersworth did have it while I was there. There was talk to do away with longevity but the police union had it in their contract for a long time. The concept is simple, the longer you have been with the department, the larger your bonus check. Now, we are not talking a great deal of money but at least it is something to help pay for Christmas.

When I arrived at Somersworth, New Hampshire, I received a $1,000 bonus for having a Master's in Science degree in Criminal Justice. This was the only community that I knew of that provided for a bonus such as this. They should have kept it because a few years later they city did away with the practice. They were looking at the money they were spending and were looking for ways to save the taxpayers some money. The idea behind incentives is to attract quality personnel and to keep them. Often, the town fathers forgot about the original intention.

Specialized training is another concept that should be mentioned here. Professional enrichment should be on going in an organization. Each department or agency should concentrate on the interests of the individual. They should look at the big picture not just filling a shift with a body. I always liked to find out what were the special interests of my officers.   You can do it very easily with a questionnaire to elicit their interests. This way you find out what top employees are interested in and as the opportunity presents itself, you can provide the officer or manager specialized training. If individuals like what they are doing and the department or agency shows a genuine interest in them, then they are more likely to stay with the organization.   Many officers and managers become dissatisfied because they believe in their mind the department or organization do not care about them. If this is the case, then key employees will start to look else where for another department or agency.

If police departments or any other organization have an area for the officers and staff to maintain their physical conditioning, it is good. I believe that if departments or organizations mandate that their officers or staff is physically fit then something should be provided to help them. Many officers or staff members do not like to hang out at the police department or organization so there should be some alternatives.   Providing an individual or family membership or discounted membership in a local health club would benefit the officer or employee, his or her family and the community. The city or corporate may balk at the idea but look at the benefits. The officer or employee maintains his or her physical conditioning and is less likely to injury his or her back. Look at why an officer or most employees becomes injured. Most of the injuries are to the back that results from a lack of exercise or inactivity.   The officer who is off-duty is exposed to the public in a positive way. They get to see him or her off-duty in a different environment other than work. They see him or her as a real person.

Unbelievably some police departments require their officers to purchase their own firearm for duty. This was the case in Fort Lupton, Colorado. I imagine it is a common practice with small police departments. To make matters worse there were different types and calibers. The officers were able to pay for their firearm through payroll deduction. I was somewhat shocked to find out this was the practice. Making individuals spent money out of his or her pocket is definitely wrong. The officer probably does not have much to begin with anyway. Even when I started in law enforcement, I had to purchase my own uniform, leather gear and equipment. At least my original department in Bristol, Connecticut issued the firearms. I guess that is what I had to do if I wanted the job. My thought is if we expect our officers to do the job, then we need to issue them the tools to accomplish the task including the issuing of a department firearm and ammunition. Fortunately, I convinced the City Council to purchase a firearm for all officers. Everyone should be trained with standard issue firearm. Of course, the officers would be trained with department issued ammunition for the firearm. I cannot see making them pay for their own ammunition.

Paying for college tuition is a very big incentive. Many communities already have tuition reimbursement in place but very few take advantage of it. The truth is that many communities have a plan in place but there is little or no funding. I call it a "Ghost Program," just "Smoke and Mirrors" to impress their personnel. There are too many hurdles an individual has to go through to get approval to take a college course. They say, "The heck with it- it is not worth the trouble." Communities do not make much of an effort to advertise this incentive. It is too bad because this incentive should be exploited more to draw the qualified candidates. The Armed Forces including the National Guard advertise paid tuition in their recruitment program. It would be a good idea for police departments and other organizations to do the same thing. We know how expense college tuition is, so why not use it to recruit police and manager candidates. If municipal governments and other organizations truly mean what they say about paid tuition then they should put forth the effort and do it.

Let us recap the incentives mentioned so far, and they are as follows:

- Signing Bonus
- Insurance
- Birthday
- Take Home Car
- Christmas Bonus
- Specialized Training
- Health Club Membership
- Department Issued Firearm
- College Degree bonus
- Paid College Tuition

The incentives could be a blessing in disguise for the police or sheriff departments or any type of organization. Generally, there is not much thought that goes into it. Recruitment is taken for granted but during times when it is difficult to attract qualified police candidates or other managerial personnel, it would make better sense to utilize this strategy. Some of the larger police agencies and perhaps even non policing agencies are already doing this in their recruitment campaign. The smaller and large police agencies should take advantage of it too.

Written Training Agreements

Some police chiefs may disagree when I mention written training agreements but why not have the person you are about to hire sign a written training agreement? Many departments and corporations now routinely use this document to insure a person will stay at least two or three years. Others say it will not work because you cannot force anyone to sign a contract. They say it is like slave labor. No, I say if a person wants a police job then he or she will sign the agreement. I never had any problems with any of these officers refusing to sign the training agreement. Because of the recent trend in personnel going from one department or organization to another, it makes sense to have them sign the agreement. This is only one tool to help the police chief and/ or top executives keep their quality personnel for a few years. There are many samples of agreements that are already being used so you can ask or have your Town or City or even a Corporate Attorney draw one up after you have given your input. I truly like training agreements and they do work.

The following is what I include in the training agreement for law enforcement personnel when I was chief of police. The city agreed to purchase uniforms and equipment, provide academy and field training upon being hired and training for professional development. If the department sent the officer to the police academy then you can include the cost of tuition and the salary paid while he or she was there. If the officer successfully completes one-year probation then he or she agrees to stay at least two years before leaving employment unless terminated with cause. I will guarantee you one thing; this agreement will make the employee think twice before leaving the department too soon.

I proposed having the officers sign a training agreement in Florence, Arizona and at first, the Town Council did not agree with me. They saw the light after I reported an officer that went to work at the Sheriff's Office after he was only with the department less than one year. After I explained how expensive it was to recruit, select and train the officers, they quickly agreed something should be done. I sold them on the idea. They modified the plan for only one year past probation, so in effect, it was a two-year commitment. At least it was better than one year and it solved the problem for the time being.

It is a known fact that small departments are a training ground for larger departments. As I stated previously I cannot blame the officer for going to a larger department for more pay and greater opportunities for advancement. However, fair is fair. If an individual intended all along to jump to another department after he or she received valuable training then he or she may have to pay up for violating the training agreement.

One officer in Fort Lupton, Colorado decided to leave to go to a Metro department. Our department was a well know training ground. The officer had previously signed a training agreement but decided to leave before its completion. He was shocked, to say the least, when he received a bill from the city in the amount of about $6,000 to recover the cost of uniforms, field training and training he had received. His attorney tried to paint a picture that the big city was trying to take advantage of the little guy. The City Council, I may add, was very supportive and told the City Attorney to force the officer to abide by his contract or suffer civil consequences. The City was very serious about collecting and was prepared to bring this matter to court. However, before this civil action could be taken the former officer's attorney offered a settlement and the offer was accepted. The former officer agreed to pay several thousand dollars as to the agreed upon settlement. I just want to make it clear that the training agreement needed to be honored. I was glad to see the city took a stand on this issue. Why have training agreements if you are not going to enforce it? All it took was for me to take action against one, so it showed everyone I was serious about the agreement. No one left early after that.

Recruitment and selection can be a pain free experience for the police chief or manager if it handled correctly. Again, where police chiefs and managers go wrong occurs when they take unnecessary risks and circumvent the process. Most departments and organizations have written guidelines in place. If you do not have written guideline then you should take the time to develop and implement them. My best advice is to follow your own procedures. If you do other than what is written then you should change the guidelines to reflect your practice. Eventually someone will remind you of the deviations. Remember always be professional.

Chapter 10
Dealing With Police Unions

When one hears the words police union, some police chiefs breakout in a cold sweat. Police unions have been around for a long time in many states, but some states are a "right to work" state and they do not have unions. I have worked in both, unionized and non-union departments. Unions are predominantly in New England, the Mid-West and California. In Bristol, Connecticut we had a closed shop or other words everyone had to join a union and was affiliated with AFL-CIO. There was no choice in the matter. Unions organize to bargain for better salaries and working conditions. There are other reasons but these two are the primary reasons. The real issue is that management was not taking care of their personnel. The attitude was "us against them" mentality. Some of the real union rabble-rousers would brag about how they gave the chief a hard time. Let me tell you these employees would submit a grievance for any reason. It was truly pathetic to think that most of these individuals who were active with the union were the least productive of the employees. They were the ones who needed the help of the union the most.

Management can coexist with the Police Union. It is just another way of life and you have to live with it. My former police chief in Bristol, Connecticut was excellent in dealing with the Police Union. He always seemed to manage to keep everyone happy and he did so with communication. The key to success in particular with police unions is keeping the channel of communication open. Actually the chief had an open door policy and anytime someone was upset about an issue they could just walk in and discuss the issue. Let me tell you I was paying attention all the years he was there. He had to be a patient man but you know something, there were never any major problems or dissatisfaction with the chief. He probably brought along a few tricks of the trade when he came from Hartford, Connecticut. Hartford Police Department had very strong unions and they still do. If there was an issue, he always seemed to smooth it over. He was that good. Where police chiefs go wrong occurs when there is a communication problem, rumors start flying and before long it is too late for damage control. It usually spells the end for the police chief. There will be more on the communication problem later.

Now, police unions as a rule are generally beneficial for everyone. They are supposed to represent the entire union body but in some cases, they do not. In my case, I will relate an experience that happened to me when the police union was a no show. They left me to fend for myself. No union representative came running to my aid. Fortunately, for me I survived and resolved the issue myself. There is always a lesson to be learned. **You cannot depend upon the union to survive** is the morale to my story.

The Fishing Expedition

Now, I am not knocking the unions and unions have their place when it comes to salaries and working conditions. Some police departments, I agree, need the unions to prevent the abuses by management. When I needed the union the most where were they? A long time ago during the summer of 1971 I did something stupid and I admit the punishment was what I deserved. Here is the situation. I was walking a beat on the third shift when the area officer in a marked cruiser stopped to pick me up. He wanted me to go fishing with him at the local reservoir in his area and just happen to have the fishing equipment with him. I know it sounds stupid already. If I had any sense at all, I should have told him to forget it. Having been on the department just over a year I was still brand new and was trying to get the guys to trust me. Peer pressure can be detrimental to a new person trying to fit in. This individual had been with the department for three or four years. I think most of you can relate to this. We drove to the reservoir and fished for a while and went back to the downtown area where he dropped me off. Oh, in case you are wondering I did manage to catch one fish. He told me not to tell anyone. When we got off shift it seemed everyone knew about our fishing expedition including the chief the next day. It seems that one particular officer did not like this guy and decided to spread the word.

The next day this officer told me that the chief was going to call me into his office so I should get my story straight. Other words, he wanted me to fabricate a story. Let me tell you I was very scared. I wondered how I had been so foolish to fall into a trap like this. One sergeant who I had a great deal of respect for pulled me to the side and told me to tell the truth. He said the chief knew the whole story anyway. You know something that was the best advice that I could have received. When the chief called me into his office and asked me about it, I told the truth. The other guy went into the office and spun a story and that was stupid because I told him I was going to tell the truth. This guy got himself fired and I received a one-week suspension and one-year probation. I took my medicine like a man and the embarrassment along with it and I stayed clean ever since. It was a valuable lesson for me to learn. **Do not do anything that you will regret later. Do the right thing.**

Here is the point about this story. Where was the union? Here I was a young officer not knowing enough to call a union representative. No one volunteered to come forward to help in my situation when I needed someone to talk to the most. Here is the real story. Later I found out that no one liked this particular officer. He was a thorn in management's side and he even aggravated some of the union people. I was the pawn for management to help get rid of this individual. This was a golden opportunity delivered on a silver platter to management saying, "Here is your guy. Do want you want with him." Later I found that it was a common practice for some officers to go fishing while working the night shift. Everyone knew about it and nothing happened to these officers. It was a big joke. It was a very valuable lesson and expensive one learned about the dynamics and politics of the police union and management. It was a win-win for both sides. Unfortunately, it was at my expense. I could have avoided this situation by just saying no.

The story does not end here. About 10 years later a different chief wanted to clean out the old disciplinary files and he offered everyone to petition to have any discipline permanently removed. I requested to have my discipline removed and the chief agreed to remove the suspension from my personnel file. In addition, he agreed to return the file to the affected officers. Everyone received his or her file except for me. The chief told me that he had misplaced the file and could not find it. By this time, I had advanced to the rank of Lieutenant. I was glad to have the file removed from my personnel record but it appeared suspicious to me. Why all of a sudden he could not find the file? I suspect the real reason is that he did not want me to see some information in the file. I did not question him about it again. **Sometime you just have to forget it and move on.** I think that at the time union and management collaborated to get rid of this individual but could never prove it. I never saw any written notice of neither the charges nor any of the accusatory reports. The chief kind of hinted to me that basically I was "railroaded." The union officials were still there and I think he did not want to make waves over something that happened in the past. Looking back it was a good move on his part. This was contrary to how the union operated at the time. I guess it depends upon who you were before they would do anything.

These reflections made me a stronger person in how I interacted with the department personnel and in public. Without realizing it, this incident made me a better person. I never ever agreed to be involved in any type of police misconduct. I decided if I was going to get myself fired, I did not need anyone's help. There was always that one incident, the famous fishing expedition to always remind me and for a few years after that, the joke of the department. I never ever got involved with union activities. I began to distrust the ulterior motive of certain union officials. I would be very cordial to them but not trusting.

The union, especially in Bristol, Connecticut had their own agenda. They could have been a vicious bunch. I was smart to keep my distance. Even when I attended union meetings there was just a certain amount of information presented before the union body but there was more going on behind the scenes that I could ever imagine.

I agree there is a place for police unions but sometimes they go too far in protecting the malcontents and problem officers and yet are a no show when certain officers are involved. They protect those they want to protect and others have to take care of their situation themselves. I made up my mind that I would not play games with the police union and I would **treat everyone fairly**.

Bargaining in Good Faith

The union ultimately wants the city to bargain with them in good faith. There are a great deal of dynamics going on between the union and the city. The bottom line is that the police union wants to negotiate a better contract for the regular members while the city wants to keep their tax base down. In Somersworth, New Hampshire, my department personnel were organized as an association recognized by the state as a bargaining unit. Later, they jointed the International Brotherhood of Police Officers to strengthen their bargaining position. The Berwick Police Department across the river from us was affiliated with the Teamsters. In the late 1980s and early 1990s I saw a migration of professional unions moving through New Hampshire. The reason was obvious. New Hampshire communities had a high tax base and it was difficult to get anything from the municipalities so police departments formed unions. Matter of fact, the department heads formed into an association, also known as the union. I guess if you knew the history of the community a little better than you could understand more clearly.

When I was in Somersworth, New Hampshire, I was not directly involved in the bargaining process with the Police Union. The City Manager only called upon me as a resource person and it was usually in the form of a phone call to answer a question or a meet briefly with the manager and city negotiator before the actual bargaining session. Actually, the City Manager did me a big favor. There was no way I would want to get involved in the bargaining session, especially when the session turned into heated discussions. Besides, I had a stake in how the bargaining sessions turned out. I wanted them to get more benefits and pay increases. My suggestions for any chief or manager who was thinking about being directly involved with the bargaining session, my answer would be not do it.

I was there in Somersworth for three of their contracts and each time during the negotiations, there were bitter feelings. Each time these officers came back saying the city was screwing them. Even when there was an agreement by the city with the police union, the officer still felt they were held hostage by the city and were getting screwed again. The City Council mandated that there would not be any retroactive pay for anyone and this alone added an extreme amount of pressure during negotiations. The union members kept saying it was an unfair labor practice but the complaint never went anywhere. Going through negotiations is not fun and I can specifically relate it to my time in Bristol, Connecticut. The feeling towards the City was the same in Bristol as they were in Somersworth. At least when an agreement was reached the officers received retroactive pay.

There were times when my officers would come to me and ask for my opinion. I told them to accept the best deal they could get. I knew that the city would not settle any contract for more than three percent and that was a given. Of course, the union was asking for usually around eight percent. They were always far apart. You want to know the real dynamics. Generally, if the city delayed the agreement for six months to a year or longer, they would save at least three percent for the taxpayers. Prior to negotiations with a union, the City Manager would have a closed door meeting with the City Council regarding the parameters of negotiations. They would usually tell him three percent and no more. Both sides will sit through negotiations for many months or even a year to eventually settle for what the City Council wanted in the first place. They actually vote on each contract after the union ratifies it. They rarely agreed to anything outside the parameters given to the City Manager. In reality, the Police Union should have settled for the first offer by the City because it was usually the highest. Of course, during the negotiating game the city will always try to have the union give up something in return. There was not much to give up anyway in the union contract. Why not cut to the chase and say this is what you are getting and no more?

In Somersworth, New Hampshire the union had a provision in the contract that all disciplines in their personnel file would be removed after one year, provided that there were no repeat offenses. This was a good provision for the malcontents, marginal or problem employees. Even employees who were involved in misconduct were protected. It was very difficult to terminate an employee if you were to follow progressive discipline. If someone was involved in misconduct that warranted a suspension, the disciplinary matter had to be removed from the personnel file after one year. You did not have to remind the employees, they were usually at the door on their one-year anniversary day. After the discipline was removed from the file, they would start over again. It was comical to think about it. One sergeant always got into trouble during the fall just before hunting season. He would get suspended for one or two days and a year later the suspension was pulled from the file and he would start over again.

The police union never wanted to give up this provision. I suggested to the City Manager many times to give up something in return to get the provision out of the contract. I do not blame them for wanting to keep it. The people who were responsible for getting this provision into the contract in the first place are in management positions now. I always say, "What goes around comes around."

Holding the Cards

When the city is negotiating with the union, they are holding all the cards. They are bargaining with the power. The city has the deep pockets and they are controlling the negotiations. The longer it takes the more money they will save the taxpayers in the end. The City Council will take their time because there is no rush to settle any contract. They know that eventually the Police Union as well as the others will settle the contract. Just thinking about it, they had an arrogant attitude. The people in the community were more sympathetic towards saving taxpayer dollars than giving city employees an increase in pay. The City always agreed to a three-year contract and the first year it was a freebee because they saved money. There was no retroactive pay ever paid out while I was there. In my mind, it did not make any sense. I would have tried to settle the contract as quickly as possible and get on with the business of policing the community. **If you treat your employees right in the first place and pay them what they are worth, you would not have these union issues and long drawn out negotiations.**

There were times when the Police Union filed unfair labor practices to the state. No problem, the City just sent their City Manager, City Negotiator and Labor Attorney to Concord, New Hampshire to argue the issue. The union would have to use their union attorneys to argue their side. On the other hand, just look at the money the city could have saved in attorney and negotiator fees if they had been more reasonable. Just remember, time was on their side. The longer it dragged out the more money they saved the taxpayers. After about a year had gone by the city was ready to settle with the union. This happened each of time was wasted. You would have thought the union could have approached this dilemma better. It was in our best interest and the community to get my personnel back on track.

The city knew that it was illegal to strike. The most the union could have done was to have a ticket blitz or initiate the blue flu. The first was not an option because the community would not stand for it and fortunately, they never had the blue flu. I think the city intentionally utilized a delaying tactic. I did not say it at the time but I believed the city bargained in bad faith. They knew that the police union's demands would be high and they would never accept the first offer by the city. As I had stated, the city holds all the cards.

The only other action taken by a police union was in Bristol, Connecticut. During an impasse with negotiations one year, the union decided to have a ticket blitz. It truly was not successful because only a few officers participated but it got the attention of the media anyway. I do not know if it helped or hindered negotiations. In my opinion, union job actions are not very effective. They tend to alienate the community.

In my role as police chief, the union saw me as the good guy in this case. In many other departments where the chief takes more of an active role, the chief is looked upon as the bad guy. I think in many ways I helped settle the contracts. After awhile I convinced the union officials that the city's offer would not get any better and I was usually right. I was not directly involved and I did not mind my unofficial role at all. It was a little frustrating because it took too long to settle the contracts. My advice is to **get the city to settle the contracts as soon as possible**.

Some Problematic Issues

Dealing with frivolous grievances was a complete waste of time. Generally, when an employee submits a grievance it will be of one of the following issues: money, working conditions or equipment. The issue was always money in Somersworth and Bristol. This should come to as no surprise. Usually the grievances in Somersworth were not related to the contract at all. It was in my best interest to always follow the contract. Whatever money was owed to the employee, I made sure they received it. There are other issues that come up were not in the contract. If an officer did something beyond his or her ordinary duty, they wanted to be compensated for it. When an officer field trained a new person, he wanted to be compensated for it. These issues should have been addressed in the contract to make it easier. I eventually got approval for an additional five percent while the officer was being field trained.

For a few years, a touchy issue was the rank of detective. Eventually a separate pay grade was added between police officer and sergeant, but only while the person was acting in the capacity as a detective. It was deemed a temporary assignment and not a promotion at the time.

Officers in Somersworth got two hours pay at time and a half in the event they were called in for any reason. It was called "Call Back." It was reasonable especially if an officer was called in to administer the intoxilyzer test on a drunk driver. If the officer completed the assignment in thirty minutes he could go home. It was not a bad deal. Other officers looked at the "Call Back" as an opportunity to get some free money. Sometimes the officers would try to get "Call Back" prior to the beginning of their shift if they were sent on a call or try to get "Call back" on the end of the shift. Sometimes these guys were just plain greedy. They would try to interpret the contract and twist the language to their liking. It did not work and I denied the grievances and stated it was not in the contract.

One little trick that I picked up from my former chief and it worked very well for me was to make the grievant wait the full 10 days for my answer. According to the union contract the police chief had 10 days to answer a grievance. In almost every case, I gave a written response on the tenth day. Some police chiefs I knew would get angry especially when a frivolous grievance crossed their desk and they would fire off a response right away. I think that it is just human nature to answer right away. I would advise them to **wait before responding** because you might write something that might hurt your case later. Just do not let your emotions get in the way. When I give my answer, I give a complete fully thought out and complete response. Besides, I like to make them think about it for a while. Nothing infuriates them more than not hearing anything or not having some acknowledgment from the chief. I do not even discuss the situation with anyone other than getting input from my captains for background information. If someone got impatient, I told him or her I was in the process of answering the grievance. I already knew what my response would be from day one but I did not tell them anything. It was fun and I admit it. Besides it was my hidden message that if I was going to play the game, it was going to be my way. I could see the expression on their face just dying to ask me, "Well chief what is your answer?" One certain captain would ask why I did not respond right away. I told him I was thinking about it. The real reason was that the union person would ask the captain. The captain, who was officially "non-bargaining," sided with the union on many issues. He often sympathized with the union. He just wants to be liked by his personnel. In a way this is good. I understood where he was coming from so I was careful about what I said to him.

Anyone going into a unionized department for the first time has to have a clear understand of the dynamics going on all the time between management and the union. I still call it **gamesmanship** on this level. The union officials will always test the chief to see how far they can push him or her. You have to remind yourself to remain professional and it is not personal. You have to appear nothing they say or do is bothering you. Deep inside it sure hurts, but do not show it. If you show your emotions, the union will then turn into piranhas and will turn up the heat on you. The union can make life so miserable that many police chiefs call it quits or be instrumental in getting the police chief fired. They can be a powerful organization and you **cannot take them lightly or underestimate unions.**

The former police chief from Berwick, Maine and I were good friends. We collaborated on an Explorer Post, Community Policing and many other issues. His union, the Teamsters gave him nothing but a hard time while he was chief. His heart was into it but he could not get along with the union. The ironic part about it was he was once active with the police union. I guess they got angry with him when he would not give away the store or the taxpayer's money. Eventually he just called it a day and resigned. He is now teaching for a Community College the last time that I checked. The point is that so many chiefs become frustrated that they eventually quit. You have to be crazy to put up with all the abuse.

Every now and then, I was reminded of "Garcia." When I first went to Somersworth, I was introduced to Garcia. Prior to my arrival the officers were required to report for roll call 15 minutes prior to the beginning of their shift with no compensation. Other words, it was free time for the department. The police union filed a grievance that eventually went to the State Labor Board. They ruled that the officers should have been compensation for the time and I agree. If the officers work the time then they should get paid. This issue had already been decided in **Garcia v. San Antonio Metropolitan Transit Authority Et Al., 469 U.S. 528 (1985)**. The United States Supreme Court held that the San Antonio Metropolitan Transit Authority employees have the protection of the Wage and Hour provision of the Fair Labor Standards Act. It was an expensive proposition for the city because they had to pay out thousands of dollars to the police employees. Usually, anytime there was a money issue the name of Garcia was mentioned. I guess it was supposed to scare me.

Many police, sheriff departments and many other types of organizations do not compensate their employees for the time worked. Many times an employee is not give a choice between overtime and compensatory time off at the same rate. A sheriff department in Arizona routinely scheduled extra shifts for the deputies but it was only for compensatory time off. I could not understand how they got away with it for so long without anyone complaining. I believe they were afraid to complain in fear of losing their jobs. There are many police, sheriff departments and other organizations alike that do not comply with the Fair Labor Standards Act. Sooner or later someone will complain and the municipality, county government or organization will have to pay. I can understand why officers or any worker would want to join a union.

In Somersworth, if an employee was not satisfied with my answer the next step was the City Manager and after that, the Personnel Advisory Board. The Board had the final say unless the union wanted to take the issue further to the State Labor Board. I must have been doing something right because I never lost a grievance before the Personnel Advisory Board nor the State Labor Department. The intent was to always treat my employees fairly and compensate them when they worked. There was no real mystery to it. If an employee had a good argument for compensation, I listened to him or her. If it was reasonable then he or she got paid. Of course, I always conferred with the City Manager on any money related issues.

I remember in Bristol, Connecticut when I was burnt on a compensation issue. At the time I substituted for another lieutenant scheduling officers for overtime and regular duty assignment while she was on vacation. In Bristol there was a great deal of scheduled overtime on each shift and it was very competitive. It was so sophisticated that the hours for each officer were posted and everyone was in rotation, starting with the least amount of hours. Everyone on the list was called and if there was no answer the response was indicated as a refusal. In my example, the officer filed a grievance because a person with more overtime hours was asked to work before he was. In his grievance, he said that it was unfair because he was available to work and had not been asked to work. He felt that he should have been compensated at time and a half for eight hours. Thinking back about it, he was the type who never worked much overtime and I was sure that I had called him. I was shocked to find out he won his grievance. All he had to do was come to me and asked for a shift and I would have given him one. There was another lesson learned here. There are **individuals who will take advantage of every situation**. Apparently, this individual saw an opportunity for some free compensation.

One thing I found out when I was working in Bristol for so many years was the level of greed in the police department. There were individuals who cared more about how much money they could make during the year than about service to the community. Service to the community became secondary. I was naive to think that individuals would be happy to have a job as a police officer to serve the community. Something was lacking and it was called dedication. Do not get me wrong. I like to make money too but I enjoyed serving the community. I thought I would mention this issue here because I think the original concept of the union was good but it later evolved into one of self-serving.

One thing about unions is that the networking is very good. Unions tend to share information with other unions and in my next example, it worked to the detriment of my friend who became the police chief in Newtown, Connecticut. When he became appointed as the new police chief in Newtown, some of his personnel were curious about him so they called some of the union officials in Bristol. I knew this happened because some of my friends in Bristol told me. I can imagine the message was not good, since he was not popular with the union anyway. His new department employees had already received a negative image of him before he started. I felt sorry for him because he never truly had a chance to succeed. Eventually the police commission terminated his employment as their police chief. The union played an active role in getting rid of him. It was a shame because he was a talented individual and had much more to offer the police department and community.

Unions can create a great deal of trouble for the police chief especially if they do not like the person. My former police chief in Bristol was a master at getting people to know him. He was a likable guy and that helps in the long run. Again, **communication is the key and having an open door policy is required.** I did not leave anything to be taken for granted either. I did not stay in my office. I walked around and spoke to my personnel so they would get to know me better. Nothing is more suspicious than a mystery chief or manager who hides in his or her office all day. Actually, this is a theme that I mentioned all the time, **"managing the department by walking around."**

If a Police Chief or executive has union problems and it was publicized in one of the local newspapers, I would be willing to bet that the main problem was communication. He or she has isolated oneself from the Union. It is a fatal error and a recipe for failure. Surely it will happen soon or later. Granted, there are some Union Officers who are a pain in the neck and on paper they are sometimes marginal employees. You have to remember these individuals were elected to their position by their union body and are thrust into leadership positions even though they usually do not carry any formal rank. There were a few occasions when I had to discipline the union president and there were a few times when he criticized me. You know there were many times I did not want to talk to him at all; he just annoyed me. However, I was very cordial to him and always communicated with him. I acted very professional even though there were times I had to restrain myself.

Just like a high school teenager, this union president would test me to see how far he could get. One day he came to work with a designer haircut like some of the younger teens would get at the time. He had designs cut into his hair like arrows. His wife had dared him to do it. At the time, I did not have a specific rule to cover haircuts so he had me on this one, but the next day I amended the rules that governed dress code, and in particular haircuts. I ordered him to get rid of the designer haircut. He complied and that was the end of it. Neither he nor anyone else submitted a grievance. I am sure if it happened in Bristol, Connecticut, then there would have been a grievance. There was one time when the chief in Bristol allowed one officer to have a beard. Now, normally police officers did not wear beards while in uniform at least in Bristol. After he allowed one then a few others grew one too. Management could never put a stop to it even to this day. It was a change in their working conditions now.

These were examples of the types of games some individuals will play to see what they could get away with. Unfortunately, the police chief has to devote a great deal of time and energy to these silly issues. You would think that some of these individuals would have better things to do. Imagine if all their energies were focused in trying to prevent crime, society would probably be better off. Expect some of your employees to play some games with you. I have seen the officers do it in Bristol and actually experienced it in Somersworth as well. You have to remain calm and keep smiling and not show them they are getting to you. Do not be surprised when you find some trying to play games with you. This goes for any management position.

It was different in Florence, Arizona and Fort Lupton, Colorado. These states were considered right to work states and unions were not allowed. Some larger agencies formed associations but there was nothing to mandate them to bargain with the city or town for a contract. It did not bother me in the slightest to not have to deal with a police union. What a big difference! It was almost too good to be true to not have to worry about having to deal with the games the union likes to play for the time being. It can wear you out after awhile and sometimes I do not see how some chiefs can last for so long.

Many departments have supervisor officers in the same union with the patrol officers. I see a problem with this. In my mind, it is very difficult to supervise subordinates in the same union. This held true for Bristol, Connecticut and Somersworth, New Hampshire. I am sure there are similar situations occurring in police departments as well as other organization all over the country. In Bristol, they even have lieutenants in the same union. My question is how can you effectively supervise someone who is in the same union? It has to be difficult. Now, some departments have a separate supervisor's union and that is much better.

There had to be incidents of violations of rules and misconduct that never got reported. I can relate to this specifically. It happened every day in Bristol. If you were part of the click or a union brother or sister then you were protected. However, if you were not one of the boys then your incident got reported. It was just that simple; there was no equity. If you recall, my fishing expedition is a good example. If the incident occurred with one of the union pals then it would never have gone anywhere. After observing what happened throughout the years, I think that it was a valid statement. The union boys took care of their own members in the "click" and it was an unpleasant fact. If you were outside this close-knit circle then you were fair game for management. The "good o' boy" network was live and well even in New England.

Sometimes I had a hard time envisioning managing the department when all your management staff is with the union except for the two captains. I suspect that this is a problematic issue with many police departments and other organizations. Perhaps, if the city had taken care of their management staff or management cared more about employees, then there would have been no problem.

What a Deal!

I do have to thank the union many times for giving me the opportunity to retire early. The union put in a grievance on behalf of all the union members, which at the time I was a lieutenant and in the union. I truly did not realize what was going on until the union reached a settlement with the city. For years, the city took five percent out of our gross pay for retirement. The union argued that it was not equitable because if a person had worked substantially more overtime than one who did not would pay more into the retirement fund during his or her career. They argued the five percent should have come from the officer's base pay. I never thought about my contributions to the pension fund but apparently, someone else did. I have to agree they were right in this case. I think what everyone was looking for was the excess pension contributions returned to the men and women of the department. The city in their infinite wisdom offered to return the pension contributions, give a credit in time towards retirement or a combination of both. When the city notified me that they were giving me a credit of nine years or about five thousand dollars in cash, I told them to keep the cash and I would accept the time. With the time credited to me my total time on the department put me over the 25 year eligibility mark. In short, I could retire anytime after having spent just over 18 years on the department. They made me an offer that I could not refuse. Who could turn this deal down? Christmas came early.

Even though I benefited from this deal somehow it did not seem right. However, the deal was sanctioned by the city. When happened next was unbelievable. Over the course of several years, there was a mass exodus from the department. Many veteran police officers retired with only 15 to 20 years to pursue other ventures. The city lost a great deal of experience and suddenly younger officers like me were thrust into higher management positions. I was eventually promoted to captain because all the captains retired. Being captain put me in a better position to eventually become police chief in another community. So in effect, I retired and was able to collect my pension and salary, otherwise known as "double dipping." What a great deal. I certainly joined the cause and I thanked the union many times. If the city was smart, they should have paid the excess pension contributions and everyone would have been happy. I do not think they realized the ramifications.

In this one instance, the union did well for everyone concerned. I am sure some of these individuals were not thinking about me. They were mainly thinking of a scheme to get more money out of the city. As it turned out, it was not only a jackpot but also a bonanza for me.

Just thinking about it from a chief's point of view, it was a big headache. The police chief in Bristol handled it very well. He just refused the grievance and let the city handle it. He was out of the loop and was not affected by it one-way or the other.

Managing in Bristol had to be a difficult environment to manage. Over the years, slowly but surely, the city bargained away management's rights. Take for example the management right to dictate the assignment and where it will be. If the chief wanted a special patrol, he had to discuss it with the union first. Imagine you could not do something that affected the distribution of manpower without discussing it with the union. It was a change in their working conditions, a grievable offense. Another costly item was police dispatch. Two sworn officers manned each shift and on the second shift there was a sergeant. For years, the city wanted to convert slowly over to civilian dispatch like most other police departments across the county. The city could save tens of thousands of dollars if they had converted over to civilian dispatch. In addition, the fire department has their separate dispatch. Just think of all the money that could be saved if they had a combined Public Safety Dispatch. Officers would be put back on the street where they belonged and fire fighters would be added to the trucks. The domino effect would be additional savings from not having to staff overtime shifts on patrol. The city negotiated with the unions for a long time. Recently, the unions agreed to combine both dispatch centers into one Public Safety Dispatch Center. I think this was an excellent move and it will benefit the city for years to come. The union was always willing to bargain but they always wanted something in return. This was the major hurdle. It was a very expense proposition to fund both dispatch centers.

If that was not problematic enough, the police chief had to deal with the police commission in order to get any policies approved. Any disciplinary matters had to be eventually resolved by the police commission. So the chief not only had to negotiate with the union but also with the police commission. He managed to do it though. After the chief left in 1988, the department went through two more police chiefs from the outside. Neither one stayed more than three years. After they left the city finally went with an inside candidate. So far, he has managed to get along with the union and has been very effective. It is a big plus in his favor. As long as the **police chief communicates** effectively with the union, he will do well in situations that involved the union or dealing with union related issues.

In Somersworth, New Hampshire, it was much easier to manage a police department. I had all the management rights and I did not have to negotiate with the union on assignments or shifts. We used civilian dispatchers in our Public Safety Dispatch Center. We dispatched for the fire department as well. Sometimes there were complaints but the fire chief and I worked out these issues. One of my main problems was the captain who I had transferred to take over the supervision of dispatch. He did not like having to dispatch for the fire department. Apparently, he could not see the big picture. The more that the police department's dispatch center did for the community, the least likely the dispatch function would have been turned over to the County. As you probably already know, many counties have taken over police department dispatching. The town or city saves about $200,000 or more while they get dispatching service in return. It is a good deal for the town or city but not necessarily more efficient. I have heard many complaints about county dispatching over the years primarily that they are too busy to handle all the radio traffic. Civilian dispatchers work out very well as long as they are trained. In Florence, Arizona and Fort Lupton, Colorado, we were the Public Safety Dispatch Center. In each case, I used civilian dispatchers.

I have not even discussed probably many more problematic issues here. Each chief or manager will have to deal with these issues as they come up. They may not be as complex as the one in Bristol, Connecticut dealing with the pension fund contribution but each one will require much thought. My advice is for a police chief or leader to think long and hard on each issue before rendering a decision. When a decision is finally reached, it will have a long lasting effect. Sometimes a hastily made decision on what was thought a simple issue may have long reaching consequences on future actions. Be careful of the advice from your staff.   They might mean well but they may not have all the facts or understand the ramifications. There were times when I wished that I could have thought longer before making a decision. Take your time and make the right decision.

In summary, the following is my best advice:

- Think long and hard on each decision.
- Be careful of the advice from your staff.
- Take your time.
- Be mindful of long reaching consequences.
- Make the right decision.

Some Positive Issues

Even though I had mentioned some problematic issues there are the positives. In the real world, there is nothing perfect so why should unions be perfect? As I had stated earlier unions can have a useful purpose.   As I became more comfortable in working with the police union in New Hampshire, it became less nerve-wracking. If you work it right, it can be a win-win situation for both sides. It does not have to be adversarial; it is not us against them mentality.

I accomplished many things in Somersworth, New Hampshire with the help of the police union. We evolved from a mismanaged and a poor public image police department to one that the community was proud of. It was accomplished only with the help of the men and woman of the police department. It was to their credit that we were successful. True there were some "bumps in the road" along the way but we overcame them after we got to understand one another better.

I tried not to paint a picture of doom and gloom if you happen to be in a department with a police union. It only appears that way because the 5%'ers take up much of the chief's time. There are usually no problems at all with the greater majority of the personnel.

Oh, No! A Storm

Have you ever wondered about what happens when there is a "Vote of No Confidence" by the union directed at the police chief? Perhaps, you have read in the newspaper or heard on the television that a local chief was the recipient of the vote of no confidence or you experienced it yourself. There is no doubt that this could be one of the most stressful periods of your life. The vote of no confidence can have a detrimental impact on the police department and community. It will be a big story for the media. So, what do you do? I have seen the city manager, police commissioners and city council members rally around their police chief. All too often, usually there is a hastily prepared news conference detailing their support for the chief and how dare the union vote no confidence against their police chief. Actually, they have to come out and support their guy. What do you think they are going to say? Let us fire the police chief.

Let us examine these issues because we can agree there is much more to the story than just a vote of no confidence. Now some unions will use it as a ploy during their negotiations but deep down there could be some serious problems that should not be taken likely. Yes, police chiefs can survive the proverbial vote of no confidence but many more will either resign under the pressure or eventually be fired. Realistically, take for example a professional baseball team. It is much easier to fire the manager than fire the entire team. What the owners look for is chemistry between the manager and his players. Another hires managers fired from one football team. It happens all the time. It is not because they are terrible. It is the same rationale between the police chief and his personnel. When police chiefs go through the interview process, the City Manager or City Council is looking for someone with the same philosophy but also have the chemistry to get along with his or her personnel. Sometimes it works out and other times it does not.

These events can be analyzed and prevented. If the police chief or top executive takes the attitude such as the heck with them, the "us against them" mentality, it will spell the beginning of the end. Matter of fact, many of these issues hit the papers and anyone can follow along to see want happened. There are many warning signs that the police chief or manager should be made aware. Many times it could be in the form of a breakdown in communication, stalled union negotiates for a new contract, accusation of unfair labor practices, perception of unfair disciplinary practices and many others. Actually, it could be in many forms that could have an accumulative effect but the main problem for a police chief is the lack of communication between the police chief and the union. There is no doubt that this is the number one issue.

Let me tell you what happened to me that could have easily turned into a union vote of no confidence against me. I thought everything was going well and it was during one of those periods when the union was without a contract. Tensions during the negotiating session were running high. At one point the City Manager told me about one of my sergeant making an implied threat about bringing a firearm to the negotiating sessions. Now, it cannot get anymore tense than this. Incidentally, I did speak very tactfully to the officer about this complaint. I advised him that it would not be a good idea to even hint about any violence.

One day the captain who sympathized with the union all the time, came into my office and asked to speak to me. He stated that the union was requesting a department meeting with me to discuss some problems in the department. I asked him about the issues and he said he did not know. I said to myself, sure. I told him, "No problem, set it up for the afternoon." I think that I caught him by surprise because he expected me to say the heck with them. It would have been all the ammunition the union needed. I figured this captain was trying to set me up again and I knew that he knew the issues. His friends in the union talked to him all the time. There was no mystery about it.

I decided the best way to counter would be to take the offensive and address the issues head on. At precisely 3:00 p.m., I walked into the training room and the entire department was present even the ones off duty. The room was full of people and every seat was taken. I could only hope for this type of participation all the time. Because the union requested the meeting, the city did not have to pay overtime. Without a doubt I have to say that this was the most stressful and nerve-wracking experience of my life. I would not wish this upon on my worst enemy. No police chief should have to go through an ordeal that I had to go through. They asked if they could be frank with me and I told them absolutely. I stood in front and answered question after question. During this time I kept my control and responded candidly to their questions. It started out tense at first because I believed that many thought there was going to be a vote of no confidence. The meeting turned into a fruitful discussion of all the issues. I could not ask for anything better. The dynamics of the department were suddenly reversed in my favor.

Many of the issues that were brought up were minor riddled with rumors. They were mainly frustrated because of the stalled negotiations. As you already know, these little rumors can lead to bigger problems if the personnel believe them. Some of them wanted to believe the rumors. Many of the issues dealt directly with negotiations that I had no part of. Many of their issues dealt with the city manager. There was not one issue that directly involved me. Near the end of the meeting I suggested a meeting with the city manager to clarify some of their concerns. I did ask the city manager after the meeting if he could address some issues with my personnel and he accepted even though I had previously briefed him about my experiences. In fact, I have to give him a great deal of credit for appearing at the meeting. It was nowhere near hostile as my meeting had been. The city manager handled himself very well but he made one statement that infuriated them later. He told them if they did not like working for the city then they could seek employment elsewhere. I wish he did not say it because a few of my personnel eventually left the department. I felt like saying it too. **Sometimes, you have to know when to keep your mouth shut.**

My meeting lasted about an hour and a half. Let me say after the meeting was over with I was stressed. I had dodged "a big bullet." They were ready to steamroll me over and hang me out to dry before the meeting. After the meeting, it was a completely changed group. Several of the officers after the meeting thanked me for taking the heat and answering some tough questions. I survived the ordeal. Coincidently, I got a telephone call from one of the reporters from our daily newspaper asking me if it was true that there was a vote of no confidence against me. I told him there was no such vote. He seemed surprised because he was sure there was and I told him to check his source again. When I saw the reporter the next day, I just smiled. It was the last time the union called a meeting.

Knowing that several individuals had tried to set me up including the captain, I showed up for work the next day like nothing had ever happened. My secretary commented that I should have taken the day off. She knew what I had to endure. I was polite and cordial to all. During the weekend the association had their annual picnic at the lake and I attended as always. Actually, going to the picnic was the last place I wanted to go but I knew that I had to make an appearance. I could see certain individuals were having their private conversations about me in their group and I am sure the topic of discussion was me. They were still trying to figure out what happened and I just carried on as if nothing had ever happened. Actually, it was comical to see the expression on some of their faces. The last thing that I wanted to do was to show them they were getting to me. I played the part; my game face was on.

In reality the whole episode could have been avoid had they been honest with me from the very beginning. All that some had to do was ask me directly about these rumors. Apparently, there were some who had different agendas. Police chiefs and managers should be aware of some of the underlying issues. Sometimes only the superficial reasons are mentioned in the beginning and you have to probe deeper to get at the real issues. Many of these issues can easily be blown out of proportion. It is amazing to me one or two individuals will intentionally start rumors to get everyone fired up and just wait for the fallout. **Just be calm and maintain your composure.**

If the police chief ignores these telltale signs, then it will spell trouble. I have seen it happen too many times to police chiefs and in each case, they had a police union. It is a common ploy by the union to seek attention through the media, city administration and the community. Obviously, when this happens they are looking for something.

Many chiefs take the wrong approach by circling the wagons too soon. He or she will align themselves with the city manager, city council or police commissioners. They will rally around the chief as I had stated earlier. It is possible to survive. I have seen one chief who survived two actual votes of no confidence. However, many more will not survive. Eventually, if there is a continuing problem, the city manager may force the chief to resign, retire or eventually terminate him. It may take six months, a year or longer but I can assure you one thing, something will happen.

My friend who was police chief in Connecticut had undergone a vote of no confidence. It was a heart wrenching experience for him and his family. The family suffers too. There could be no doubt the union was after him. The union members continually went around the chief to the police commissioners. After listening to them for so long, I guess after awhile the police commissioners were starting to believe the complaints.

We use to speak once in awhile about it and I wished that I could have done more for him. I was afraid the ultimate disgrace was about to happen to him. It was a matter of how long he was going to survive. Now, if someone wants to get rid of you they will find a way. The commissioners started with poor evaluations. They began to criticize him for things beyond his control. At one point they had enough to bring him up on charges and put him on administrative leave with pay. They eventually gave him his hearing and terminated him. His captain, the second in command was elevated to acting chief. Now it should not come to any surprise that the captain was promoted to chief. I am not saying there was any funny business going on but I cannot help being suspicious after my ordeal with one of my captains in New Hampshire. It is not unusual for an officer with command rank who would have aspirations to be chief. I encouraged this natural progression but I would hope the command level officer would not conspire to help remove the chief before his time.

Another police chief in New Hampshire had undergone the usual vote of no confidence. He was an outsider, just like me and had gone in to make the department better. He had a tough union. No matter what he did, the union was never happy. The person who had a hand in getting him removed was his captain, the second in command. He told me several times that he had trouble with him. His ordeal is similar to many other chiefs all across the country that faces this dilemma.

It is possible to head off a vote of no confidence. There are some revealing signs that you should be aware of. The obvious sign is that everyone is quiet for a few days and no one is coming to you for anything. It is as if no one wants to associate with you because you have the plague. The more obvious is that rumors are circulating the department and even the council members are asking you questions if your personnel are happy.

The following is a brief guide to follow if you should get a vote of no confidence:

First of all, do not panic. You can survive it.

- Seek out the union leadership and invite them in for a meeting.
- Keep the lines of communication open.
- Find out the Real Issues.
- Dispel the Rumors and get the facts right.
- Keep a low-key approach.
- Keep the City Manager, Police Commissioners or Council Members informed.
- Do not have a news conference just yet for a show of support until you have made every effort to reconcile the differences. You may alienate the union even further.
- Do not run to the Media. If they ask you then you can give them a brief statement that you are working out the problems with the union.
- Always show respect and be professional.
- Do not take it personal.

Police Officer's Bill of Rights

Every so often we hear something about the Police Officer's Bill of Rights. Many states have already legislated the bill of rights while other states are considering it. Colorado if you recall is a right to work state and there was a big move to legislate the bill of rights. Police chiefs were against legislating it and someday there will be a provision for it. In the unionized states, you better believe that they have had the bill of rights for a long time.

What is the big deal about the Police Officer's Bill of Rights anyway? I certainly would have been made aware of my rights when the chief brought me up on charges for a fishing expedition during the early 1970s. As I stated early, I never got a notice of the charges nor an offer to first speak with a union representative. I did not even know the process. The next thing I knew I was before the Board of Police Commissioners at their mercy in executive session. This is just a simple example why the bill of rights evolved anyway. There were too many police officers brought up on charges with little or no opportunity for any type of defense. These officers were at the mercy of the police chief. No, police chiefs could no longer do what they want when it came time for discipline. There was no equality. Individuals were not treated the same. It was as obvious as to what was going on that you could predict what was going to happen. It depended upon who you were or who you know.

The reason these rights were legislated in many states and considered by others is the inequality and mistreatment of police employees when they were brought up on departmental charges. Police officers had a new tool at their disposal. In terms of fairness and equal treatment, police chiefs were mandated to follow the police officer's bill of rights. When this was first brought up in Colorado, I did not have a problem with it. It was not tying the hands of police chiefs as some people thought but it was more like treating your employees fairly. Some have lost sight of when they were new police officers. How would you like it if someone brought you up on some trumpeted up charge without knowing what to do? My principles guided me to do the right thing. I always treated people the way I wanted to be treated. I always reflected back to 1971 when I was brought up on charges and disciplined. It was fortunate for me that the police commissioners were lenient with me. They could have very easily dismissed me and I would not have known what my rights were at the time. At least an employee should be given a fighting chance if that was the case.

In my policy and procedures, I stated the employees' rights and how the investigation would be conducted. It did not matter if it was legislated or not, I practiced it anyway. I thought it was only fair to have the employees know what to expect.

The following is an excerpt directly out of the Fort Lupton Police Department's Policy Manual that I had specifically written that I found might be helpful to you:

Chapter 14- Internal Affairs

General Interrogations Procedures:
a. A law enforcement officer may not always be entitled to counsel or representation prior to or during interrogation. However, during any investigation of a serious nature, which could lead to dismissal from law enforcement service, and/or criminal action, the officer being interrogated shall be afforded the opportunity to be represented by legal counsel or accompanied by a representative of his choice.
b. It is the department's view that representation by counsel or the officer's other representative to observe under this procedure is limited. It is not intended to turn an investigation or interrogation into a "due process" hearing. Rather, it is to provide an opportunity for counsel or the officer's representative to observe on behalf of the officer that the interrogation is conducted in a fair and objective manner. In addition, the officer has the right, during the interrogation to briefly confer with his attorney or representative regarding questions presented to him. If a

request is made for private consultative, this should be honored so long as it does not unnecessarily impede the progress of the interrogation.

c. Attorneys or representatives should not interrupt the interrogation by raising objections to questions or by making statements for the record unless the objection is based upon a procedure that violates the rights of the officer under interrogation or investigation.   Any representative who interferes with or impedes the progress of the interrogation or investigation shall be asked to leave.

d. Employees under interrogation shall be required to answer fully, completely and accurately all questions posed, so long as the questions specifically and directly relate to the performance of his official duties. Compelled statements and/or answers by an officer may not be used in any criminal prosecution as evidence; however, they may be used for departmental administrative purposes, or to impose disciplinary action.

e. Any employee who fails to answer questions shall be subject to administrative charges based on his/her refusal to answer.

Interrogations during Criminal Investigations

f. The Miranda Warnings will be given when the employee being interviewed is under arrest or is likely to be arrested as a result of the statement.

Administrative Statements

a. When an investigation is not criminal in, or where criminal prosecution will not occur, members shall be informed that the interrogation will take place for administrative purposes only and a Garrity admonishment will be made.

b. The employee shall be advised that he/she is required to give a statement for administrative purposes and he/she is entitled to all the rights and privileges guaranteed by the City of Fort Lupton Personnel Rules, laws and the constitution of the United States and the State of Colorado.

c. The member or employee will be advised that refusal to answer questions which relate to the performance of official duties or fitness for office will make the member subject to departmental charges which could result in dismissal from the Fort Lupton Police Department.

d. Further, the employee will be advised that if a statement is given, neither the statement nor evidence, which is gained by reason of such statement, can be used against him or her in any subsequent criminal proceeding. However, such statement or evidence may be used against him in subsequent departmental charges and disciplinary action.

e. The investigator will ask the employee if he/she understood the requirement to give an administrative statement. If so, the member or employee will be requested to furnish the statement.

f. If the employee declines to give the statement, a direct order to give the statement will be given by the interrogator. An employee or member who continues to refuse may be immediately suspended from duty.

Conduct of Interrogations

a. All interrogations shall be conducted at reasonable hours, preferably at a time when the officer is on duty, unless the seriousness of the investigation is of such a degree that immediate action is required.

b. The employee under investigation shall be informed of the nature of the investigation prior to any interrogation and who will be conducting the interview.

c. Interrogating sessions shall be for a reasonable period and shall be timed to allow for such personal necessities and rest periods as are reasonably necessary.

d. At the request of any employee(s) under investigation, he/she shall have the right to be represented by counsel or any other representative of his/her choice who shall be presented at all times during such interrogation whenever the interrogation relates to the employee continued fitness for duty.

e. The formal interrogation of an employee under investigation, including all recess periods, shall be recorded, and there shall be no unrecorded questions or statements. Employees shall be entitled to a copy of their own statements and tapes made during the course of an internal investigation.

f. If the employee under interrogation is under arrest or is likely to be placed under arrest as a result of the interrogation, he/she shall be completely informed of his/her rights prior to the commencement of the interrogation.

g. In the interest of fairness to the officer under investigation, the department will make <u>no statements</u> until such time as the investigation has been completed. In the event the employee under investigation, or his/her counsel makes public statements concerning the allegations under investigation, the department shall respond in any manner it deems appropriate.

h. If the employee is ordered in off-duty, he/she will be entitled to compensation according to the City's Personnel Rules.

Conclusion of Internal Investigation

a. As soon as practical, the employee shall be notified that the Internal Investigation had been concluded and a decision regarding the matter will be forthcoming.

Operations Commander Responsibility

a. The Operations Commander shall be responsible for the Internal Affairs Function.

b. A thorough report shall be submitted upon completion of the Internal Investigation to the Chief of Police for review and approval, and subsequent action, if necessary.

Internal Affairs Records

a. The Chief of Police shall maintain all Internal Affairs Records and will secure them in a locked file cabinet in the Chief's Office. Records that are over three years old may be stored in the locked Records Archives Room in the Police Department Basement.

b. If there is any action requiring disciplinary action, then a copy of the investigation and disciplinary action will be placed in the Employees' personnel file.

The above policy and procedure actually represents much of the language in the Police Officer's Bill of Rights. I wanted to make sure that each one of my personnel knew what their rights were and how the investigation would be conducted. In effect, no one had to legislate the police officer bill of rights for me. I had already implemented them. Another consideration that I had not already mentioned is the State Labor Department. During my time in three departments, I never lost a disciplinary case during the grievance process to include the State Labor

Department. I cannot remember any case going that far. I always tried to be thorough and fair.

All and all dealing with police unions is not bad. I have had good experiences with and without unions. Using common sense goes a long way. I like to think that I treated my personnel fairly.

Chapter 11
Police Internal Affairs

Police Internal Affairs are one of the most important functions that a police department could have. The department's reputation in the community could be tarnished because of one incident. It takes a great deal of hard work to change the image of the department around. Some individual's opinion in the community will not be changed no matter what you do. Your reputation is on the line and it is up to you whether you will do something about the violation of the rules and regulations, different types of misconduct or even the commission of a crime. What you do or not do will affect the reputation of the police department for years.

There are many police chiefs, as well as executives alike, and you probably already know some that are either blind to what is going on or they do not want to know. It is like the philosophy now in the military about gays, "Don't ask, and don't tell." Of course no one wants to have any problems and that is just human nature. If you avoid some of the telltale signs or you do not do anything when a problem is brought to your attention, then it may hit you suddenly like a ton of bricks. Some people think if you ignore the problem long enough, it will go away. This is wishful thinking. Everyone will be on your back for an explanation including the media, the community, and the city manager and council members. If the situation is very serious and you did not do anything then, it will eventually cost you your job.

Every so often, officers read about police corruption in someone else's department or in another state. When it hits closer to home then one might think more about it. You think that it will never happen to you but it can. When you are in your office, you do not know for a fact what is going on each shift, 24/7 (24 hrs a day, 7 days a week). It is impossible to know everything unless someone tells you about it. What if the media finds out about it first? Take for example the Rodney King incident. Everyone knew what happened to Rodney King because it was televised on every major network station all across the country. What was ingrained in everyone's mind was the severe beating that he had received by the Los Angeles Police. To be fair, there were other police departments represented there as well. There had to be some indicative signs that this one was not a remote incident of police brutality administered by the late night shift. It sure hit home when someone videotaped the beating. How can you dispute what was seen all over the country. The Los Angeles Police Department had a reputation of one of the finest police departments in the country. As a result of this one incident this police department's reputation came under fire. It seems that the beatings on the night shift were commonplace. It was a brand of old fashion police justice. The rationale was that their case was going to be dismissed or nothing would happen. You do not forget about the bumps and bruises. The police chief eventually resigned due to the adverse publicity and the heat put on him by the police commissioners. Someone had to take the fall and guess who it is going to be most of the time? You are right; it is the police chief.

What about the New York City Police Officers that decided to test their new stun gun? They thought they could use this device to help illicit a confession. It was a problem when the two prongs of the stun gun were put on the skin the electric current would leave burns marks on the skin. At the time these stun guns were a new tool for law enforcement. The real purpose was to incapacitate unruly individuals who were resisting arrest. Leave it to some officers to find a new use for stun guns. They were now used as instruments of torture. I thought using torture to obtain a confession was last used hundreds of years ago or in third world countries. When officers first heard about the incident with the New York Police Department it did not come as a shock. The police department has a reputation for being corrupt. In all fairness given the size of this police agency more than 30, 000 sworn officers it is very difficult to police the police. However, in recent years it has been much better. When these incidents hit other smaller agencies, it becomes more of a shock. In New York it is more of a way of life. I have to give New York credit though they managed to root out a great deal of corruption. Considering the size of their police force, it is a monumental task.

I can recall an incident in about 1964 that happened in Bristol, Connecticut. The revelation of a burglary ring consisting of police officers on the night shift woke up the community. Who would have ever thought that police officers would be involved in burglaries? Everyone in the community was shocked. This revelation not only rocked the community but also severely tarnished the image of the police department for decades. Some police officers were breaking into stores, removing merchandise and putting it into the trunk of their police vehicle. They would either find the break-in later or let the owner of the store report it. This scheme had gone on for years until one day a telephone call was made to the media by a person purported to be a milkman making deliveries. The milkman was rumored to be a police officer. I could believe an officer was so fed up and frustrated that his only alternative was to call the media to get something done. Obviously he could not go to his lieutenant because he was reputed to be involved. The State Police was notified and they did an investigation. A total of 10 officers were fired or resigned. Even to this day many people in the community remember the scandal that rocked the community. I could recall a few times in my career in Bristol when a citizen mentioned, "you guys were nothing but crooks." It kind of hurt when he said it but he was partially correct. Even though a number of police officers were fired or had resigned they did not get them all. A few lucky ones managed to get away with the crime. It took many years to get over the stigma of a corrupt police department and there is some reference even to this day. The media had a field day. It not only made local and state news but it attracted nation wide attention.

The corruption in my opinion had an opportunity to grow in the department because of an antiquated seniority system that is even prevalent today. Everyone bids for shift according to seniority. The most senior officers would end up on the day shift and the junior officer would end up on the night shift. The only rotation was between second and third shift. Even then officers could elect to stay on a particular shift. Other words, the same officers worked a particular shift. There was very little moving around from shift to shift. You can easily see the potential for misconduct when the same officers are stuck on a shift with nothing much to do. At that time, there was not much crime and many times an officer could go through the entire shift without a call for service. With the same officers working a shift they developed camaraderie with one another and coupled with boredom, well you know what could happen next? The potential for police misconduct is still there even today.

After this major incident you would think that a department could take the hint and clean their own house. After I went on the department in the later part of 1969 I cannot remember any other corruption investigation. There were never any on-going internal investigations into police misconduct. There were only sporadic investigations when something was brought to the police chief's attention, like my fishing episode. Another incident involved two police officers with a girl and allegedly one had sexual intercourse with her while on duty. The incident was brought to the attention of the chief by another police officer. Right, you guessed it; these guys were not popular with the union. Both these individuals were fired. The other guy was caught up with a situation with his partner and kept his mouth shut. It was too bad because he basically was a good officer. The point is, how often did these types of incidents take place and nothing was done about it? Every so often you would hear rumors about rendezvous with a female and where was management? They had to hear the rumors too.

Periodically, when someone truly messed up and so obviously, that management had to do something. There were very few written reprimands ever issued. I cannot remember ever seeing one or another officer getting one. One sergeant clearly messed up when he found himself involved in a political campaign. He discovered some dirt on a mayoral candidate by using the department's record system and disseminated it to the local media. Now, you have to admit that this was pretty dumb. He not only admitted it but also was arrogant about it. It was pretty sad to think that he did not think he was doing anything wrong. However, he crossed the line and involved himself in politics. The police chief had no alternative but to fire him. Just think if he had kept his mouth shut there would not have been anyone the wiser. No one would have ever known. He probably thought that his behavior was acceptable and no one would do anything. Little did he know when he got himself mixed up in politics it was a different ballgame. Perhaps, you can relate to a few incidents such as this.

Most police departments are small so they do not have a luxury of having a separate Internal Affairs Division. Usually the function falls to the police chief who many times have to investigate or assign the investigation to someone else. Sometimes the chief is so busy he does not have the time to do a thorough investigation.

In June 2001 a police chief resigned from a police department in New Hampshire. He allegedly had an affair with a female who was involved in a domestic squabble and I had already mentioned this in another chapter. Anyway, the selectman contracted with a management consultant firm to conduct a management audit of the police department. After several months they issued a 59 - page report criticizing the management of the department. As quoted in the Fosters Daily Democrat, they stated, "The department is stuck in a 20-year old policing model." You cannot say it anymore succinctly than the way they put it. They went on to say that there were no policy and procedures regarding the internal affairs functions and there were no files on any internal investigations except for two. These two files dealt with the chief and his defense against the charges.

The only department that I took over that had an internal affair function was Fort Lupton. They had a policy and procedure on internal affairs and there were a number of files so it appeared they were doing a good job with it. The other two departments were a different story. There had no files at all. Somewhere along the line there had to be some investigations but when I checked there were no master files. I guess it was whatever the police chief wanted to do.

What is being Corrupt?

At this point I think we need to talk more about the problem, the extent of the problem and exactly what is it? First let us take a look at the definition. As defined by the American Heritage Dictionary, corrupt is marked by immorality and perversion and being dishonest.

I do not believe that there are an immense number of corrupt police officers. When the news does break the story is so wide spread that it appears the entire department is corrupt. The nature of crime ranges from the serious to less minor offenses. We hear about the most serious offenses. For example, there was media attention regarding a police officer that got himself arrested for statutory rape. He was from a police department in North Carolina. He got involved with a young female, age 15 and he was 23 years old. Ultimately he resigned but he had to answer to the charges of rape. It was a foolish thing to do and another black eye for law enforcement. The police chief did a smart thing when he contacted the State Bureau of Investigation to conduct the criminal investigation part of it.

Internal investigation covers more than just corruption in the police department. It includes a multitude of wrongdoings including violations of the rules and regulations of the department and personnel rules of the city or town and violations of the town or city ordinances and crime. If left unchecked, the **little problems can easily escalate into bigger ones**. This is where the chief has to pay attention to what is going on and initiates an investigation when there are wrongdoings.

Some will disagree and do nothing about minor misconduct that is clearly identified in the department's rules and regulations. Most departments have in their rules and regulations a provision against accepting any gift or gratuity. Everyone knows that it is not ethically or morally right to accept gifts from the public. Yet, these practices are widely accepted by police officers all over the country. The badge does not give a license to get free stuff. Very rarely are these provisions enforced. Many departments have a provision that they cannot even accept a free cup of coffee or meal but it is an accepted practice. I know a department that is nationally accredited and know for a fact they have this provision in their policy manual. However, their officers would routinely go into a restaurant and accept a meal at half price. I was in the same restaurant and after having finished breakfast the witness recognized me as the police chief of Somersworth and shouted to her co-worker, "Does he get half price?" I quickly told her I did not get a discount and felt embarrassed when all eyes were upon me. I later had a conversation with the owner of the restaurant about half price meals to police officers and he stated that he appreciates the good work all officers do and this was one way he showed appreciation. He had a point. However, what do you do about the provision about accepting gratuities in your policy and procedures manual? The question is do you continue to overlook it? If so, then this provision should be removed if it is to be continually ignored.

So is it all right to accept a meal at half price or a free cup of coffee when you do not solicit it? Is it still a violation at this point of the department's rules and regulations? Where do we draw the line? Even though a rule is in writing, the police chief sets the tone whether a practice is acceptable for not. If you have something in writing and no one including the chief follows the rule you probably should not have one because sooner or later you will get burnt. **A rule is only as good as those who abide by it**. When management audits are done on police department they not only look at the policy and procedures but their customary practice. This is true when departments are undergoing their national accreditation process or if there is a management study being performed. What they will discover is that much of the time the customary practice does not match up with the rule. This is going to spell trouble sooner or later. If the cup of coffee is acceptable then say so. Let us not put the blindfold on so we cannot see what is going on. Police officers are pretty clever in seeing what they can get away with. Sooner or later they will travel into the gray area and cross the line. It may seem too minor or insignificant to bother but the chief should be making a statement when this happens. It does not take long for something to get out of control. My opinion is that there should be **zero tolerance**. There should be no exceptions. If you are going to have a rule then enforces it. I know it is the hard line. There should no wheeling and dealing, discounts, half-price or free anything. Police officers should be treated like any other customers asking for a service. The owners of businesses who provide these favors to police officers are looking for something in return. You remember the following saying, "There is no free lunch?" It is true that sooner or later they in turn will ask a favor. Generally, they will ask the officer to cross the line and do something totally inappropriate.

These types of moral dilemmas go on all the time. Unofficially, the department says it is tolerable even though, technically, it violates a policy. Knowing about it and saying nothing can lead to trouble later when the technical infraction turns into a bigger problem later. When you are driving by a restaurant and I do not care where it is, focus your attention to the number of police cruisers in the parking lot. If there are several, I would be willing to bet that the meal is half price or there is some type of discount.

When I was in Bristol, this type of activity would go on all the time. Sometimes it was so outrageous it was hard to believe. Take for an example an off duty veteran officer bring his family into a restaurant and when it was time to pay he would say, "I am a police officer." I wonder if he left a tip. It did not take long for the restaurant to change their policy. This same officer would go into the back door at McDonald's and take out a large order without paying. Imagine the nerve of this guy. How could he take advantage of people this way? Of course the image of the police department was tarnished even more. This is an example of one individual taking advantage of an accepted practice. It was hard for me to believe that management did not know what was going on. They probably got their free coffee or their meal at half price and who knows what else?

Around Christmas time during the early 1970s the Bristol Police Department was always buzzing with activity. It is not what you think with the busy season and all. No, officers from the day shift were making their annual rounds to area businesses picking up bottles of liquor. It was hilarious to observe the contest to see which officer would bring in the most liquor. Liquor by the cases would be brought into the station in plain view of everyone. There was never a word said about it. This was an accepted practice at the time that quickly died out after the new police chief took over. I wondered how many bottles of liquor the captain and the police chief got. There was no question in my mind that they got some. I was glad that I never wanted to get involved. This practice was so common they thought nothing of it. What a way to set the example for the younger officers or public perception of police for that matter. I thought it was wrong to place the blame on the merchant plain and simple. In my mind it was like blackmail, coercing them to make their contribution. The police officers were acting like the bagman in a crime syndicate. I have to admit everything was better with the new chief. Just thinking about it, some of these guys actually had the audacity to take advantage of people while wearing their badge. Now, I am just speaking of one department. Just take a look at the extent of the problem when many police departments were doing it all over the country.

Another type of misconduct involved a young officer in Somersworth, New Hampshire. It seems that he got friendly with a young lady who had received several parking tickets. He just voided out the parking tickets and destroyed the records in the file. When we asked him about "fixing parking tickets" he at first denied the accusation but then confessed saying that he was just doing a favor for a girl. I think he was just trying to impress her and maybe he did but it ultimately cost him his job. He was on probation so it made termination much easier. I guess he was not thinking and did not value his job very highly. We only found out by accident because someone else was looking for the records and started asking questions about it.

Another example of misconduct - in actuality- floored me, because I did not expect it from this individual. You never know when, which, how or why a person would actually fool you. He was a clean-cut family man. I would have never suspected in a million years that he was dirty. When I was in Fort Lupton, Colorado, my investigator decided to take cocaine from the property room. This guy was using coke on and off the premises and was taking the drugs from the drug pile to be destroyed. I guess he tried his best to destroy it and had his own private supply. We would not have found out about it if he had not been for a guilty conscience. He called me up one afternoon wanting to meet with my lieutenant and me to discuss a matter. He showed up at the appointed time with his preacher and the rest is history. I will go into detail later to discuss the scope of the investigation.

These examples I can cite repeatedly. It never ceases to amaze me how some individuals can think so little of their profession and become involved in some type of misconduct or corruption. **The three B's are the downfall to cops, "Broads, Booze and Bargains."** I think misconduct and corruption extend more than what we think in many police departments. Some are minor transgressions while others are more severe. Minor meaning violations of the department's rules and regulations to the more serious including actual criminal offenses. This reminds me when there was a police officer in the 1970s that happened to be with the Hartford

Police Department in Connecticut. After completing his shift he traveled to Springfield, Massachusetts, a short distance away to commit armed robberies. He was just trying to supplement his meager income. He eventually got caught like they all do. The more severe the more news worthy it becomes. Besides, everyone likes to read about a little police scandal. It hits the community even harder when they find it involves their community.

There are moral and ethical questions that come up that could undermine the efficiency and morale of the police department. Case in point: In Florence, Arizona it was brought to my attention that one of my officers was dating a high school senior. I actually heard it from a few citizens that were aware of what was going on. I called this officer into my office to ask him. I told him, "Tell me that it is a joke and it is not true you are dating a high school senior." He stated, "Yes, it was true, but she is 18 years old." This young girl was in a special education class at the school. I asked him if he knew about it and he said, "Yes, she only has a minor problem and should not really be there." I was amazed because he had an answer for everything. I told him this conduct was unacceptable as a police officer and it must cease and desist immediately. He failed to heed the warning. People in the community were disgusted with his behavior and they wanted something done about it. In addition, this officer had some other problems. In fact, added his problems together, lead to his termination. Rarely do I get involved with someone's personal business but when it tends to undermine the community trust and embarrass the police department then it becomes my business. In my mind, dating a person in high school is unacceptable. It appears that the police officer was taking advantage of a young, innocent girl. I do not care if the person was of age or not. There seems to be no end to moral and ethical questions.

You can see why there is mistrust and lack of faith in many police departments. Many police chiefs and executives have worked hard to make police work an honorable profession and all it takes is a few bad apples to caste a negative image. The negative image is like a plague and can last for years like in Bristol, Connecticut. It takes more work to undo the damage caused by a few corrupt police officers. If you want to take the pulse of the community to see how the public perceives your police department, just take a survey or start asking questions. Many people do not trust the police plain and simple. How can the people have faith in their police officers? This will be discussed in greater detail later on in another chapter.

Police officers need to be held accountable for all their actions. The Law Enforcement Code of Ethics as endorsed by the International Chiefs of Police is a statement that all officers should hold dearly that is stated as follows:

Law Enforcement Code of Ethics

As a law enforcement officer, my fundamental duty is to serve the community; to safeguard lives and property; to protect the innocent against deception, the weak against oppression or intimidation and the peaceful against violence or disorder; and to respect the constitutional rights of all to liberty, equality and justice.

I will keep my private life unsullied as an example to all and will behave in a manner that does not bring discredit to me or to my agency. I will maintain courageous calm in the face of danger, scorn or ridicule; develop self-restraint; and be constantly mindful of the welfare of others. Honest in thought and deed both in my personal and official life, I will be exemplary in obeying the law and the regulations of my department. Whatever I see or hear of a confidential nature or that is confided to me in my official capacity will be kept ever secret unless revelation is necessary in the performance of my duty.

I will never act officiously or permit personal feelings, prejudices, political beliefs, aspirations, animosities or friendships to influence my decisions. With no compromise for crime and with relentless prosecution of criminals, I will enforce the law courteously and appropriately without fear or favor, malice or ill will, never employing unnecessary force or violence and never accepting gratuities.

I recognize the badge of my office as a symbol of public faith, and I accept it as a public trust to be held so long as I am true to the ethics of police service. I will never engage in acts of corruption or bribery, nor will I condone such acts by other police officers. I will cooperate with all legally authorized agencies and their representatives in the pursuit of justice.

I know that I alone am responsible for my own standard of professional performance and will take every reasonable opportunity to enhance and improve my level of knowledge and competence. I will constantly strive to achieve these objectives and ideals, dedicating myself before God to my chosen profession . . . law enforcement.

International Association of Chiefs of Police

I hold the Law Enforcement Code of Ethics true and dear to my heart. I take it very seriously and in my last two communities; Fort Lupton, Colorado and Florence, Arizona I had a framed copy that hung on my wall. In addition, as part of the National Accreditation Standard also for the State of Colorado Accreditation Program, I stated verbatim the entire code of ethics in my policy manual. I wanted my personnel to read it and understand it. To me, this was one of the most meaningful statements ever crafted by the International Association of Chiefs of

Police. It is a profound statement that, in reality, enhances my philosophy about the profession of law enforcement.

There seems to be no end to infractions of the rules and regulations and even violations of the laws. I seem to have run the full gambit from the minor to the severe. Generally, at some point the chief will have had the opportunity in his or her career to conduct investigations into misconduct or corruption. The question is how many, how often and how severe? The result is that the officers misuse his or her position for personal gain or favors. What is the chief going to do about it? How you perceive misconduct and what you ultimately do, sets the tone for the entire department. Many of these misdeeds go from looking the other way when a crime takes place, frequenting with known felons, to actually being involved with crime.

Public Opinion

Public Opinion can make or break the department. Sometimes public opinion can be very damaging beyond repair even though the police chief and other staff members is trying to make things right. Just ask anyone about his or her local police department and you will find out. I discovered that people are very vocal and quick to form opinions. It may have resulted from one traffic stop to being a victim of a crime but the impression is still there. Once people form their opinions, it stays for a long time.

When I was interviewed for the police chief's position in Fort Lupton, Colorado I wanted to know what people thought about their police department. I wanted to find out whether the perception was good or bad. I asked one Hispanic individual who I later found out that he had been released from prison have had numerous contacts with the police officers. What he related was not totally good or bad. Basically, he said that he did not have any problems with the officers. Other people in the community related that they had a favorable impression of the officers while some people spoke of some dirty cops tipping off local drug dealers. Whether it was true or not, it was the perception and I wanted to change it. The City Administrator, the Mayor and City Council Members also heard about the rumors too. They also wanted me to do something about the problem.

Believe it or not, I actually had one person come into my office to talk to me about problems in the community. The next thing I know, he was calling some of officers' crooks. I told him if he had any information or evidence of criminal behavior, that I would initiate an internal investigation. He then stated, "You guys would not do anything anyway." He then went off on a tangent and asked, "How come we do not have a Hispanic police chief." It kind of stunned me for a second because he went from crooked police officers to a Hispanic police chief. I politely told him the city council made the decision and selected me. The next thing I said to him was that it is time for him to leave. I was not going to accept being insulted by him or anyone else.

A few bad apples in the police department can wreck havoc with the reputation of the police department. Doing nothing or ignoring drug dealers is sometimes perceived by the community as serious misconduct. Perhaps it was only a perception because of the amount of drug trafficking in the community. Rumor had it that drug dealers had a free reign in the community. Maybe the officers did not have probable cause at the time. It was hard for me to believe that officers would ignore the obvious. Some serious questions had been raised, however. If I were to make some impact in the community, I would have to set about the task to resolve them.

Every time I managed police departments there were always questions about morale and integrity of the police officers. I believe one of my strong points is the ability to clean up a problem-ridden department. I wanted to change the negative public image of the department. Take it from me, no matter how bad a department appears from a public perception standpoint, it can be turned around. It might take some time but it can be done.

There can be no question that the police chief must keep his own house in order first. It cannot be "do as I say, not as I do" mentality. It is very difficult to enforce the law when police officers are breaking the law themselves. It is more like a double standard in the community.

Using the Media

There is no police chief I know that likes to air his or her dirty laundry. Every time the media found out about police misconduct they would be knocking at the chief's door to get answers to their questions. My first inclination is to tell them absolutely nothing but I did come to my senses quickly. When a police chief keeps silent or refuses to make a comment it appears that he or she is trying to hide something. I try to provide enough information for them to write their story. Let us face it, if the reporter does not get the facts from you, then he or she will find another source. I would rather have the reporter get the facts right the first time.

Generally, when the reporter is looking into police misconduct, I never volunteer any information about the officer or incident. I allow the reporter to ask the question, limiting the scope and then I provide a limited answer. I always say the incident is under investigation. I try to minimize the damage and at the same time appear to the public that I am trying to get to the source of the matter.

Most of the time the police chief will not acknowledge one way or another whether there is an internal affairs investigation into misconduct or even state it is a personnel matter. I think police chiefs ought to rethink their position further and take the offensive. If no one knows about the internal affairs investigation that is one thing, but sooner or later, someone will find out and get in touch with his or her local news reporter. Every time I hear a police chief or City Manager say that he or she cannot say anything because it is a personnel matter, I think otherwise. The first thing comes to my mind is what are they trying to hide? I think that you have to avoid the perception that you are trying to hide something because it smells like a cover-up. The minute the media smells a cover-up they will be all over you like the plague.

As I recall, each time there was a major internal affairs investigation some how the media found out about it. I was not surprised when they came knocking on my door. The last major incident in my last community, Fort Lupton, Colorado involved my investigator who took cocaine from the evidence room and used on and off the premises as I had earlier stated. This made me think long and hard about the possibility of cops tipping off the drug dealers. It was not long before I got a call from the media asking me questions about the investigation. This was an embarrassing moment for the police department and community. I knew that it would make headlines all over the state. Do not underestimate for a minute that you can hide these investigations from the media for long. When I was asked, I released the bare minimum amount of details and prefaced it with the incident was still under investigation. I told the public that we would do everything possible to uncover the truth. This bought me more time but I knew they would be back later to find out what I did. When the investigation had been completed, the community knew what action I had taken. The officer's employment with the city had been terminated and the criminal investigation by the sheriff's office was on going. Eventually it was reported the officer had been arrested by the sheriff's office. Actually the media made the department look good because of the action that I had taken. It was an opportunity for me to send a strong message about using and selling drugs in the community. Use of drugs by anyone including officers would not be tolerated and strong enforcement action would be initiated. The community and the City Council liked my response to the media and strong message. I took a hard stance against drug abuse. The negative news turned into a positive message to the community.

I handled the media the same way in my other departments as well. Sometimes I got lucky and the media did not find out about these incidents outside the community. Take for example: when my officer became involved in a DUI incident with a known prostitute in his truck in Phoenix, Arizona. This officer's actions could have been a very embarrassing incident for local law enforcement community. However, the incident was handled very low keyed and gratefully there were no inquires this time. If they were to ask me questions about the incident then I would have been truthful about this ordeal.

Even after I left Florence, Arizona the police chief who replaced me had several rocky bouts with the media. He had to handle questions regarding the complaint against him by his officers about favoritism and discrimination and to make matters worse, a shooting incident involving one of his officers.   After reading of the accounts in the media, it looks like the media had a field day with him. He even got the Town Manager involved in addressing the media. He was unprepared to answer the questions posed by the media. All and all, the situation could have been better handled. It appeared the police department was trying to hide something. One of the officers shot an alleged fleeing felon from an apartment complex under construction. While we are on the subject, the apparent action may have been a violation of the department's use of force policy and State Statute. All the officers were well aware of a United States Supreme Court decision in the matter of **Tennessee v. Garner**, 471 U.S. 1 (1985) when it was permissible to shot at a fleeing felon. The following is what the Supreme Court ruled:

> *"Where the officer has probable cause to believe that the suspect poses a threat of serious physical harm, either to the officer or to others, it is not constitutionally unreasonable to prevent escape by using deadly force." Thus, if the suspect threatens the officer with a weapon or there is probable cause to believe that he has committed a crime involving the "infliction or threatened infliction of serious physical harm", the use of deadly force is permissible. If the officer does not have probable cause to believe the above, reasonable, non-deadly force must be used to affect the arrest.*

I wanted to go into detail about the Supreme Court decision to point out that a series of inaccurate statements can lead to further trouble. Sometimes it is best not to say anything in situation when a police officer is evidently wrong only to the extent the incident is under investigation. If you do not know or you are not sure about the details just say so. If you guess, you might regret your statement later on. Sooner or later, the real truth will come out. Shooting incidents can be rather tricky. Before you release information of shooting events, make sure you know all the facts and that the city or town attorney had a chance to review the town or city's response. The real issue: Did the officer know about the use of force police and in particular, the requirements for a fleeing felon situation? He knew about it because he had been trained on the use of force policy. Did the officer fear for his life? If this was the case then the officer would be justified in using deadly force. Of course this point never came out because the town council had stated they had never approved the Department's General Orders. It seemed that there was a great deal of confusion because the police chief never revised the general orders that I had previously written.   Incidentally, the Town Attorney had previously approved the orders involving liability including the use of force. If the reporter had been more diligent and asked more questions in the community, he would have uncovered the real truth. As it was the case, he only got part of the truth. The reporter did not realize how close he came to breaking a bigger story.

I think that you can agree honesty is the best policy. I did not lie to the media and if they asked a question that I did not want to respond to, I would just say, "I can not answer this question because this matter is still under investigation."

The best way to learn how to deal with the media is to look at the styles of other police chiefs to see how each handled the situation. When I was in Somersworth, New Hampshire I learned very quickly. Of course, my captains would advise me not to tell the media anything. If I had listened to them the media would have eaten me up alive. I wanted to be honest and forthright with the media. I wanted to project an open and honest image to the public and I was going to use the media to help me do it. It was important to me to regain the trust that had been lost long ago. I wanted to project an image of confidence and leadership not only to my police department but to the community as well. The community had to trust someone and I wanted it to be me.

I observed enough police chiefs around the county and state to know which ones handled the media very well in all kinds of situations. The ones who handled the media poorly, found themselves in difficulty, not only with their council members or selectman but the community. At first I did not feel very comfortable in dealing with the media because Bristol, Connecticut did not prepare me for my new role. I made up my mind long ago that I was going to be truthful with the media. Getting caught in a lie is a fatal error that could accelerate your departure very quickly. Over time and with each media situation I encountered or experienced, I became very accustomed to speaking officially to the media. In addition, you get to personally know the reporters in your area and likewise they get to know you. Even when they made minor mistakes in a news article, I did not call their editor to print a retraction. I think I had a mutual respectful relationship with all the reporters. I can honestly say they treated me fairly over the years.

A police chief gets burnt when he or she tries to pull a fast one or tries to deceive the reporter. Saying information "off the record" to qualify an earlier statement may be acceptable but it all depends upon the relationship with the reporter. The rule is if you do not want to see it in print, do not say it. When you read about an undisclosed source it may in fact mean someone close to the investigation or the police chief who has first hand knowledge about the incident.

The City Manager and City Council Members do not like to be surprised from reading about the serious misconduct or corruption in the newspaper or see it on the TV nightly news. Sometimes police chiefs forget to keep elected officials informed and some problems could develop from it. I always made it a point to bring the City Manager and City Council Members up to speed regarding an incident.

In the eyes of the public, the police chief will look better if it appears he or she is doing something about misconduct and corruption in their community. Saying nothing may imply another message too. It may seem as though the department is covering up the incident or the alleged incident was acceptable. It is an opportunity to send a message to the community as well to the members of the police department that there will be zero tolerance towards any type of police misconduct or corruption.

The following is a quick guide when the media inquires about police misconduct or corruption:

- Be ready to answer questions by the media.
- Seek the advice of other Police Chiefs you know and respect
- Have a brief statement ready.
- Above all be <u>honest.</u>
- Only release information when absolutely necessary but hold back information critical to the investigation.
- Watch what you say "off the record," it could get you into trouble.
- It is better you do not say anything "off the record."
- Keep your City Manager and/or City Council informed. They do not like the surprise of reading about it in the newspaper.
- Upon conclusion of the investigation if, you are asked by the media tell them the action you took.
- Keep Smiling.

Preventing Police Misconduct & Corruption

Police departments often times take the persona of the police chief. The men and women of the department will carry out the will of the police chief or supervisor. If the chief, supervisor or manager hides in the office and ignores the minor transgression by the police officer, then they will assume the wrongdoings are satisfactory. There is no police chief or executive that I know who is fond of personnel problems. It is a fact of life. However, if you have personnel working for you, there will be problems and the more personnel in the department, the more problems there will be. The police chief or leader cannot ignore these problems and tribulations can certainly escalate out of control.

The philosophy of the police chief is very important. It sets the tone for the rest of the department. I consider myself a fair and honest person but, at the same time, I do not tolerate police misconduct or corruption. I had set the tone in each of my three departments about my philosophy during my first week. Often when a City or Town hires a new police chief, most of the time the agency will go outside the department. The person coming into the department is not known, so it seems more credible to convey a new philosophy. It is not to say the inside candidate for the police chief position is not competent but everyone knows him or her. Who knows what skeletons that the person may be hiding? By doing things this way, the town fathers bring in a new face and fresh ideas. I think it is much easier to convey the message, which will set the groundwork for the new policing philosophy. It is critical that the chief discuss police misconduct and corruption early on. I always told my personnel there would be zero tolerance. All zero tolerance cases brought to my attention or discovered by me ultimately would be investigated. This way, my personnel knew right up front how I felt about police misconduct and corruption.

Establish the Internal Affairs Function

I think a **policy and procedure on Internal Affairs Investigation has to be written or revised and put into the policy manual**. Not only this policy and procedure but also all the policies in the policy manual need to be reviewed and revised as soon as possible. If the department does not have a policy manual, one needs to be put together one as soon as possible. I consider this the bible of the police department, the nuts and bolts, so to speak. It is only fair that your personnel know what is to be expected in different situations. If you borrow a policy and procedure from another department, like many others do, then make sure you revise it according to your needs. Nothing irks me more than various departments copying another order without making any changes. How lazy can you be? There has to be some modifications because each department is different and unique in its own way.

Each time I developed a **comprehensive order for the Internal Affairs Function**. Even though I did not have a separate function, I designated my lieutenant, the 2nd in command to be responsible for the function. When I was a captain with the Bristol Police Department I was in charge of the Support Services Bureau along with a separate function for internal affairs investigations. Do not make the mistake like many chiefs and executives by conducting the investigation themselves. It does not matter who you put in charge as long as you have confidence in their ability to do a good job. The police chief needs to review the investigation and decide on the next course of action. It does not make sense for the chief to conduct the investigation, review the results and also decide on the punishment. It is like the chief being the judge, jury and executioner. There needs to be an appearance of fairness and I am sure you would agree.

I keep referring back to the chief who had replaced me in Florence, Arizona because he provides an excellent example what I am mentioning. He took away the investigative function that I had assigned the lieutenant and decided to do many of the investigations himself and in some cases assigned to his investigator. He did the investigation and decided what the punishment would be. He did this all without changing the general orders. Guess who knew that he was not following the policy and procedure? You guess it, his personnel. He never bothered to change any of the orders except by deleting my name and adding his. The moral of the story is being smart and do it right.

The following is a brief excerpt of Chapter 14, The Internal Affairs Function of the Fort Lupton Police Department that I had rewritten and put into effect stating clearly the policy statement or philosophy and outlining part of the procedure:

Internal Affairs Function

The policy of the Fort Lupton Police Department shall be to investigate all types of complaints and alleged serious misconduct against police employees. The investigation of these complaints through standardized procedures demonstrates the department's desire to provide honest, efficient police service and inspire public confidence. The department calls for the assumption of innocence until a preponderance of evidence indicates misconduct, the fair and impartial investigation of all complaints and allegations of misconduct; and a progressive, positive disciplinary process that mitigates and eliminates continuing inappropriate behavior.

Procedure

The Internal Affairs Function shall be established to conduct and/or supervise investigations in the following circumstances and/or situations:

- *When an allegation or complaint of serious misconduct is made against the department, its members or employees.*
- *In any breach or suspected breach of integrity of the department, including but not limited to violations of the law by members and/or employees, the compromise in any case which the department is involved, the unauthorized release of confidential information, and matters of a similar nature.*
- *In any case in which a Fort Lupton Police Officer has been killed or injured by the willful or deliberate act of*

another person.

- *In any case in which a person has been killed or injured by the willful or deliberate act of a Fort Lupton Police Officer, whether on duty or off duty.*
- *In any case which involves allegations by another employee of the police department or other town employee?*
- *In assisting any member or employee of the department by investigating cases of personal harassment, threats, and/or contrived situations which could be harmful to the interests of the employees involved.*
- *When assistance is indicated to aid other police agencies, whether Federal, State, County, or municipal in which there is an investigation of a police employee in illegal activity.*
- *To research and gather information for the city when the city is enjoined in a lawsuit involving the actions of police employees; and to render similar assistance when a civil suit is brought for damages allegedly incurred through the actions of a police employee.*
- *To undertake the investigation of any matter at the direction of the Chief of Police.*

Generally, Internal Investigations, and those upgraded from the routine complaints against police personnel, shall be investigated primarily by the Operations Commander under the direction of the Chief of Police.

- *Complaints investigated under the provisions of these procedures shall be confidential in nature, and may be reviewed only with the permission of the Chief of Police.*

- *Generally, violations of the rules and regulations observed in the supervisor's presence or minor infractions discovered by the supervisor or division commander will be handled in accordance with the disciplinary procedures. Nothing in this procedure shall prevent a supervisor or Division Commander from invoking an emergency suspension in special circumstances or instituting disciplinary action when deemed necessary and appropriate. Any questions or conflicts as to the seriousness or type of investigation procedure shall be resolved by the Chief of Police.*

The employee under investigation will be issued a written Notification by the Chief of Police that will include:

- *the Allegations*
- *Employees' Rights & Responsibility Requirements*

The above policy and procedure reflects my philosophy and conveys to the employee what it is, the types of investigation, under which circumstances and who is responsible for the investigation. There is even a written notification by the chief when an employee is the subject of an internal investigation. In addition, later in the order the employees' rights during an investigation are clearly stated. Even though I wanted to set an example for others to see that police misconduct will not be tolerated, I also wanted to make sure my personnel had every opportunity for a defense and explanation of his or her actions. I did not want to give the appearance of a kangaroo court-like atmosphere.

Enforce the Policies and the Rules & Regulations

If you are serious about doing internal investigations, then you have to insure that the department's policy, rules and regulations of the police department and the personnel rules of the city are followed. It may seem insignificant to you but you have to investigate minor violations of the rules and regulations and **be consistent**. There is nothing that gets an employee more upset than getting called on the carpet for something and when someone else does the same thing nothing happens. You have to be careful about the appearance of favoritism. If this is the case, then there is going to be a problem with credibility. My goal is to treat everyone as equals and at the same time being fair with the employee.

Before I get into the specifics on how the investigations will be conducted, I wanted to relate to you a true story about one investigation that I started within a short time after taking over the Fort Lupton Police Department. One officer brought to my attention that a sergeant who had been close friends with the former chief had been accumulating and using earned compensation time that he had not earned. It appeared there had been a fraudulent use of earned compensation time. When I discovered this, I called the Weld County Sheriff and asked him if his investigator could conduct a criminal investigation in the fraudulent accumulation and use of earned compensation time. I might add that the response was almost immediate. Before I knew it, the investigator was knocking at my door. I explained the problem and he immediately commenced a criminal investigation. The sergeant was officially notified that he was under investigation and he was more than cooperative with the Weld County Investigator. At the same time my lieutenant conducted the administrative part of the investigation. At this point the investigation became bifurcated; one being the criminal and the other part the administrative. Anything derived from the criminal can be used for the administrative but any incriminating evidence derived from the administrative cannot be used for the criminal investigation. It is two separate and distinct processes. The sergeant was advised of his Garrity Warnings for the administrative investigation and signed a form acknowledging this. The following is a brief explanation to illustrate the point of the Garrity Warning:

> *The phrase derives from a 1967 U.S. Supreme Court decision related to employee rights. It is a warning given by an employer to an employee during an employment investigation that includes:*
>
> - *Requiring the employee to answer questions related to their employment or risk disciplinary action, and the consequences for failing to do so could result in job loss for refusing to comply.*
>
> - *Assuring the employee that information gained under the threat of job loss will not be used against that employee in a criminal proceeding.*

After the criminal investigation had been completed, there appeared to be many discrepancies but not enough to rise to the threshold to warrant a criminal complaint. Apparently there were enough doubts whether he intended to defraud the city and it appeared the fraud was committed with the full consent of the chief. The former chief was not available, so my lieutenant could not ask him some key questions regarding the department's policy on earned compensation time at the time. It appeared that much of the time earned was not recorded anywhere as it should have been. Because there was some doubt about the intent and there had been some obvious violations of department and city rules, that it was necessary for me to only suspend him for 40 hours without pay and forfeit 40 hours vacation time. The employee acknowledged that the punishment was fair and that was the end of this episode. Matter of fact he asked me, "Chief do you want me to resign?" I told him no, it would not be necessary. In my mind this matter had been concluded. I gave him the benefit of the doubt. This employee became a productive and valuable asset to me. I never regretted giving him a break.

There was another incident involving the former court clerk in Fort Lupton. She had been in charge of a program called Shape-up, a program geared towards the youth. It involved taking selected youth to a prison for a specialized program for juveniles at risk. I will go into the specifics of the program later because it was definitely worth discussing. The City

Administrator had terminated her for other reasons and he turned the program over to me to administrate. The program depended upon funds from donations, the city, school and parents. There appeared to be some discrepancies in the accounting of the funds. After seeing there was a possible embezzlement of funds, I contacted the Colorado State Bureau of Investigation. The agent reviewed the documentation and had many questions himself. This case was still pending further review when I left Colorado in 1999.

Even though the city had very good accounting, the problem develops when the employee solicits additional funds. There is always a potential for abuse when one person is handling the money and there is no check and balances. After the program was turned over to me, I developed a better way to account for the donations. It never ceases to amaze me how many times people get into trouble over a small amount of money. It is just too easy to pocket the money **when there is no official control over the funds.** When there are checks and balances in place there is less opportunity for abuse.

I always made it a practice to **never** personally handle any money. In Florence, Arizona there was no petty cash fund at the police department. If funds were needed, all one had to do was make a request to the Finance Office. Actually, it was not very cumbersome. When the other police chief took over the reins of the department, he reinstated the petty cash fund. Problems developed when too many hands dipped into the fund. There was no control person. In Fort Lupton, Colorado, my secretary was responsible for the petty cash fund. The expenditures had to have a receipt in order for the officer to be reimbursed for a minor expense. The intent of the petty cash fund was to make minor purchases and not to circumvent the purchasing system in the Finance Office. The system worked very smoothly and there were rarely any discrepancies. I would personally check over the record each month before reimbursing the petty cash fund.

If you are made aware of police misconduct or corruption, you need to initiate an investigation when there are violations of the rules and regulations even for minor violations. If your personnel know that you mean business then the potential for abuse will be much less. In other words, if they know you will do something then they will not do it, plain and simple.

Inspections - Keeping Everyone Honest

How can a police chief or manager effectively prevent police misconduct and corruption? I say it can be done through inspections to keep everyone honest. **Supervisors and personal inspections by the police chief is the key to prevention.** Everyone has to be actively involved from the Chief all the way down to the police officers. You and I know police officers are reluctant to inform on another officer because of the blue wall of silence. They should report conduct that officers recognize as being definitely wrong. All the supervisors should be checking, but the most important of all the supervisors is the sergeant in the field. The sergeants develop a rapport with their officers and they will usually follow his example. If he or she is lax, then that attitude will be conveyed. If some minor misconduct is acceptable then the officers will do what ever it is according to the norm.

One famous is example was the Rodney King incident. Everyone by now is well aware what happened. Mr. King received a severe beating by the Los Angeles Police Officers that was video taped. There were other police departments that were involved in the high-speed pursuit that culminated into a gang type beating. When I first saw it on the televised news, I was in a state of shock. I could not believe that police officers could give such a severe beating to another human being without killing him. When it was all said and done, a number of police officers were disciplined and some were charge with a crime. One sergeant and an officer were convicted of a civil rights violation in Federal Court. In addition the City of Los Angeles and the police department was sued and had to pay a judgment in the millions of dollars.

The officers rationalized that they had to use this force in order to subdue Rodney King. I think and many others have the same opinion that the force used went way beyond reasonable. These guys were way out of control. Hey, this was a common sense issue. People who saw the videotape were not fooled and neither was the jury in Federal Court. They almost killed the guy. Where was the sergeant who was at the scene? He was standing around with all the others watching the beating take place. He did nothing to stop it. The real issue was this type of behavior condoned on a regular basis by the supervisors on the night shift. It appears that they had not problem beating Mr. King with the supervisor present. How often did these or other officers administer the night shift justice? I will submit to you that this culture evolved on the night shift as normal behavior by officers. The **supervisor has to be held accountable** for the actions of his or her officers.

If the supervisors had done their job long ago to begin with - by disciplining officers who abused citizens - then the Rodney King incident would never have occurred. It was a situation that had gotten out of control very quickly. Who knows what might have happened if the video camera had not been there and how long this situation would have gone on?

The supervisors need to be held accountable in the chain of command. The chief needs to make a point that discipline will be taken against a supervisor if he or she should have known there was police misconduct or corruption and failed to take action

Many police departments still rotate their shifts while many other adhere to the seniority rule. Staying on one shift too long with the same officers could be a problem and can lead to police misconduct and corruption. One can get stagnant being on a shift for so long. There are always discussions of how long one should stay on one shift. The answer is whatever works best in your situation. I have had departments rotate their shifts from one to three months. Rotating shifts is better all the way around because the officer will be exposed to various types of activity on each shift. It is not good to keep all the rookies on one shift. There should be a blend of the new to the more experienced on each shift. Shift rotation is easier, especially when it comes to supervision and the chief will sleep better at night.

Another tool that is available to the supervisor is drug testing. Years ago, it was unheard of to have a police applicant take a drug test as part of his or her pre-employment physical. Today, however, it is the norm with the widespread drug use all across the country. It became even more apparent to have more than just the pre-employment or just cause when my investigator in Fort Lupton, Colorado became addicted to cocaine. If you recall, he was the officer who took cocaine from the evidence room and using on and off the premises. As part of the investigation by the Weld County Sheriff's Office, the officer was ordered to take a drug test. The drug test came back from the lab with a positive result. This was no big surprise because he admitted drug use, but the drug test was part of the investigation.

Because drug use in any organization is a real problem, **I developed a random drug testing policy that was approved by the City Administrator and the City Council and put into effect.** The policy was easier to implement because there was no police union. The following is the policy statement for **Random Drug Testing** that I used in Fort Lupton:

It is the policy of the City of Fort Lupton that the critical mission of local

government and law enforcement justifies maintenance of a drug free work environment through the use of a reasonable employee drug testing program. The public has a right to expect that those who are sworn to protect them and those civilians who work with them is at all times both mentally and physically prepared to assume their duties. There is sufficient evidence to conclude that the use of controlled substances and other forms of drug abuse will seriously impair an employee's physical and mental abilities, and thus their job performance.

If local government employees and public safety employees participate in illegal drug use and/or drug activity the integrity of the City Government and Law Enforcement professional is threatened. Public confidence is further weakened by the potential for corruption created by drug use.

Therefore, the City of Fort Lupton shall maintain a drug testing program to detect illegal drug use.

Those of you who have a union may have to negotiate this provision because they will say it will be a change in their working conditions. I say it is a management prerogative. Your legal counsel for the city or town can advise you accordingly. The policy was first implemented in the police department and later expanded to citywide. The policy and procedure explained how it will be done and the selection process used. It stated that two employees a month would be randomly selected to undergo the test. The key is random. If you select the same individuals all the time without going through a process, then it is no longer random. Matter of fact, it would be discriminating against certain employees. Each department employee and later expanded citywide was assigned a number. The numbers were computer generated using a computer program at different times of the month. There are probably other programs that will do the same thing. Sometimes it was done in the beginning, the middle or end of the month so that the employee could not predict a pattern. The days of the week varied as well.

When a person's number came up he or she was tested and the specimen was sent to the lab. The turn around on the results was usually one or two days. Even though some employees' numbers came up for two consecutive months there were no complaints. It is the luck of the draw and my personnel understood the way it worked because I had explained it to them. When my number came up in the computer program I was tested for drugs, as well as everyone else. I wanted everyone to know and made a point that the policy included the police chief too. No one was going to be exempt, including me. The policy would not have worked if I had made excuses that it was not meant for me or I was too busy. If it was good enough for my personnel, it was good enough for me. As the leader, I felt it was my duty to set the example.

The program ran smoothly but there could be some drawbacks. If you forget to do the unannounced drug testing then it could lead to some problems. Even with everything going on you have to schedule some time for it. It is too important to forget about. **The key is consistency with any policy**.

Training

The last part of the equation in the fight against police misconduct and corruption is training. There has to be on-going training that involves all personnel. Everyone needs to be reminded of the implication of misconduct and corruption and the long reaching consequences. If the community is to maintain their trust and support of their police department, the community need to know their local police department is corruption free and are doing everything possible to keep it that way.

Training, using the Law Enforcement Code of Ethics as a guide, will serve as a basis for other advanced training. Ethics must be included in recruitment, in-service and roll call training. Even a 10 minute message during the roll call will go a long way in combating police misconduct and corruption. The message needs to be continually reinforced.

In summary, the most effective way for the police chief and other leaders to effectively control police misconduct and corruption is the leadership example that he or she exhibits and the levels of accountability that are in place. The police chief is the key and the chief as well as the supervisory must set the example for everyone to follow.

Chapter 12
Citizen Complaints

Because of the nature of our business is dealing with people problems, people are going to complain. Problems seemed inevitable. Making people happy all the time is virtually impossible. The reason I do not get too upset when people complain about police officers is that complaints could be anything from a misunderstanding, miscommunication or people were not very happy with their service they received by the police officer. Many complaints originated from negative police contacts. I can not think of anyone who likes to be stopped by the police and get a ticket for a traffic violation. The focal point of this section will be to better understand the dynamics of complaints and how to handle them.

The reason why people get upset and complain much of the time is the lack of empathy and understanding by some police officers. I cannot tell you how many times a person did not like the officer's attitude or he or she was rude. Often times the officer's negative demeanor might be the cause of the complaint, while other times it may be a perception or a mechanism of the citizen to get some attention. Often complaints are unfound or simply not true. However, I remember a few officers were outright rude and some even went as far as belittling citizens. There were many citizen complaints after someone was arrested. In my mind the people file complaints in the hopes of having their criminal or motor vehicle violations dismissed by the court. This seemed to be the case in Fort Lupton, Colorado. I suspected that many people prevailed with this tactic when they complained to the prior police chief. This tactic did not work with me. Their criminal or traffic case would still go to court, while I would tell the citizen their complaint would be investigated. Of course, most complainants would be looking to have their case dismissed. The greater majority of complaints against police officers were rudeness.

It seemed many complainants lined up at the door in Fort Lupton, Colorado to make a complaint against a police officer. I truly did not have to remind people they could make a complaint if they felt like they were not getting the service or were not being treated properly. My concern was for everyone to be treated with respect at all times. This was not too much to ask of officers. The complaints seemed to zero in on one or two officers all the time. It appeared to me after checking into the complaints that the officers were only trying to do their job.

This reminded me of a situation as captain in Bristol, Connecticut. Some officers would never have complaints lodged against them. After being captain for so long, the answer was simple: the officers did not do anything to get themselves into trouble because they would take the path of least resistance. There was never any pressure put on these guys to do their job. One lieutenant use to joke around, but was serious about the motor vehicle statistics. This officer related to other officers in the department after averaging the total monthly motor vehicles arrests amounted to a quarter of an arrest per man per month. These statistics from 100 officers in the police department were pathetic. Now when you think about this, there were quite a few officers who were not doing anything at all, while only a few officers like myself, would make a number of motor vehicle arrests per month. Which officers do you think received the complaint? You guessed it - the officers doing the work. One citizen complained about me targeting high school children speeding on the main thoroughfare from the high school. The captain called me into his office and talked to me about the complaint. I could hardly believe my ears. It was like I had a crystal ball on the radar unit telling me who were the high school children and who were not. I knew the captain had to talk to me so he could report back to the person who made the complaint. Who do you think sent me to the vicinity of the school to run radar because of a speeding problem? It was management. I went back the next day in the vicinity of the high school to run radar again. I never heard anything more of that complaint. Some citizens were complaining because I was doing my job. These citizens forgot the real reason I was there was to slow down the traffic so the young motorists would not get into an accident. Traffic safety was the main concern.

Keeping in mind what I had gone through when I was a patrolman, I wanted to convey the message to officers that people are going to complain whether you do your job or not. Either way, people will complain. Some people complained about certain officers using unethical tactics. It was obvious many times when a complaint was made by a reputed drug dealer who wanted to shift the heat somewhere else. The officers were just starting to make a dent in the drug trafficking in the community. Officers, including myself, were starting to see the results and the people were more comfortable in the community. Along with the hard approach against drugs, there would naturally be more complaints against police officers. You cannot have it both ways. If the officers are doing their job there will be complaints. The trick is to ensure they are doing the job right and not infringing upon any rights of the citizens. Officers have to comply with the law and the crooks do not...yea right.

I informed officers to do whatever it takes to do their job and keep the streets safe. I told officers not to worry about the complaints because complaints were my concern. I also told the officers that I would not be calling them into my office each time to chew them out just because a citizen made a complaint. In my way of thinking, the officer is not automatically wrong, like the way some police chiefs think. I must have said the right words because all the officers responded in a positive way. Every two or three days, officers were making good drug busts. You see, the officers were limited in the amount of discretion used after stopping a motor vehicle. Officers had to call their supervisors even if there was probable cause to search the vehicle. Sometimes a supervisor was not immediately available. The process was too time consuming and cumbersome for the officers. After a period of frustration, the officers did not bother to stop motor vehicles unless absolutely necessary. The motor vehicle arrest went up about 200% and so did drug arrests. Imagine a correlation between motor vehicle stops and drug seizures. I conveyed that patrol officers do the majority of good drug busts after a motor vehicle stop for a moving traffic violation. I was truly proud of the way the officers had responded. Everyone was happy with the results including the Mayor and City Council members. Each had originally directed me to do something about drugs in the community. We were beginning to make an impact.

Just to make sure everything was running smoothly and citizen's rights were not violated, I personally reviewed each report and made periodic inspections out in the field. Officers under my command would never know when I would show up. Many times these inspections occurred during the late evening hours. Actually, I was impressed with the way the officers professionally conducted themselves. The officers were experienced and each was well aware of the search and seizure laws.

In the three departments I managed, I made a concerted effort to investigate all citizen complaints. Any time a citizen was dissatisfied with any services by the police department; my philosophy is to find out why. **Encourage citizens to make a complaint if dissatisfied and each would be investigated.** My lieutenant, 2nd in command would coordinate investigations. Either he or a sergeant would investigate a citizen's complaint and file a report reporting their finding. **The last part would be a response to the citizen and a letter written outlining their complaint and the results of the investigation.** If the officer was at fault, an apology on behalf of the department was made and the citizen was reassured that the police would try harder next time. About 90% of the times, the officer conducted himself or herself properly. Complaints were usually found not sustained or unfounded. I was not surprised because people will misplace the truth to get out of going to court or pay a fine.

Oops, You're on Tape!

There was another time in Somersworth, New Hampshire a citizen complained that one of my officers was rude to her in the police lobby. Now, if you knew this officer like I did, the complaint could be true. He said, "Chief, I was nice to her." This is one time where the ultimate decision had to be based on he said, she said. In the police lobby there was a sign in large letters, "Notice, All Conversation Recorded." I would like to add that this was perfectly legal to record conversations as long as the public was put on notice. Of course this may vary from state to state so you might want to check with your town or city legal council. This was an easy investigation because all we had to do was play the tape to see what was exactly said. The tape was very clear and it proved that, if anyone was rude, it was the complainant herself. The officer was calm and polite for a change. It was nice to know he handled himself very nicely.   I called the complainant after the investigation was completed and asked her to come to the police department to talk to me. When she came into my office and took a seat I asked her to listen to the tape. Her expression said it all. She knew at that point she had been caught. In so far as I was concerned, this was the end of the case.

Now, there are some people who just will not go away even when they are dead wrong. One long time resident, who was friendly with one of the council members that did not care for me, made a complaint that officers were harassing his son. Now, his son was an adult and should have made the complaint. Nevertheless, I agreed to look into the complaint. The complaint was assigned to my captain and he investigated the complaint. He reported that the officer in question stopped this person's son for an equipment violation. The windows of his vehicle were tinted in violation of state law. There was no doubt in my mind about the violation. Anyone could see the windows in the car were too dark   Even though the father was informed that the officer was doing his duty and the action took was correct, this individual was adamant that the police were wrong. The father just would not take no for an answer. I told the father that I could call the Department of Motor Vehicle (DMV) Inspector to check the vehicle for a violation and we would abide by their decision. I already knew it was a violation and the law was clear about it. The Motor Vehicle Inspector only took about two minutes to arrive at the same conclusion. The citizen even argued with inspector too. Even after all these years it is still funny to think about that argument between the DMV Inspector and the father. The DMV inspector thought we had set him up. Some people you cannot please no matter what you do. No doubt, the father reported back to the council member that officers were harassing his son. This one was a no win situation and I was satisfied each officers had done the right thing.

Quality Service

My intent was to focus on **customer service**. The concept is simply to provide quality service to the citizen.   It is not something new; the private sector had been doing it for a long time and why not the public sector? I increased public awareness regarding complaints about police services by using the media to get my message out. In addition, I **developed a brochure that outlines department philosophy and the process involved in the investigation of citizen complaints.** Each citizen making a complaint would be given a brochure outlining what was to be expected during an investigation. It also detailed the citizen's responsibility. It was only fair to put on notice a person who comes forward with a false complaint. If a false complaint could be proven then he or she could be charged with a misdemeanor. At first, the officers thought I was trying to solicit complaints but this simply was not the case. The officers in Somersworth, New Hampshire were more suspicious because of their involvement with the dreaded union. After I explained what I was doing by letting the **public know that the department had a complaint process in place** and that we would probably not receive a sudden influx of complaints. It was true we were not bombarded with complaints. The personnel in all departments like the clause about taking action against anyone making a false complaint.

It was just the opposite in Florence, Arizona. There were virtually no complaints at all. I thought it was a little strange that there was no documentation about any complaints. I thought it would be proper to advise the people in the community that they could make a complaint against a police officer if they were dissatisfied with the service or with the way they were treated. I wrote about citizen complaints in my weekly column for the Florence Reminder. The following the text of the article:

The Complaint

*The citizen complaint has always been an area of concern for law enforcement. Citizens wonder what would actually happen if they would make a complaint against the police officer. Would the police suddenly retaliate against them or would the police just go through the motions? Will there be a cover up? These are all valid concerns. However, I approached citizen complaints as a break down in service, misunderstanding or our fault where we just "dropped the ball." Yes, we, the police are human too and can make mistakes. I have instituted a procedure whereby a citizen who is dissatisfied in any way can make a citizen's complaint. **The goal is to improve services, and we need to know the problem so that we can correct the problem. If we do not know there is a problem, then we cannot take measures to make it right.** There will not be any cover-ups nor will we just go through the motions. Every complaint will be assigned and investigated.*

A citizen who in their opinion was not treated fairly, or properly and with no respect, or not satisfied in the way a criminal arrest, traffic stop or an incident was handled by a police officer can make a citizen's complaint in person, or by telephone. We will even meet with the complainant at a different location. We will ask the complainant to give a written statement and name witnesses, if any. We will even investigate an anonymous complaint in so far as giving it a cursory look to see if any laws have been violated. Not that we are soliciting complaints, but it is important to know if we are doing anything wrong. You should keep in mind that the police are only as good as the information they get.

If we receive a citizen's complaint, I will **assign a control number and write a letter of acknowledgment to the citizen.** *The complaint will be assigned to the patrol sergeant or Operations Commander depending upon the severity. The usual time line for an investigation is about two weeks. Upon completion of the investigation the complaint will be given the following classification:*

- *Unfounded: The allegation is false or not factual.*

- *Exonerated: The incident complained of occurred, but the accused member's actions were lawful and proper.*

- *Not Sustained: Insufficient evidence to either prove or disprove the allegation.*

- *Sustained: The allegation is supported by sufficient evidence.*

- *Partially Sustained: Allegation partially supported by evidence.*

I will **write the citizen a letter as to the outcome of the investigation, and outline what we will do to prevent another occurrence.**

I was attempting to briefly outline our citizen's complaint procedure. Hopefully, you will see that I am serious about improving not only the quality of service, but also the quality of life in the Town of Florence. As always, if you have any questions please feel free to call me or simply stop by to say hello.

The article in the newspaper helped somewhat but Florence was by far a strange community. There had to be some dissatisfaction about something. There were very few complaints. The rumor mill thrived in the community and even more so because it was a small close-knit community. What set this community apart from the others were the political dynamics. Florence generally received their influx of winter visitors, also known as the "snow birds" beginning to arrive in November. Some of these people eventually stayed year around and became involved in politics. They began to wield some of their power. There was a power struggle between the people on the hill or "snow birds" and the town's people. You would think people who were retired would not want to get involved but there were a few power hungry people. There was always a struggle between these two factions. They were so into their own world that they thrived on every little rumor in the community. Rather than go to the source of the problem and ask questions, some chose to believe their source.

I brought up this problem with the rumors at this point because the council members would come to me with their complaints about perceived problems with police service or a complaint against a police officer. This community was very difficult to read in this regard. It was kind of a no win situation for me. A constituent would complaint to a council member who would then complaint to me. I would discuss our complaint procedure but it seemed to fall on deaf ears. Members of council could not seem to distinguish between the concepts of second and third hand information or hearsay information and fact. The town council was their own worst enemy; they were ignoring the process.

Here is a good example of what I mean. Several council members were complaining about a particular officer harassing children in the downtown area. However, during my time in Florence no one actually came forward to register a citizen complaint about the officer. This officer almost single handedly reduced the vandalism in the downtown area. The complaints of vandalism went down to almost zero and the incidences of drinking and drug use in the downtown area was almost negligible. This officer and a few others did a very good job in resolving the problems in the downtown area. You would think the council members would be happy about the results. One or two commented that the children will just go out into a nearby secluded desert area to drink. The message was like - underage drinking is acceptable in their minds to drink in the downtown area. I thought to myself, "Are you kidding me?" I wondered which "planet" they were from. As a police chief or executive you will have to deal with behaviors and thought processes such as these.

Let's Party

There was one particular parking lot near the police department where the children congregated at night. During the evening hours, the children would yell, drink and smoke dope. It became so bad that a couple who live in a house bordering the parking lot went to a council meeting to register their complaint. It developed into something so horrific that these kids began throwing beer cans over the fence. I advised this couple to go before the town council to register their complaint. What a mistake that turned out to be. I could hardly believe my ears after listening to their complaint when one council member said, "You knew what it was like when you moved here." I could not believe it. The council members actually insinuated that it was perfectly all right to party in the parking lot and annoy the neighbors. Little did these citizens know that some of the children hanging out in the parking lot were children of some of the council members. I thought to myself, "What idiots." I actually felt embarrassed for this couple in the way the elected officials acted. Just imagine: these people are actually running the community. Now there are some good town managers and some bad ones. My town manager would just sit there and not comment at all. I guess public safety and keeping order went out the window. They were sending a different message to me about keeping order. I guess I could never figure them out.

I can understand why some people would not make a complaint. People believed then and now that their complaints would be heard by deaf ears. The town council was supportive of the efforts of the police department only when it did not affect their families and friends. Everyone else was fair game. This was hard to believe, but it was true. The people in the community knew this and everyone seemed to accept this fact. No one would come forward to do something about the situation. It was the status quo of the community.

There were some people who did make few complaints against police officers but there were few and far between. In the meantime the town council would continue to hear from the people in the community about some problems with the police. It was frustrating to me in trying to change their way of thinking. The council seemed to rely on rumors. Originally, when I had first moved to Florence there was a different town manager and town council. There was a sense of better compatibility, which was the reason why quite a bit of money was spent to bring me to Florence in the first place. The Florence community wanted to change the "good o' boy" system.

If you recall, the Town of Florence had a recall of the Mayor and three council members. A recall, if you are not familiar with the term, is where the voters petition to have another election against selected or all council members. Usually there is dissatisfaction among the voters and the new candidates solicit voters to obtain signatures on a petition to mandate a new election. A person does not have to wait for the regular election. It is expensive but some people do not care about the cost. This practice is popular out west and in particular, Arizona. To be honest with you, being from the East I never heard of the term until I arrived in Arizona. Three months later there was basically a new council with a completely different philosophy and their first course of action on their agenda was to fire the town manager. It was a shocking realization that anything can happen, especially when you were dealing with politics.

There are some managers who are truly good bosses. One manager once said, "Being a manager is easy, you surround yourself with quality staff." I always remembered those words. During my three months working for Bill Galletly, I found Bill to be one of the finest persons and one of the best managers I had ever worked for. Bill eventually found better working conditions and a home in Clinton, Oklahoma. I was happy for him. My only regret was not working for him longer. As a team, Bill and I could have done more for the community. Bill was a gentleman right to the bitter end, even when he thanked the council for giving him an opportunity to serve. In contrast, when the town council did not renew my contract, I was too shocked to say anything. Bill's vision was to make changes in Florence to better the community and some people did not want to change. The community resisted change that ultimately led to the recall. However, Bill did leave his mark in the community.   Most of Bill's ideas were incorporated and adopted by the recall town council.

My point is that many times the **political dynamics changes in mid-stream**. It is just a way of life in the political game. Originally, I was brought in to make changes, to create a system of fairness and provide equal treatment for the entire town's people.   Police officers were going to move far away from the "good o' boy" mentality. There was no longer going to be a protected few. The law was going to be applied equally and fairly, which was all together a different approach for this community.   I made a big point about creating an atmosphere that officers were catering to the public and more important, try harder to provide quality service to its citizenry. Along the same line, I wanted the community to complain if they are not pleased with police services. People were beginning to like the changes in Florence.   The change was different from what officers, citizens and councilmen alike had been accustomed to.

However, there was only one citizen person that would report complaints about suspected maltreatments of police officers.   This citizen was the mother of two brothers that officers often arrested for various crimes. The mother complained that officers were picking on her sons because they were black. My lieutenant conducted an investigation and did not find any evidence that the two boys were being singled out because of their race.   As a matter of fact, arrest charges usually varied from serious robbery and burglary to assault with a dangerous weapon.   Both were eventually sent to prison and they did not have to go very far. The prison complex was only about one mile away.   Apparently, there was no deterrent factor even though the prison system was nearby. The mother thought the police were still picking on the boys. These guys were always involved in something. One morning a four wheel all terrain vehicle was stolen from a nearby home. The ATV ended up in the backyard of the two boys who seemed always involved in criminal activity. No police action was taken because no one actually saw who drove the vehicle. It was obvious that one of the boys took the ATV and went for a ride on it. The boys were lucky this particular time because they got away with committing a criminal act.

Everything changed with the "recall" council. The community seemed to have regressed back to the old way of doing things - like taking care of their own. On the surface the town fathers said they were all for equal and fair treatment for all citizens but behind the scenes, it was a different story. I, overall, sensed that the police department could have done a much better job in dealing with citizen complaints given the type of political environment. I was also hoping citizens could have gotten better cooperation and had more confidence in their police department. Many improvements had been made including how people regarded the police department, but there was still room for much improvement.

Handling citizen complaints in Fort Lupton, Colorado and Somersworth, New Hampshire were much better. The complaint procedure in fact worked the best in Fort Lupton. Each police department actually had a good citizen complaint process in place and I just fine-tuned it.

Conversely, there was a time in Fort Lupton before my arrival whereby the citizen complaint process just came to a screeching halt. Apparently the interim city administrator did not like the prior chief and ordered him to bring all the internal affair and citizen complaint files against police officers to his office. The city administrator decided that the process was not fair after listening to complaints by some police employees. In addition, the city administrator ordered there would not be any internal investigation until further notice. Now, how absurd can this be? I never had known anyone to arbitrarily stop internal investigation because of an employee complaint. The whole process was circumvented. It appeared that the investigations were required to go through the interim city administrator's office. This was a period of frustration because supervisors could not investigate and take action against any police officer for allegations of misconduct or citizen complaints. It was like a freebee because these complaints were now going to be ignored. This did not last long thankfully because the City Council did not like what was going on either. The City Council removed the interim city administrator from his position and appointed someone else. The internal affairs and citizen complaint component was returned to the police department where it belonged. When I was appointed police chief, I retrieved the internal affairs and citizen complaint files from the former interim city administrator's office and locked them in the records archives. Because there was no master list, I did not know what files had been removed. At least, I could safeguard the rest.

What happens if you ignore citizen complaints? It is like a double-edged sword. If you have many complaints, people may perceive the department as doing something wrong or if you ignore the complaints then people will have less faith in their department. I do not worry about getting too many complaints because this is usually not the case. I want to investigate these complaints to prevent them from escalating into severe police misconduct or corruption. If you ignore the problem it has a tendency to get worse over time. I want people to have trust and confidence in their police department. You already know some departments have a horrible reputation in the community. If you do not know about your department's reputation then it is time to get into the community to find out. Often times your personnel do not want to be the bearer of bad news. Officers do not want you to "kill the messenger." I rather hear about the bad news sooner than later so that I can do something about it. If the people in the community have a perception that police officers cannot trust their local police departments then you have a great deal of work to do.

A police department's reputation means everything not only to the community but to the outside world as well. In Somersworth, New Hampshire, it was well known throughout the state that this police department was a "dumping ground" for police chiefs. It was a scary thought for me knowing that every chief since 1970 to when I had been appointed in 1988 was terminated for one reason or another and one of the reasons was the "Coca Cola Caper." Other chiefs had made fun of Somersworth. I like to think that it was through my efforts after a great deal of hard work that opinions began to change. I made a concerted effort to change public opinion about how the Somersworth Police Department conducted business.

Public opinion can be changed. The new chief coming into the community has an advantage. He or she is not carrying baggage from previous departments. If so, then adverse information will be discovered during a background investigation. Everyone will be on his or her best behavior because everyone is nervous about how one is perceived by the new chief. It is an opportunity to convey a new philosophy or reinforce an old one regarding expectations and ethics. At the same time the public will be looking for greater things to happen and expectations will be higher. Citizens will be looking for the police department to break out of its old mold if the citizenry were unhappy with law enforcement performance. The expectations may be higher by the public but I think it is easier to plant new ideas and philosophy to bring the department to a higher level. I was exited to think that changes could be made to the police department and was optimistic to think the police would eventually be accepted. Having faith and trust in a police department means a great deal to a community and it was definitely by desire to reach a certain expectancy goal because it was attainable.

One positive thing about exciting your department's personnel about change is a change in attitude. **When officers are exited about change their attitudes are channeled into something positive.** A good attitude about ones job performance and more important - about themselves - reflect in lowered or less citizen complaints. I found this to be true in each police department. I realized the more officers felt wanted and part of the organization, the better the performance. **There is definitely a correlation between poor job performance and citizen complaints.**

Policy & Procedure

The best way to keep everyone honest is to have a Policy and Procedure on Citizen Complaints. The following is a policy statement on citizen complains:

> *The policy of the Fort Lupton Police Department shall be to investigate all complaints by citizens against police personnel in a timely manner. This complaint procedure will be an administrative procedural step to draw management's attention to problem areas deserving investigation, training,*

supervision, and other administrative actions. The procedures established herein are intended to assure the prompt and thorough investigation of complaints and allegations, to clear the innocent, establish misconduct and facilitate appropriate administrative action in the public interest, the interest of the police department, and the interest of the employees of the department. The department calls for the assumption of innocence until a preponderance of evidence indicates misconduct; the fair and impartial investigation of all complaints and allegations of misconduct; and a progressive, positive disciplinary process that mitigates and eliminates continuing inappropriate behavior.

The policy statement in reality states the viewpoint and sets up the procedure. The policy informs everyone what is to be expected and the consequences. I never actually got into the practice of soliciting complaints except for a few occasions when we stumbled upon some misconduct and some chiefs may disagree with me on this point. I think there are enough complaints without trying to solicit more. I would rather remind people they can make a complaint if dissatisfied with police service or did not like the way they were treated. I prefer this approach much better. Other than doing a survey on customer satisfaction, if the police chief calls up someone asking if he or she is satisfied with police service it could undermine morale. I can understand the intent but one has to be very careful about perception. It may look like the chief is soliciting complaints against a certain police employee. I have seen these types of situations get turned around on the police chief where it looked like it was more harassment and discrimination. Everything may be legitimate but now the chief is on the defense trying to explain his or her actions. If a certain employee were shirking his or her duty, sooner or later, someone would be making a complaint. I found this to be true most of the time. I would wait until a complaint was made.

There was an on going complaint while I was in Fort Lupton. A police officer sued the city for discrimination because he alleged a certain sergeant, under orders from the previous chief, tried to solicit a complaint against him. The couple allegedly was approached by the sergeant asking if they wanted to make a citizen's complaint for poor police work against the officer. The officer was approached by the couple and told him what the sergeant had said. Whether it was true or not, I do not know, but this along with other complaints could have an accumulative effect in a lawsuit. I always waited until there was an official complaint. I imagine it is the smart way of doing business. Soliciting complaints can be more harmful to the police agency. My advice is to wait. One saying that I often use is "if you give someone enough rope, they will hang themselves." Inevitability, this statement is a true fact, most of the time.

The following are examples of language that I used in the procedure:

Procedure

Scope of Investigations of Complaints/Allegations: The incidents which are to be investigated pursuant to the policies and procedures herein are:

- *Alleged violations of Federal Laws or Codes;*
- *Alleged violations of Colorado Criminal & Traffic laws.*
- *Alleged violations of the City of Fort Lupton's Ordinances, and/or Personnel Rules & Regulations*
- *Alleged violations of the Fort Lupton Police Department's policies, procedures, rules, regulations, general orders, administrative memorandums, or lawful orders issued by authorized members of the department.*

Types of Complaints/Allegations to be Investigated:

- *Those reported to supervisory or command level personnel by employees of the department in writing.*
- *Those referred by a citizen in writing or in person.*
- *Those reported by an anonymous citizen. <u>Note:</u> Anonymous complaints may or may not Be investigated. It would depend upon the seriousness of the allegation and other factors. The Chief of Police will make the final decision whether an investigation will be conducted*

Anonymous complaints can be a problem as well. Some chiefs and managers will investigate all complaints including those filed anonymously. I do not want it to appear that it is going to be a witch-hunt. Unless there are special circumstances, a person must come forward to make a complaint. My thinking is that if someone was serious about a complaint then he or she would not have any problem in giving their name and address.   Personally I do not put much faith in anonymous complaints. At the very most, the complaint will receive a cursory look and possibly be dropped.   However, what could change is if suddenly there were several anonymous complaints about a certain officer taking money or propositioning young ladies during a motor vehicle stop. Now, with this added information on such complaint may warrant further investigation including a sting operation.

Using an undercover police officer from another jurisdiction would be ideal in this situation.

I found that the general orders worked very well and also conformed to national and state accreditation processes. Obviously, I had gone into greater detail concerning who was going to investigate. The Operations Commander was responsible for coordinating investigation but the supervisors were also accountable. I wanted the sergeants to get into the practice of completing the Internal Affair/Citizen Complaint intake form. The form gathered some basic information about the complainant, the officer and description of the incident. I certainly did not want any of my supervisors referring the citizen to someone else the next day. I hate anyone passing the buck. If someone wants to be a supervisor then he or she should accept the responsibility.

Generally, each complaint had a time limit of about <u>10 days</u>, which was more than adequate to investigate minor complaints. In the event a supervisor needed more time all he or she had to do was ask. There were a few occasions when it was difficult to contact the complainant.

When my reviewed complaints had been completed and I had made a decision, I wrote a letter to the citizen informing him or her of the results. Even if the officer was wrong I did not tell the citizen what the discipline would be. At this point I would state the matter would be handled internally and there were areas brought to management's attention that could be addressed through additional training. I always invited the citizen to either call or visit me in person if there were any additional questions. Only a few people who filed a complaint were not satisfied with my response.

On such dissatisfied complainant example occurred in Fort Lupton, Colorado. One citizen complained about the way a burglary investigation was conducted by my investigator. No matter what, the citizen was not going to be happy with the results. One evening, someone entered her garage and stole her motor vehicle and drove it to a neighboring community, the City of Thornton. Actually, the vehicle was found parked at one of the resident's driveway. There were no witnesses nor would anyway admit to driving the vehicle. My investigator, being a nice person picked up the complainant and drove her to the location of the vehicle. At this location is where the situation got ugly. The complainant could not understand why the police just could not enter the house to look for suspects. The complainant did not understand the police needed probable cause to enter the home. People are protected against unlawful search and seizure in violation of the 4th Amendment to the United States Constitution. One person was taken into custody but the case never went anywhere. There simply was not enough evidence to establish probable cause to make an arrest, never mind proving a case beyond a reasonable doubt.

After reviewing the investigation by the Lieutenant, I wrote to the complainant that my investigator had acted properly. Actually, the only mistake made was picking up the complainant and transporting her to the location of her vehicle. The complainant disagreed with my finding and made a complaint to the City Administrator. The administrator set up a meeting within a week and called everyone into the conference room to rehash the entire episode. When the meeting was all over that the administrator agreed that this citizen's complaint was fully investigated and allowed the initial findings to stand. I also sensed that the administrator realized he should never have gotten involved with the complaint after it had already been completely investigated. I went on to advise the investigator that it was not a good idea to bring the complainant to the location of the stolen motor vehicle until the investigation had been completed. I guess you have to read people a little better. Most people would have appreciated the effort by the investigator, but not this person. Nothing I or anyone else could have done to change her mind. I presume if I had fired the investigator then maybe this complainant would have been happy. Sometimes these complaints can be very frustrating. This lady was not going to be happy about anything we were trying to do. Maybe she would have been happy if we had violated someone's civil rights. Maybe she could have been named in the civil suit too.

Nevertheless, no matter what you do, you cannot please everyone. I was always guided by the principles of doing the right thing. Having a procedure in place and following it helps with the explanation to the complainant. A procedure also helps the City Administrator or Manager in understanding the process involved.

I had provided some good examples of several citizen complaints that I had been involved with. The main point is to **investigate all citizen complaints that are brought to management's attention. The following are some dos and don'ts that may assist you in dealing with citizen complaints:**

The Do's:
- Develop a good Policy and Procedure
- Develop and display a Citizen Complaint Brochure
- Advise the citizens of your philosophy on complaints
- Investigate all citizen complaints
- Treat everyone with dignity and respect
- Investigate as expeditiously as possible
- Report the findings to the citizen as soon as possible

Correct the problem even if it means additional training for the officers.

If you are not satisfied with the investigation take a second look.

- Once completed, file the investigation and put it away under lock and key

Now, the Don'ts:

- Don't argue with the complainant.
- Don't reveal your disciplinary action, if any.
- Don't offer any excuses or rationalize the officer's action.
- Don't volunteer information that may lead to a civil suit.
- Don't discuss the investigation with others except with the investigator and sometimes the City Manager on more serious cases.
- Don't play politics with citizen complaints.

The goal for citizen complaints is bring to management's attention potential problem areas that could be resolved through training. Most citizen complaints that find their way into the chief's office are the result of a traffic stop. In each case, the citizen asserted that the officer was rude and/or used profanity. In some cases, I believe this to be true. Some officers are rude and do use profanity towards citizens. Many citizens in fact are belittled by the officer, such as chastising drivers for making a stupid traffic maneuver. Maybe the officer's remarks are true but certainly the officer's word selection used can be in a more diplomatic and dignified manner. Why should the officer go down to the level of a cynical citizen? Usually these encounters will certainly result in a citizen's complaint.

The above complaint will be investigated but the result will be "not sustained." Reason being, the complaint cannot be proved or disproved without any additional witnesses. This results in the officer's word against the motorist's word. This complaint will go no farther because the officer will receive the benefit of the doubt. Now, if there are other complaints regarding rudeness or disrespect filed against this same officer even if the complaints are "not sustained," the police chief may have a ticking time bomb on his hands. **Frequent complaints accusations of rudeness and disrespect should be a clue that the police chief may have a continuing problem with this officer.** If there is only one complaint and no others then the complaint may be more unfounded or the officer corrected his or her demeanor on his or her own. Sometimes motorists will lie to get out of a traffic ticket. On the other hand, the officer may have been rude and disrespectful towards the citizen. It may be worth keeping your eye on this officer and monitoring his or her motor vehicle arrests more closely.

One indisputable way to help resolve some citizen complaints and to keep these complaints to a minimum is to have a video camera installed in the cruiser to monitor the traffic stops and the conversations. Having cameras installed is a good idea to keep everyone honest and on his or her best behavior. **The video camera also protects the officers against any false accusation.** One cannot dispute what is recorded on tape. Some states have different laws on recording conversations between two people, so you might have to seek advice from your city or town's legal counsel to be in compliance with the law. There is not harm in advising citizens that he or she is being video taped during the traffic stop, in cases that require two-party consent. Either way, the tape will provide additional evidence to show probable cause for the traffic stop and resolve very quickly any accusations regarding rude and disrespectful treatment. As they say, "A picture is worth a thousand words" and even more so with taped conversation. The officer using the video camera no doubt will be on his or her best behavior.

The video cameras mounted in the police vehicles will be the resolution to the problem of he said or she said scenarios. The tape can be either the officers or citizens' witness. One does has to be careful that the videotape has not been tampered with but there are various ways to handle this problem. **Each department should have a policy and procedure on the use of the video camera and the supervisor should be checking to insure the officer is complying with the requirements.**

Citizen complaints can also be handled very easily. The mission statement is a very critical piece of information. **The mission statement reflects the philosophy and attitude of the department.**   The following is an example of a mission statement that I used in Fort Lupton, Colorado:

Mission of the Fort Lupton Police Department

The primary function of the police department of the City of Fort Lupton and the reason for its existence is to protect life and property, maintain social order and enforce the laws of the State of Colorado and the Ordinances of the City of Fort Lupton.

We will serve and protect all people within our jurisdiction with respect, fairness and compassion with customer service as our approach. We will investigate problems and incidents, seek resolutions and foster a sense of security and safety in our neighborhoods.

234   Patrick L. Cote

We will maintain the public trust by holding ourselves to the highest standards of performance and ethics.

We are dedicated to providing a quality work environment and the development of its members through effective training and leadership. We will foster an atmosphere that promotes employee well-being.

Working in partnership with the community, we will continually strive to improve and enhance the quality and delivery of our services within our community.

Keep in mind that the mission statement is a very serious document. Some police departments do not have a mission statement. However, I strongly recommend every police department should have one. I had the help of my department personnel, the Police Committee and citizens in helping me to craft the mission statement. I widely publicized the mission statement including displaying a framed copy in the police lobby. I think it helps to know how the public will perceive the police department and to move away from the notion, "They are not going to do anything anyway."

If the citizens understand what law enforcement are doing and the citizen complaints are investigated honestly and fairly, then the department should realize a good reputation. All people want is a fair shake and have someone in the police department listen to their concern. Often times citizens perceptions are shaped by the attitude of the supervisory person taking complaints against the officer(s). Some police departments have a terrible reputation regarding handling of citizen complaints and I can understand why. Officers do not take citizen complaints very seriously. If people are generally satisfied with fair treatment, fewer complaints will be received or heard by the political powers to be.

Hopefully, I have given you some insight into handling citizen complaints. **The most important thing is to look into public dissatisfaction so that the entire police department can improve services to the public.** Everything will fall into place.

Chapter 13
The Disciplinary Process

The disciplinary process ties in the previous two chapters, Internal Affairs and Citizen Complaint investigations. People always ask is discipline training or is it punishment? Some will argue that it is strictly training. I will argue that it is both. Everyone desires a second chance assuming the violation is not so severe that it would warrant an outright dismissal. It is like my philosophy that the person committing the violation of the rules and regulations would learn from their mistake but suffer some penalty, so in my mind it is both.

The next part of the equation is not so simple. What is the appropriate punishment in a given situation? It becomes a little tricky if the department does not use a code of conduct as used in Bristol, Connecticut. My former chief in Bristol actually implemented it after the police union agreed to it. It set forth all the violations you could think of and the penalty for a first, second and third offense. Overall, I think it was good because it took all the arbitrariness out of the decision-making as to what the appropriate punishment will be. The union seemed to accept the penalty and why not? Every conceivable type of complaint was in black and white along with the penalty. Everyone knew what the penalty would be for a particular offense. The guesswork was taken out of it. The next part was trying to get the supervisors to report violations of the rules and regulations. Sometimes this was more complicated because the supervisors were part of the union too. The follow through was questionable though. You can have all the rules in place you want but if no one enforces them as in the case of Bristol, you might as well throw out the rulebook.

What I found difficult was trying to decide the appropriate penalty for a particular offense without having any standard to go by. I always had trouble dealing with this issue especially since the employees' fate was in limbo while a decision was being contemplated. When I was suspended for a week without pay as a result of my fishing expedition it caused me to reflect more. I know what it is like to live from payday to payday just barely making ends meet. I had to tighten the belt when I was out on a payless vacation because of my actions. This experience certainly made me think twice about doing anything foolish in the future. It was a well-learned lesson. A one-day suspension would have been more than enough for me. When you suspend someone and while they may deserve the punishment one hundred percent their family feels the effect too. The food and other essentials are suddenly taken away and the family might perceive it to be the police chief's fault.

This is especially true if the penalty seems overly harsh. If you do not believe me just ask someone for his or her opinion. It is fair to discipline but sometimes there is overkill. Some employees receive such a penalty that there may never recover. Other words, the employee may just give up and not do anything. The employee is there just for a paycheck and little else. You probably already know some individuals with bad attitudes. A bad attitude is contagious. The idea behind discipline is to change the behavior of the employee into something more constructive. The police chief or leader has to find the right recipe to channel the employee into positive behavior.

The question remains what is the appropriate punishment for a particular violation of the rules and regulations? I go through a great deal of agony in trying to decide the proper course of action. If I had listened to my staff in each of my departments, I probably would have fired three times as many. In Somersworth, New Hampshire I quickly realized what the disciplines the captains were recommending in most cases were extremely excessive. The culture of the police department at the time was to impose severe discipline to employees who had committed infractions of the rules and regulations. What are you going to do fire everyone who made a mistake? We made enough mistakes ourselves. The prior police chief in Somersworth was more of a hardliner, which is where the harsh disciplines come from. I realized that their judgment was flawed and I would have to make the judgment for myself on a case-by-case basis. Without rhyme or reason, the captains were recommending terminating individuals, in my opinion, for not very serious offenses. Of course, it was a different story if the offense involved one of their friends and the recommendation was far more lenient. So in effect, it depended upon whether you were one of the "fair haired" boys or not. This was especially true; I hate to admit, in my former department in Bristol, Connecticut.

Being from a unionized police department the chief had to be very careful with the disciplinary practices because each decision would be scrutinized. If the discipline in the eyes of the union were not fair then they would go through the grievance process and take it all the way to the Connecticut State Labor Department. Many cases that had gone to the State Labor Department and some of the decisions were reversed. Sometimes it was hard to believe. Take for example, one police officer decided to do a little drinking while off-duty and got involved in a motor vehicle accident. He not only was drunk but also left the scene of the accident. We arrest people for that and throw them in jail. The police chief, after giving the employee due process, fired him for misconduct. Even though this individual was a friend of mine, I have to admit he got what he deserved. The union filed a grievance and it went all the way to the State Labor Department. In their infinite wisdom, they reinstated the officer and gave him back pay with the exception of about two weeks or so suspension without pay. Everyone was puzzled over that one. No one could believe that he got reinstated. The State Labor Department felt that this officer did not deserve to be fired because there were no disciplines in his personnel file. Maybe they felt he deserved a second chance. Some situations do not deserve a second chance and perhaps, he should have stayed fired. This brings up an interesting question. What do you have to do to sustain a termination of an employee in the eye of the labor department?

A few years later this same officer was involved in a fatal accident. He happened to pass a vehicle on the right and did not see a person on a bicycle. There still was a question in my mind as well as others whether or not he had been drinking. At the time another agency, the State Police, should have been called to investigate this accident. In this particular case, our own police department did the investigation. Who knows if he had been drinking or not? As it turned out he had not been drinking but the thought crossed everyone's mind. Stranger things have happened. Anytime one of your police officers becomes involved in a motor vehicle accident, another agency should be asked to investigate. It is not to say there will be a cover-up but why give someone the opportunity to criticize your department. The smart thing to do is to have a complete impartial investigation. Having someone else make an independent determination will not taint the outcome of the investigation. During my stint at three police departments where I was police chief, I made it a practice to call another agency to conduct the investigation if one of my officers were involved.

There should be no exceptions such as in my case one day when I got involved in an unfortunate accident involving a motorcycle. At the time I had just left Western Auto in Dover, New Hampshire and was towing a brand new bass boat to my home about three miles away. Little did I know that the wires had been crossed, so when I put my right turn signal on to turn onto my street my left turn indicator was flashing. A motorcyclist following close behind decided to pass me on the right. He went onto the soft shoulder and ran into the bass boat as I making the turn. I dragged the poor fellow about 30 feet before I stopped. I kept hearing "stop" and when I looked into my rear view mirror I did not see anything at all. I finally stopped, got out of my vehicle and observed a young male and his motorcycle underneath my trailer. Fortunately, he was not very badly hurt, just a broken leg but it could have been much worse. My officers when they responded to the motor vehicle accident were surprised to find that I had been involved. I directed the officer to notify dispatch to contact the New Hampshire State Police to conduct the investigation.

Guess who showed up a short time later. You guessed it, the media. My accident made front-page news the next day, so you can see why it is important to have an unbiased investigation. As it turned out the young fellow got a warning for illegally passing on the right. Western Auto assumed responsibility for inadvertently crossing the wires for the turn signals. I have to admire them for doing the right thing. Even though I was not held responsible for the accident, I still felt terrible about the whole thing.

I like to think of discipline more of a positive reinforcement of the rules and regulations. Depending upon the seriousness of the offense would dictate the penalty. I like to use the progressive discipline model for discipline. Everyone desires a change to improve performance so the levels of discipline should be incremental. If the individual keeps repeating the same mistake then the penalties should be increased dramatically up to a point where termination might be considered. Other words, if the employee is dumb enough to keep screwing up then the police chief or manager will have to take necessary measures to fire the person.

Going too fast!

In Somersworth, New Hampshire, I had mentioned earlier that we had hired an officer from another police department. It looked like on the surface we were getting a quality individual and his work did reflect it for a while. Apparently, this officer had a heavy foot and liked to go fast with his lights and siren on. I wondered if he thought he was a racecar driver. We should have taken a closer look at him and checked further at the other police department. Guess what? He had similar problems. While this officer was still on probation, he was going to fast on an icy road and slid off the road into a utility pole causing some damage to the cruiser. The captain issued him a written reprimand for his accident. Next, this officer was involved in a more serious accident. This officer received a call to respond to a burglary alarm at a store in the downtown area. While in route to the call traveling at a high rate of speed he took a turn too fast and struck a utility pole. This time this officer totaled the vehicle but he did not get hurt. The officer was wearing his seatbelt and it was a miracle he was not killed at the rate of speed he had been traveling. This officer had been previously warned, so it did not come as a big surprise when I terminated him. I was disappointed that I had to take this action because overall, I had to look out for the safety of my other officers and above all, the safety of the citizens.

Sometimes, the employee messed up so badly that there was no choice but to terminate him or her. There were times when I wanted to give the employee a break but what can you do when they put themselves in this position. I was never thrilled about terminating someone and having to go through the testing process all over again. Whenever possible I would try to issue a written reprimand first, depending upon the seriousness of the violation. There were many times when the employee took the decision right out of my hands. I look at it this way. They fire themselves.

In Florence, Arizona, I had to terminate an officer for being stupid. If there was such an offense, this guy should have gotten a prize. I had briefly mentioned this incident earlier but this is the officer who fell in love or is it lust with a high school senior. The girl was 18 years old but she was in a special education at the high school. I had heard about it from a citizen in the community and thought he was kidding. I called the officer into my office and asked him about it. He said, it was true but she was an adult. I tried to explain to the guy that the girl was still in high school and people were making fun of the police department. We were trying to maintain a good image in the community and this one incident could hurt us. It did not faze him when I pointed out to him she was in a special education program at the school. He had an answer for everything. He said that she just had a minor learning disability. I told him it was not a good idea to date the high school senior. I told him to cease and desist because we already looked bad enough in the community. I said, "Why don't you wait until she graduates high school?"

In addition, I asked the officer about his cell phone bill. He was in the rears to the tune of about $3,000. Normally I would not have intervened so early but he was the one who asked to be on the cell phone plan sponsored by the police department's account. The employees received a special rate because they were employees of the town. I never had any problem with anyone not paying his or her cell phone bill until this officer came along. He never paid the bill from day one and this guy was enforcing the law. I cannot understand how anyone could do this. I told him he would have to take care of the bill because the town would ultimately be responsible. Doing a good deed for your personnel can suddenly turn around to bite you as in this case. Sometimes people will take advantage of your good nature. Who knows, I probably should have told them to find their own cell phone service. It only takes one person to spoil it for the rest of your personnel.

My warnings were ignored. He continued to see the high school senior and after hearing about it I called the officer into my office. At this point I had had enough and suggested to him it would be in his best interest to resign because I was going to move for a dismissal. He submitted his letter of resignation the same day. The ironic thing about it was that they broke up about two weeks after he submitted his letter of resignation. His foolishness cost him his job. The sad thing about it was that he was doing a good job. He found another police job with a police department on an Indian Reservation near Mesa. He lasted only a couple of months with the department. This former officer tried to get on with other police departments but he was never successful. The last I heard he was working on a train going back and forth from Arizona to Texas. This was a sad ending to once a promising career.

Civil Court

There are times when you have more than enough evidence to terminate someone for violations of the rules and regulations. When is it appropriate to accept a letter of resignation instead? This dilemma comforts police chiefs and mangers all the time. The question remains whether the police chief or manager should go through the agony of the disciplinary process or take the lesser evil approach, the letter of resignation. My answer is it depends upon the situation. Not that I mind when the situation calls for it but dealing with personnel matters will take up a great deal of the chief's or manager's time. I found this to be very true while dealing with disciplinary matters in each of my previous departments. I would reflect back to how my previous chief in Bristol, Connecticut would handle disciplinary matters. Many times my former chief accepts the letter of resignation. Sometimes I would ask him why he did not just fire the individual. He said, "Why fire him and suddenly find yourself at the State Labor Department or Civil Court?" After thinking about it for awhile, he did have a good point. When a case goes to the state labor board the police chief or manager finds the table is now turned on him. He is now on the defensive trying to explain his actions leading up to the dismissal. The union would certainly file a grievance to contest the discipline and take it all the way to the State Labor Department. When a person submits a letter of resignation, the process is over. The person leaves the department and the discipline problem has been successfully concluded. The only problem I can see is if the former employee now says that he or she had been pressured into resigning from the department.

In order to avoid this argument I had my second in command or another ranking officer in my office to act as my witness and I always tape-recorded the meeting. Therefore, it did not appear I was trying to gang up on the individual I always offered to have him or her bring in someone for support. Most of the time they were embarrassed enough so they usually declined my offer. I always gave my employee a way out and it took me a while to get to this point.

In Somersworth, New Hampshire after I terminated the officer for being involved in a motor vehicle accident with a marked cruiser, the union president came into my office and asked if I could speak with him about it. I never agreed with the union president very much on issues but he did make sense on this one. I did not like to think about unions. I can understand their position to bargain to get better wages and benefits but many times, they push management excessively far. When they try to negotiate to dilute management rights, then it is time to draw the line. He asked if I might consider allowing the officer to resign from the department instead of being terminated. The officer knew he had truly messed up but he was willing to accept the ultimate punishment. He was worried about getting another job with a termination on his record. After thinking about it for a couple of minutes, I agree to allow him to resign. I had already accomplished my goals and that was to remove him as an employee for the sake of the community. This former officer had been punished enough and I did not want to ruin him for live. He deserved another chance like anyone else but somewhere else.

If the job was for another police department, I hope they would be smart enough to do a thorough background investigation on him. They would just have to ask the key question. "Is your former employee eligible for employment at your agency?" If you reply no, then you need not say anything else because you could find yourself in civil court. Many departments are too careful because they only will release basic information about a former employee. Everyone is paranoid about being sued. On the other hand, more bad officers are being hired without thorough background investigations so a department will find themselves in civil court anyway. It is a situation where you are "dammed if you do, and dammed if you don't." Actually I do not have a problem in telling another chief the truth about a former employee. If they want to sue over it, then my attitude is "Go ahead, make my day."

I present a choice to the officer if the situation was bad enough for violations of the rules and regulations of the police department to warrant a termination. If the matter was of a serious nature, like a criminal offense, then the employee can forget about it. In this case, I will certainly go for termination. I would go into detail about the circumstances and the specific charges related to the incident. The employee at this time would have an opportunity to explain him or herself. I explained that I will move for termination but there is a way out. I will allow the employee to resign in lieu of being fired and it is usually the end of it.

I use to think that is the coward's way out. Why let the employee resign when you have the person dead to rights? Besides, he certainly deserves what you are about to dish out. In the traditional way of thinking, a police chief or executive may have his or her employee dead to rights and it may appear to be a solid case until it goes to the State Labor Department or Civil Court. After they start to dismantle your solid case piece by piece then you will realize how easily this all could have been avoided. You will see how a solid investigation can fall apart. Your previously fired but now reinstated officer with back pay will now be a disgruntled employee. He or she will poison the minds of the other employees.

First, they will look to see if your former employee had received due process. I have done it both ways, a formal hearing when I was in New Hampshire to a less formal process in Arizona and Colorado. Which is better? It depends on whether you provide due process in each case. Obviously, the more formal hearing will take more time. Everyone should be familiar with the Loudermill Hearing and the following is an excerpt of the decision:

In 1985, the United States Supreme Court decided Cleveland Board of Education v. Loudermill, 470 U.S. 532. The decision was heralded as a major advance in the job security rights of police officers and other public employees.

Loudermill affirms the principle that a non-probationary police officer may not be terminated; or, otherwise disciplined so as to lose significant pay or reputation, without certain procedural steps. These include a pre-termination notice of the charges on which the discipline is based, an opportunity to review the evidence, and a chance to respond to the charges all coupled with post-termination procedures, which provide for a due process review.

The Loudermill decision does not discuss the type of hearing as long as it is a **fair process**. I am all for it because I would not want to be deprived of my rights where due process is concerned. It is the reasonable thing to do. First, let us get back to Somersworth's process. I quickly learned after I took over as police chief that the union would challenge me regarding various disciplines. When internal investigations were completed and after my review, I put into writing the charges when necessary and a date to report to my office for a hearing. Usually the person reported with his union representative and both captains were present during the hearing. My hearings were tape-recorded. After the charges were read the employee was allowed an opportunity to explain his or her side of the issue. Sometimes these hearings got too lengthy only because the union representative would make a presentation on behalf of their union member. Upon conclusion, I would render my decision in writing. It did not take a rocket scientist to figure out the reason the employee was in my office in the first place because he or she violated rules and regulations of the department. There were no if, ands or buts about it, they were guilty. I want to hear what the employee had to say. As chief, I had to play the game.

In Somersworth, the employees truly got their breaks. The union knew how to play the system. If the union was not happy with my decision and most of the time they were not, then they would submit a grievance to the City Manager and he in turn would conduct his own hearing. The union wanted me to delay the implementation of the discipline but I never did. I always had the employee serve their suspension first. What did the union think they were in court or something? The City Manager would rule in my favor and the police union would request a hearing before the Personnel Review Board made up of citizens from the community. They would continue with their grievance even if their case was an outright loser. By this time, the employee had already received two hearings and now he was on his third full hearing. The decision of the Personnel Advisory Board was final and binding. The board always ruled in my favor. I never lost a case involving a disciplinary matter. Even though the board's ruling was final and binding, it was not. The employee could always appeal to the State Labor Board or Civil Court. I have been to the State Labor Board on a few occasions and they ruled in my favor too. I always decided to take the reasonable course of action. If I had carried out the penalties my captains wanted me to take then I would most certainly been a guest of the State Labor Board more often. These decisions in my opinion were reasonable, which is why the boards ruled in my favor.

I can see having one disciplinary hearing but having three is far too much. It was that way in Somersworth. The question is at which level is an employee entitled to a disciplinary hearing. If I gave the employee a hearing at my level then once you are at the level of the City Manager it should have been more of a review of my decision only. No, we had to have a hearing at that level too. Sometimes I felt that I was on trial and not the employee. Somehow the union people would try to shift blame on the police chief or leader. They would try to paint a picture of a witch-hunt. The employee should shoulder their share of the responsibility. I always tried to refocus and remind everyone why the employee is there in the first place. He or she had violated rules and regulations of the police department that necessitated disciplinary action in the first place. Sometimes the hearing at the City Manager's grievance hearing would turn into a heated discussion. I think there were times when the union would intimidate the City Manager and they realized they were getting to him. After a few hearings like this, he would shorten the grievance hearings. The Personnel Review Board conducted hearings as well. I think they went beyond their role. All they were supposed to do was review decisions by management to make sure the employees had been treated fairly.

No one can say that the employees in Somersworth were not treated fairly. They truly received their due process but I think the city went way beyond the intent of Loudermill. The union would always want a full-blown hearing like a trial with each session tape-recorded. I thought it was ludicrous to have three separate hearings. After a while, I scaled down my hearings. I was spending far too much time on disciplinary matters than I wanted. Other important matters need my attention more like the safety of the community. I will be honest with you, these personnel matters were wearing me down. At first I was a little sad to leave Somersworth but not sad to leave all the aggravation. I suspected the union was trying to get me to lose my cool but I never did. There were certainly times when I wanted to give them a piece of my mind but I always remained professional. I kept telling myself it was only a game and there was nothing personal.

Unions can definitely have an impact in the outcome. Take for example an internal investigation that I personally conducted in Bristol, Connecticut just prior to me being selected as police chief in Somersworth, New Hampshire. I investigated an allegation that one of the officers was involved in smoking marijuana while on and off duty and snorting cocaine. Now, the source of the allegation came directly from the officer's estranged wife at the time. While this officer was working the night shift, he would stop at his home for a few minutes and smoke marijuana. His relatives were more than willing to discuss the situation. Of course, when I interviewed the officer he denied it. I completed my lengthy investigation and submitted it to the police chief for his review. There was no doubt in my mind or his that the officer was using drugs on and off duty. The chief called him in and immediately suspended him pending the results of a hearing before the Board of Police Commissioners. I thought to myself: this is a "slam dunk" case. With all my statements from witnesses, how can I miss this one? The wife and relatives of the officers were more than willing to give me a blow-by-blow description of what happened.

The City of Bristol paid for my expenses to attend the hearing. As they had me waiting for my turn to go into the hearing room, apparently there was a last minute deal between the attorney of the officer and the Board of Police Commissioners. Instead of him being fired for drug use, he would agree to a suspension of two weeks without pay and not be eligible for promotion for three years. In addition, he would have to undergo weekly drug testing. I could not believe it. In my mind, the board did not discipline the officer according to the code of conduct. This individual deserved to be fired but instead agreed to a plea bargain. I guess they were afraid to go to the State Labor Board and civil court.

Just think of the leadership example the Board of Police Commissioners set. They sent a message to everyone else that drug use is not so bad. This particular officer took his punishment and eventually rose to the rank of lieutenant and then captain. On a positive note, he did seem to turn his life around and I have to give him credit for it. However, what kind of leadership example did he set for everyone else? I can see giving someone a second chance but this is one situation where he should have been terminated. The Board of Police Commissioners wasted my time in bringing me back to Bristol for the hearing. They did not even thank me for making the long trip even though they paid for it. It was like a circus like atmosphere. They should have just made a deal with him in the very beginning instead of playing games. This was politics at its worst. I wondered if they followed through and tested him once a week like the Board of Police Commissioners directed. One thought had crossed my mind as well as others, what condition would the officer be in when he was backing up another officer.

It was a different world to leave the unionized police departments in the northeast and head west to first, Florence, Arizona and to Fort Lupton, Colorado. Both are right to work states.   Other words, if they wanted to terminate your employment they could.   There were no unions or formal representation of employees. Generally, if someone was not happy with a termination he or she could always take the matter to civil court.   After being accustomed to union environments for so long, it was quite refreshing to be where there were no union officials breathing down your neck. Not that I was intimidated, but they can get to you after awhile.

After looking more closely at the Loudermill decision, I decided to scale down the hearing at the police chief's level. I still gave the notification of charges in writing and the order to report before me. I always made sure my second in command was with me as my witness. When the employee did report at the appointed time I discussed the charges and the investigation. I gave the employee an opportunity to present his or her side. When the informal hearing concluded, I issued my decision in writing as to what the penalty will be.

The Penalty

Determining the penalty was a little tricky. In each of my three departments, I did not have a code of conduct as in the case of the Bristol Police Department. If you recall they spelled out exactly what the penalty would be for a 1st, 2nd or 3rd offense for a particular violation. Having a code of conduct would have made it much easier to render a decision.

I thought about the penalty long and hard. Above all, I wanted to treat the employee fairly. If I had appeared to be too harsh then it would have sent a negative message to the rest of the employees that the police chief was a headhunter. I wanted to send a message to all employees that negative conduct will be dealt with accordingly and it serves as an example that inappropriate behavior will not be tolerated. Sometimes I would discuss discipline at my staff meetings and for fun I would say, "Pick a number from one to ten." How can anyone arbitrarily pick a number of days for a suspension without pay? When does a situation call for one day as opposed to five days? There are some departments that give 30 days off without pay. If you have to go to that extreme then perhaps he or she should have been fired.

In Florence, Arizona and Fort Lupton, Colorado I sought the advice of my second in command as what might be the appropriate penalty. In addition, I looked at the employees personnel file to check his or her prior disciplinary record and just as important, some of the positive things he or she has done for the department. The letters of commendation and positive comments from citizens have to mean something. More often than not, many police chiefs do not take into consideration the employees' personnel record. I did not want to come across as a strict disciplinarian or one who is too lenient. In each case where I was contemplating a suspension, I would first discuss it with the town or city manager. Usually in a manager and council form of government, the manager would have the final say because he or she is the personnel officer. I wanted to feel comfortable with the discipline whether it was a one-day or week suspension without pay. The goal was to punish the employee for violations of the rules and regulation but at the same time, I wanted them to learn from their mistakes. I wanted to salvage the employee and redirect him or her into a positive direction. If the violations were minor then a written reprimand would be sufficient. I truly did not take joy in suspending someone. Sometimes my personnel would think I was too lenient but whatever the case I was generally satisfied with the outcome. Most of the time my employees did not repeat their mistake; my tactic worked. Why go for the termination of employment when it is not necessary.

Types of Discipline

Take a look at the types of discipline that I used in my policy and procedure's manual at the Fort Lupton Police Department. It is important to know the types of discipline because not all is negative. The following are some excerpts:

CHAPTER 15

Discipline

Discipline has as its immediate purpose the channeling of individual effort into effective and productive action. Discipline may include such activities as encouragement counseling, training or the imposition of negative sanctions. Violation of departmental policies and procedures may result in disciplinary action. Violation of departmental rules will result in disciplinary action.

Positive Discipline

Positive discipline may be defined as that form of training and attitudinal conditioning, which may be used to reinforce desired conduct or alter behavior without invoking punishment. These may include:

- *Training - Provides a positive mechanism by altering the behavior of the affected departmental member by providing insight or review into the correct methods of police operation and conduct. Training should not be administered as punishment.*
- *Counseling - Provides a positive method for seeking change in employee behavior. At times the supervisor must assume the role of counselor to the subordinate.*

Employee Commendations, Awards for Merit, Valor or Compensation, and employees deserving of special recognition. Fort Lupton Police Employees may be recognized by the below criteria. (See Awards Program Chapter 2.9)

- *Commendations by supervisor given to employees for above and beyond normal duties, example: Citizen*

Letter of Commendation. Signed copy to employee and personnel file.

- *Meritorious and valorous action shall be recognized by citizens, other officials or supervisors and brought to the attention of the Chief of Police. Example would be an employees' heroic act while on duty. The police chief shall then determine the appropriate award to vary from official letter of commendation; Employee of the Quarter Certificate; A plaque, or city council recognition.*

It is important to mention positive discipline because there needs to be rewards in addition to punishment. I had implemented various types of employee incentives, such as the Employee of the Quarter, Commendations and a Metal Program for meritorious service and valor. **It is important for the personnel to feel a part of the organization and recognition is a must.**

Negative Discipline

Negative discipline may be defined as that form of discipline which takes the form of punishment. When positive methods of discipline fail to produce compliance, negative discipline must follow to preserve the integrity of the department. Punishment is the first step in the process of removing the subordinate from the organization for the good of the service.

The department will adhere to the following requisites of punishment:
- *Punishment must be fairly and impartially applied.*
- *Certainty of punishment must be understood.*
- *Punishment will follow swiftly upon detection of misconduct.*
- *Punishment for similar breaches of conduct must be consistent.*
- *Punishment is not only provided to train the affected employee, but to train the department as a whole.*

After the assessment of the investigation and a determination of findings, the employees' supervisor(s) will make recommendations for training and/or disciplinary action. The concept of progressive discipline will be followed, except that serious infraction(s) may receive severe disciplinary action commensurate with the infraction(s).

The above reflects my philosophy.   There should be recognition for good behavior. All too often, the employee does not get the recognition for exceptional performance. I think it should be a two-way street, recognition for doing something positive and negative for misdeeds.

Professional Standard Review Board

Some chiefs and managers may be against this because they do not want anyone to know the business of the department in particular personnel matters. As an option, I included a Professional Standard Review Board in special circumstances in order to get an impartial viewpoint. Why not get some help in some of the more difficult cases. The following is an excerpt of this section of the Fort Lupton Police Department's policy on discipline:

> *The chief may refer the case to a Professional Standards Review Board in certain situations to make a determination of a violation and make a recommendation.*
>
> 1. *The Professional Standards Review Board may consist of*
>   a. *Two police officers*
>   b. *One police supervisor*
>   c. *One citizen*
> 2. *Selection process for review board: All department members will be voted into service by their peers. Alternates will also be selected to serve in the absence of the member or in case a member is the subject of a complaint. The police chief may select a police committee member to serve on the review board. The police chief will select the citizen member to serve making the best, most objective possible choice from the community at large.*

> *The Professional Standards Review Board may study all investigative results. They may meet and request further interviews of complainants, witnesses, subjects and other principals.*

> *The Professional Standards Review Board may recommend disciplinary and/or corrective action the police chief may institute sanctions more or less severe than those recommended.*

The selection makeup of the board is up to the chief. You can have more civilians and less police officers or have an equal number. I find that the civilians can do a very credible job in reviewing disciplinary matters and can provide guidance during difficult times. We have heard it all before. The police department in many cases gives the appearance of a secretive organization. You can help to dispel this notion if you decide to use civilians in special circumstances. It is just something to consider. Some of the larger police departments are already doing this so it is not a new concept, but it is new to medium and small departments. Whatever action the police chief takes also needs to be reasonable in the eyes of the public. Believe me, there is nothing sacred when it comes to city government. No one can ever keep his or her mouths shut. Take for example, the information coming from the closed door of an executive session before or after the City Council Meeting. The word always got out of these sessions. No one is supposed to talk but the council members do. I always found out what went on all the time behind closed doors. Police officers can never keep things to themselves. It seemed the minute that I was finished speaking to an employee everyone knew what happened. Most of the time the person receiving the discipline told everyone what happened in the chief's office.

Just think of the repercussions when the word gets out to the council members and the community. If the employee does not think that he or she got a fair treatment then the message will be negative to all his or her friends, relatives and others who will listen. A great deal of damage can be done if the perception of the treatment is not fair. Most of the time, when a council member heard the news regarding a discipline, they usually said, "Good Chief." In Fort Lupton the Council Members would also say, "Do what ever it takes to straighten out the department." I just smiled when they mentioned it and it was reassuring that I had their continuing support.

Is Evaluations Necessary?

The last pieces of the puzzle are evaluations. Some police departments do them and some do not. When I was with the Bristol Police Department for 18 years, my performance was never evaluated by a supervisor nor did I evaluate anyone when I was a supervisor. It seems silly to think about it now but it would have been nice to know how I was doing. I just assumed management was very happy with my performance. As long as no one rocked the boat, everyone was happy. This was considered the norm in Bristol. I do not know if they are doing evaluations at this time or not.

When I was going to graduate school at the University of New Haven, I developed an evaluation system for police officers including supervisors. I thought as well as others that it was a good tool to begin the process of evaluations. Even my former chief was impressed with the document, but the evaluation system did not go anywhere. The evaluations would first have to be approved by the union because it was a change in their working conditions if you can believe it.

I received my first opportunity to use my evaluation system after I had arrived in Somersworth, New Hampshire. After staffing my evaluation system with my personnel, they seemed positive about it because it was performance based. Other words, it was an evaluation on job performance and each task was broken down into acceptable and unacceptable performance. I like the evaluation because it gives an opportunity for the employee to know exactly where they stand on acceptable performance. The evaluations were performed once a year but more often with probationary employees. It was an opportunity for the supervisor to have a one on one chat with subordinates regarding his or her performance. The evaluations could have been more productive if they were attached to merit increases. When you have a union, this becomes more difficult because their percentages are locked in for everyone even marginal performers. In my opinion, if an employee is not performing up to standards then they did not deserve a raise.

The evaluation is not a tool for discipline but you certainly can use the results to support a disciplinary case. It can also point out potential disciplinary problems and implement corrective behavior. An evaluation is a tool to point out the strengths and weakness of an individual. It is an opportunity for the individual to learn his or her weaknesses and to work on them. At the same time, management learns of these weaknesses and there may be a common denominator for a group of individuals. It is an opportunity for management to provide training programs to correct these deficiencies. It is a two-way street: the employee can work to improve his or her performance and management can provide training to assist with the employees' development.

When I traveled west to Arizona and Colorado, they were already using evaluations for their employees. These evaluations were tied somewhat into merit increases but generally, everyone in Florence, Arizona received their merit increase anyway. The problem that I saw in Florence was that the evaluation form was for a city employee and it did not zero in on job task for a particular department like the police department or fire department. The evaluation forms were flawed but it was better than not having one. Everyone expected to receive his or her raise. Everyone received a written evaluation except for me, if it makes any sense. Because the Town Council had appointed me, the Town Manager decided it was best for the council to evaluate me. I did not argue being the local, humble public servant. It did not make any sense, since the town manager saw me on a daily basis and who would know best? When it was time, the council met with me in executive session before a council meeting to discuss my evaluation. Now, this was about seven months before my contract would be up for renewal. I was surprised because they gave me a rave review. They gave me compliment after compliment and overall they were very pleased with my performance. They never discussed any criticism. Usually during an evaluation the evaluator would discuss any weaknesses and areas for improvement, but in this case there were none. They gave me a $3,000 raise and I was very pleased. One council member asked when my contract was up for renewal, and one mention the exact date. I should have noticed it but I was just ecstatic about my raise. Little did I realize that they were not going to renew my contract anyway?

The point is that some evaluations could be false and it is a problem in itself. Many evaluations are flawed because the supervisor does not want to tell the truth. The truth hurts sometimes but then you have to be honest to the employee in all fairness. If you are not going to be honest with evaluations and you are just going through the motions, then you may as well "can" your evaluation system. Just give the employee their raise.

The evaluation system in Fort Lupton, Colorado was a fair system. The new City Administrator established a new evaluation system that he probably borrowed from his previous place of employment. Nevertheless, it was a good one. He even offered to replace his if I had come up with a better system for the police department. He would give it consideration. I have to admit even though he was new at being a city administrator he had the makings of being a top rate manager. The evaluation system was tied directly into a merit system. I thought about making revisions on the evaluation system that I had developed but had not come to that point yet when I left the fair city of Fort Lupton.

Even if evaluations are not tied into a merit system, it still is a good management tool for the chief or manager. If it is an accurate evaluation, you will know more about each person and how they are performing. If there are any weaknesses, you will know as well as any potential disciplinary problems. It may be an opportunity to intervene early before a matter gets out of hand.

In summary, **discipline is a two-way street** - there can be some good and bad points. I do not know anyone who takes joy in disciplining someone but it is unavoidable. Unfortunately, there are times when you have to make an example of one or two employees for the good of the police department. Personally, I think when the police chief or manager is assertive in disciplinary matters there are less problems with his or her personnel. The opposite is true when the personnel can see management is reluctant to doing anything. If this is true, there are those individuals who will try to get away with everything. Just take a look at a chief who runs a tight ship or other words, do not overlook even small infractions of the rules and regulations. It may seem petty but this type of agency has very few disciplinary problems. The more that you do in the beginning, the better it will be in the long run.

There are so many tasks involved in running a police department that handling disciplinary matters is an integral part of the system. It is very easy to criticize a police chief in how he or she manages a police department and even more so in how he or she handles disciplinary matters. Other people are watching what you do. If you mishandle a disciplinary matter your personnel and more important the public will view it negatively. Just look how fast the last two chiefs from Los Angeles went down hill. It was a perception on how they handled specific incidents. They were well-respected, very able police administrators. A good example is the Rodney King incident. Everyone is well aware of what happened and need I say more? When the going gets rough, the chief takes the heat and unfortunately, it will cost him very dearly. He or he will ultimately get the "golden handshake or outright terminated. Intelligence does not play a factor; it is the politics of the situations. It depends upon who is more expendable, the police chief or the politician. Handling disciplinary matters effectively is a task that can no longer be ignored. The better you handle these types of situations the better it will be for you in the end.

Chapter 14
Patrol Operations

The patrol division is the "backbone" of any police department. Most of your personnel and resources are assigned to patrol. During the course of my career, I have had the opportunity to visit many police departments and view their operations. Some are better than others. It seems the larger the police department the less they see of the chief. It should not be that way. I will never forget the words of Earl Sweeney, a well-respected leader in law enforcement circles across the country and more important, the former Director of the Police Academy in New Hampshire. He said two profound statements that had a tremendous effect upon my management style. First he said "You manage best by walking around" and he said, "Put the shoe leather to the pavement." What does this have to do with police operations? I had already discussed it earlier in the chapter on management styles. It has everything to do with police operations. Matter of fact, this is one area you need to pay close attention. This is not to infer that other areas involved in policing are any less important.

What did he truly mean? I had just come from the Bristol Police Department and my former chief's management style was such that he stayed in the office except to take a coffee break. This occurs when he surfaced and he would chat with personnel for a few minutes. It is fine to depend upon your personnel for daily or weekly briefings but are they telling you everything and being honest? Are they telling you what you want to hear or are they just "sugar coating" it because they do not want to upset you? If you are going to be held accountable for what goes on in the department and the city, it is your responsibility to know. If you have the trust and confidence in your staff then there is no cause for worry. I understood what he was telling me. It came over loud and clear. I do not know if the other chiefs in the room understood but it was a simple concept he was telling us all during a management seminar. Earl Sweeney has had many years of experience as a police chief before he became the director of the police academy. He was relating his experience why he was successful. It is not by accident that one person is more successful than another. Sometimes experience is the best teacher. Some chiefs probably blew him off but I was paying close attention. Many of those police chiefs who were in the room with me are no longer in policing. They ran into some misfortune and many resigned or got fired. Maybe they should have been listening closer. What he said made perfect sense to me in all this madness of trying to be a good police chief. It was not that I felt I was better than anyone else was but I had a desire to succeed as police chief.

Do You Feel Lucky?

I did not want to stay in my "ivory tower" and depend completely upon my personnel for consultations and briefings. My patrol captain in Somersworth, New Hampshire was reluctant to tell me anything except for bad news. I realized that he was still bitter about being passed over for police chief and I hoped it would get better in time. I made up my mind that I was going to **make my own luck**. I did not feel confident enough to be lucky so I made it my business to find out what was going on in the police department. I had to laugh sometimes. This guy would come into my office and say, "Chief, can I see you for a minute." Matter of fact, I found out what he was going to talk to me about because I had already found out. Most of the time what he said was not a surprise. His behavior was predictable. After having gone to the Federal Bureau of Investigation academy for management staff and chiefs, you would have thought he would have come back with all kinds of new ideas, suggestions and new programs. No, he had zero contributions. I tried to ask him about some of these programs and he said, "They don't work." I said to myself they do not work if you do not try them. This individual was the ultimate pessimist. I was disappointed that he never bothered to utilize his knowledge to improve patrol operations. He was part of the management staff that I inherited. Just a side note, the sheriffs have it right. They usually bring in their own management staff that they can trust and depend upon after being elected into office. In municipal government, it is much more difficult to fire your management staff. It takes a time and documentation in order to remove someone. During this time there could be damage done far beyond repair.

After about a year or so watching him, I decided to reorganize the department to be more efficient. I was not going to take any more chances. I took away this captain's patrol duties and transferred him to be the Support Services Commander in charge of the building, vehicle maintenance, and dispatch. It was the only place I could put him without screwing things up too badly just short of termination. The "janitor" as he called himself, could not mess up too badly because I watched every move he made. Had I stayed there longer I probably would have made another move, but this time he would have been out the door. I put the other captain in charge of Operations including Investigations and the Patrol functions. After making this move, I could see a drastic improvement and felt more comfortable with it. I guess the point is **can you trust your staff to do the job?** I cannot emphasize this enough; you need to have he right person in place in charge of a specific function to do the job. The former captain in charge of patrol operations was not a bad person. He was a good spirited likeable person, who was thrust into a position beyond his abilities and he could not realize it. Do you know someone like this? When a new police chief takes over a police department, he or she is going to inherit a management staff, good or bad. It takes some time to figure out whom you can depend upon. If you are so lucky to have a good staff then your task in developing the department further and bring it to a new level will be much easier.

Now, some police chiefs will say they are too busy with administrative functions to be out there every day and that is why they have supervisors. This is very true to a point but you cannot afford not to be. I use to hear it all the time but it is just an excuse. Sometimes police chiefs are caught by surprise when there are problems. Many of these problems could be dealt with early on before they become insurmountable.

No one likes to admit they have problems. Police officers and supervisors in the field are responsible for their own area and they tend to be protective. They want to deal with problems and keep to themselves. Who wants to admit to the lieutenant or higher that they cannot deal with problems and need help? It is just human nature to deal with the problem by yourself. Sometimes these issues get out of hand and chiefs wonder why they were left out of the loop and suddenly it was a major problem. Just recall when you were a police officer. Would you dare tell the sergeant or police chief that you could not handle a problem? It is very difficult to do. It is not in the human psyche to admit failure especially a police officer.

Protect and Serve

One of the basic functions of the police department is to "protect and serve" the public. You see this motto on many of the marked police cruisers and literature across the country. This profound statement says a great message but sometimes we forget what it is all about. The public has high expectations for their police force. They expect that they will be protected at all times and criminals will be apprehended when they commit crimes. They also expect the speedy recovery and return of stolen property. Get this; the public also wants to be kept informed. Is this asking too much? Are we living up to the motto, "Protect and Serve?" Clearly now, we do not live up to the expectations of the public. It looks good on paper or emblemized on patrol car doors, but in actual practice, this is one area that can be drastically improved. People make fun of police officers all the time drinking coffee and eating donuts.

Just think about where all the complaints originate. Most of them originate from the patrol division. People usually complain about the attitude or rude treatment of the officer. Generally, there is dissatisfaction with police officer being unsympathetic to the needs of the citizens. Sometimes police departments are their own worst enemy. We teach police officers to be suspicious even to the point where the complainant is thought to be lying. We can certainly improve in this area.

After being in Bristol, Connecticut for so long, I had the opportunity to witness attitudes of police officers and how they treated citizens. This was an example of a daily routine of a police officer in Bristol. I would be willing to bet the attitudes have not changed very much. At the beginning of every shift, the officers going on duty would make a coffee run. The first order of business for the day was to meet your fellow police officer at the border of the district and talk for a half hour or so, unless of course, there was a call for service to interrupt this important dialogue. Sometimes, depending upon the time of day, there would be a third officer. Now, people are not stupid... they know what is going on. The general public tends to stereotype police officers as the "Dunkin Donut" men, eating donuts and drinking coffee all the time. It is probably not fair to put all police officers into this category because not all officers do it, but it does seem strange that this label has stuck all over the country. Just check it out and hear all the jokes yourself. People see police officers parked side by side all the time drinking coffee. When are they protecting the public? If they are "shooting the breeze" for an hour or so, there is very little protecting going on. Some will say they are passing on information. Maybe the police officer thinks the public is not aware of what is actually going on.

During their eight-hour shift there was very little actual police work, there is some patrolling, very little traffic enforcement and some calls for service. I was considered strange and not trustworthy because I did not want to participate in the coffee breaks. I always made an excuse since I was more eager to do real police work. In between calls for service, there are several more coffee breaks during the course of the shift. The lieutenant in charge of the shift would expect everyone to put miles on his or her cruiser, at least 60 miles during the course of their shift. I guess management figured the officer would be forced to patrol in the neighborhoods and be visible. Where was the sergeant when all this was going on? They were required to check with each of their subordinates at least three times on every shift and sometimes they did not check at all. Their concept of patrolling may have sounded good but in actual practice, there was just "aimless" patrol without any purpose.

It was funny to think about how these guys tried to circumvent the system by trying to keep management happy with the miles. If someone had many miles he sometimes passed some to the next shift so that officer would not have to drive as much. Near the end of the shift, if someone was short of miles even during the gasoline crunch during the 1980s, they would cruise the perimeter of their district several times at a fast speed until they had the proper mileage to turn in. One officer was creative enough to the extreme that he jacked up the rear end, wedged the accelerator down to put the rear wheels in motion, and achieved his mileage that way. These officers worked hard to get out of work. Just thinking about it now just makes me realize how much the pubic was getting shortchanged. It was not a new phenomena but a culture that had developed over the years. The concept of protecting and serving had been forgotten. The only challenge was to see how much money they could make by pulling overtime shifts and working extra duty construction jobs. The almighty dollar was the rule of the day. It was truly sad to think they had forgotten what law enforcement was all about. Maybe times have changed and the emphases are more on "protect and serve" the community.

The sergeant is supposed to set the example for the police officers, right? Well, one example, I was embarrassed to have witnessed a particular incident. I backed up a sergeant who stopped a car for a traffic violation. Apparently, it was a stop sign violation. It should have been just another ordinary traffic stop, when I heard the sergeant swear at the motorist and saw him point to his stripes and say, "See these stripes." I wanted to just crawl into a hole and die. Any police officer for any reason, let alone a traffic violation should belittle no one. Why not just issue the ticket and let the person be on his way. I am sure this motorist told all his friends about how he was treated by Bristol's finest. The sergeant thanked me for backing him up and I went about my business. I never said a word about it. Do we know how our officers are treating motorists during traffic stops? Many of the complaints and bad feelings toward police officers originate from a routine traffic stop. I have more examples but you get the general idea.

It was not my purpose to humiliate any department but only point out problems due to a lack of productivity, concern for the citizens and the stereotype image of the police officer.   Further, I might add, not all departments are like my examples. There are many good police agencies out there but the number of bad ones far outweighs the good ones. As I had made my journey around the country, the impressions of police officers were still the same. Police officers want to see law enforcement as a profession and many departments have achieved this goal but the overall opinion of police officers is poor to fair at best. It is not by accident why people feel the way they do about the police. Many police officers have worked hard at trying to perform police duties but the negative attitudes by the public still persist.   Just ask around the community how the public perceives the police department.   Studies will tell you people have more confidence in their police department than ever before. They certainly did not perform the studies in any of my former communities. Some people still hold a low opinion of police officers and it gets worse with negative contacts such as a criminal or motor vehicle arrest. The feelings are the same or even worse in my new community. My new community appears to have a professional police department but you cannot tell from the citizens. Many have a poor opinion of the police officers. The objective is to keep the negative opinions to a minimum. It is almost impossible to win over one hundred percent of the people. I think that it is too bad because police departments are their own worst enemy. They have the power to do something about this negative label, yet they have their "blinders on." If the supervisors ignore the way citizens are being treated in the field, the problems will get worse.

A new police chief or manager going into a new police department needs to find out about the culture of the department, type of service and the overall impression of the quality of service to its citizens. The chief or manager might find themselves doing more damage control than providing programs for the citizens. There needs to be a way to find out what is going on and locating people that will tell you the truth, is just as important. No doubt, it will be a challenge. However, the police and community working together can change the negative perception of the police department.

Doing Your Own Assessment

In each of my prior police department, I did an overall assessment of its operations, in particular, the patrol operations. I wanted to find out for myself the present state of the department. I interviewed my management staff, personnel and even other city employees and citizens. I needed to know the problems if I were going to do something about it.

I did a complete assessment from top to bottom including riding on patrol to see for myself what was going on. I put into practice what Earl Sweeney told me about **"managing by walking around"** and **"Putting my shoe leather to the pavement."** In order to find out exactly what is going, on you have to get out there and check things out for yourself. It seemed like a common sense thing to do. If I were going to succeed at being police chief, I would have to create my own luck. I went out into each of my communities and walked around. I made it a standard practice to get out of my office to find out what was going on. I spoke to people and was able to get valuable information about the community and more about the police department. I used this information to improve the operation of the department. Getting input from the citizens, I found to be a valuable resource. Matter of fact, when my personnel were looking for me, they would say I was doing my "Walk About." I guess they watched "Crocodile Dundee, too and coined a new phrase for me. I kind of like the phase because they were beginning to understand what I was doing. It was not to waste time to shoot the breeze but to get information. The key was to **get the community involved**.

In Somersworth, New Hampshire patrol operations was more reactive than anything else, like many other police departments. There would be a call for service and the assignment was given to a police officer to handle. At the time, there was no concept of directed patrol where a police officer would patrol previously identified problem areas. What a new concept! At least in Bristol, Connecticut we were assigning directed patrols during the shift. Their idea of patrol was to ride around and maybe make some traffic stops in the beginning. Actually, the idea of riding around and being visible is not new. O.W. Wilson, the author of Police

Administration discussed the concept of "omnipresence." If while on patrol you gave the impression that you were everywhere, the crooks would go somewhere else. Actually, they just waited until the officer drove by and broke into the building. There needed to be a new school of thought. Just riding around the neighborhood and just being visible was not very effective. Something else had to be done to make patrol operations more effective. I knew that I would have my work cut out for me in Somersworth. It was not that they did not know how to conduct police work but the old school of policing had to be changed. Besides, the town fathers did not hire me to keep things status quo. They saw a need for change and I was about to change some things. Slowly but surely I made some changes. I was introducing my personnel to a new philosophy.

What type of assessment should be performed in the department? It is just as important to find out what they are not doing as what they are doing. What they were currently doing was a product of the old school of thought. The following are some suggestions in making an assessment of the patrol operations:

- Type of Calls for Service.
- Time spent on Calls for Service.
- Quality of Written Reports.
- Quality of Preliminary Investigations?
- What Calls do not require a report?
- How the officers handle Calls for Service?
- How much time to hand Calls for Service?
- Number of Traffic Arrests per shift?
- Type of Self-Initiated Activity?
- Any other assigned duties?
- Number and type of citizen complaints.
- What are the officers doing with uncommitted time?

These were just some ideas. You do not have to do anything formal but taking notes is a good idea to begin planning for improvements. I discovered that there was a great deal of *uncommitted time* and it should not be a big surprise because this was generally the case in small and medium size police department. Rarely do police officers run from call to call every day of the week. Granted, there are busy periods and everyone understands this. There is too much uncommitted time that the officers should be using more constructively.

Getting the officers more involved in using *uncommitted time* would be a feat in any department. Everyone likes to take a break from the back-to-back calls and do nothing for a while like take a coffee break in previous examples. It is this notion of doing nothing is what needs to be changed. Officers use to complain how busy they were taking calls for service and so forth. When you stop and analyze what they are doing you will find, just as I have, there are times that cannot be accounted for. Back in Bristol, management directed all officers to write down the times, locations and what they were doing on a shift. First, no one looked at the "Officer's Activity Report. Secondly, many of the officers just outright lied about their activity. I called it "Creative Lying." The only time someone decided to look at the activity report was when an officer was in trouble for something. The whole thing was a joke and no one took it very seriously because the supervisors never followed up, plain and simple.

The next idea was the concept of "Directed Patrols." Now, this was a good idea and it forced the officer to use some of his or her uncommitted time. The officers were directed to respond to troubled areas and document what they did. Now, some officers did it, others went through the motions, and did the "Creative Lying" bit. The management of the department did create more paperwork and the officers were not happy about it. Anytime there was a change they would always moan and groan. It was a typical human nature response. The program could have worked much better if they had instructed the supervisors to follow up and report their findings. Upper management should have been checking the supervisor's work also to make sure the task was being performed.

The lessons of past experiences were carried with me to Somersworth, New Hampshire and I used them in my other departments as well. I made changes along the way such as having the officers **complete an activity report without the hourly description.** I did not want to force my officers to lie about it. There was the concept of directed patrols that I had implemented as well. In each case, I held the supervisor accountable for checking the paperwork.

The main point is that the *uncommitted time* needed to be channeled into more of a constructive effort in each of my former police departments. It does not take one to realize and numerous statistical studies to show there is much more *uncommitted time* than committed time. There is certainly management software from different vendors that will break it down for you. You will know exactly what they are doing and how much time they are spending on a given task. Now, I understand some officers will be busy from start to finish on a shift but there are certainly down times. Not everyone is busy one hundred percent all the time.

I even went through the trouble of doing a statistical analysis of the types and numbers of motor vehicle arrests performed by each officer for each month. Some officers consistently wrote more traffic tickets than others did month after month. I was not surprised, since this was true in Bristol as well as the other departments. If these officers were consistent from month to month and handled the same number of calls as the other officer, why did they not write just as many tickets? It is a good question but they will tell you they were not a traffic person or they do not like to write traffic tickets. Not that I wanted anyone to manufacture motor vehicle arrests, but is it not their job to be watching for moving violations while on patrol? Is it not their job to make the community safer by enforcing traffic violations? In each of my former departments, I made it a point to have everyone involved in enforcing traffic laws. I figured it was not too much to ask. There were some officers in the beginning when I first took over a department that they wrote very few if any tickets during the month. I instructed the supervisors to ride with the officers who were not producing. Getting officers to do more motor vehicle stops for violations was a good opportunity to check for other criminal activity.

Now, someone will accuse our department of having a traffic ticket quota. I never suggested, hinted or ever required anyone to meet a traffic quota. I pointed out that during the course of the month while on patrol there should be no problem in observing traffic violations even by accident. The purpose of traffic enforcement is to reduce the number of injury accidents because of a moving violation; however, there are other good results. Because of increased enforcement, my officers were able to arrest more drunk drivers, and drivers operating under suspension and a host of other violations. More important, the officers were able to make a significant number of drug related arrests as a direct result from an initial moving violation. If an officer was not doing anything for the month, I wanted to know why. It was not asking too much for an officer to come to work to be more observant and to take action when the flagrant violations were there.

Another area that I improved upon was parking ticket enforcement. In Somersworth, New Hampshire, they had parking tickets but the Parking Enforcement Officer, a non-sworn officer or commonly referred to as a "Meter Maid" wrote the bulk of the tickets. Typically, police officers do not like to write parking tickets. It is too beneath them, or so they thought. In Florence, Arizona and Fort Lupton, Colorado, unbelievably, they did not have parking tickets. It did not take me long to design and implement them. The idea was to get the officers out of their cruiser more often. We were getting more complaints about vehicles parking in the handicap parking spaces and it was time to enforce the violations. Again, here was another opportunity to increase contacts with citizens.

I found out many of the officers were not assigned to specific areas. Patrol officers were just roaming all over the city and taking turns responding to calls. They would merely wait around for something to happen. They were not responsible for any one area and I changed that. I created patrol districts in each community and made the officer responsible for each assigned areas. Yet, this was another new concept incorporated into the patrol division. At first, they could not understand the significance but after a while, they saw the light. I wanted them to get to know their area better and, hopefully, get to know the business and people as well. During the evening shift, the officers were not checking businesses like they should. While checking these businesses they would find some problems such as breaking and entry into a building or even vandalism.

While waiting for something to happened, why not initiate some activity. It was a different concept but being more aggressive on patrol can lead to better things. *Self-initiated activity* can be one of the most productive activities during the shift. I have seen it so many times where a police officer, being inquisitive, stops a motor vehicle for a routine traffic violation, and suddenly the stop turns into a major felony arrest. Now, you are not going to get this way if all you are doing is driving around and drinking coffee. I am not opposed to taking a coffee break but there has to be time to do some police work, like protecting and serving the community.

I had an officer in Fort Lupton, Colorado who approached me one day and asked me if he could do some drug enforcement. It was like music to my ears. He understood the reputation of the police department where someone allegedly was tipping off the drug dealers. Here was someone who wanted to do real police work. He said that he did not like drug dealers and wanted to do something about it. I told him I would provide all the support possible. I emphasized traffic arrests and convinced him most of the drug arrests are made from routine traffic stops during the evening hours. I quickly made a believer out of him after he made several good drug arrests after a few motor vehicle stops. This officer was a "go-getter." He convinced a few other officers to join his quest and soon we had our own mini drug task force on the night shift.

Handling the information was easy. One other sergeant on the night shift knew what was going on beside me and sharing that information with others was on a need to know basis. Some other officers felt hurt but the overall results far outweighed a few hurt feelings. After a while, they understood the need to know basis. The local drug dealers were starting to get hurt by our drug enforcement. I could not have set it up any better. Patrol operations can be fun. The City Council told me numerous times about the wonderful job we were doing. It was gratifying to know someone appreciated our efforts. We were addressing the City Council's goals in reducing drug trafficking in and around our community.

In addition, I told the officers that in the event that personal property was confiscated during a drug arrest, we would initiate an asset forfeiture process. Any asset turned over to the police department by the court would be sold and the proceeds would go into an asset drug forfeiture account that would be used to buy more police equipment. The city administrator, I might add, approved the drug forfeiture account. He like the idea in using the account to buy police equipment, but the requests had to go through the City Council for approval. City Council did not have a problem with it either. Why not use the drug dealer's money to buy more police equipment to fight drug trafficking in and around the community. Everything worked out as planned. The officers loved this idea and they worked harder. I actually enjoyed every minute of it myself.

A distinguishing incident happened one day and I have to mention it here. One fellow had his vehicle turned over to the police department by the court because he was found guilty of selling drugs. Typically, we would sell the car to the highest bidder after advertising it for a week. One evening this fellow saw his former vehicle parked in the police parking lot. He probably had too much to drink because he picked up a large rock, slowly walked up to the vehicle and threw it through the windshield. After throwing it, he just calmly walked away as if nothing had happened. The only problem was that the entire episode was on camera. He did not know we had a camera overlooking and video taping the events in the parking lot. He was arrested nearby and was brought to the police department for booking. When he went to court, just to add insult to injury, he was required to pay restitution to the police department to replace the windshield. It was ironic to think that he had to pay damages for a vehicle he once owned. He felt somewhat foolish but we did collect. Actually, everyone joked about it for a long time and every once in a while an officer would remind him. It was one of the lighter moments. He certainly had a bad day and would quickly like to forget about it at least until the next time he was arrested. There was justice and we were starting to reap the benefits.

Everything came together very quickly in Fort Lupton. The officers understood the concept of patrol and they wanted to work. The only problem I saw, and it was frustrating, was losing good personnel to another department in the metro area. I could not blame them though because they would be making much more money than I could pay them. I wish I could have paid these police officers more even after the City Administrator conducted a compensation study to tell us we were paying officers much lower than other departments. I did not need a compensation study to tell me this. He needed documentation for the City Council to consider revising the city's compensation salary scale. Fort Lupton was a training ground for police officer pure and simple. Until the city paid just as much as a metro department, they will continue to lose good officers, even today. Even after I left the department, they lost two more officers to a metro department. This metro department took three of my best officers. I guess it speaks well of the quality of officers that we hired and trained.

Word does circulate to other departments in a positive sense when police departments have good patrol operations. When the officers are excited and look forward to going to work, good thing happen. The Patrol Division becomes a more cohesive unit and even the public can see the enthusiasm. It was exciting to see a transformation from a mediocre to highly skilled police operations.

I wish it were that easy in Florence, Arizona. Basically, I had to rebuild the police department. We had to recruit, hire and train new officers to fill the existing vacancies. It was a challenge to say the least, but it was rewarding to see a transformation of a poor agency into a respectable one. There was nothing but confusion and chaos in that department. They were dying for some leadership. Had I had remained police chief longer than two years, who knows how far the police department would have advanced by now? What took two years for me to build up the chief who replaced me tore it down. The department reverted back to the confusion and chaos as it was before I took over the department. That chief failed to see the concept in what I was trying to do. If he had asked, I would have told him what I was trying to accomplish. The first thing he did was to have the officers not run radar and ticket speeders as my officers had done. He did not want the town's people to be harassed and get tickets. The patrol operations were in confusion and disarray. Not that I was the greatest thing that ever came along, but I knew how to make the system work. On the positive side during the two years I was there, the patrol operations came together. We had accomplished many things together.

Making a Commitment

My secret in improving patrol operations after making my initial assessment was to **work within the system**. Other words, without threatening to fire or discipline the officers right away and carry a big stick, I worked with them to improve and encourage what they should be doing little by little. All supervisors were new. It took a great deal of patience and perseverance to make the system better. When I took over everyone was in an acting position. My lieutenant was new to law enforcement. He had been full time for about eight years in his second career. He had loads of expertise in the management field and performed very well. He knew exactly what I was trying to do and he was enthusiastic. He was weak in some areas but that was no problem, I would train him as well as the new sergeants. I knew it would take some time to rebuild the department and my personnel were all for becoming a professional police department.

The town's people and the town fathers liked what they saw. The officers had been transformed from riding around on patrol to something more positive. We were actually providing good service to the citizens. One positive thing that the citizens like was the personalized approach to vacant home checks. We did the same thing in Fort Lupton, Colorado and Somersworth, New Hampshire. The winter visitors in Florence did not have to worry. While their home was vacant during the off-season, the officers checked their home during their shift. If there were any problems, we would give them a call to their out-of-state residence. The senior citizens, or commonly known as the "snow birds," complimented us all the time.

If the police department has a poor reputation, the first priority is to rebuild the trust. The police chief and other executives have to **"police the police" first** before anything good will happen. It is just common sense. How can the public trust the police if they think they are nothing but crooks. Maybe it is not true or there are only a few bad apples but it is the perception by the public that hurts the police department's image. If there is a problem, the chief along with management has to clean it up.

One indicator how the police treat the public is the number of citizen complaints. It was important to know how many citizens complaints and the seriousness of these complaints. If there are a number of complaints, you can feel certain that many more go unreported. Probably a citizen reports one out of every five complaints. If the same officer is involved in a number of them then perhaps there is a problem. As I had earlier stated in another chapter, people will complain to get out of a ticket. If use of force is involved and there are complaints as a result, it would behoove the chief to take a closer look. What I did in every agency was to initiate a use of force report by each officer that had to use force to make an arrest. Matter of fact, the International Association of Chiefs of Police endorses the use of force report and encourages agencies to report the numbers of use of force incidents. The software was free at the time and it would have been interesting to find out the extent of the problem all across the country.

Requiring officers to use the use of force form will automatically take care of most of the complaints of excessive force. The supervisors need to review the reports and follow up and ask questions on questionable use of force tactics. At first, the officers were suspicious of management for using the use of force forms. I told them frankly the purpose and they would see that the number of use of force complaints would be reduced. Actually, it keeps everyone honest. The officers saw that I was right after I gave them an explanation. They have to understand that management was not out to get police officers in trouble. If someone were using excessive force in making an arrest this person would eventually get into trouble anyway. The complaints were already there. Once the complaints regarding excessive use of force have been resolved, the police department can proceed to the next level. If the public can see the chief along with other leaders have been cleaning up the department, this will certainly instill more confidence in the department. You have to pay attention to what the officers are doing.

Police officers have to keep in mind the goals of law enforcement first and foremost is to protect the public. Everyone should be able to venture out into his or her neighborhood at any time of the day or night and not be afraid of being a victim. People are afraid to be a victim and this thought permeates the young and old. My vision was to make our community safe and I developed strategies to accomplish this objective.

The patrol operations would be the key for success. I wanted to use crime prevention techniques to target problem areas, and in particular, criminals. Many of these principals are not new. Crime prevention techniques was utilized beginning in 1829 by Sir Robert Peel in the first modern police department in England. Some police chiefs call it different names but the strategy is **crime prevention**. Organizing the patrols in different areas to reduce crime is the true essence of policing.

Crime prevention is very important along with the return of stolen property. Citizens like to get their property back on a timely basis if the stolen property had been recovered. There is nothing that gets citizens upset or irritated more than by keeping their property for years when it should have been released. Now, the property should not be appropriated for the department's use while the case is going through the court system. Take for example, when I was appointed as police chief in Florence, Arizona and when I took over the office on my first day I noticed a large television with a property tag on it in my office. It was stolen property that never had been returned to its rightful owner. I told the detective responsible for property control to put the television and anything else that was property back into the evidence room where it belonged. I wondered how much of the stolen property had left the department. I understood why the people did not have any faith in their police department

Another area that was a problem was a citizen turning in firearms to the police department because they did not want to keep them any longer. In Bristol, Connecticut, many of these guns never made it to the property room. Many, I am afraid to say, went directly to the officer's locker. People use to speak of turning in guns and I wondered why they did not make it to the evidence room. After a while, I kind of put two and two together. Here was another situation that management knew about it but did nothing to stop or prevent these occurrences.

One police chief got himself fired in the early 1980s in Somersworth, New Hampshire. Citizens turned in firearms and he eventually would sell them at a gun store in Kittery, Maine. He eventually got caught at it after someone complained. Getting greedy eventually cost him his job. When I took over as Police Chief in 1988, I found an antique firearm in my desk. Not that I was paranoid, but I thought it was strange after all the problems they have had. I thought these officers were trying to set me up by leaving it in the desk. I figured it was a test to see what I was going to do with this firearm. During my first day, I called the sergeant who had been interim police chief into my office and asked him about it. He had a surprised look on his face as if he did not know what I was discussing. He did not know how the gun got there. I told him to take the firearm, fill out a property report and put it into the property room. I could just imagine what would have happened if I had kept it there and wondered when they were going to spring the trap on me. Maybe they were going to try to blackmail me at some point. Anyway, had this been their little plan, it did not work.

The moral of the story is making sure **all of the property and evidence is properly accounted for and inventoried.** It goes along with taking care of your house first. If the citizens find out that the police are playing games with the property then they certainly will lack trust in their police department.

All our statistics from the Uniform Crime Reports or Incident Based Reporting comes from reporting known crimes from different town and cities. From there, we make comparisons from one city to the next to see how we are doing after all. We keep track of the statistics or stats all the time. If the numbers look good, we try to impress the politicians. Are we reducing crime across the board all over the county? The reports tell us that we are reducing crime. I never relied very much on statistics, if they were accurate or not because it was a double-edged sword. One year the chief can be the hero in reducing crime in the community and the next year the goat because crime went up. I was always humble about it and qualified the statement by adding, "We will try our best to keep crime down and there are no guarantees." Even if crime had gone down in some areas, trying to convince a victim of a serious sexual assault that crime in the community is down was futile. I am sure the victim will be impressed. It would be the wrong thing to say.

I think it would be fair to say that crime prevention is an important concept. One police department that I had interviewed for to become chief had a crime prevention office next to the police lobby. One of the interviewers asked us to describe the office next to the police lobby. I thought the person was kidding. Having a crime prevention office is nice but the responsibility of crime prevention rests with each officer, not a showcase office. Having one person in charge of crime prevention is fine and many departments already have crime prevention specialist but what is the patrol operations really doing about it? Each officer has to demonstrate crime prevention in his or her area.

Targeting problem areas and zeroing in on suspected criminals is what crime prevention is all about. If you concentrate in an area long enough, the criminals will move to another area. It is like the reputed gang problem in Fort Lupton, Colorado. People were actually terrified of the so-called Hispanic gangs and I suspected some of the police officers were too. One time, gang members actually drove to a person's house, went inside and dragged out a young male. They beat him up in front of his mother. The police were called to the scene but they did not do anything. They just took some names, addresses and basic information and that was it. There was just a minor report on the incident. In the meantime, the young male had to go to the hospital for treatment of his injuries. He could have been a victim of a homicide. Now something is wrong with this picture. The reputed gang members would drive into the community, pick some fights, some serious, and peddle their drugs and no one would bother them. It seemed we were always trying to get an arrest warrant after the fact.

I believe in old fashion police work and it can be very effective. I called a meeting with my staff and declared war on the gangs. It was time that we took back our community. Our responsibility was to protect the citizens and we were doing a poor job at best. I got word to these gang members that anytime they came into our community the police were going to stop them to see what they were doing. Sure, this could border on harassment. I figure this minor inconvenience is far outweighed by the greater good, namely keeping our citizens safe. Further, I told our officers that if there was probable cause to make an arrest there was no need to wait, make the arrest and bring them to jail. If we had an opportunity to confiscate and impound their property such as their motor vehicle, then we would do so. The idea was to inconvenience them much as possible. There had to be a consequence for getting involved in crime in our community. After a few confrontations with these gang members, the problem quickly went away. The gangs saw that we were serious and they decided to terrorize others in some other community. It only took a few months to take care of the problem. This problem should have been resolved long before my arrival with aggressive patrol. The citizens appreciated our efforts and there were never any complaints of harassment.

Discussing gang problem reminds me about graffiti in some of the neighborhoods. We set about the task to do something about it in Fort Lupton. The objective was to remove the graffiti as soon as possible. We had developed a city ordinance to make the owner of the property responsible to remove the graffiti, if in fact, the person responsible could not be found. In addition, we included a provision to make it illegal for a minor to purchase a can of spray paint. We were somewhat successful in eradicating graffiti and often times the owner of the property was the city. They were slow in removing it on a timely basis.

The City of Phoenix, Arizona did it right. They enacted a city ordinance to remove graffiti. This program was highly successful not only in Phoenix but in other communities as well. As soon as someone "tagged" an area, the city crew would be right there to paint over it. It sends a message to the property owners that the neighborhoods will be kept graffiti free. You cannot say that about many other communities.

The "broken window theory" holds true. This theory holds that physical deterioration and an increase in dilapidated buildings leads to increased concerns for personal safety among area residents. If the property is unsightly because of broken windows and accumulated trash then it will invite others to contribute to the unsightly mess. If the building is cleaned up and the neighbors do likewise then the entire neighborhood looks respectable. More important, the property values remain the same. Another component that the city council was adamant about was strictly enforcing the Zoning Ordinance regarding code violations. Why bother with junk cars and accumulated trash? Like the "Broken Window Theory," it may start with a small mess and before you know it, the little mess suddenly turns into a big mess. The Code Enforcement Officer was on people all the time to get rid of their junk cars and to get rid of their trash. The code was so strict that if people left their empty trash containers on the street too long they were issued a citation for the violation. The City Council was very concerned about the way the neighborhoods looked to visitors in the community. They wanted to convey a good impression about the community to encourage people to move their home or business into the area. Other communities followed suit. Some even call it blight control. Actually, you could go anywhere into the community and not find any slum like conditions or any property with junk cars and trash. The code even included a provision to insure the owners of property cut their grass and weeds. Some people will say it was strict and they were right but we had a respectable looking community that anyone would be proud. More people took pride in their community and reported violations of the code more often than crime.

When I first arrived in Fort Lupton, the pieces of the puzzle were already there. All it took was for me to bring things together. The Zoning Code was not strictly enforced; it was selectively enforced. I used what was already there to clean up the community. I figured if the citizens took pride in their community again then they would get more involved in crime prevention.

The chief must first concentrate on the little things that annoy people. If you take care of the little problems first, then everything else would fall into place. I wanted the officers to thoroughly patrol their patrol district and report any problems. This included doing security checks of buildings to make sure they were secured and had not been vandalized or burglarized. Sometimes you have to remind officers of the basics involved in doing good police work. Concentrating on crime prevention is the key. Preventing crime is just as important in making a number of arrests. Other words, instead of being reactive all the time responding to crime that had already happened why not take a more proactive or aggressive stance and try to prevent crime? This to me was more logical and was what I hoped to accomplish in my former communities. Traditionally, police department were set up to be reactive to crime so some reeducation had to take place. The public had to be educated as well. I always kept the public informed about our crime prevention initiatives either by a letter to the editor or an interview by a news reporter. I encouraged people to report not only crime but also any problems they neighborhood. I told them if their local police department did not know anything about their problem, then the police cannot do anything to help them. Improving the quality of life in the community would be a major impetus of our patrol operations. There will be more on this in another chapter.

Thinking more about police operations made me realize that if people are going to support their police department they must first have confidence and trust in them. This is what is lacking in many communities. It was always an uphill battle for me but I think I was successful in this arena. People in each community were beginning to have confidence and trust in their local police department. This is the true essence of "To Protect and Serve." It is kind of like reinventing patrol operations again. Sometimes officers have to be reminded about the purpose of patrol and how it can best serve its citizens. Sometimes it is a long road but the current or new police chief must take steps to win back the community. Now, take a look at some patrol methods, some of which are typical and some different but equally effective.

Patrol Methods

There are different ways to accomplish the patrol mission and different patrol methods, some of which are very effective. The traditional methods of the marked and unmarked police cruisers and the beat cop are still being used today but now we have to resort to other types of patrol tactics. In small and large police departments, the methods of operation are limited but agencies can be creative.

Sometimes you have to be creative when certain situations arise. While in Somersworth, New Hampshire, we had a problem like any other community with underage minors purchasing beer from supermarkets and the mom and pop convenience stores. It was not so much a deliberate violation but more of a nonchalant attitude about checking for the required identification. We used what we called a "Tic-Tack" patrol to check the liquor establishments. We used underage operatives to go into the store to make a purchase while a plainclothes officer and a marked police cruiser was nearby. It seemed to work very well. We were able to make a number of arrests of adults selling liquor to minors. In order to deal with a particular problem you have to be creative and be flexible with your patrol force.

In the early 1970s I participated in a special patrol called "Team Patrol" in Bristol, Connecticut. The same officers worked in a particular area every day to get to know the people and to deal with the crime problem. Little did we realize that we were actually performing *Community Policing*. The reason I mention this now was at the time we were able to vary our patrol techniques. We realized we were having a problem with marijuana smoking parties in the park during the evening hours. If we drove a marked police cruiser into the area, they would just hide everything. We just could not catch them until we changed our tactics. One evening we changed into plain clothes and set up surveillance in the wooded area overlooking the parking lot where all the pot smoking was taking place. It did not take long to catch them at it and finally we were able to clean up the area. The only casualty was me. I accidentally lay in a poison ivy patch while taking up my surveillance post. In the dark, I was not able to see the poison ivy and got it all over my neck and face. Oh well, I was very itchy for a couple of weeks, but it was worth it to get the druggies out of the park. I guess when it comes right down to it; we will do anything to get results. The Team Patrol concept went away after the Federal funding dried up. It was unfortunate because the powers to be at the time failed to see the effectiveness and the community involvement aspect of this patrol technique.

In Somersworth, New Hampshire, the police bicycle was just starting to come into the picture. Only a few departments at the time had a short of bicycle patrol, and I saw the necessity of having one. No one could see it at the time but you cannot beat an officer on "stealth" patrol. Some people thought it was silly, even our Public Works Director until he observed two officers on patrol bikes swoop down on an individual on a busy street corner in front of a market. Before this person knew it, he was down on the ground being handcuffed. The officers knew that there was an arrest warrant out on the individual. The Public Works Director told me, "Seeing was believing." He was suddenly convinced that the bike patrol was an effective tool for law enforcement. During the early 1990s the police bicycle was still a novelty but the police officers liked its versatility. If you cannot sneak up on criminals on foot then a bicycle is a consideration because you can get into an area before a marked cruiser can and quickly close the gap on a criminal activity. Many police departments use the bicycle patrol and it is very effective.

Learning from past mistakes, I always ask if officers have experience in riding a bicycle. It seems like a silly question, but I got burnt. During the last day of training, one of my officers fell off his bike and broke his arm. He was going to be out of work for at least one month or more. I asked him how he managed to break his arm. He said, "I never rode a bicycle before." He could have volunteered the information prior to training but wanted to attend the training. So it seems not everyone knows how to ride a bicycle. **Remember, you cannot take anything for granted.** After this experience, I always asked the question. It never dawned on me that this individual never rode a bike before the training.

After I left New Hampshire and went to Florence, Arizona, I set up a police bicycle patrol on a part time basis for special patrol situations, functions and parades. It worked well too but in Fort Lupton, Colorado, the officers simply loved using the bicycle. We used the bicycle as often as we could but some days we had to park it because there were days when we were shorthanded. There were many situations when the officer on the bike got to the complaint or alarm first because he could take short cuts and go in places that the cruiser could not. The police bicycle is one of the most effective patrol methods that a department can use. I understand fully that small police departments do not have the luxury of having a bike patrol every day. Sometimes there is only one patrol and many police departments are in this similar situation. Similarly, some medium size police departments may feel the pinch as well.

A police chief facing a manpower shortage can still have a police bike patrol even if it is on a part time basis for special situations or problem areas. It shows that a police department can be very multitalented when the time comes. This was the case in Bristol, Connecticut when we were having a problem with unregistered dirt bikes being operated on private property. We quickly took care of this problem in short order by equipping an officer on a police dirt bike. It did not take him long to clean up the area by issuing a number of citations to the violators. After a few weeks of chasing them down, he was hard pressed to come up with any more violations.

These were some examples of being creative to take care of problems in the community where the traditional foot patrols and marked police cruiser rendered ineffective. Some police chiefs are still in the old school of thought. They utilize the same traditional patrol methodology, using a marked police cruiser most of the time and a walking beat man some times, day in and day out. They are inflexible and unwilling to change. The officers get energized and eager to use different methods to combat crime. If the officers are doing the same thing day in and day out, they get bored. Now when you induce a challenge and vary the patrol technique then patrolling becomes more interesting.

Other departments have gotten very creative; such was the case in Dover, New Hampshire. They found a way to institute a mounted patrol in their downtown area and parks without entwining it in their budget. I thought it was very clever the way they did it. Someone donated two horses and the stables near the downtown area. The entire program was funded through donations. The patrol was used for crowd control for specific functions but mainly for community relations. The children loved the horses. Overall, it was a big hit. This was just another example of being creative for patrol operations. **There has to be flexibility to change as the need arises.**

Scheduling

Scheduling officers to fill a shift can be a very a frustrating experience especially when there are not enough officers to fill existing positions. What is the best schedule for the police department? It all depends what works best for the department and officers. Rotating shifts once a week can be very taxing on the body and hard on the family. Many police departments still rotate their shifts and some do it on a monthly or quarterly basis. I personally like the rotation once a quarter or every three months.

The next question that comes up was how many hours per shift and the workweek? Some departments have 8, 10 or 12 hour workdays. It did not matter to me as long as my officers like it. In Somersworth, New Hampshire, we were fixed to the eight-hour workday because of the union contract. The officer would have gone to the 10-hour day in a heartbeat but this provision would first have to be negotiated into their contract. It seems the captain always had trouble with the schedule. I tried to help him by purchasing a book with all kinds of schedule configurations. No, he kept to his old ways. A leader has to be open to new ideas.

Out in the western part of the country police departments seemed to use the 10 hour day/40 hour workweek for the schedule and this was the case in Florence, Arizona and Fort Lupton, Colorado. It was a good schedule and everyone seemed to like it. Who would not what this shift when you can get four days off in a row? It was not a bad deal. The only thing we had to be careful about was how long officers can work past their scheduled shift. Working 20 straight hours is never a good idea. We use to split up the shift and let officers work five hours overtime as a last result if someone called in sick at the last minute.

In Bristol, Connecticut, there was an abundance of overtime. There were times when you can work everyday if you wanted and there were plentiful private duty or construction jobs available everyday. The local newspaper, the Bristol Press publishes the salary each year of top paid city employees. Each year these employees would try to break the previous year's record; it was an on going contest. Most of the top 10 every year were police officers. A police officer many times headed the top spot just about every year. The department heads including the police chief, upper level management and the mayor many times did not break into the top 10. The officers earned their money by working overtime on shifts and construction jobs earning premium pay for traffic control. Police officers, sergeants and lieutenants were eligible to work construction jobs every day. Some lieutenants changed the hours of their work to work these construction jobs. My question is the following: how can anyone be effective working patrol if he or she already worked 8 or 10 hours on a construction job standing on their feet all day? There is no way they can be effective. When they go to work, they are generally too tired to do anything. I know because I used to work these construction jobs and found them to be too taxing on my body. I stopped working them because I did not want to put myself or anyone else at risk because I was too tired.

I know officers are still doing the same thing in Bristol. I am surprised they never get hurt more often. After being there for so long, luck does play a factor. Heck, if they have the opportunities to make some money why not go for it? The management practice in this case is not sound. Because management allowed it for so long, it would be difficult to change. The police union would file a grievance, since it would be a change in their working conditions.

Learning from experience, I was always concerned about the officer's alertness and effectiveness for duty. Besides, it is an officer safety issue and should be common sense. Sometimes officers lose sight of it when it comes to the almighty dollar. I would not let the officers work long shift such as double shifts or working construction jobs prior to their shifts. I just did not want my officers to get hurt because of some foolish mistake or not being alert. How many times have we heard about some police officer getting hurt because they worked too many hours or got hurt at their other job? It happens far too often and the police chief needs to have some control over it.

One issue that always comes up is "moonlighting" for police officers. Moonlighting is police officers working another job to supplement their police salary. I wrote a policy and procedure for police officers working another job other than their police job. Each person had to receive written permission from the police chief to work another job. My concern was a conflict of interest and how many hours would the person be working? Working as a bouncer in a local bar is not a good idea. If the officer did not have a conflict of interest and it did not interfere with his police duties then I generally gave permission. Some police chiefs think they should not get involved. It becomes my business when I am looking out for my officer's safety. My feeling is that officers should be paid enough so they would not have to work these outside jobs. I used this argument very effectively in getting my officers in Arizona and Colorado a substantial pay increase. I never did like the idea of "moonlighting" very much but I certainly could appreciate the reasons for it.

Which schedule is better? **The best schedule is the one that fits the overall needs of the police department** and the shifts configuration providing the most efficiency. The result is the type of service provided to the citizens would be the determining factor.

Getting Back To Basics

Sometimes we realize the patrol operations are out of sorts. Often it is the same boring thing every day. Falling into a routine is often the makings of a disaster about to happen. We hear about incidents where a police officer was assault or killed because he or she let down their guard. How often have we heard about some police officer getting hurt when he should not have? The police chief should recognize these tell tail signs that not all is well. I continually ask questions of the supervisors and police officers to see how things are going.

In my travels all over the country I have had the opportunity to observe many mistakes by police officers. Sometimes police officers forget about officer safety. Many times, they bring it up themselves and quite often they too let their guard down. Many good things can happen because of a good motor vehicle stop but some bad things can happen as well. I have see many officers after pulling the motorist over letting them sit in the front seat of the cruiser along with the officer. Now, how crazy can this get? I have seen good agencies like the State Highway Patrol in North Carolina do the same thing. I think officers are just asking for trouble. Officers discuss officer safety issues all the time but sometimes it gets thrown out of the window. All it would take is a split second to shoot the officer while he or she is writing a ticket. Officer safety issues need to be practiced all the time. I guess when you do the same thing day in and day out it is easy to develop bad habits and be complacent. This is where training and constant follow-up by supervisors come into play.

One problem that I see is that police officers should be more aggressive. I do not mean being rough and tough, but being more inquisitive and checking out people and vehicles more often. These inquisitive types are the ones who come up with the big arrests all the time. Just think if officers took the time to fill out a field interview report and turned it into the detectives. There is no doubt that more crime could be solved. The little things break down the effectiveness of the police department. How can we get the citizens to cooperate when we cannot get our police officers to buy into it? I even went through the trouble of designing a fill in the blank type form to make it easy, and it was the same old story. Some officers did it and some did not bother.

If you see a suspicious looking person loitering around a street corner late at night, why not ask him some questions? It may not mean anything then but it may mean something to the detectives. This individual may very well be a key figure in a burglary. Such was the case back in Fort Lupton, Colorado when a sergeant stopped a vehicle late at night in the downtown area. It seemed suspicious the way they were driving so he decided to stop them. When he approached the vehicle, he observed a bunch of coins in plain sight. As it turned out after further questioning these individuals just broke into an ice machine near the public works facility. Solving this case perhaps would never have happened if it were not for the curiosity of the sergeant.

One area that the police chief and managers alike should look at is the **preliminary investigations**. Some officers develop some bad habits in the way they approach these investigations and often times this is where you hear the criticism from the public. Police officers often resort to being "report takers." What I mean is there is very little investigation going on just recording some information for a report. The citizens get upset because they rarely hear from the police officer about how their case is going. Often the phone calls to the police officers are not returned. I use to hear the complaints from the public and I always reminded my officers that it was important to return the phone calls. It is not asking too much to keep the citizen informed.

Doing poor preliminary investigations are a problem all over the country. I even had the opportunity to have knowledge of a burglary investigation in my area in North Carolina. The Deputy Sheriff took a report of a burglary that occurred at a residence in the county. The perpetrators took a safe out of the bedroom closet and made off with it. The safe contained over $20,000 worth of jewelry, old coins and cash. You would have thought that this would have been considered a major crime and the detective would have been called out. Nope, there was none in this case. Detectives went to the residence the day after the burglary but did not do anything, except write a few notes about the incident. The victims did not hear any more from the Sheriff's Officer for six weeks. The victims ultimately started complaining about the service and I truly could not blame them. Even the report fell way short. There was only a brief paragraph with some basic information and even then it was inaccurate. They may have called it an investigation, but in reality there was no investigation at all.

Just think about how your officers are conducting their investigations. Are the supervisors checking the work of their officers? Are the supervisors responding to the crime scene too if the officer is inexperienced? These are important questions to ask. The police report is an important document but it is an area where police officers fall short. This usually results in criticism from the public. All too often, the supervisor accepts the report and it becomes the police department fault. If the report does not have the information, the supervisor should be returning the report to the officer for further follow-up. Asking the officers to write a thorough report is not too much to ask. I have seen officers try to get out of doing reports to the extent that I had required a report for everything. I took away the discretion.

Another report I would like to mention is a case management system for follow-up investigations. Not ever investigation should go to the detectives. Officers on patrol should be doing more follow-up investigations during their non-committed patrol time. Often times the officer develops the mindset that the detective will be working on the case anyway so they put a half-hearted effort into it. The supervisor should see to it, the officers not only do follow-ups, but that they do it well. The case management system will prioritize the investigations as well as checking the progress.

One problem that I would like to discuss here is taking a report of a crime over the telephone. Some police departments are so big that they have resorted to taking some crime reports by telephone even burglaries. I think from a community relation's standpoint this is bad business. I know departments are busy but there is nothing like a personal contact. How would you know if the complaint is false or not?

When officers write a report they have to keep in mind the five W's: who, what, when, where, why and of course, how. If they can write a report containing this information then the quality of reports will improve. What can police departments do to improve performance? Police departments should concentrate on the basics, such as everything learned at the police academy. If we concentrate on the basics then everything should take care of itself. There should be more training in preliminary investigations, accident investigations, handling domestic violence and report writing just to name a few.

Police departments must undo the bad habits of police officers and concentrate more on training, **getting back to basics**. It has to be an on going effort by all, a **team effort** in order to "serve and protect" the public.

Chapter 15
Criminal Investigations

The Criminal Investigation function is almost as important as patrol operations. One works hand in hand with the other yet investigations can be very frustrating for the police chief and managers alike, especially in small police departments. It was frustrating trying for me to develop the investigation function in all three police departments and I will explain why. The most problematic was finding qualified police officers to be a detective. Some want to be detective but they do not want to do the legwork. The focus of this chapter will be how some organizational problems were handled in three of my former departments.

In Somersworth, New Hampshire, I had a captain in charge of Investigations with two other detectives, one handled felony investigation and the other juvenile cases. In addition to the normal flow of cases, there were many bad check and forgery cases. The captain had developed a good case management system to monitor the flow of investigations and follow-ups. The system worked very well because this captain had been with the department and had the experience and dedication to do a good job. The key was finding the right person for a detective's position. Just because a person tests well on an examination for detective in some agencies, it does not mean he or she will be a good detective. I have seen some high scoring officers who became detectives that did not do anything. They were there for the prestige and nothing more.

Before I go on about my former departments, let me first discuss my experiences as a detective. Early during my career, I became a temporary detective in the Bristol Police Department. It was more of a training period but if you produced, you had an opportunity for a permanent appointment when a vacancy occurred. I say permanent as long as you produced. The Lieutenant in charge of detectives, Buzz Barton was a tough talking old time cop but he knew his business and I learned a great from him. My partner and I worked the second shift and every so often, we would have to spend some time in the office trying to catch up on paper work. This lieutenant would always pop in unannounced to check up on what we were doing. I wondered if he was trying to catch us goofing off, but I thought he cared about what we were doing. He made it clear that he did not want to catch anyone hanging around the office doing nothing. He was a results orientated type of detective. He made everyone work and he quizzed everyone about his or her case. There were times he knew the case better than I did. I probably got my work ethic from him. Lieutenant Barton was a leader and an excellent detective in his own right. He expected his detectives to do a thorough investigation including canvassing the neighborhood or business district looking for witnesses. He expected each detective to do his own legwork and if you slacked off, somehow he would find out about it.

As I had stated earlier, the position was considered a lateral assignment and at that time in the early 1970s there was no additional pay. If you were fortunate enough to be selected, it was considered a "plum" assignment. The detective served at the pleasure of the lieutenant and if you did not obtain results you could find yourself back in the blue suit again on patrol. Each detective had a heavy load and was expected to solve some cases, make some arrests, execute search and seizure warrants, as well as recover stolen property. The lieutenant kept us very busy and it was one of the highlights of my career. I loved detective work and when the time came to accept a promotion to sergeant, I had to make a difficult decision but the result was my accepting the promotion and going back to patrol. When anyone asked what I liked doing the best and I would respond without hesitation by saying, being a detective.

It was a pleasure to see this lieutenant working a case. He was a master craftsman in his own right working in his elements. Many officers would complaint that he was too tough, but I say he was effective during this time. If you could see him using his skills during interviewing and interrogations, you would have thought he wrote the book. He convinced criminals to confess and they were happy to do so. He said many times, "I am like a priest wearing the collar and hearing a confession." He would tell them, "You may as well tell me everything" and they did. He was simply amazing. Why cannot others have the same work ethic? Many of these techniques that I used in the three police departments where I was chief came directly from him.

The City of Bristol was growing fast and they kept adding police officers to the police department. The Patrol Division was growing and so was the Detective Division. Bristol spoiled it when they went away from the appointment to a promotion with a pay increase. This happened during one of their contract negotiations and I knew it would happen eventually. When a vacancy occurred in the Detective Division, an officer would have to take written and oral board examinations. The person who scored the highest was the winner. Just because someone scored high does not make the person a good detective. Do not get me wrong. Not everyone fell into this category. There were some good ones but there were some bad ones too. Take for example when I was a captain in charge of the Support Service Bureau, I was in charge of the department during the evening hours including Saturday. One Saturday I was working, I walked into the Detective Division and found two detectives playing chess. Now, both of these individuals were working overtime. After I chewed them out I told them if they did not have enough work to do then they could go home. They chose to stay and work some of their cases. I did inform their lieutenant about it. I am sure he took care of the problem. There was just too much of a lazy fare attitude in the department. I think it is the result of being unionized for so long combined with the loss of management rights. I am not knocking the union and they have certainly served their purpose in getting additional pay and better working conditions. However, there is a time and place for everything. They were upset at me, but it is not too much to ask officers to do their work especially when they were being paid at time and a half. This would never have happened during the Buzz Barton era.

I am a firm believer in having the detective's position by appointment only serving at the pleasure of the person in charge. I know there can be abuses to the system but it can work. I know in medium and large police departments it is primarily a promotion to detective. The only way you can demote someone is with cause. In some unionized police departments like Bristol, it would take an act of Congress. Very rarely did anyone get fired or demoted in Bristol. In each of my prior departments, I appointed a detective and while he or she was there the person would get an increase in pay. In the event a person was reassigned to patrol, he or she would revert to their former pay scale. All too often, a person gets promoted to detective and after a while some of them become complacent. I am trying to be nice but some could not solve their way out a paper bag on their best day.

For almost a year, I was the Commander of the Detective Division until the chief decided to transfer me to the Traffic and Planning Division. The plan was to move his lieutenants from division to division to get an all around experience. It seems that I was the only one moving around. After this, he transferred me to Training and Planning. He always attached the planning component to my title because I was more useful to him. It is not a bad idea to rotate your command staff so everyone has experience in every phase of the organization. The police chief's and manager's responsibility are to develop his or her personnel to the extent that you were training your replacement. I hope that this person does not replace you sooner than you think. Anyway, my point is that it is good to periodically change Commanders of the Detective Division. It is good to get new faces and fresh ideas to enhance greater productivity. Smaller departments do not have this luxury but sometimes change is good.

Even though the chief transferred me to a new assignment to gain a broader range of experience, I was disappointed to not have stayed longer. I thought that I was productive and even introduced a new Case Management System that assigned cases by solvability factors and track investigations. I think what helped my transfer was some political pressure from some of the influential figures in the community. Here are the details of the event. One evening one of my detectives called me about a situation at a local carnival. One of the workers was conducting a game of chance for money on the midway. This was a complete violation of the law. There was a roulette type wheel, the person would place a bet on the number, and the winner would be paid in cash. This was clearly gambling in plain view of everyone. The detective was instructed to take enforcement action and to confiscate the gambling devices. I thought it was an excellent arrest; there were plenty of witnesses and evidence. This was a slam-dunk and boy was I wrong. The next day you would have thought I had committed a crime. The owner of the carnival was like the "Godfather" who was very influential in city politics. No doubt, he called the mayor and police commissioners who in turn called the police chief. Even though it was the right action to arrest the individual for gambling, the city fathers did not like it. Now, I have to admit I was confused. For years, the police department strictly enforced the gambling laws and now things were different? I could not figure it out at the time but I do understand now. You see it was selective enforcement. It was proper to arrest certain individuals for gambling except for the untouchables. Apparently, the "Godfather" was one of the untouchables and I did not realize it. I was naive to think the law was to be enforced equally and fairly without bias. It was a good lesson to learn.

I made up my mind at the time that I would not play favorites. I supported the detective in making the arrest and never regretted the decision. You have to **believe in your principals** and stick with them. After all the fuss and commotion that I caused there were never any more incidents of gambling for money at the carnival. I guess we were effective after all. I believed that no one is above the law and still believe it. Being in charge of the Detective Division comes with awesome responsibility and I believe I did meet it. You have to do the right thing. The chief transferred me to another division to broaden my experiences but I did believe this gambling arrest did help him to make his decision quicker.

Actually more experiences in Bristol as a detective and later as the Commander of the Detective Division provided me with the broad base of knowledge to effectively direct the operations of the Investigations Division in three departments. You may laugh but many of the things that I initiated were the complete opposite in Bristol. This brings up another point. **What may work in one department may not work in another.** The system in Bristol worked but it could have been better.

The Investigations Division in Somersworth, New Hampshire was very efficient. I had some "go-getters" who were interested in getting the job done. Consequently, there were few complaints from the public about not solving crime. We did not solve all the crime but we were effective in solving many serious crime. Being new as a police chief, I felt comfortable with the operation of the Investigations Division. The captain had expertise as a polygraph examiner and it certainly helped many of our investigations. Not too many departments that I knew of had the luxury of having a polygraph examiner in their police department. Many times, you could have someone else do the test but then you would have to wait a few weeks for test results or for an examiner to become available.

Even though I was comfortable with the operations, I still wanted to improve. I asked many questions to understand why they did things in a particular way. A department should never stand still and rest on its laurels. It was nice they were solving some crime, but the tables could be quickly turned around if the detectives were just sitting around and doing nothing. The quality of investigations can always be improved. I wanted to make sure that we sent our detectives to specialized training so they could do their jobs better. Fortunately, our area was not in a high crime area so we did not have to do too many violent crime investigations.

One quirky thing I changed in Somersworth, New Hampshire was the responsibility of the evidence and property function. When I took over the department, the patrol captain was responsible for various functions including evidence and property. He was the evidence custodian. This did not make sense so when the opportunity presented itself I switched the evidence and property to the captain in charge of Investigations. Actually when I reorganized the department, I changed the functions of both captains so this captain had the Operations Division including the Patrol and Investigations Divisions. It seemed a logical change. The move worked very well and the evidence and property was where it should have been in the first place.

Another problem from a staffing point of view was that there was a captain, a sergeant and a detective in Investigations. At one time, the detectives carried a rank of sergeant. It makes no sense at all to give someone a rank of sergeant just so they could have a pay raise. I feel that a sergeant should be a supervisor not a detective. There are many police departments that still do it and I personally think it is the wrong approach. Nevertheless, eventually the sergeant was transferred to the Patrol Division.

When I went to Florence, Arizona I was in for a culture shock. After the department has been decimated with resignations, it was going to take some time to build it up. A female officer had been assigned temporarily to Investigations prior to my arrival. This was a small department with one investigator. I decided to keep her assignment as a detective because I liked her quality of work. She was dedicated, caring and truly liked what she was doing. She was also in charge of the evidence and property room. Because I believed that she had the aptitude and a desire to learn, I thought in time with additional training she would have been a first rate detective. Some of the other officers did not like her in this assignment but in reality, she was the best person for the job. In time, she solved some cases and I see the progress being made. Even after a permanent chief took over after my departure she was left on patrol and was even more discouraged. In my opinion, they ruined a good police officer and her potential to be a very good detective. Some police chiefs can make matters worse without trying too hard. You have to know what you are doing first before any changes should be made.

Personnel Changes

The Council members did not like the aforementioned female officer for some reason and the first action that the interim police chief took after my departure was to replace her with someone else. He certainly killed morale very quickly. Her replacement was not a "ball of fire" and I hear he did not do much at all. Sometimes you have to put a square peg in a square hole for a good fit. This officer selected for Investigations was better suited for the Patrol Division because he was good at traffic enforcement. My suggestion for a new police chief going into a police department for the first time would be **not to make any personnel changes unless it is necessary**. There should be a period of observation and assessment to see what is being done, the type of cases, quality of reports and if any cases were being solved.

In Florence, the challenge was trying to outwit the den of thieves at the end of Main Street. These two brothers were involved in everything, burglaries, thefts, stolen property and drug trafficking. One by one we were able to make good cases against them, which incidentally, landed them in prison not too far away. At least they could take turns staying in the state prison complex in Florence.

Trying to catch these individuals proved frustrating at time. The younger brother was so bold that he stole a quad-all terrain motorcycle from the owner about three streets away about 6:00 am. It was an unusual time but he was probable still high from partying all night. We found the quad behind his house. We knew he was responsible for the crime but we could not prove it. We would have looked foolish arresting his mother or father, the owner of the property. At least we recovered the vehicle but there would be another time and place.

Murphy's Law

Usually I stay pretty upbeat and optimistic until I received a phone call one evening in Florence. Murphy's Law hit me again. If anything else can go wrong, it will. Nothing surprises me anymore. It seems problems in police departments never go away. The dispatcher informed me that our evidence room was on fire and the mayor was at the scene. Our set up for the evidence room was strange. It was located in a separate building behind the police department. By the time, the fire department arrived and extinguished the fire we lost half of the evidence room. Most of our property, evidence and records went up in smoke. The fire marshal determined that the cause of the fire was electrical, but being suspicious, I still wonder about it. Somehow, the air conditioner developed a short and it went up in flames. The fire ruined a good computer including most of the records. It would be a monumental task to replace everything. Naturally, I was wondering what was going to happen to our criminal cases?

When I think about these events, it seems strange. The mayor never went to any of our crime scenes until now. The sergeant who was in charge of the shift probably gave her a call directly. In any event, I thought the circumstances were very suspicious. In hindsight, I probably should have gone with my hunch and called in some experts to investigate the circumstances of the fire. It was possible to have a fire because it was an old structure. At the time, we were in the planning stages to move the police department to another location. The town hall was going to move into a new facility.

The timing was terrible. We were at a point where we were making good progress on cases. My detective was doing a good job but we could have done better. The Patrol Division was not providing critical information that the officers developed on patrol. I thought large departments had the conflict between the patrol and detective division. There was just too much resentment and conflict between the two groups. Back in Bristol, officers would intentionally withhold information just so the detective did not get it. Some patrol officers had the attitude that they would do all the work and the detectives would get the glory. It was too bad but this was the prevailing attitude. Do not kid yourself for a minute. These conflicts still exist in small and medium size police departments too. This female detective was starting to shine. She had taken the initiative to reorganize the property and evidence room and it looked good. Some of the officers were jealous. The fire could have been electrical but it was too much of a coincidence.

It is crucial to have an exchange of information. The more information exchanged the better for the overall goal to protect and serve the public. I could see many of the patrol officers resented having a woman in the detective division. She could have done a better job providing she had gotten support from the patrol officers. This situation is a familiar story. It occurs in just about every department. **There is a need for there to be more teamwork between patrol and investigations.**

Achilles' Heel

I have seen some property and evidence rooms that looked like a disaster hit it. Take for example, in Bristol, Connecticut we had one officer in charge of the evidence room and it was a joke. When the court called to have a piece of evidence brought to court I thought he would have a coronary. There were many times I can recall when he could not find the evidence. The officers thought it was funny, but in reality, it was a sad state of affairs. It was almost a miracle if anyone could find any evidence in the mess. However, he had time to shoot the breeze every day with his friends including the captain. I wonder how many cases the court dumped because of him. Evidence and property was all over the room. Some was piled high in the corner, put in a box or shoved in a corner. When he finally retired because of health problems, they found a unique storage for fingerprint cards. When he got behind, he put hundreds of fingerprint cards in the false ceiling in his office. This officer was a liability to the department and management never did anything about it.

The evidence and property room can really be an Achilles' heel for any agency. If your evidence area is not secure and policy and procedures are lacking then you certainly can have problems. Take for example in Fort Lupton, Colorado when I found out my clean-cut investigator was stealing cocaine from our evidence room and using on and off the premises. If you recall, he had been taking the cocaine from the evidence to be destroyed pile from cases that had already been disposed of by the court. All we needed at that point was an order from the court to destroy the drugs and make arrangements to do it. This guy was disposing the drugs on his own and no one the wiser. Matter of fact, if he had not felt guilty about it and confessed to the crime it may have been some time before we made the discovery. I do have to give him credit for coming forward to tell me about it.

When the investigator confessed his crime, I knew it would take some time to dig our way out of this hole. The reality is that this could happen to any police department and I cannot emphasize enough to make sure there are controls in place to prevent this from ever occurring again. Missing drugs were a problem but what about all our cases that were waiting for a disposition, trial or plea bargain. In any event, we stood a chance to have all our cases compromised. I contacted the Weld County Sheriff to send an investigator to conduct a criminal investigation to assess the damage done. At the same time, our police department did an administrative investigation, which ultimately led to the termination of the investigator.

We did a complete inventory of the evidence and property room. In order to make a criminal case against the investigator we had to determine which cases he took the cocaine. The former investigator provided valuable assistance to the investigators. We were able to account for most of the cocaine. Quite fortunately none of the current cases waiting for a disposition was compromised nor any of our other criminal cases. We were quite fortunate in this regards. The sheriff's investigator did make a good case against the former investigator and it was resolved quite effectively in court. The former employee received a suspended sentence and probation, which was fair under the circumstances. What a way to go. He got himself addicted to cocaine and now he would never be able to go into law enforcement again. His once promising career was finished. This incident could happen to any one.

Because of this incident, I was able to take a good, hard look at our evidence procedure and the security of the evidence and property room. We were able to improve all areas. I thought we originally had a good one, but apparently, it was not good enough. It was far better than previous departments but there was no check and balances. Other words, there was no one checking on the work of the custodian of the evidence and property room. The chain of custody was very good. We had a room specifically for processing and packaging evidence. We had all the packaging materials and forms necessary to document the evidence and fill in the blanks to show the chain of evidence. All evidence was secured in a locker and the evidence custodian would catalog it and store it on a shelf in the secure evidence and property room.

Another area I looked at was the security of the evidence and property room. Even though the room had a dead bolt lock, there were security issues that required some necessary improvements. The police department was located in the municipal building. Other administrative offices were on the same floor but the basement was accessible through the police department or administration. Any one could access the basement through the administrative side and go into the area of the basement where the evidence and property room was located. We added combination locks to the door leading into the police department portion of the basement. The last part of the improvement was revising the policy and procedure addressing evidence and property to include checks and balances. The Operations Commander, a lieutenant, would conduct an audit of the evidence and property room on a semi-annual basis. The Lieutenant would submit a report detailing the results of the audit and suggestions for improvement. Now granted, it was a great deal of work to do an audit but absolutely necessary. There has to be a check and balance. In addition, there should be spot inspections of the Property and Evidence Room to insure its integrity. It is critical that the Policy and Procedures are followed. If at any time a defense attorney found out that there are problems with storing and cataloging evidence, they would have a field day in court. Many cases that your personnel work long and hard on will become a casualty of the court's dismissal of cases. Why have sloppiness ruin many cases. Now is the time to take a proactive approach to make sure the reliability of the Property and Evidence Room is intact.

Another step I had to take was to find a good replacement for the investigator's position. At the time, I appointed a female police officer that had prior experience and she was enthusiastic about her new assignment. She along with some other officers did a tremendous job with the audit and reorganizing the evidence and property room. Sometimes it is like a crapshoot, you never know how a person will work out. Eventually due to some problems with investigations, I eventually transferred her back to patrol. I will discuss these problems in more detail later on. At the time, I only had one person in charge of Investigation but I was working on a plan with the city administrator to add a second person and have a sergeant in charge of Investigation. This way there would be accountability and a second person was needed to assist with investigations. It would take a while to fill the position because we were always in the hiring mode to fill existing police officer positions.

Everyone has problems with handling evidence. Even in North Carolina, I recall the Sheriff's Department lost a significant amount of evidence and was the laughing stock of the community. The Sheriff's Department deputies confiscated about 5,000 pounds of marijuana after a major drug arrest. It had been stored in a secure trailer or so they thought. Someone found out about it and managed to make off with about 2,000 pounds of marijuana. Apparently, the secure trailer was not in a very secure area. Someone got the bright idea to bury the remaining 3,000 pounds at the local landfill. Some unknown persons went to the location, dug it up and made off with the remaining marijuana. Who knows for sure whether it was an inside job or not and the Federal Bureau of Investigation was conducting an investigation. I suspect that it was an inside job. I do not know if any arrests were made. How can anyone let 5,000 pounds of marijuana just walk away? Someone in administration should be held accountable. No one was held accountable, but it was an embarrassment for the Sheriff's Department.

Another example of a poor procedure in handling evidence and property is at one of the area police departments in North Carolina where I use to live. I had the opportunity to visit the police department and while talking with a detective, the question came up about handling property and evidence. Each officer is his or her own property and evidence custodian. When they seized any evidence after documenting it they secure it in their personal locker. What is the police chief thinking? I wonder how many other police departments handle evidence this way. It is an accident waiting to happen. Any good defense attorney could certainly make a case about the way the evidence was handled and stored. If I were a defense attorney this would be the first area I would attack. Why subject your department to criticism and possible lawsuits because of inadequate work. The police chief is ultimately responsible for the conduct of the department and this includes everything. The buck stops at the top.

The following are suggestions for the police chief and top executives who want to insure they do not have the Achilles' heel:

- Have one person accountable for Property and Evidence.
- Insure the Property and Evidence Room is secure.
- Insure the chain of custody is followed through documentation of the evidence.

- Have an audit of the Property and Evidence storage area at least on a semi-annual basis.
- Periodically do a spot inspection of the Property and Evidence area
- Quiz the Evidence Custodian on the procedure and ask questions regarding specific cases
- Insure property and evidence is secured in evidence lockers and not the officer's personal lockers.
- Insure the department has a Policy and Procedure on Handling Evidence
- Insure that the supervisors follow-up and check the work of their subordinates and report any problems.

It is important to insure the integrity of the property and evidence system. If the officers follow the procedure properly and if the supervisors do their jobs then there should not be any or less problems.

Know When to Ask For Help

Many small and medium size police departments have limited resources and the investigation function in a small police department only has one or two personnel. A small department can quickly become overwhelmed if they suddenly have a major crime on their hands to investigate. Major crimes can quickly overwhelm even medium and large police departments. Their resources can be taxed to the limit.

Everyone knows about the JonBenet Ramsey murder investigation in Boulder, Colorado, which is about 25 miles west of Fort Lupton. Early on, the Boulder Police Department wanted to conduct the investigation by themselves. They did not want any outside help. Many police departments are like this. They look at their own community as theirs and do not want any outside interference. This was the original mentality. The Denver Police Chief once told me that he had offered his homicide investigators to Boulder to assist with the investigation. They told him he had it under control and no thanks. Now, what kind of sense does this make? Here we have Denver Police Department investigating many homicides during any given year compared to maybe one every couple of years for Boulder. It is not hard to figure out who had more experience in homicides investigations. If the decision were mine to make, I would have quickly accepted all the help that I could muster. Boulder Police Department has a respectable Detective Division but **when you need help you have to know enough to ask for it.**

My purpose is not to rehash the JonBenet Ramsey murder investigation because it has been done constantly in the news media, reinvestigations by the Boulder County District Attorney's Office and the Grand Jury. However, where the Boulder Police needed the help the most, was early on in the investigation. There was no doubt the crime scene had been contaminated and as a result, much of the evidence had been lost. Whether any one will ever find the person or persons responsible and bring him or her to justice it is anyone's guess. The best and the brightest have worked hard to solve this case but at this point, there seems to be a stalemate. There have been many personnel changes at the Boulder Police Department including replacing the police chief and the commander of the Detective Division. Maybe some day we will find out who was responsible for the murder of this beautiful child. Just think the results may have been different if the crime scene had been properly handled in the very beginning. I always said the detectives are only as good as the information they received and this includes the results of the analysis of the evidence found at the crime scene.

The date September 11, 2001, "The Attack on America" will be forever be engrained in everyone's mind. It will be one of the darkest hours to remember. Terrorists hijacked four passenger airliners and struck terror in the hearts of millions of Americans. Two of the planes struck and collapsed the twin towers of the World Trade Center in New York City, a third struck the Pentagon in Washington DC and the fourth crashed into the ground in Pennsylvania. The intentional crash into the World Trade Center where thousands of people or killed and injured not only created the largest disaster in the history of the United States but the largest crime scene as well. Even the New York Police Department, the largest police department with over 30,000 sworn police officers in the United States would require assistance from all over. The jurisdiction would not doubt be under the Federal Bureau of Investigation because the hijacking was originally a federal offense. Even the FBI with its vast resources would require assistance from other police departments not only in the United States but also all over the world. The point is that an agency is never too large to ask for help. In the days following the terrorists attack the FBI quickly gathered evidence to determine who was responsible. Thousands of Federal agents and support personnel have been investigating and gathering evidence. This type of crime and crime scene could easily happen again. Law enforcement has to be prepared to deal with these crimes of such a magnitude.

This investigation with the cooperative effort of federal, state and local law enforcement ultimately lead to the conclusion of those responsible for this heinous crime. Never in our history have we been a target of a terrorist attack of such immense proportion. The bombing of the federal building in Oklahoma City is now pale in comparison to the destruction of the World Trade Center. The United States is vulnerable to terrorists attack to the extreme that we have never witnessed before.

Law enforcement will under go new challenges in the future with the potential of mass homicides so present in our society today. Never in our history have we even dreamed of the tragedies that we have witnessed today in our society and there may not be any relief from the carnage. We have witnessed the following in such a short period:

- shooting of innocent victims in our schools all over the United States
- the bombing of the federal building in Oklahoma City that resulted in the scores of killing of innocent victims
- the mass murder of innocent victims of the doomed airliners, the victims at Pentagon in Washington DC and the thousands of victims at the World Trade Center in New York City.

Where will it all end? Nevertheless, wherever these crime scenes take place the police departments will need assistance from many law enforcement agencies, fire departments, and emergency services working together as a team.

Today we live in a different society compared to 30 or 40 years ago. Many departments just had to investigate the routine crime and occasionally a serious crime such as a homicide, especially in small departments. I can specifically relate to Bristol, Connecticut, a medium sized police department. Bristol was considered a safe city to live in because there was very little serious crime years ago. None of these crimes were too overwhelming. Now it is a different ball game. Police departments now have to investigate much more serious crime than ever before. Small and medium size police departments are not immune to serious crime. Crime from the inner cities has now moved into rural areas. With the potential for increased crime from extremist groups, we now are facing new challenges in investigating crimes beyond our wildest imagination.

A New Approach: Criminal Investigation Task Force

Police departments will have to rely on one another for assistance and many are doing it already. Departments have already shared personnel resources in the County in the form of Drug Task Force and SWAT teams. We know most police departments are small averaging less than 10 sworn officers all across the country. Many departments are only a one or two man operation. We need to take the cooperative effort to a new level in our present day of violent crime. My thought is to have a Criminal Investigation Task Force in the County to investigate violent crime. Why not share personnel and resources to investigate serious crime. Some departments have made an attempt to do so in trying to share information on a regional basis, or in some cases, forming a task force to track down a serial killer. In my mind it makes more sense to share personnel, equipment and more information.

Now, already you are probably wondering who was going to be in charge? This question always comes up and it may be a determining factor in not having a task force because of the issue of jurisdiction. I can tell you from previous experience many police departments are very possessive regarding their investigations and it is a sore spot. The Regional Criminal Investigation Task Force could be run like the state or county drug task force by designating a person in command and one in second in command. I believe police departments could do a better job with their investigations if they pool their resources. The result is better investigations that ultimately lead to the arrest and conviction of criminals. We cannot forget about improved service to the community.

I cannot tell you how many times I called for outside assistance in criminal investigations. Every time that I became a police chief in a new community, the chiefs would offer their assistance anytime I needed it. There were times when I had to make a call. I will never forget the police chiefs of the major city in Phoenix and Denver offering their assistance to me any time I needed it. All I had to do was ask. They were honestly and truly sincere. When I was the police chief in my former communities, I made it a point to offer my assistance anytime a new police chief took over a nearby department.

The point is one investigator can only do so much in a major criminal investigation. When you add personnel from other departments and other resources, you are more efficient and effective. I do not know why police departments do not do this more often. I guess I already answered this question, being possessive about their territory.

Limited Resources

Each department small or large has to deal with budget constraints and have limited resources for investigations. Getting back to small departments, many only has one or two detectives to handle the caseload. There is only so much one person can do and so often expectations are high. Let us face it, not every department can get a helicopter. How else can a department get additional equipment when you needed it the most?

A police chief has to take the initiative when it comes to equipping the department with the resources to do the job. In each of my communities, the town or city councils were very supportive with my budget requests. There has to be a great deal of patience and understanding of how city government works in order to obtain these items. The police department is only one department competing for its share of the revenues that go into the general fund. I was quite fortunate to have so many of my budgetary requests approved by the city council. Simply put, I prioritized the needs of the department in terms of essential equipment and each time the council voted to approve my budgetary requests. I did not get everything, but pretty close to it. All I did was to establish a need and provide an explanation how the equipment was going to be used. After that, I just followed the city's procedure in going through the purchasing policy.

When I went to Fort Lupton, Colorado there was some equipment that was laughable. I thought they were kidding when they showed me their booking camera. It was sad to see some departments having to resort to substandard equipment but it is the reality that many police chiefs have to face. The police officers were using a disposable 35 mm camera for mug shots in the booking room. The department did not have a mug shot camera. When I showed some council members some of the equipment we were using such as the disposable mug shot camera, it did not take much convincing on my part to have the council approve a new mug shot camera. Sometimes you have to fight for necessary equipment.

One thing that upsets the town or city councils are police chiefs who does other than what they say they are going to do. Trying to circumvent the city's purchasing policy will certainly land the chief in hot water. Even after I left the department in Fort Lupton, I had previously convinced the city council to purchase two or three AR 15 rifles in the event of an emergency. These assault rifles would have been used as part of our Special Operations Response Team. The interim chief tried to get approval to buy another type of assault rifle after several department members talked him into it and they quickly changed their mind. The city council can sometimes be fickle. I told him that the council had already approved my request and why did they have to change? Instead of having three assault type rifles available in emergencies, they now had none. You see I understood the dynamics of politics. You have to know your city council. I knew how to play the game and what it would take to get essential equipment for the department.

Before I had arrived in Fort Lupton, the city council was suspicious of the police department's purchasing practices. Some equipment was purchased with funds approved by the council for other purchases. Expenditures were made for capital items not approved by the council. I could see why the previous chief got into trouble with the city council. They simply did not trust his purchasing practices. Even after I took over one council member devoted much of his time going through the purchasing requisitions and invoices to track some of these expenditures. Somehow, some of these records mysteriously disappeared.

I made it a point never to play games with the town or city council. I purchased exactly what was authorized and no more and had followed the city's purchasing policy to the letter. Even when these items were approved in the budget for the fiscal year, the funds could not be spent yet. Each time that I wanted to make a capital expenditure for a piece of equipment, I had to go before the city council to explain it again to get authorization to spend the funds. It amounted to getting the approval twice, once for budget adoption and again at the city council meeting to get their final approval to spend the funds. After I bought a piece of equipment such as the new booking camera for mug shots, I invited the council members to see it. Whenever we made a significant purchase, I made it a point to show them. Putting on a little show is good for the police chief. The council members are interested in knowing the equipment was purchased and it was now being used. Nothing aggravates council members more when they realize the equipment is just sitting in the corner or basement doing nothing. They do not like to waste money. Based on the department's history, it was important to win their trust and confidence. After a while, they did have confidence in me and they relied on my judgment. I think that I was successful in this regard. Sometimes I wondered about it because it was smooth sailing to get their approval. I thought it was important to discuss some of the political dynamics here because if you cannot convince the town or city council to approve expenditures for equipment then your job as a leader will be more difficult to achieve.

I always found a way to obtain additional resources for the department. I borrowed equipment from other departments and the sheriff's office especially for drug investigations. There were times when we had to borrow a body wire and night scopes to assist us doing drug investigations. It worked out very well until we were able to purchase some of these items. I might add, these departments were more than willing to lend it out as long as they were not using it. I did not want to depend on someone else's timetable so I looked for other ways.

I found it extremely useful to use State and Federal Grants and the Asset Forfeiture Process. First, let me discuss Asset Forfeiture. One of the reasons why the officers were so conscientious in fighting drug trafficking because they knew that any assets seized from suspected drug dealers would eventually be turned over to the police department. I presented a plan and got approval to set up a special Drug Asset Forfeiture Account for the police department. These monies would only be used to purchase police equipment and pay for some specialized training. The city administrator and city council loved the plan because if was another source of revenue for the police department. However, I still followed the city's purchasing policy. I did not want to give the impression that I had a pot of money and I was going to do whatever I wanted with it. I **kept the council involved in the purchasing policy.**

In Fort Lupton, my officers quickly learned the process in applying for asset forfeiture with the county and the D.E.A. (Drug Enforcement Agency) out of Denver. Matter of fact, the D.E.A. was more than willing to do all the paper work for a cut of the action. They received about 20% to take care of the paperwork and to arrange an administrative hearing on the asset forfeiture. In the few cases we were involved with the Feds we were quite successful. Every time we seized a motor vehicle in a drug case and the title was clear we would go through the Asset Forfeiture. We were starting to develop a sizable fund. I used the money to make purchases of equipment to help us with drug and criminal investigations.

Applying for Federal and State grants is another option to help obtain resources. It takes a great deal of paper work but I was quite fortunate to have a sergeant in Fort Lupton who was good at it. This sergeant was extremely dedicated. He would work on the grants and somehow manage to file them on the day they were due. He sometimes put me on the spot because I needed to get approval to apply for a grant because sometimes the grant needed matching funds. I convinced the city administrator that if the Federal or State government approved the grant they would eventually have to vote to approve the award anyway. We just made a copy of the grant to include in their information package and that seemed to satisfy them. There are many grant funding opportunities available for different programs including the Department of Homeland Security. All you have to do is find out about these available funds and sometimes that is a trick in itself. I use to subscribe to a service, the IACP Net based out of Minneapolis, Minnesota, available to all law enforcement agencies and for our size department it cost $500.00 for the year and it was good money well spent. The IACP Net included the latest grants available through the government. It is an excellent service with the latest information for the police chief executive. The IACPNET.com is worthwhile. It helps the chief and managers as well to keep up with the latest changes

Another source often overlooked is military surplus equipment. All you have to do is to call your state's procurement office to find out the procedures involved. It can be quite rewarding because there are certainly good equipment waiting to be found. Police departments have obtained vehicles, computers, M-16 rifles and much more. All one has to do is to visit the military installation near you to see what is available. Sometimes it will be a wasted trip because you cannot find anything good, besides crates of gas masks. It is a way of converting some of this military surplus equipment to police department use. It can be cost effective for the department to do so. I have just one piece of advice. Just **be careful about what you select**. The vehicles may or may not be any good. The military vehicle would have to be outfitted for civilian use, repainting and more unexpected cost can be incurred to get the vehicle road ready. The cost of repairs might be cost prohibitive. Many police departments including my former departments have taken advantage of this program. Most of the time the price is right, free most of the time or at a reasonable price. The following is an excerpt from the **United States Code**:

> ### Sec. 2576. Surplus military equipment: sale to State and local law enforcement and firefighting agencies
>
> ▪ *The Secretary of Defense, under regulations prescribed by him, may sell to State and local law enforcement and firefighting agencies, at fair market value, pistols, revolvers, shotguns, rifles of a caliber not exceeding .30, ammunition for such firearms, gas masks, and protective body armor which (1) are suitable for use by such agencies in carrying out law enforcement and firefighting activities, and (2) have been determined to be surplus property under the Federal Property and Administrative Services Act of 1949 (40 U.S.C. 471 et seq.).*
>
> ▪ *Such surplus military equipment shall not be sold under the provisions of this section to a State or local law enforcement or firefighting agency unless request therefore is made by such agency, in such form and manner as the Secretary of Defense shall prescribe, and such request, with respect to the type and amount of equipment so requested, is certified as being necessary and suitable for the operation of such agency by the Governor (or such State official as he may designate) of the State in which such agency is located. Equipment sold to a State or local law enforcement or firefighting agency under this section shall not exceed, in quantity, the amount requested and certified for such agency and shall be for the exclusive use of such agency. Such equipment may not be sold, or otherwise transferred, by such agency to any individual or public or private organization or agency.*

We almost had a vehicle when I was in New Hampshire. The vehicle was supposed to be in good running condition, but when we got there, it would not start. The vehicle was left there and some other agency probable got it. I found that some of the military personnel were not very helpful. Your state's national guard would provide you with some information to get started.

Assistance from Patrol

There is no doubt about it that the Patrol Division can be a valuable asset to the Detective Division. When small police departments have only one or two detective to investigate major crimes in order for the system to work, the patrol officers and investigators have to work together as a team. It takes a gigantic team effort to find all the pieces of the puzzle to solve crime and ultimately bring the criminal to justice.

There are so many different types of investigations that it becomes a major task to juggle and manage the caseload. People, even patrol officers, do not realize what is involved in doing an investigation, case preparation and finally preparing to testify in court. Now, we are just speaking of one case.

I always wanted to involve patrol in investigations as much as possible. Many times I was able to augment investigations by using patrol personnel to assist. They absolutely loved special assignments. It got them temporarily away from their day-to-day duties to help the investigator to work on a case. I can think back to my detective days when I was with the Bristol Police Department. It was quite an opportunity even if it was only for 90 days to work in the Detective Division. Many of the department's personnel got their start as a detective by first working the temporary training assignment. It was an excellent morale booster and everyone looked forward to being picked for the assignment. I do not know why it stopped after a few years. I had to admit management had a great idea and it was too bad they did not continue it.

The idea of a short-term training assignment was and still is a great idea. I took this idea and used it many time in my three former departments where I was police chief. It may be difficult to accomplish in small police departments but the benefits will be greater. The training idea was phenomenal, they could not have planned it any better. The personnel rotating in and out of the Detective Division not only got on the job training from an experienced detective but a better understanding on how the system worked. Patrol officers do not see what happens after they did their preliminary report. They do not see the legwork that follows such as locating and finding witnesses, more in-depth evidence analysis, report preparation, arrest warrants, search and seizure warrants and much more. There is no better way for a detective to learn that from the hands on approach. You can get the basic book knowledge but then you have to apply what you learned.

If I had an opportunity to use patrol personnel on a major crime, then I would do so. Sometimes I would just have the patrol officer continue the investigation with the detective. This way the officer sees beyond the preliminary investigation. The police chief has to find a way to be creative and **using patrol officers to help with major investigations** will be a morale booster. Police officers on patrol get discouraged because they start an investigation and hear no more about it unless an arrest is made and he or she may have to appear in court. If there is information in the preliminary report crucial to the investigation that led to the arrest of the perpetrator, sometimes he or she is left out of the loop. Patrol officers accuse the detective of being "glory hounds" and the detectives say the patrol officers are "cry babies." Instead of being accusatory towards one another why not, work together as a team to put the bad guy in jail. I am convinced we can solve much more crime if everyone works together. It may be difficult but it can be done.

Just to make sure my officers were getting recognition where it was deserved, I constantly reminded my supervisors to recognize their personnel and write letters of commendation.   When I was in Somersworth, New Hampshire one officer approached me and asked if I had looked at a burglary investigation. I had not and told him I would take a look. It caught my eye because he did an outstanding job. Actually, he caught a person committing a burglary, made the arrest and submitted all the paperwork. Everything was tied together very nicely. There was one problem; no one told him he did a great job. Often we are quick to remind officers of their mistakes and when they do something good not a word is mentioned. I found this to be quite ironic. I asked the patrol captain if he was going to recommend a commendation. He said, "I was thinking about it." I told him after he thinks about it for a minute, write a letter of commendation for the officer. There is nothing that can kill morale quicker than not recognizing someone when he or she should be recognized.

In each of my previous departments, I instituted a Field Interview Cards for my patrol officers to use. If the officers contacted a suspicious person on the street or in a vehicle, during their shift, I wanted my officers to complete the form and turn it in at the end of the shift. This was a good way to involve the patrol officers. Stopping and interviewing suspicious people is a good way to identify unsavory looking characters. Now, I am not saying that it is right to single out a certain race or ethnic group of people. No way would I encourage or endorse racial profiling. When I say check out a suspicious person it does not matter what is the race of the person. Any one can commit a crime and an officer aggressively patrolling his or her area can make a difference. The suspicious person the officer is interviewing may very well be planning to commit a crime or may have just completed it. The investigator may be looking for the individual and it may be the last piece of the puzzle. The officer can be a great help in helping to identify suspicious persons and known criminals in the area. Documentation is important.

Charleston, South Carolina took it one-step further.   They had identified convicted felons and kept taps on their whereabouts. Statistically convicted offenders are multiple offenders and by keeping an eye out for them and asking questions about what they are doing may have kept crime down. Some people may say it was harassment and the American Civil Liberties Union may say it was an infringement of their individual rights. It must have been effective because they were able to keep crime down. I do not think it is harassment or an invasion of someone's individual rights; it is good preventive police work.

Police officers need to be more assertive and diligent in completing the Field Interview Cards. I personally believe the **patrol officers and investigators working**

together can solve more crime. Police departments should utilize patrol officers more often in assisting investigators with major crime investigations.

Case Management and Solvability Factors

It is important for the police chief especially in a small department to have a game plan on what cases the investigator will handle utilizing solvability factors. Everyone knows by now that the department should not devote all its resources to investigate every crime. Some cases should be assigned to the patrol officers for follow-up while the more serious cases are assigned to the investigator based on priority and solvability factors.   Solvability factors are nothing more than information that would provide clues to the identification and subsequent arrest of a perpetrator of a serious crime. Some information is better than others are so this information has to be assessed to determine its usefulness.

It is important to have a policy and procedure and the following was taken directly from the Fort Lupton Police Department's Policy Manual that gives a good example of case management and solvability factors:

CHAPTER 5
INVESTIGATIONS

Criminal Case Assignment and Responsibilities/Review

All police reports will be submitted for review and approval to police sergeants and/or Police Chief.

A police supervisor will review the completed reports daily.

Assignment Alternatives

- *Police Patrol personnel may be assigned cases for follow-up work at the discretion of the reviewing/assigning supervisor. A copy of the assigned investigation will be forwarded to investigations with the assigned officer's name and the appropriate FR number.*

- *Police Patrol personnel will be subject to the same time frames as investigative personnel for completion of follow-up work.*

Police Patrol personnel can be assigned cases under the following conditions:

- *When suspects are known and arrest is appropriate and when such suspect resides inside of the city limits;*
- *When follow-up work is totally inside of the city limits;*
- *When a case is so detailed or involved that the original reporting officer would be able to follow-up the case with less difficulty than an investigator;*
- *When a case has drastically limited follow-up potential that can be more easily handled by patrol personnel;*
- *At the discretion of the assigning supervisor.*

Investigative personnel will be assigned cases for follow-up when such cases are not assigned to patrol officers. Cases assigned for follow-up will be closely monitored by supervisory personnel. Investigative personnel will normally be assigned cases, which conform to the following:

- *Serious crimes requiring detailed evidence collection, statements, interviews, and long term follow-up work;*
- *Cases which require follow-up work outside the city.*

Prioritizing Cases for Assignment

"C" Designated Cases

- *Cases which are designated as "C" cases will be followed up by a supplemental report and required action within 30 days of the assignment date;*
- *The case packet including assignment sheet and supplemental reports will be returned to the assigning supervisor within the 30 day period.*

"B" Designated Cases

- *Cases which are designated as "B" cases will be followed up by a supplemental report and required action within 15 days of the assignment date;*
- *The case packet including the original case and assignment sheet with supplemental reports will be returned to the assigning supervisor.*

"A" Designated Cases

- *Cases designated as "A" have the highest priority for attention. These cases require immediate attention with follow-up action and supplemental reports submitted within seven days of the assignment date.*

- *The case packet including assignment sheet, report, and supplement reports will be returned to the assigning supervisor within the 10 day period.*

Priority Designation Requirement

Basis for case prioritizing

- *Police cases are prioritized according to various weighted factors.*
- *The primary consideration for such prioritizing is the solution probability;*
- *Investigators or persons assigned follow-up work should be assigned only cases, which have a chance for solution. This will decrease case loads and increase solution rates. Its effects benefit the department and community alike.*

Supervisory Function

- *Supervisors will analyze cases for priority factors.*
- *Officers will ensure that their initial reports contain pertinent information for determining solvability factors.*
- *The following are **solvability factors** that will be considered:*

1. *Arrest*
2. *Immediate availability of witnesses*
3. *The suspect could be named*
4. *Information about the suspect's location*
5. *Information on suspect's description*
6. *The suspect could be identified*
7. *Information about suspect's vehicle*
8. *The vehicle plate number used in the crime is known*
9. *There is traceable stolen property*
10. *There is significant physical evidence*
11. *There are identifiable latent fingerprints - presence of evidence technician who indicates a priority judgment that good physical evidence is present.*
12. *A significant M.O. (modus operandi) can be developed*
13. *It is reasonably suspected that there is a limited opportunity to commit the crime.*
14. *A judgment by the patrol officer that there is sufficient information to conclude that anyone other than the suspect could not have committed the crime.*

15. *A judgment by the patrol officer that there is enough information available that, which a reasonable investment of investigative effort, the probability of case solution is high.*
16. *There is reason to believe that crime would arouse public interest that public assistance would lead to crime solution.*

The system we developed was one way to manage and prioritize the criminal cases. It is important for the supervisor to follow-up on the case assignments to check its status. The more serious cases would be assigned to the investigator. This system worked very well in Fort Lupton and we used something similar in Florence, Arizona. The important consideration is to **develop a case management system**.

Types of Investigations

What should the Detective Division or Investigations responsibility be? There is no doubt that the investigator should be responsible for all the violent Part I offenses in the Uniform Crime Report such as Murder, Forcible Rape, Robbery and Aggravated Assault. Some Detectives Divisions are large enough to separate crimes against persons and crimes against property. The small departments do not have this luxury and tend to investigate all serious offenses. The other property Part I offenses in the Uniform Crime Reports such as Burglary, Larceny, Motor Vehicle Theft and Arson are important too but obviously, the violent crimes have a higher priority.

Drug investigations in Fort Lupton, Colorado were starting to pick up. Officers were enthusiastic about investigating drug trafficking in the area. We were starting to get a great deal of drug intelligence not only for our community but other communities as well. One day I had received some information about drug trafficking in a nearby community of about 500 people. The drug sales were going on at all hours of the day. Anyone who wanted drugs, namely cocaine, could get it. It just so happened that my wife and I attended church services in this community on Saturday evening. It was not unusual to see people from other communities attending mass. I took the opportunity to drive by the residence several times to gather information about the layout of the premises. This community was at the south end of the country and when I called the County Task Force they were interested but not enough to take action right away. I contacted the Adams County Drug Task force to get some assistance because this community was not in my jurisdiction. They were very interested and eventually got the Weld County Drug Task Force involved. It did not take long because shortly thereafter they made a sizable seizure of cocaine and cash. I told them it would be easy pickings. They finally believed me and took action. It was a good feeling to help someone in another community.   The Sheriff's Deputy only occasionally patrolled this community. The drug dealers felt safe to do whatever they wanted. The person who gave me the information lived next door to the drug trafficking location and the people in the neighborhood were getting fed up with the drug related traffic. They were afraid for their children and some would not venture very far from their home. The drug sales were so brazen that this woman could see what was going on looking out her kitchen window at different times during the day. In fact, she had her husband erect a fence to shield them from the unsavory looking characters that they would see. One person even had the gall to walk over to her property and ask if the person was home. It took effort on my part but I was happy to do it. I get the urge to assist with investigations and in this case, I was not going to turn my back. I could have easily said it was not my jurisdiction. My patrol officers and investigator were involved in this operation.

Actually investigating drugs is a full time job especially with the amount of drug trafficking in the area. The County Drug Task Force was noticing what we were doing and wanted to get more involved. This was a change. There was a time when they did not want to work the community. They did not know whom to trust. I was pleased that we were able to turn this program around. Fort Lupton now had a good reputation not only in the community but also in law enforcement circles.

We were able to accomplish some good deeds in Florence, Arizona. Some of the investigations turned out very well. One officer with his K-9 was assigned to the Pinal County Drug Task Force. This turned out to be a good move because this officer was able to stop vehicles carrying drugs coming across the boarder from Mexico into Arizona. On two occasions, this officer made two sizable seizures of large quantities of marijuana. One vehicle had over 500 pounds and the other about 225 pounds of marijuana. Our investment in the drug task force paid huge dividends. Even though our department was small with one investigator, I was able to utilize the drug task force in our area. Using other resources helped keep our crimes down including drug trafficking.

If I was able to assign an officer to the drug task force in Colorado, I think we would have done a better job and would have realized significant results sooner. I was not able to provide an officer because of our manpower problems. There was always someone leaving to go to a higher paying department. The **drug task force is an excellent way to supplement your drug investigations** in your area. Generally, the drug task force investigates drug trafficking in the communities that assign an officer to the task force. Actually, I cannot argue with that philosophy because I would expect the same thing. I could not complain too much because I could not spare an officer.

All the patrol officers were busy besides the investigator. Overall, we were doing a decent job in investigating crime. We were starting to see some results because overall the crime in the community had gone down even though it was the trend all over the country. I do give credit to my officers for doing a good job. Our solvability rate was sometimes higher than the national average and I always thought we could always improve on it. An aggressive highly trained and experienced investigator should be able to make an impact. True, not all the crime can be solved but we sure can try.

A small and even some medium size police departments can be quickly overwhelmed if there is a crime spree. One of the reasons why the solvability rate in small police departments is low is the obvious, one or two investigators can only do so much. If more time is taken to investigate violent crime then the other crimes will have to take a back seat. The community does not understand and become impatient. I have heard many times from the citizens about never hearing about their case. At the very least, there should be a process in place to let the citizen know about the status of their case even if there are currently no leads and the investigation has been suspended. No one wants to hear that his or her case is unimportant and other cases have higher priority. Where the citizen is concerned, there is nothing more important than him or her being a victim of a crime.

Each department must develop a method to inform the citizen of the status of their complaint. Some departments have the luxury of having additional clerical staff to help them with this task, while smaller agencies do not. Each officer had the responsibility of conducting their own follow-ups on investigations assigned to them by their supervisor. The investigator gets assigned the serious cases and the patrol officers the rest. This system worked very well but occasionally we did receive a complaint. In addition, our department in Fort Lupton, Colorado had a Victim Assistance Coordinator that worked with victims of crime and I will talk more about this later in another chapter.

Most of the time, the investigators were busy investigating child molestations, some forcible rapes, aggregated assaults, occasionally a robbery and mostly burglaries. Sometimes I would become impatient with the progress of the cases because of the time it took to investigative them. I was at a point where I received a status update from my investigator when it was apparent we were not making much headway on some important cases. If you recall, this female investigator replaced the investigator who I eventually terminated because of theft of cocaine from the evidence room and using it on and off the premises. Every Monday morning I had a conference with my investigator to review the status of them. I thought it was necessary because I did not like how she was handling some of the investigations, one of which ended in a complaint to the city administrator. It was probably more of a personality conflict, but I thought she could have handled herself better during a burglary investigation. This was the case where a motor vehicle had been stolen from an unlocked garage and the keys were left in the ignition. The woman's purse was also left in the vehicle. There were no signs of anything else being disturbed. This was a strange case. The vehicle was later recovered in another community and the detective picked up the owners of the vehicle and transported them to the location of their vehicle. The victims did not like the way the investigation was conducted and how they were treated. There was no evidence that the victims had been mistreated and I might add the detective went out of her way to accommodate them.

I was satisfied that the detective treated the people decently. They were upset that nothing was being done about getting the persons responsible for stealing her vehicle. The suspects managed to cash some of the stolen checks that were in the purse. With all the available evidence, I think that the female investigator could have been more diligent in pursuing this case. What bothered me about it was the crime scene itself. In my mind, it was highly unusual for someone from another community to go directly to her home and manage to go into the garage and steal her vehicle. I think the daughter knew more about it than she was telling. After everything settled down, I waited a short time and then transferred the detective back to patrol. I thought it was necessary because the job was not getting done. There are times when the police chief has to make a move for the benefit of the department.

In all fairness, the detective was involved with numerous sexual assault and molestation of child. It seems that we were getting a new case every few weeks. Each case required countless number of man-hours to properly investigate the case. If some other cases come in then many others sometimes received minimal investigation or those cases had to be put on hold. In the previous example, the detective was trying to be accommodating to the victims and little did she realize it was a no win situation. They were unreasonable with some of their requests and the victim's husband had a negative prior contact with the detective. At this point she should have sought some advice.

The investigator will get some unusual requests from time to time. For example, a female came into my office to complain that nothing was being done about her investigation. She said about 20 years ago her brother, who now lived in Fort Lupton, Colorado sexually assaulted her when they had lived in Iowa. Her brother was working with children and she was afraid that he would be assaulting them. A records check revealed that her brother did not have a criminal record. I advised the female that her complaint had originated in another state and it was beyond the statute of limitations. She did not accept the fact that the police were not going to do anything. Some people no matter what, you cannot please. She would stop by the police department from time to time making the same complaint.

Investigators will get unusual requests, assist other police departments and take on a large caseload. It takes an experienced investigator to manage the caseload. What happened when the investigator becomes overwhelmed? On occasion, it could very well happen, so occasionally you have to provide additional help from the patrol officers. Temporary assignments can be made and perhaps getting an assist from the Sheriff's Office would be very helpful.

Cultivating an officer to become a good detective or investigator does not happen over night in a small police department. It requires patience and understanding. Sometimes I caught myself being impatient and would literally bite my tongue not to say any negative comments to discourage the investigator. The Detective Division in Somersworth, New Hampshire was good to begin with but became better while I was there. I was making good progress with the Investigations or Detective Division in Florence, Arizona when the Council Members began to interfere. I think it was mainly jealousy stemming from an officer who was talking directly to the Council Members. In Fort Lupton, Colorado, I think overall significant progress was made. The division was expanded from one to two investigators with a sergeant in charge. The investigators could handle more criminal cases including more drug investigations. The Property and Evidence Room was secure and a good policy and procedure developed for handling evidence was now in place.

The Detective Division is something the police chief cannot take lightly. Every function is important in the police department but it would benefit the chief if he or she paid particular attention to the operation of investigations. I did not take anything for granted. I reviewed the reports of the investigator to insure we were doing quality work. I was pleased with the job the investigators were doing in all my departments.

Chapter 16
Community Policing

Community Policing during the last ten years or so has taken off and many police departments have adopted this new policing philosophy. We **will** explore the concepts and how this new policing philosophy has not only helped my communities but others as well. It seems to be the new buzzword in policing. Even the town and city managers have joined in this new quest. During the early 1990's the new city manager in Somersworth, New Hampshire did not know what the term meant. He thought that perhaps it was just another gimmick. Police Departments were always experimenting with new programs with the intended end product being - to reduce crime in their area. Some of the programs were very impressive but some never went anywhere.

What Is Community Policing?

The philosophy behind community policing is very simple. It is a partnership between the police and the community to work together to reduce crime in their community. Everyone seems to have their opinion of what it is and there are now many books written on the subject. What may work in one community may work very well, while in others, it may not work at all. The police chief has to be careful in how to progress from a traditional to the community policing style. The transition may be excruciating slow and some officer will never buy into it. How can you motivate the officers? The discussion in this chapter will focus on the community policing issues in my former communities, what worked and some suggestions for improvement.

Everyone can agree that the overall goal in the community is to reduce crime and the fear of crime. We want to have our citizens feel safe and when they do not, they ultimately put pressure on the council members, mayor and city manager. I use to hear it from the public. Can you do something about crime? You can tell people that crime has dropped over the past 10 years according to the Uniform Crime Reports published by the Federal Bureau of Investigation annually. Generally, the people will not be impressed if they had been victim of a crime. Being a victim of one crime is considered one crime too many.

In the traditional style of policing the police officers in their marked cruiser would ride around and this in turn would help to drive the criminals away. People had second thoughts about "omnipresence," appearing to be everywhere. The thinking was if the police appeared to be everywhere being highly visible then the crime rate would go down. No, the criminal would wait until the officer drove by and then commit the crime. Studies demonstrated that the traditional methods of policing were not effective and other strategies had to been incorporated. The police were trying to fight crime by themselves.

The police were trying to do the job alone and it was not working. Why not use the community to help the police to solve some problems. If the police and citizens worked together then perhaps they can be more effective.

Traditional Policing: The Good Old Days

Let us look at some of the more traditional styles of policing, some of which were very effective. During the early part of the 1900s police departments used the beat cop especially in the large cities. As populations grew, the police departments expanded their patrols to include a marked police vehicle. This transition continued and there came a time during the 1970s when these beat cops were starting to move into the marked police vehicles. Other words, many communities moved their beat man and put him or her into a marked police vehicle to cover a wider area. The crime rate was rising rapidly all over the country and police departments were responding by increasing their patrol motorized patrol force. It made sense to the police administrators at the time by throwing more officers at the problem. As more officers were being moved into marked police vehicles they did not realize that they were losing the interpersonal relationships with the public. There were now more police officers but the crime rate was still rising. Something else had to be done about the problem.

Police departments were already doing components of Community Policing and they did not realize it. The "Beat Cop" was an integral part of the policing system in many communities. Many police officers thought the cop on the beat was a waste of time and manpower. Everyone wanted a piece of the action and wanted to go into a marked police cruiser. Even early in my career during in the 1970s in Bristol, Connecticut it was not fun being on the beat on the third shift having to walk from call box to call box during a snowstorm. The instructions from the sergeant were clear. Each officer had to walk his beat, make his ring, direct traffic during rush hour and handshake the doors of businesses after they closed for the day. These were the expectations. If a door was found left unlocked the owner of the business was called to come to his or her business to secure the door. None of the younger officers particularly liked walking the beat. However, the old timers on the day shift like the walking beat and usually requested it. Usually the same officers worked the walking beats and the others in a marked cruiser patrolling a district. The day shift officers had seniority and they always worked the best area. The officer with badge number one worked the same beat every day from Monday through Friday. He had paid his dues and this was his reward as an unwritten rule.

Back then, it did not make any sense but it does now. Officers working the same beat day in and day out got to know the people in their area and they handled all the problems. When there was a problem, a merchant would call the police dispatch and ask to speak to the beat cop. Very rarely was there a formal complaint logged on the police daily complaint blotter. These "old timers" would handle the complaint unofficially. No one knew what it was but the problem was handled. I even worked the day shift walking beat occasionally. I would fill in occasionally on overtime when the regular beat man got a day off. One day I got a call to see a local merchant on the beat. When I got there, he asked me if I could do his bank deposit for him and to bring back his change. I declined and told him I could not do what he had asked because it was not part of my duties. He said, "The other guys do it all the time."

One popular beat cop was Officer Bob Watson. At the time, he happened to be the only black officer on the department. Looking back now, he was the essence of community policing. You see, back in the old days many departments were already doing what they are trying to do now. It is like reinventing the wheel with a new slant to it. Some of the management staff did not care for Bob because he did not issue very many parking or traffic tickets or even criminal arrests. I like to use him as an example because he was effective in a different way. Everyone in the community knew Bob Watson and he was very popular with the kids. We are realizing now that issuing tickets were just one dimension; there are many other dimensions involved in being the complete police officer. When Officer Watson was on the beat, there were never any problems. He took care of problems unofficially. Rarely did he have to make an arrest when he went to a disturbance or domestic violence. The other old timers performed similarly in this regards but Bob was the most effective.

From a personal point of view, my father owned and ran a restaurant in Bristol, Connecticut during the 1950s and 1960s. He remarked to me one day about a situation where two guys from Waterbury, which is located about 20 miles away, would show up in the late afternoon just before closing. He never saw these individuals before and my mother and father were getting very nervous about the way they were acting. Did he call the police to make a complaint? No, he called and asked Officer Bob Watson to stop by because my father wanted to speak to him. After my father related the story to him, Officer Watson had a talk with the two individuals. What was discussed I do not know but these two individuals never came back to Bristol again. Officer Watson handled the problem and there was never any complaint logged at the police department.

I remembered Bob when I was in High School. He was a people person and he even spent time with me playing basketball. I think that he influenced me a great deal and his enthusiasm motivated me to become more interested in law enforcement. Even with the other students, he was popular. He was excellent with the kids because he took the time to understand how they felt and what problems they were experiencing. He was credible because he genuinely cared about people. Even after I began to be promoted and started climbing the promotional ladder, I began to understand Bob's method behind the madness. I simply let Bob do his job and never got after him because he was not issuing enough tickets. It was a sad day when Bob Watson decided to retire because we lost an excellent community-policing officer. He was the essence of community policing. If other departments had more officers like him, our communities would be a better place to live. I think we can relate to someone who had a positive influence in our lives and Bob was one of them.

In 1971, the Bristol Police Department stumbled upon another policing concept called "Team Policing." The police department was able to obtain a federal grant to fund an experimental team patrol concept. The thought was to put the same officers in a patrol district everyday to help reduce the crime rate. The grant funded additional equipment, training and overtime. The equipment included a three-wheeled type vehicle that helped to patrol a shopping plaza and a low-income project in the district. It looked like an ice cream truck and many of the officers did not like it. The citizens generally poke fun at the officers driving it asking if they had some ice cream. The top speed was about 35 M.P.H. and it shook your whole body when you drove it. It was like someone punching your kidneys during your eight-hour tour of duty. I did not know anyone who liked to ride this weird looking vehicle. Everyone thought up some excuse to get out of this assignment.

However, it had the potential to be a good idea. No one ever took the time to explain the importance of a mobile beat man. A person could cover a small area very quickly and still have the interpersonal approach of the beat man. The problem was that we did not get any training. No one took the time other than an initial orientation to talk about the program. The supervisors were not involved as much as they should have been. The program was effective but it could have been better.

The same officers worked the area, which happened to be the most crime ridden in the community and most problematic. Much of our serious crime, domestic violence, assaults and drug related offenses were coming from there. These officers began to know the people in their area. It seemed that we were going to the same complaints day after day talking to the same individuals. The people in our area especially the low-income area, the famous Davis Drive knew us by our names. We responded to one domestic in particular, it seemed like a weekend occurrence. We knew the wife and the combative husband. We knew every time we responded to the residence that we were going into a battle. He knew us by name and it did not matter. When he sobered up the next day, he always apologized. I could not understand at the time how anyone could live in a hostile environment. This guy was a construction worker and a good provider for his family during the week. It was the weekend when this guy would go crazy after a bout drinking all night. Everyone at the time knew the couple and responded to their address so I think it was helpful that we understood the situation. We thought for sure that we would be responding to a homicide one day but it never escalated to that point.

Sometimes being too familiar with certain troublesome individuals can appear to hurt the program. We were always contacting a white male in his late teens who was always in trouble. He and his friends were involved in drugs, alcohol and assaults. His mother thought the police were picking on her son so she decided to call the FBI to complain about a civil rights violation. Her son would always get arrested for some crime so she probably thought she could put some heat on the police. Her plan did not work. The FBI paid a visit to our fine community twice to investigate our team members and each time everyone came out clean. The reality was that no one was intentionally harassing this person. This kid was always stupid enough to get into trouble in the same area. However, on the positive side we were able to keep the crime from getting worse. I could imagine what may have happened if this person was allowed to run wild. He was frustrated because he could not do what he wanted to do in our area. We just simply displaced crime; he would go elsewhere to commit it.

The team members can handle certain situations as they say fit even to the extent of altering the method of patrol. Sometimes we used our imagination to handle a certain situation. One day we decided to do something about the pot smoking in the park during the evening hours. Every time we drove a marked police cruiser into the area to check them we could never catch them. One evening we decided to change to civilian clothes and watch them from the wooded area. When it got dark, my partner and I snuck into the woods and crept up on them. I lay down in some vegetation and watched them through a pair of binoculars. It was apparent after a while that they were smoking pot and that was when we called the marked cruisers to move in. We were able to make a number of arrests that evening and eventually cleaned up the problem. There was no more pot smoking in the park. There was only one problem; I did not realize that I was lying in poison ivy. I had poison ivy all over my face, neck and hands. I was hurting for a week or two but it was worth the effort.

During this period police work was actually fun. Everyone looked forward to going to work and doing something different. The sergeants allowed some creativity to get the job done and overall we were quite successful. There was many times where the officers used their ingenuity to solve a particular problem. I believe we had made a huge impact in our area.

Sadly, after one year in operation the Team Patrol ceased to exist. It was apparent the federal funding ran dry. I thought the Team Patrol concept worked very well and I was disappointed that it was not continued. Looking back on the program now we were actually doing problem orientated policing. With the approval of the sergeant, we were able to adapt our patrol practices to solve problems in our area. We were solving problems without the partnership of the community. We did not realize it at the time but we missed a golden opportunity. The component missing was community involvement. The police like always was trying to do it all alone.

After the year had been concluded, the officers were switched around and we reverted back to working different patrol districts. We were back to the reactive patrol. Someone would call in a complaint and the police would respond to it. Imagine we were doing something that worked and it was suddenly dropped without explanation other than the funding ran out. If management had taken some initiative, they could have continued this patrol technique and built upon it. Management killed a productive program.

During the 1980s everything remained the same but with an added twist. One of the captains came up with the concept of "Directed Patrol." In addition to patrolling his area, he was given an assignment or a series of assignments to check problem areas and to spend some time patrolling there. This was again another component of problem orientated policing. We had the making of breaking new ground. This was the latest trend in policing by concentrating on problem areas. If the officers had taken it a little more seriously, we could have done a better job. No one wanted to be told when and where he or she was going to patrol. Some of our guys were resistant to new ideas and they were just going through the motions. The captain had the right idea though.   This new patrol concept would have worked better if there had been a training session. If the officers had a better understanding on how it worked and the reasons for it then they would have been supportive. There was no follow-up on the directed patrols other than indicating the areas patrolled on the back of the Officer's Activity Report. The officers were generally not truthful in their report. Many times they did not bother to check the directed patrol area and the sergeant did not follow-up. Most of the time there was no follow-up from the lieutenant to the captain. It would have worked better if the officers were required to fill out a specific directed patrol form that was checked by the sergeant. The **fatal error was no accountability**.

The only other attempt to begin working with the public in Bristol, Connecticut was setting up Neighborhood Crime Watch programs.   There were some crime watch programs but not nearly as many as they should. The concept for this program was good. It asked people to help the police by being the eyes and ears for anything suspicious in their neighborhood. They were encouraged to call the police and in the beginning, the police did call. The detective doing the program thought all he had to do was give a presentation to a group of neighbors and the program would exist on its own. The problem with this program as well as many others was not enough involvement with the police. These neighbors have to be nurtured over time to have a thorough understanding. You just cannot have a neighborhood meeting, put up crime watch signs, and expect to have a Neighborhood Crime Watch program. After a while, the people will revert back to their normal practice. It takes a great deal of work to institute and maintain a Neighborhood Crime Watch program. It is a great idea but if you are not committed, the program will be doomed. Why do it, if you are not going to do it right? The problem here was a lack of follow-up and no accountability. On the surface, we were working with the public but in reality it was "window dressing."

I mentioned several examples of worthwhile programs in the 1970's and 1980's in my former department. The programs could have worked with more effort. Other police departments were experimenting in programs but generally, there was no earth shattering results in new patrol techniques. I thought it was important to discuss these programs because they were actually components of community policing. Management was dabbling with the components, but the pieces were never completed to form the picture of the puzzle. Little did police departments realize that the beat man was an integral part of the community policing system? They were actually solving problems before anyone realized what they were doing. Management at the time was busy looking at the measurable results such as how many parking tickets, written warnings and traffic tickets were issued. There was too much emphasis on quantifiable results, which was only one aspect of policing.

When I say many of the problems were "window dressing," I mean just that. It looked like the police were trying to do something but nothing more. There was no real attempt to identify and deal with problems in the community. Just think what may have happened with more forethought and planning. The department could have been a trendsetter in contemporary policing practices. The department would have to follow the lead of others. I may have been critical but the reality was at the time other police departments were very similar.

In the 1990s the Community Policing concept really evolved to what we know it today. The federal government gave away millions of dollars to police departments all over the United States to add more personnel and adopt the Community Policing principals. The task was left up to police departments to develop programs that involved the participation of the community. Communities were able to get additional manpower, training and technology as long as they made a commitment to Community Policing.   Many departments initiated their own version of community policing.   Some were similar but not the same.   Some may call it community policing but in name only.   No two programs were alike simply because no two communities are the same.   I will discuss my three former police department's Community Policing initiatives.   Each department was different but in the end my last department, Fort Lupton was where everything came together.

Bicycle Patrol

I can remember when police departments were first using the 10 -speed bicycles in New Hampshire early in the 1990s; everyone thought it was a silly idea.   It is funny how this type of thinking was stereotyped.   The new buzzword, "Community Policing" started circulating in law enforcement circles.   Police departments were trying to understand the new policing philosophy.   People heard of it but did not understand the concept.   I understood after relating back to the Team Patrol days with the Bristol Police Department.   On the surface, it looked like another gimmick to try but this time there was merit to it.   I could see it would be a great opportunity to get closer to the citizens.

In Somersworth, New Hampshire I was able to implement a police bicycle patrol with a donation of two 10-speed bicycles from Wal-Mart.   I have to say this corporation was very interested in helping their community and when I asked them for a donation they did not hesitate.   In the beginning, we were able outfit the bike with equipment and assigned an officer to a bike patrol on a part-time basis.   My personnel were not too thrilled about peddling a bicycle around until I formed a committee to have them check what other police departments were doing.   They not only came back more enthusiastic but helped formulate the policy and procedure.   Because it was different, people in the community were somewhat skeptical.   We used the bicycle patrol for parades, special details and the annual "Children's Festival.   The officers really got their exercise because part of the city is hilly.   Somersworth is still known as the "Hilltop City" and they are not kidding.   We did not do as much as I liked because we could have done more.   At least we were making some progress but it was good public relations.

I implemented a bicycle patrol in Florence, Arizona.   It was not very popular during the long summer season with 100 plus degree temperature every day.   Everyone would say it was a dry heat, but hot is hot.   We were able to utilize the bike patrol for parades, special occasion and certain patrol situations.   Being in a small department it was difficult to implement on a full time basis.   Other larger police departments were doing it on more of a full time basis.   Many of the Metro police departments in the Phoenix area were routinely using police bicycle patrol.

As time was going on police departments were accepting the police bicycle as an excellent community-policing tool. The traditional beat man can only cover just so much territory in his or her area but now the beat man is more mobile with the bicycle. He or she can patrol anywhere, downtown area, parks, and schools and off the road. The bicycles were going into areas not reached by police patrols. Now that the police officer was out of the marked police vehicle, he or she was approachable. The idea behind "Community Policing" is to get to personally know the police officer and vice versa. It is just common sense. People are generally more open when they get to know you.

We were doing this a long time ago and did not realize it. Back in Bristol, Connecticut, the merchant in the downtown area would call the police station to speak to a certain officer on the beat. If he had a complaint, the officer handled it informally. The merchant usually did not call the police department first to lodge a complaint. The reason he wanted to speak to the officer about his problem was that he liked and trusted the officer. People are generally not open to strangers. I wanted the officer on the bike to be more responsive to the needs of the citizens. This was a different concept because now we were asking police officers to talk to the citizens and find out about their problems. It was opposite of what the officers were trained to do, respond to only to complaints made to the police department. They did not understand the true significance. They were going to solicit complaints.

What I was trying to do was to get the officers to deal with the problems on their own before they became big problems. I wanted them to be creative and take the initiative. I realized it would take an effort to retrain the way they were thinking. Police officers are normally trained to be reactive, only take action when there was a complaint. Now we were asking them to do something different to deal with problems on their own. Too many police officers relied on their supervisors to make decisions for them all the time. The time for the handholding was over. Getting across a new philosophy would take time and effort.

The bike patrol in Florence was just one component of the "Community Policing effort. Over time, the community like the patrol and were getting use to it. I realized it was an excellent way to get closer to the police. The bike patrol worked even better in Fort Lupton, Colorado. When I first arrived, the officers already had a bike patrol. All I had to do was continue what they were doing and budget for better bikes and equipment. The officers were enthusiastic about it and wanted to ride the bikes more often but the lack of manpower stopped me. I had to staff the marked police units first. There were many times when we patrolled during the shift as part of the normal patrol. We were able to patrol the parks, schools, downtown areas and other hard to get to areas. This program was a success. During the later part of the 1990's police departments all over the country were using the police bicycle. It was a resounding success and an integral part of the community-policing program. It was slow to catch on but now police departments wanted to use the bicycle patrol. Some council members were looking at it from a cost effective standpoint, a way to save gas but I was looking at it from a community relation's standpoint. Our motivations were different but who cares, they were buying into the new philosophy.

While on routine patrol, the officers were able to catch more people in the act of committing crime than ever before. The crooks were always looking for the marked police vehicle now we have them second-guessing. Now they are looking over the shoulder for the quiet riding and hard to spot police officer on the bicycle. In Fort Lupton I cannot tell you how many times we snuck up on shady looking characters doing a drug transaction or caught them in an area where they were not supposed to be. If a police department does not have a police bicycle patrol then it is time to implement one even if it is only on a part-time basis.

Park, Walk and Talk

One program before I implemented the Bicycle Patrol in Somersworth, New Hampshire was the Park, Walk and Talk. When the officers were not responding to calls for service and just riding around, I wanted them to park their marked cruiser in the downtown area, walk the area and talk to citizens. Again, it was important to get to know the citizens. Many officers lived out of town and many people did not know them. I thought it would be a good way to get to know the citizens better.

One day I was walking around the downtown area in Florence, Arizona after I had first arrived doing my famous "Walk about" and had stopped in one of the stores selling southwest jewelry. After talking to the owner for a while, he asked if the officers could stop by his store and introduce themselves because he did not know any of them. This person was a winter visitor and only operated his store during the winter when the other winter visitors or "Snowbirds" were in the area. It was sad to think that this person in this small community did not know any of the officers except for a few after being in the Town of Florence for a number of years. It did not take long for me to implement the park, walk and talk program. The objective was to get the officers out of their cruisers and to walk the downtown area. Some did it more than others, but overall it worked very well.

I did not have to do much convincing in Fort Lupton, the officers responded to my requests very well. Many of the officers were already stopping in the downtown area and the merchants already knew most of the officers. The community seemed to like most of the officers but the city council wanted community policing. Whether they realized it or not they were already doing many of the components. What the department needed at that time was better leadership and more coordination. Many times the left hand did not know what the right hand was doing. The sergeants individually were doing their own version of community policing. Many of the programs they were doing were good. All I had to do was make them better. The Park, Walk and Talk program worked very well. What I wanted them to do was to solve problems on their own and work with the citizens more. They were always getting guidance for everything.

What use to bother me when people would ask, "Why don't the officer smile and waive to me?" It was a very good question and I could not answer it. Many times the officer on patrol does not look friendly and it should not be so. There is no reason the officer cannot be friendlier. We need to change this type of behavior. If the police are to be treated with respect then they should do like wise. If police officers are friendlier then the citizens will get to know them better and have more respect. It is only common sense. Actually, this is one theme that keeps reappearing again that I will keep exploring when I discuss other programs. I not only heard it then but also heard it in other parts of the country including North Carolina and Louisiana. People in general when the conversation comes up about their police department very few have anything good to say. Changing the way of thinking does not happen over night so police departments have to work at it very diligently.

Neighborhood Crime Watch Programs

The Neighborhood Crime Watch program can be a very good program and in my experience it did not work as well as it should. In all three of my previous police departments, I started a neighborhood crime watch program and each time it got a cool reception. There were some people interested but not enough to devote manpower but I did not give up. I think the reason for it was that there was not enough burglaries in one area to have people get excited about. Some people just want a Neighborhood Crime Watch Sign in their neighborhood and this alone will not prevent burglaries. Generally, people get excited after the fact when they had been victimized and now they want action.

Some police departments in other communities do it very well but in others, the program fails, like in Bristol, Connecticut. There was interest but very little follow-up. The crime prevention officer has to be involved continuously with the neighborhood groups. The purpose behind the neighborhood crime watch program is to get the neighbors interested enough to call the police in the event they observe suspicious persons and vehicles in their area. The police want the citizens to get involved and be the eyes and ears of the police. The objective is to get them more involved and have them call the police. If people got more involved in their community then without a doubt, there would be less crime and more criminals would be caught in the act.

Having the sign is nice and it looks pretty but what it takes a cooperative effort by the people, meeting on a monthly basis to discuss issues. There needs to be a continuing coordinated effort by the department. Just because a neighborhood organized into a neighborhood crime watch program does not mean it will succeed. The **people have to be kept informed** of what is happening. One of the best ways to do this is in the form of a **monthly newsletter** to keep everyone informed of the latest happenings and other interesting tidbits. Actually, people are nosey and want to be kept informed. Just seeing the police officer occasionally will not do it. Is the Neighborhood Crime Watch program working? If it is slow in getting people together what needs to be done? If there are suspicious persons or vehicles, in the area do the police get called and the other neighbors notified? The police needs to follow-up and let them know what they found out. What gets me angry about these programs is that people are left guessing. It would not hurt to call the person back and thank them for their effort. A little encouragement means much to the neighbor. If a newsletter is going to be published, one suggestion would be to have one of the neighbors designated to do it and the police officer act as the liaison. The police officer would provide the latest information on crime prevention and information on burglary rings working the community and anything else of interest. The person responsible for completing and disseminating the newsletter could fill the rest of the information with information about the neighborhood, such as people on vacation or sick. The last bit of information that is not performed too frequently is a telephone tree. If something is happening there should be phone calls made to the neighbors to put them on alert. The police officer is critical to insure the people keep their interest in the crime prevention program. There should be a conscious effort by the officer and continuing support by the police department to make the Neighborhood Crime Watch program a success. Many police departments start them but fizzle out after a few months and they ask themselves why. I know why, we help to kill the program. It is doomed to fail after it gets started and the reality is it does not have to be so.

People are so involved in their lives that sometimes they quickly lose interest or there is no support from the crime prevention officer and police department. I think the key to successful neighborhood watch programs is the following:

- Meet on a regular basis at least once a month.
- Designate a watch captain.
- Frequent follow-up visits by the Crime Prevention Officer.
- Monthly or Quarterly Newsletter by the Neighborhood Crime Watch.
- Police Department providing continued support services, such as signs and other materials.
- Open communication by the Police Department.

- Telephone tree to alert neighbors.

The Neighborhood Crime Watch program is a vital component of Community Policing. Let it be a real partnership by maintaining an open dialogue with the neighbors. With the officer working with the neighbors and getting to know them he or she will be helping them solve other problems in the neighborhood. Yes, they can help solve some crime but more they would be working together to solve other problems. In my communities, we did not get that far because of a lack of interest. Just think of the possibilities; the sky was the limit.

Business/Home Security Assessment

What usually compliments the Neighborhood Crime Watch program is the business and home security assessment. In all my communities, I made available a security assessment even if there was no crime watch program. In Somersworth, New Hampshire, I specifically had an officer trained in crime prevention techniques and he would go out into the community providing an assessment and helpful crime prevention tips. He would teach people how to **"target harden"** their home or business. It many plenty of sense to me but only a few people took advantage of it. We kept offering the service and still there was only minimal interest.

We even offered to lend out inscribers so that people could etch their name or partial social security number on their valuables. Occasionally, someone would ask to use the inscriber. Our "Operation Identification" should have had more impact and it was not the lack of information about it. Every opportunity that I had to promote our crime prevention programs, I took advantage of it. Again, I was puzzled why there was a general lack of interest. If there was a rash of crime in the neighborhood then I believed the situation would be different.

Help Stop Crime

In Somersworth, New Hampshire, we came up with a "Help Stop Crime" program. Like other communities, we wanted people to report crime and call in tips using a special phone number. Rewards were available. You can use catchy phrases like, "If you see it, report it." I used this one in Florence, Arizona. There crime stopper programs that can be organized in the community where they would collect donations in the community to be used as rewards for helping to solve crimes. It is another way to involve people.

Are Crime Prevention Programs Successful?

Preventing crime has to be an on going effort. I came to realize after trying to do crime prevention programs in three communities, people do not get very excited unless they have a vested interest, which usually means they had been victimized or there is a violent crime wave and people are afraid to leave their house. I have spoken to other police chiefs about their programs and some had come to the same conclusion. The programs were good but more people should have been involved. Sometimes I was at a loss as to why these programs were not more successful. Some of our neighbors are so transient that people rarely get to know their neighbors very well. If you do not know your neighbors very well, then why should you care? Somehow, we have to get past this and get people involved. If there is a community newspaper, this should be brought to the attention of the people. I recognize many people do not get their community newspaper on a regular basis.

Ways to Improve

If there is a will, there is a way. An aggressive police chief should find ways to kindle some renewed interest in crime prevention. One way to get key information out to the public would be through a **Community Newsletter**. The city manager in Somersworth, New Hampshire to his credit started a community newsletter. It was a great idea no if, and or buts about it. He recognized many people did not buy the local paper and wanted to keep people informed. Once a quarter a newsletter was mailed with the water bills. Each department in the city was required to submit information for the newsletter and it was a good opportunity to discuss programs and crime prevention. It was more work but it was worth the effort. Some of the other department heads groaned about it. I thought it was a great idea.

I tried to get the Florence Town Manager to do a community newsletter in some form but he declined for some reason. He did not want to bother with it. In Fort Lupton, Colorado, the city administrator started a Community Newsletter and it was received very well. Why not keep the city informed through the newsletter. Every time the city administrator wanted some information for the newsletter, he would remind me that space was limited. I just smiled and walked back to my office. I usually cranked out plenty of information for the newsletter. He would give me his shifty eyed look and smiled. I told him he would have to edit out the material he did not want but it was all important. It was another great opportunity to showcase our department and discuss programs. When I asked people if they read the newspaper or watch the city council meetings, I found very few did. I would bet the majority of people did not follow what was going on in their city or even cared unless you raised their taxes. There was a general lack of interest in their community. As in Florence it was the same but worse, a few people controlled town government and they created havoc. People did not like what was going on but as long as they were not affected, they did nothing.

I did not let the lack of a newsletter in Florence stop me. I found a way to disseminate information to the public through the local newspaper called the "Florence Reminder." One day I approached the editor of the paper and asked him if I could write a **weekly column**, called **"Crime and Prevention."** He certainly did not mind because he was always looking for stories. Every week I wrote an article. In all there were about 40 or 50 articles on different topics. It was a great deal of work but it was fun to do. It was an opportunity to showcase our department, discuss crime prevention programs and other issues affecting the city. It was a resounding success. People were always coming up to me and complimenting me about the week's article and asked what I was going to write about next. Even after I had left the department these articles were still accessible in the newspaper archives.

This leads me to the next area where the citizens can find out what is going on in their community. The **Police Department's Web Page** on the Internet was an excellent tool for law enforcement to showcase the department and crime prevention issues. Even if your community is cool on the idea of a Neighborhood Crime Watch program, the police department's web page is a good way to get people informed. If they do not want to get involved then at the very least they can get educated on crime prevention. It does not have to be an expensive proposition. I always found people who were willing to design the web page for free and the software in use today makes it very easy to do it yourself. However, it is nice to involve the community in helping to design the web page. Some departments use high school students to help and I was working on this idea in Fort Lupton.

After I got to Fort Lupton, Colorado, I wanted to have a police department web page. I thought it was important for the citizens to find out what was going on in the community. One resident in the community and his business partner volunteered to design a web page. I provided the information and they put it together. The local power company hosted the police department's web page as a community service. So, you see if there is a will there is a way. The police department web page was very well done. It provided information about department programs and its officers. There was even a fill in the blank type form for a citizen to report a crime, problem or concern. They even had the opportunity to email me to chat about problems. You would be surprised the number of people who will read your website.

One citizen who was handicap and home bound in a wheelchair emailed me about a speeding problem on his street. We were able to do something about it because of his email or otherwise we would never have found out about it. He acknowledged his gratitude in helping with a traffic safety problem.

Every time I did something positive or initiated a new program, I informed the **news media**. They were always looking for human interests stories and of course anything news worthy. Rather than have them poke around looking for negative stories my philosophy was to give them positive information. What better way to showcase the department again and let the citizens know what was going on by using the news media?

There are always ways to improve the department's crime prevention program. Each community is different so it may take some time to find out what works and what does not. Including your officers in the discussion to come up with suggestions would pay dividends. If the officers are directly involved in these programs, they will try to make it work. They do not want to get a label of failing. No one wants to fail so why not do something creative to add a different twist. With all the latest technology there is always something worthwhile to try. **The main thing is do not give up**.

Citizen Ride –A- Long Program

One of the best programs that I initiated in Florence, Arizona and Fort Lupton, Colorado was the citizen ride-a-long program. It worked well in both departments and there were times we were getting so many requests in Fort Lupton that we had to reschedule for another day. Matter of fact, I encourage everyone, young and old to ride on patrol with a police officer for four or eight hours. Anyone wanting to ride would have to complete a request to ride with an officer, a fill in the blank type form and a waiver. Some naysayer will criticize. What if a civilian rider gets hurt? Well during the four plus years I had been doing it no one got hurt. I guess there is always a first time for everything. The officers never put the civilians at risk and everything was outlined in the policy and procedure manual. If a cop can come up with something negative then they will find a way. I recognized some officers did not like to have a civilian ride with them, but I left it up to the supervisor who the civilian was going to ride with.

The Civilian Ride-A-Long program ties into the community policing. I wanted to dispel the notion that the police department was a secretly run organization. People even today are suspicious about how their police department operates because they do not know what is going on. Why not let people find out for themselves. I encourage people and council members to ride with the officers to see what was going on in the community and to have a better understanding how a police department functions.

Some departments do not allow civilians on ride-a-longs, period. However, they should reconsider to allow this practice. If you want to get people more involved in crime prevention efforts then you have to find other ways to perk their interest. Riding with the officers or spending some time in the dispatch center will sure help the cause in the end.

The Police Committee

When I first arrived in Fort Lupton, there were provisions for a civilian police committee in the City Ordinances. They were volunteers appointed by the City Council with no authority at all except in an advisory capacity. We had a committee in name only and nothing was happening. I recognized this as an opportunity to involve civilians in an advisory capacity. It took a while but I managed to get some civilian volunteers plus a council member. We met on a monthly basis in my office. The previous chief and the chief who replaced me did not recognize the potential. They simply delegated a sergeant or lieutenant to attend the meeting. You can see how quickly people can lose interest if their police chief is not interested. If I wanted this Police Committee to be effective then I had to spend time to nurture the committee. The people who volunteered countless number of hours did an outstanding job. Their purpose was to help improve the operation of the police department. I recognized it was so important for me to be there that on a few occasions, when my duties conflicted with scheduled meetings, I rescheduled the date of the meetings in order to be in attendance.

The two most dedicated committee members were Carol and Chris Criswell of Fort Lupton. They attended almost every meeting and assisted with some of the community policing activities. As I understand it, they are still involved. One excellent activity was the **"National Night Out"** that was held across the street in the park once a year in August. There will be more on this later. Incidentally, the "National Night Out" was held during the same time by other police department across the United States. One time we needed someone to wear the Crime Dog costume and Carol Criswell volunteered to wear it in the hot sun. We always teased her about it and it was a great deal of fun.

I think that in the time I was there we managed to accomplish a great deal. It was positive to have citizens caring about their police department. Some police chiefs may look at it as a threat but not me. Once a month I advised the committee on the latest happening around the community and police programs. They provided some insight and good ideas. I appreciated their help. One time they came to my rescue. Some parts of the police budget were in jeopardy of being cut including funds for a new police cruiser and they showed up at the council meeting to express their support. I believed this action alone helped to salvage the police budget.

National Night Out

The National Night Out was another Community Policing program that we did once a year in August in Fort Lupton. It was a program police departments were doing all over the country at the same time. We were one of the few departments in our area to do the National Night Out. It was an opportunity to get the community interested in their police department. There was everything for the kids and adults to enjoy. There were games for the kids including a bike rodeo where we gave away free helmets. We had a host of information on crime prevention tips and techniques. The fire department was there with their robot and just for fun one of the firemen who were operating the remote control thought it was funny to squirt me with the hose. Everyone there thought it was great fun to have the police chief get squirted in the face with water. The activities last from about 6 pm to 9 pm. It was a great time and we included free food for the kids.

This is only one example to involve the community but we did not do it enough. Instead of once a year why not have other activities schedule in different parts of the city. Instead of trying to do the program alone why no include the Recreation Department. They are always looking for new ideas. In my last year in Fort Lupton, we were working more closely with the Recreation Department. The more you can get to see the police officers on a more personal basis the better the relationship it will become. I did not come up with the idea of National Night Out but, who cares. I jumped quickly on the bandwagon because I saw good things happening.

Police Explorer Scout Program

An excellent way to reach the youth in the community is a Police Explorer Scouting program affiliated with the Boy Scouts of America. In each of my three departments, I started or improved the scouting program in each department. In Florence, Arizona, there was one individual involved with the explorer program and he left shortly after my arrival. This explorer was just too gung ho about the program and he actually thought he was a police officer. Slowly but surely the scouting program was promoted in each community. There were only about six to eight high school age kids that were interested in the program.

Back in Bristol, Connecticut there was a good Police Explorer program. There were always 10 involved and they were very interested in the program. They went on ride-a-longs with the officers and on many occasions I took one on patrol with me. One day I was operating radar and an explorer scout was with me when he got a first hand look at an irate citizen. The person I had stopped for speeding was very upset and he launched into a tirade. After I obtained his license and registration, I politely told him that I would be right back. The explorer scout said, "Why did you have to take that?" I told him, "This person was upset and it would serve no purpose for me to get angry at him and besides he was going to court." Years later this scout went on to be one of Bristol's finest having just recently retired. Every so often he would always bring up this incident. He was amazed even to this day that I showed considerable restraint. I guess I left him with a positive impression.

The Police Explorer-Scouting program is a good way for those to find out more about how their police department functions. It is important to involve the youth in the community. It is very difficult to interest high school age kids in the program. There is peer pressure not to join because they think the police are using the kids as "Narcs." More police departments should be using the Police Explorer program. It is definitely a very worthwhile program to do.

Citizens on Patrol

Citizens on Patrol are a good idea and definitely a good way to get people interested in helping the department and community. We did a program in Florence, Arizona that was different from most. We were fortunate enough to obtain a federal grant without matching funds to purchase equipment for a Citizen on Patrol program. Every year our winter visitors would start arriving in November and most would be gone by the end of April. The targeted area was where the senior citizens owed their seasonal mobile homes and it was about three miles from the center of town. At one of the entrances to the park there was a guardhouse usually manned with volunteers.

The concept was to provide the senior citizens with the tools such as a golf cart and portable radios so that they could stay in communication with the police department. The framework was there and all that had to do was to get them better organized so that they could be an additional eyes and ears of the police department. We were going to provide baseball caps and t-shirts with the Citizen on Patrol logo on them. They were really excited about the idea.

One positive thing about working with the senior citizens was the ability to change some things in the mobile home park. One noticeable problem was the inept numbering system. It was a problem for a long time because the numbering pattern did not make any kind of sense. It was always a problem for emergency services to find a particular address in the event of an emergency. Once this problem was brought to my attention I worked with the post office and the town to develop another numbering pattern in sequence. The residents were all in favor of the idea. The Citizens on Patrol are not only the eyes and ears of the police but also a sounding board for other problems in the senior citizen community. Before I could get anything going, the town council decided not to renew my contract as chief of police. This was the only attempt at the Citizens on Patrol concept in Florence. I thought about it in Fort Lupton but then again I never really found the right situation for it. The situation in Florence was ideal. Today, the Citizen on Patrol concept in Florence has evolved into an excellent program. This is the true essence of Community Policing.

Citizen Academy

In Fort Lupton, Colorado, we partnered with the Weld County Sheriff's Office promote and offer several Citizen Academies. The program was well received by the citizens. A six-week program explained various aspects of the police and sheriff departments. The program culminated in a graduation ceremony. The sheriff and I was a guest speaker for one of the training sessions. Some departments run lengthy and more in depth training, but I thought ours was very effective. The citizens had a greater understanding how police departments operated. What is good about the Citizen Academy is that you can use the graduates for other volunteer type programs like the Citizens on Patrol.

The TRIAD

The Sheriff's Association came up with a great ideal called the TRIAD. It was an idea to have the sheriff's office, the police department and senior citizens working together to reduce crime and the fear of crime in their community. When the sheriff first approached me about this idea in Florence, Arizona, I jumped at it. It was just starting to take off all over the country. It was a nation wide effort to get senior citizens involved. I saw a great opportunity to enhance our community policing effort. It did not take much convincing to have our seniors participate in the program. Let me add that working with senior citizens was always a pleasure.

What is a TRIAD? It is an agreement between the Sheriff's Department, Police Department and members of AARP (American Association of Retired People) to work together to reduce crime against the elderly. No one wants to be a victim, so people are concerned about it.

Each community is no different from one another. Some people fear crime especially the elderly. Did you know that some people will not leave their home to go anywhere after dark? You probably know individuals who do just that. It is sad to think that your home can now turn into a prison for some people.

We held our first meeting with our group called the S.A.L.T. committee. It is an acronym that stands for Seniors and Lawmen Together. Ten senior citizens met with members of the Florence Police Department and the Sheriff's Department at our initial meeting to begin discussing ways to reduce criminal victimization of older persons, assessing the needs and concerns of older citizens, and establishing a broad dialogue on safety and security issues. A major purpose of a TRIAD was to develop, expand and implement effective crime prevention and education programs for older community members. The TRIAD will work to improve the quality of life for seniors by providing an opportunity for the exchange of information between law enforcement and older persons and focusing on reducing the fear of crime. The quality of life would be a reoccurring theme in the community policing partnership.

We met once a month to discuss various issues in the community. The seniors liked the program and it was an excellent opportunity to get together to not only discusses crime problems but other issues as well. The Sheriff Office's representative would make the meeting occasionally but I was not complaining. It was now the Town of Florence's program.

The program got going when I collaborated with the police chief in the next community, the City of Coolidge. The former Police Chief Kevin Harmon was a dynamic and resourceful individual. He had the vision as well as I that the TRIAD had the potential to complement the community policing program. Many times, we were at each other's meetings and several times we had a combined meeting at the Elks Club and the room was filled. Of course, we made it worth their while with a free lunch and other freebees. The program seemed to die out after my employment contract was not renewed. The chief who replaced me decided to send the lieutenant to the meetings. The TRIAD was not very active. However, on the positive side, the people are still talking and discussing the program. What happened to the Coolidge program? Their program eventually suffered the same way after the Coolidge police chief suffered the same fate as me. He fell victim to the political body. Looking back on the town fathers, they did not comprehend what we were doing for the community. In order to be a change agent you have to have the town fathers understand what you are doing. There certainly was a lesson to be learned here. They should be looking forward to change things for the better. I guess in a way we were trying to change things and we did but we were ahead of our time. Overall, it was a wonderful program, and I enjoyed doing it for them. The community was supporting the police department and we were helping the senior citizens with other issues that came up. I think it was community policing at its best.

The common denominator that I found was the support and involvement of the police chief. When the police chief went away, such as my case in Florence, these programs went away too. It reminded me of a conversation I had with the current police chief in Florence. Every time he mentions a program that he wanted to start, the council members already said I already did it. Actually, I was pleased that they still remember how effective the programs were. Maybe I was gone in body but my philosophy is still there. I guess it was a tribute to my success.

Now, in Fort Lupton, Colorado it was a different story. The TRIAD was already in place and my lieutenant was very actively involved in the program. The approach was a countywide approach and there was enough interest in it, but it would have been better if we had devoted more time and effort in our own community. Even then it was a great success. One year they honored me with a plaque for my support and dedication to the program. It was a surprise but it was truly appreciated.

While working with our seniors we identified one problem that we quickly corrected. Some of the seniors were homebound and many did not have a way of getting out. I instituted a program to check on the well being of senior citizens who were specifically homebound. Some communities in New Hampshire made it a practice to call people from their dispatch center to see if they were all right. I took it a step further by having an officer personally stop and check on the senior citizens. They truly appreciated our efforts and it did get the attention of our hometown newspaper.

School Resource Officer

Police departments all across the country utilize school resource officers. The Columbine shooting massacre occurred on April 20, 1999. Everyone by now should be intimately familiar with all the details. Tragically, there was a loss of life and the wave of the violence and aftermath left a permanent scar with many people. There was violence in schools but none could match its deadliness back then. The shooting took place only 35 miles from the City of Fort Lupton. Steps were taken by school administrators and law enforcement officers to put a plan in place to help protect the students better.

Grant funding for school resource positions were being offered like never before. If a municipal or Sheriff's Department put in a grant for a school resource officer, they were assured of getting one or more positions. Ironically, Columbine High School did have a School Resource Officer (SRO) but at the time, he was outside and out of position. If he had been inside the school when the shooting started then perhaps something could have been done and the circumstances may have been different. Nevertheless, 12 students and one teacher were killed and many others were injured. It is not my purpose to criticize what the School Resource Officer did not do, but more what could have been done from a community-policing standpoint.

The School Resource Officer's main purpose is to prevent violence and reduce crime within the school and on school grounds. Even before the Columbine shooting incident I wanted to apply for a federal grant to get a School Resource Officer. However, my purpose was not only to prevent violence, and I might add, there was very few, but to utilize the community policing principles. I made it a point to have my officers spend some time during the day in the high school, not to intimidate but to make friends with the teachers and students. The principal approached me on a number of occasions and told me how much he appreciated the presence of our officers. It was making a big difference in the high school.

Even today, police and sheriff's departments are getting a number of School Resource Officers. It is a great idea but they are not used to their fullest potential. I have had occasion to observe these School Resource Officers in action at two different high schools and I was not impressed. These officers could do so much more than just walking around and being a temporary deterrence of crime. There was still vandalism taking place and fights in the school. The student body does not respect these officers. They were looked upon with contempt and not respect. Where have we gone wrong? I taught criminal justices classes to high school seniors for college credit. I have had the opportunity to learn and observe the School Resource Officers on a daily basis at both schools. One problem that I saw was that these officers were inexperienced and were right out of the basic law enforcement training school. There had been no attempt by these officers to be visible and try to be friendly with any of the students. I asked many questions and always received the same answers. They do not like the School Resource Officer. One particular officer walks around as if the students were the enemy and it should not be a mystery why they do not like him. We have to get over the notion that the school has a hired gun to keep order.

In order to make the program more effective School Resource Officers need to keep one thing in mind and that is to **establish a partnership with the teachers, support staff and students**. Right now School Resource Officers are acting as the disciplinary arm of the assistant principals. This is not the real intended purpose of the program. I have seen these officers in action and I do not like their approach. The Sheriff Department will have to go a long way to improve what they are doing. What I saw was not community policing.

The School Resource Officer program can be improved by implementing the following steps:

- Recruitment and Selection specifically for School Resource Officer
- Specialized training in Community Policing techniques.
- Specialized training in dealing with high school age student

- Evaluation of the officer on his or her effectiveness from a Community Policing standpoint.
- Plan some fun activities with the students
- Being a friend and mentor
- Evaluate the Program

These are just some suggestions and I am sure the police chief or sheriff could come up with many more. The School Resource Officer can be used to help solve problem by being more visible and open to the students. The most important thing for the School Resource Officer to do from my perspective is to talk to the students and get to know them. Just for fun, I asked the students how they could improve the program. Without hesitation several remarked, "Get rid of him and get someone else." They say, "He never talks to us." I know the program would work in these schools if the School Resource Officers would change their approach.

The Community Policing concept is the predominant thinking in our communities. The town and city managers realize and understand what this concept means. When they are seeking to hire a police chief, they are looking for someone to work with the citizens to make the community a better place to live and work and above all, to improve the quality of life for everyone. I have described and discussed a number of significant programs that I implemented that complemented the Community Policing approach. Most of these programs were winners. There are probably many more innovative programs yet to be discovered.

Let us discuss how we can conceive a Community Policing program in cooperation with the public. I always looked for ways to improve service to the community. Existing programs have to be evaluated, modified or improved to make it work better. The best way is to get information from your staff and the public and get them involved. Someone will surely come up with an idea.

Mission Statement

The best way to convey your message and philosophy to the public is through your mission statement. Having your personnel and the citizens in your community provide input is critical to the success of your Community Policing program. It is important to convey your philosophy so that your community will know what to expect.

In Fort Lupton, Colorado I had involved the police committee in formulating the department's mission statement. Once finalized, I communicated the mission statement to the Mayor and City Council and public through the media. It was very well received. In addition, I proudly displayed framed copies of the document in the lobby of the police department for all to see.

We worked hard to produce this philosophical statement. Police Departments should be working on their own mission statement and not try to copy some other police department's mission statement. In order for it to work, you need to develop it within the organization and at the same time get input from the community.

The wave of Community Policing, as we know it today, is an essential part of our policing system. It took a while to realize that the police cannot do something about the crime and other problems without the help from the public. This type of policing can only get better. The key to any program is involvement and partnership with the community.

Chapter 17
Innovative Police Programs

Two of the most original and dynamic programs I had implemented were in Fort Lupton, Colorado. We did other programs in other departments but they were not as nearly as effective. It was always the police department initiating a program. Now given a different circumstance we were about to do something different from the traditional policing. Each time it was a program in cooperation with the Municipal Court. The Court Clerk was a dynamic, resourceful and energetic person who wanted to do more than arrange court dockets and collecting fines. I found it was very easy working with the court clerk. Young people were coming into court and often they were the same ones. She truly cared about these young people getting into trouble and one day she asked to speak to me about a program. She had been a police officer at one time so she understood how police departments operated. Here we were going to delve into a new area by collaborating with the court.

Police departments are doing the same thing day in and day out. I realize it is difficult for a small police department to develop programs and implement them. However, if there is a will, there is a way. I always found a way to fuel enthusiasm to excite personnel in the department and community. I always try to encourage and stimulate creativity. Why do what everyone else is doing? Why not be innovative and a trendsetter in your community? With a little imagination, you can do wonders. I was always open to new ideas and I believed it was worth a try. Doing the same thing, every day can be monotonous and boring.

I truly like the idea of working with our young people in our community to keep as many out of trouble as possible. If we were able to make some impact where they give a second thought about their criminal behavior, then I felt we were able to have a positive impact on their lives. **Developing a new program and getting your personnel involved can be a very gratifying experience.**

Shape-up

Shape-up was a program already developed by the Department of Corrections in Colorado and only a few departments in the Metro Denver area were involved in it. It was so seldom used that when the court clerk brought it to my attention, the program seemed like a good one. It did not take much convincing to get me aboard the bandwagon to try it. It is a program like "Scared Straight" that we so often heard about in the 1970s.

I remember the "Scared Straight" program. When I was in Bristol, Connecticut we brought a group of high school aged students to a prison in upper state New York. I personally volunteered to participate in the program. The program lasted several hours and I specifically remembered the inmates yelling at the kids. It was impressive because they got me scared. The atmosphere was very intimidating. I could not wait to get out of there. It was the last time anyone from Bristol went for a visit.

The "Shape-up" program has similarities. The program lasted two days, the first was the initial visit by the high school age youth and the second, was a visit by the youth and his parent and the police chaperones to the same facility. This approach was different from the rest because the court, parent and schools made referrals. High school age kids were eligible to participate. If a juvenile got into trouble with the police, the police officer filed out the initial screening form as a possible candidate for the program. Generally, these juveniles were first time offenders and once into court the judge who was very supportive of the program would order the youth into shape-up and pay the required $50.00 to cover expenses. Other youths could get into the program by a parental or school referral. A maximum of 12 youths could participate in the two-day program.

It seemed every week we were bringing the juvenile males to a prison in the eastern part of Colorado at the Arkansas Valley Correctional Facility located near Ordway about 50 miles east of Pueblo. This facility has 1,007 medium custody inmates. The female juveniles were brought to the Colorado Women's Correctional Facility in Canon City south of Denver. This facility has about 350 minimum custody inmates. One week it would be the youths and the next, the follow-up visit with the youth and a parent. Three members of my department and the court clerk would chaperone the kids to the prisons. The program became so popular that many guests and city officials would go along to observe the program. A car dealership in the city would volunteer two or more vans for our use. We were getting support all over the city and the program was growing.

Day one consisted of one inmate paring up with a youth. Each inmate already had a background history of their person they would be trying to influence. Each had already exhibited criminal behavior or they were uncontrollable at home. The inmates were long-time incarcerated convicted felons ranging from murder and armed robbery to lesser felonies. Some of those individuals would never see the light of day on the outside. Just thinking about the cumulative number of years these individuals had been locked up for was a scary thought.

I was interested in seeing this process first hand so I arranged to go on the first day. Each youth was given instructions about what to wear and carry on the trip.

Going into a secure facility, namely a prison, you have to use common sense. Specifically, each person was told no drugs or weapons would be allowed on the premises. Everyone walked into the lobby area of the building after waiting for someone to unlock the gate. One youth did not follow directions about the type of clothes to wear so he had to change his sagging pants to an orange jumpsuit. He felt embarrassed to wear the jumpsuit. Each youth was searched thoroughly and I think that they were beginning to get intimidated even the tough ones.

The youths were ushered into a large multipurpose room for the initial one on one. You could see it in the youth's faces. They were all scared to death. It was funny to see the youths who had an attitude in the beginning suddenly be quiet while the inmate spoke very bluntly about the youth's problem. Each inmate had been briefed on personal history of each youth including the type of trouble they got themselves into. Some aspects reminded me of Scared Straight because of the initial screaming in some of their faces. Some youths thought it was a joke but when the inmate jumped right in their face and screamed at them then it was a different story.

After about one hour, the youths and chaperone were given a tour of the prison, living area, laundry, recreation and more. When the group moved into the workout area some of the inmates would beckon the youth over to them and made sexual gestures towards them. The inmates discussed the harsh realities of prison life. I have to say that they were creating quite an impression on the kids. The kids could not wait to get out of the gym area. From there we went to visit the living area of the inmates. This particular unit had a day room in the middle and the individual two-man cells surrounded it. One youth learned earlier on the harsh reality of invading a prisoner's personal space after one inmate told him that he was disrespecting his "house" by walking in uninvited. Of course, the confrontation was set up by the inmate to act in such a way. The kids could see how cramped and how little space there was in a two-man cell. The cell had just enough room for a small metal desk attached to the wall, a sink, toilet and a two-man bunk. Imagine staying confined in a small cell for long time. These inmates were lucky to be in a medium custody facility. Some unmanageable inmates are kept in a cell for 23 hours a day. This area alone left quite an impression on each youth. After spending a few hours with the inmates, I think that they were ready to leave to go home. However, the fun had just begun.

After inspection of the prison grounds, everyone went to the inmate eating area for lunch. You guessed it. Everyone had to eat the same food the inmates ate. Watching everyone getting served by an inmate with certain portions was a sight to behold. This was not a restaurant. They could not order from a menu. They had to eat what was being served for lunch whether they like it or not. Actually, the food was not bad; it was some sort of Mexican dish. What it was exactly I could not say. The horror stories that you hear about prison food are not true. The staff at the prison takes great strides in insuring the inmates are well nourished. You really do not see anyone walking around having a look of malnutrition. Each youth was given the same amount of time the inmates were required to eat. At least we were in a segregated area.

After lunch, everyone went back to the same multipurpose room for another meeting. This time each inmate took a turn and spoke to the youths as a group. Each spoke about his life in crime and some acknowledged that they would spend the rest of their lives in prison. Some even discussed their acts of crime, including talking freely about killing someone. In order to participate in the program the prisoners had to admit their actions in committing heinous crimes. The inmates went so far to say that if they had to do it all over again, they would have made different choices. Of course, they would say that because they were now in prison. It was too late for many of them there. However, I have to give credit to the inmates for getting involved in the Shape-up program and some had been participating for a long time. It is a voluntary program. I understood each inmate had to undergo an extensive screening process by the inmates already in the program and correctional staff.

At the end of the session, the youths were thoroughly scared. They were given a homework assignment to complete prior to their next trip with their parent. They had to evaluate their life and write about making changes. Obviously, the focal point was their being influenced by others in making wrong decisions, namely peer pressure. The inmates were concentrating on the bad influences from some of their friends. They were told that they needed to make some changes in their lives or else they could end up in prison just like them for a long term or the rest of their lives. The message they were getting was very powerful. As an observer, you could not help but feel the emotion in the room. Everyone had to remind themselves these individuals counseling the youths were convicted felons and were not nice guys. They freely admitted that they were not nice people. Some of the kids who did not complete the homework assignment were chastised at the next session in front of their parents. They were told not to disrespect their parents.

It took approximately three hours to drive to the facility and the ride back was very quiet. You could tell that the kids were emotionally and physically drained. On the way to the facility in the morning the kids were talking and joking around and the return trip was just the opposite. They were no longer talking tough. Matter of fact, they were not talking at all.

The following week usually on the same day the entire group returned to the prison with one of their parents. It was usually the same routine the initial meeting with the inmate, a tour of the prison facility and the group session. This time the same inmate who spoke to a youth was paired with the same youth and his parent or guardian. The parents were equally impressed with the program. After the program went on for a while some of the city officials including the mayor went along for the ride to observe the program. It was quite a commitment because the trip began at 5:30 a.m. and ended usually around 6:30 p.m. It was a long day for everyone.

The program was by far the most impressive program that I had ever initiated. The original "Scared Straight" was impressive for one visit but the "Shape-up" program was more impressive because of the follow-up component. Let us discuss the evaluation of the program whether it is worthwhile to do and if it is cost effective for the department. Everyone is interested in the cost especially me since the department had to bear the burden of salaries and overtime expenses involved. How is it benefiting the community? Is it not a court function?

From a court standpoint, the judge and the court clerk were happy with the results. The evaluation of the program involved a questionnaire completed by each youth and the real proof was whether they were involved in anymore criminal activity. Out of approximately one hundred or so youths who were involved in the program, there were a very low percentage of repeat offenders. The goal of the program was to influence their decision whether to commit a criminal act or not. It was successful because many chose not to become involved. They were making better decisions. It was disappointing that the few could not be saved but I guess we cannot save everyone. Even then, they still had to be horrified over what they saw at the prison.

There is no doubt the police department had to incur some costs. There are always some costs associated with any program. I like the idea that my secretary, code enforcement officer and a police officer were enthusiastic about the program. Actually, my code enforcement officer's son went through the "Shape-up" program in another city. He was so impressed by the results and the change in his son that he thought it would benefit the citizens of Fort Lupton. He originally suggested this program to the court clerk who in turn came to me. The program was born. Your personnel can come up with ideas. People in the community were quick to donate to the program to pay for the gasoline, food and incidentals. The school administration even got into the act. They were recommending students who they saw as problematic to be included in the program. The prison administration charged a set $50.00 fee for each youth participant. The fee included the lunch at the prison.

As the program grew in popularity, the trips became more frequent. One trip involved going to the western part of Colorado and the other to Canon City, south of Denver. The Canon City trip was especially for the female offenders. The female inmates intimidated the female participants. When the female inmates started discussing relationships and specific inmate's roles such as the father, mother, daughter and grandmother, they really got scared. Some thought the living areas were not clean and the female inmates were "nasty."

Shape-up was definitely a program worthwhile in doing. Everyone supported the program and the City Council gave us rave reviews. The program was especially effective because most of the juvenile did not repeat their crimes and generally stayed out of trouble. In many cases, their performance in schools improved. The judge was happy because he had an alternative sentencing program. The program meets its goals.

From an operational point of view, we had to make some adjustments once a week to cover the schedule and we managed. I thought at first the other officers would start to complain but no, they were supportive of the program as well.

There was one problem that I should mention here and it was the accountability of donations. The court clerk, who truly did an excellent job in coordinating the trips, got into difficulty with the management of the funds. One day my personnel came up to me to discuss a problem with the money. They did not think the funds were being handled properly. The funds were being kept separate from the city's accounting practices and it spelled trouble. It had the makings of a "private slush" fund. The court clerk had a conflict with the city administrator over some other matters and she soon found herself without a job. I was sad to see her go because she did many good things for the city. The city administrator called me into the office to take over the administration of the Shape-up program. When I started to look over the accounting of funds there appeared to be many discrepancies and at this point, I asked for the assistance of the Colorado State Bureau of Investigation to conduct a criminal investigation of the fund. I wanted to have an independent investigation conducted so it did not appear to be a cover up. It was probably more sloppy bookkeeping than a criminal offense. I believe the former court clerk was an honest person. Some of the cash donations could not be accounted for but it could have been attributed to some lunches paid in cash. No doubt, there needed to be better accounting of the money and I sure was going to avoid this pitfall.

If you are going to use private resources such as donations from the public, the accounting practices of the city should be followed. There is just too much opportunity for embezzling funds if the opportunity is there, especially if only one person is handling the funds. Getting greedy can affect any program even popular ones such as Shape-up. The city's finance department was very helpful in setting up a special fund. The following are some suggestions to avoid this mix-up:

- Set up a special revenue account for Shape-up donations through the Finance Department.

- Draw expense money from the Finance Department.
- Obtain Receipts for expenses such as fast food restaurants.
- Require a written report including personnel and juvenile participants involved, location of facility and accounting of all expenses.
- Review of expenses by an independent person as a "Check and Balance."
- Continual follow-up of the program to assess its effectiveness

The written report and detailed accounting kept everyone honest. I did not want to give anyone the impression that the group was wasting money especially donations. It would certainly hurt the credibility of the program. It may be a little extra work but it was worth the effort and my personnel did not complaint about doing the extra paperwork. The documentation was good to show the city administrator what they were doing. Overall, the Shape-up program was one of the best programs that I have seen in my law enforcement career. We could only bring 12 students at a time. Just think of the results, if we could have increased our numbers.

Music Immersion

Our community in Fort Lupton, Colorado had a problem like in many other communities across the United States. People were getting upset with the loud music coming from motor vehicles driving up and down the streets in the downtown area and neighborhoods at all hours of the night. The speakers in the car were not normal size speakers. These things were huge. When this type of vehicle drove by it was so loud, the ground would vibrate. There was no doubt about it the noise was extremely excessive. Citizens were calling my office asking what could be done. They were getting tired from being awakened from a sound sleep. On Main Street in the downtown area these youths would cruise up and down the street all night long. Even thought there was a city ordinance against loud music coming from motor vehicles we would issue citations for violations but the problem continued. The complaints were still coming in. In fact unlike many communities if the officer clearly heard the loud music 25 feet from the motor vehicle it was a violation. In some states, the officers could not be the complainant. The city attorney reviewed and approved the city ordinance for legal issues and it was voted and passed by the City Council.

This was the first phase in our program to have a workable city ordinance. Something else had to be done to have an impact and to prevent the repeat offenders we were getting in court. Here was born another program unlike any other in the country. Our judge, Paul Sacco was an innovative type of person. He said, "He was a firm believer in making the punishment fit the crime." The court clerk, Patricia Red Earth, the judge and I collaborated to make this program work. It took some coordinating and cooperation by the officers to enforce the city ordinance. It was easy pickings. There were violations galore all over the place at all hours of the day and night. The judge wanted us to send him some violators and we certainly did. I do not think at first he thought he was going to get all those violators.

Here is how it worked. An officer would issue a citation to a motorist for loud music coming from his motor vehicle. On the specified court date, he or she would have to appear before Judge Sacco to answer to the offense. If they pleaded guilty, he would sentence them to "Music Immersion" or elect to pay a $65.00 fine. Most chose to participate in the program. The offender would still be responsible for the court fee but he or she would have to appear on Friday evening at 8:00 p.m. to listen to one hour of a variety of music most of it they usually did not like. The session was run just like a court. The person would have to show up and sit still for one hour. Some of the artists they had to listen to as an example for Barry Manilow, Wayne Newton, Barney and many others. Each month there was a different selection. If anyone seemed to like a particular song then that particular selection not included for the next month. The point was that people have different tastes in music and someone might not appreciate listening to the boom box music that most of the kids listened to on a regular basis. A police officer working overtime was the bailiff and the court clerk recorded who completed their sentencing requirement. The session ended with a song by Roy Rogers entitled, "Happy Trails to You." We have all heard it at one time or another.

The first session included about 30 young offenders and the oldest was about 40 years old. After the first session, there were no repeat offenders and each month thereafter the numbers were less.

We did not realize it at first but we were getting media requests from all over the United States and Great Britain for additional information. We were getting interest from national television stations, radio stations and newspapers. The requests were non-stop. We were getting requests for interviews every week. The judge, court clerk and I were being interviewed on a regular basis... We made news all over the country and featured on the NBC night news, Comedy Channel and many more. We made news because no one else had ever put together a program such as this. It was unique.

I did a telephone interview on a radio station as far as Great Britain. They were interested in the uniqueness purely because no one else had ever done a program like this before. They even had a segment on the Comedy Channel and the NBC

News. If there were people who did not hear of Fort Lupton, they were hearing it now. Several times the television station showed up on a Friday night with all their equipment to record a music immersion session. They even got permission from the parents to interview some of the kids.

Even though the "Music Immersion" program received a great deal of notoriety, the question remains whether it was successful or not. After a few months into the program, you could see a noticeable difference in the community. You rarely heard loud music coming from motor vehicles. The offenders kept telling us that they did not like going out on a Friday night to listen to terrible music. We picked Friday night for a reason. It is a time when they like to be with their friends so for a short time they spent time with the court.

Many communities have a similar dilemma. Many were asking their police department what could be done. I had to laugh because all they had to do was implement a similar program. We did not care if anyone was going to copy our program. Why re-invent the wheel as we so often hear. Their police departments received numerous complaints and very little was done about it.

Some departments are using decibel meters to measure the noise to see if there is a violation. I think is it ridiculous to go through this extreme to see if there is a violation. There is one department in particular that uses decibel meters to measure the noise. By the time the officer goes to the department to pick up the decibel meter and drive to the location of the complaint it is too late. The motor vehicle is long gone. Having an instrument is all well and good but it is not practical. The police department was still receiving many complaints of loud music. I remember one council member in Somersworth, New Hampshire wanted the officers to be trained in the use of decibel meters to measure the noise. He was an engineer so I was not surprised to hear his comments. I did convince the city council that the decibel meter was not necessary. We were able to get an enforceable noise ordinance but we needed a complainant. I was after a city ordinance that was not complicated and cumbersome, such as including a decibel meter.

Many police departments wanted a copy of our city ordinance. We did not have any problems with legal issues regarding the officer hearing the loud music 25 feet away from the source. You could say that there was a potential for abuse. Who would say what was too loud from 25 feet. However, it is a common sense issue. Everyone has his or her own idea what is reasonable. What is too loud? If the vehicle drives by and the music is so loud the ground is vibrating, it does not take an engineer to figure out it is a violation. You do not need a decibel meter to tell you this is violation. It should not come as a surprise but we never lost a loud music case. Most of the offenders went to the "Music Immersion" program. It helps to have a judge to support the program. Our noise complaints went down to almost zero. Now, some people thought that the police were harassing the young people but these complaints were rare. There will always be people like this. You have to trust your police officers to make good decisions.

This was another one of the best programs that I had ever participated in. The community truly appreciated our efforts in taking care of the loud music problem. Many other communities nearby were still experiencing the same problems. We realized that we had a problem and then implemented a plan to take care of it.

Laptop Computer in Cruisers

Our police department in Fort Lupton, Colorado was able to obtain a grant funding to purchase laptop computers for the cruisers as part of our community-policing program. The thought was to give the officers more time in the field instead of spending report-writing time in the station doing reports. More police departments were upgrading their technology to get these laptop computers with the capability of obtaining license number and registration information through the state's computer network. The officers would be able to obtain information quicker without going through the dispatch center. Because our dispatch center could easily handle our radio traffic, we were more interested in the report writing capability.

We had delayed implementation because of a vendor software problem. The software vendor had promised us a laptop program that was compatible with our law enforcement software and the one they had provided was not working very well. They were still working on the problem when I left the department. Nevertheless, if they can get this program going there is no doubt that it would be worthwhile. Spending more time out in the community and being visible is critical to the community-policing program. I regret that I was not able to complete the program because I had left the department. More police departments have gone to laptops computers in their cruisers and have taken advantage of this technology.

G.R.E.A.T. Program

In Fort Lupton, Colorado, we were committed to the youth in the community. We not only implemented a DARE program but also included the G.R.E.A.T., the Gang Resistance Education and Training program. In Fort Lupton, like in many communities, there are gangs and some are more dangerous than others. There were signs of gangs throughout our community with the different types of graffiti or commonly know as "tagging." Different gangs would stake out their territory. The gang problem in my view was not very serious but it could get worse if allowed to fester. There were some Hispanic gangs and some others that who periodically would come into the community to terrorize some of our citizens until we put a stop to it. You see many people try to ignore the problem and "bury their head in the sand." The gang problem will not go away and somehow these young people in the community need to change their view about gangs.

The following is an excerpt from Alcohol, Tobacco and Firearm's web page that describes the G.R.E.A.T. program in greater detail:

> The mission of the G.R.E.A.T., Gang Resistance Education and Training, program is to provide a wide range of structured activities and classroom instruction for school-aged children that results in a sense of competency and the personal empowerment needed to avoid involvement in gangs. G.R.E.A.T. is a prevention program that seeks to reduce gang involvement and curb the increasing violence permeating communities. It is not an intervention program and does not alleviate the need for continued enforcement, along with referral services.
>
> G.R.E.A.T. helps youth become responsible members of their communities by setting goals, resisting the pressure to join gangs, learning how to resolve conflict without violence and understanding the negative ramifications of gang involvement. To accomplish this program has three main components: a 7th and 8th grade curriculum, 3rd and 4th grade sessions and a summer recreation/education program.
>
> The ultimate goal of G.R.E.A.T. is to reduce gang involvement, thereby reducing violent behavior among the nation's youth. The program requires a commitment from government, education, the police department and above all, the community. G.R.E.A.T. is not the only answer, it is one of the tools with which to combine resources and positive change from the status quo.
>
> G.R.E.A.T. began in 1991 when representatives from Alcohol, Tobacco and Firearms contacted various agencies in the Phoenix area to design and implement a gang resistance program. The Phoenix Police Department, in cooperation with surrounding Valley agencies, developed a core curriculum based on reducing gang involvement. The program quickly gained attention and has become a national model. Supported by the A.T.F. and the Federal Law Enforcement Training Center, more than 980 officers representing approximately 446 agencies and 44 states have been trained to implement this program.

Every school year I had two officers teach the G.R.E.A.T program to the sixth grade at the Middle School. The Phoenix Police Department and other department in the Phoenix metro area originally developed the G.R.E.A.T. program. They recognized that they had a gang problem and they realized they had to do something about it. Over the years, the G.R.E.A.T program developed into a model for police departments across the country to use. They shared an innovative program with others. This program was well received by schools and communities as well.

There were many youths who are looking for role models and for sure we did not want them to use gang members. Many youths in the school are on the fence and some are called "want-a-bees." These young people try to emulate gang members. It would be a good bet that they know active gang members. Realizing this was the case; I worked with the school officials many times on a daily basis to bring to our attention potential problems with students. The school had a policy against students wearing anything that resembled gang identification. Matter of fact, it is very important for the schools to have a policy in place and enforce it to prevent students from wearing any type of gang identification such as a bandana, baseball cap and more.

The students liked the program and the police department was committed to make it happen each year. The evaluation of the program would be long term. Success or failure depended upon the youth joining a gang over time. Only time will tell whether this program was truly successful or not. In my opinion if you can save one child then all the time and money invested into the program was worth the effort. There has to be follow-up programs in order to make it work. People criticize the DARE program because it does not have a long-term effect. There will be more about DARE in the next chapter.

It was too soon to tell if the GREAT program was effective or not. The program was well received by the school administrators, teachers and parents. On the surface it appeared to be a good program and it would complement the Dare program. Personally, I think the GREAT program is a very worthwhile program to do but like DARE there must be a plan for the short term and the long term.

Other Innovative Approaches

Not all departments are stuck in an old policing model. Take for example the Dover Police Department, Dover, New Hampshire. They have one of the best departments in the state and it was not by accident. Some of my personnel in Somersworth, New Hampshire would say they have plenty of money to do whatever they want. This may be true but it takes commitment, initiative and a vision to be where they are at today. Even when times were tough, they had to struggle like everyone else.

One former town manager told me once, "If you surround yourself with good people, the job is easy." He said, "You turn them loose and let them do their job." His advice was logical. The Dover police chief has an excellent staff that was committed to being the best they can be. It was to their credit that they are nationally accredited and one of the best departments not only in the state but also in the country.

The Dover Police Department was committed to community policing and they saw a need to have a mounted patrol. The town fathers were serene to the idea but said there was no funding available to support this initiative even though it was a good idea. There was only one other department with a mounted patrol and that was Hampton, which was a beach and resort community. The police chief was committed to the idea of a mounted patrol so he made it a community project to raise funds to support the program. They were able to find a stable that someone donated in the downtown area to keep the horses. They raised enough funds to pay for equipment, food for the horses, veterinarian fees and training. The department did not have any trouble in finding officers to volunteer for the program. Some of the officers were experienced in riding horses while others learned to ride. This program was an instant success, especially with the kids. This was a great public relations tool and a vital link to their community-policing program. It used to be that children were afraid to approach the police, but now with mounted patrols in the downtown area, the children approached the officers all the time. The department has done an excellent job in improving the quality of life in their community.

One other program that deserves attention is their domestic violence program. Dover Police Department pioneered this innovative approach. In New Hampshire, police departments were taking a proactive arrest policy against individuals assaulting their spouse. As a condition for release, these individuals agreed to wear an electronic ankle monitoring system to insure they would not be violating the restraining order. This certainly was a different approach but it demonstrates the commitment by the department to keep their citizens safe.

Police departments have the ability to expand what they are doing by being innovative. Some police departments are small and granted their resources are limited but why not involve others? If you listen to the naysayers, they will have you convinced that you cannot do anything because of a lack of manpower, equipment, money and what ever else seems to be a good excuse. The successful police chiefs or leaders are the ones who are not afraid to get involved in the community and try different programs to see if it will benefit the department. One thing is for certain, if you do not try to improve the operations of the department then nothing will happen. The department will be just become status quo, business as usual. We have too many departments like this; we do not need anymore.

I keep thinking about the police chief in Lee, New Hampshire who resigned because of problems in the department. A management study of the department by a consultant group determined that the department was stuck in a "20 year old policing model." I call it stuck in the rut. How could anyone be police chief for so long without making improvement? I am surprised that a department can survive so long without improvements. They thought he was doing a great job. The policy and procedures had not been updated and many of the policies were 15 years old. Let me say a brief word about management studies. When selectmen or council members hire a consultant to perform a management study of police operations chances are they will find something wrong. They always will find something because they have to earn their money. If the police chief had made improvements over time, implemented innovative programs and adhered to contemporary practices in law enforcement, the management consultant would have discovered this too. However, any chief or manager will find him or herself in hot water if he or she had not made any effort to improve the operations of the department.

Why be like everyone else? A police chief or other leader who wants to make a difference has to **be innovative and try something new**. I always say, "If there is a will, there is a way." The police chief from Dover, New Hampshire had the desire and he found a way to implement innovative programs. Most of the time, it takes a sincere effort and a vision to make the community a better place to live. Getting your personnel and the community involved to help bring this vision to fruition is the key to success.

Chapter 18
DARE: Does it Work?

In the last few years or so we have heard much discussion whether the DARE program is effective or not. I am going to discuss DARE from a police chief's perspective. We have read about DARE in recent years and there have been many favorable reviews while there has been some criticism. Matter of fact, I know several police chiefs who have dumped the DARE program for another type of drug education. It must have been a bold move because they felt strong enough about it to make that choice. Why would anyone want to change from a popular nationally accepted program? There has to be more to it. There is no question about it; the program is very popular with the community. Is the DARE program a worthwhile program to promote from a practical standpoint? I will candidly discuss the good points as well as the negative ones, but first let me give you a brief overview of DARE.

This year 36 million school children around the world-26 million in the U.S. will benefit from DARE, Drug Abuse Resistance Education, the highly acclaimed program that give children the skills they need to avoid involvement in drugs, gangs, or violence. DARE was founded in 1983 in Los Angeles and has proven so successful that it was implemented in a large percent of our nation's school districts and in more countries around the world.

DARE is a police officer led series of classroom lessons that teach children from kindergarten through 12 grade how to resist peer pressure and live productive drug and violence free lives. The program, which was developed jointly by the Los Angeles Unified School District, initially focused on elementary school children. It was expanded to include middle school and high school programs.

Experiences with DARE

I implemented the DARE program in Somersworth, New Hampshire when I became police chief in 1988. It was relatively new in the state and I immediately saw that it could be a very useful program in getting an anti drug message across. Originally, it was only an anti-drug message but later it included an anti-gang and violence component. I saw it was an opportunity to get a police officer into the school and to work with teachers and parents much closer. I wanted to have them see the police officer as a friend, not the enemy.

After one of my police officers completed the training program we implemented the program in the fifth grade at the elementary school and he taught the lessons once a week for 17 weeks. Actually, it was a good choice because the officer did an outstanding job teaching the course. The students took an immediate liking to him and they looked to him as a friend. The other officers in the department were not as enthusiastic as they should have been. I think the officer got a taste of his own peer pressure because they mistakenly thought he was just trying to get out of doing work on the shift. They could not understand why he could not be called out of the classroom to take complaints at the school or go out to backup officers on the street. There was some resistance at first even with the ranking officers. The idea was to try and establish a rapport with the kids not arrest them for any given misdeed at the school. It would have defeated our purpose. I could not understand why they could not see my point of view. Little did they know at the time we were easing our way into the community policing concept and I was going to use the DARE program as an example of our partnership with the students, teachers and parents.

During the years that followed, we continued to build the DARE program but only taught it in the fifth grade. At the time I saw the importance to have a follow-up program in the middle school and school but I did not have the luxury of additional personnel to do these programs. At the end of the DARE class we had our traditional culmination ceremony. I had to admit we put on quite a show for the students, school officials, political leaders, and parents. This celebration centered on the youth's accomplishments during the 17 weeks of study. The officer selected several essays that were read by the students and he gave out awards for noteworthy achievement. It was nice to hand out the certificates to the students but what was especially special was listening to the students ready their essays. You could feel the sincerity and emotion poured into each essay. It was truly an excellent way to end the program.

The DARE program worked very well in Somersworth. If I could have expanded it, I would have but there were other considerations. I had to replace the officer's position on the street and some adjustments of the schedule had to be made. In a small department of 19 sworn officers at the time, it was quite a feat. The captain who was doing the scheduling was not too keen on the idea of losing the officer for one day for 17 weeks. However, I always say, "If there is a will, there is a way." If the police chief or manager took everyone's advice all the time, then you would not get anything accomplished. A police chief has **to do the right thing** and I was determined to do it. As it were, I implemented DARE for the fifth grade once a year. My personnel seemed to tolerate it as time went on.

My assessment of the program during my seven years in Somersworth was quite clear, it was a winner. It was a "touchy feely" type of program. Everyone felt good about it. This was an outstanding program and it was spreading throughout New

Hampshire like a tidal wave. We received rave reviews from the kids who participated, the parents, the city fathers and the community. We were complimented all the time including favorable write-ups in the local newspaper. After we gave out DARE shirts to the kids, there was usually not a day that went by when you did not see someone wearing a DARE shirt. Everyone was wearing the DARE shirt including the moms and the dads.

Did the program accomplish what we wanted? The original goal was to have the kids resist drugs after they had successfully completed the lessons. The real question is what percentage of the kids after completing the program did not experiment or use drugs? This is the question that I will attempt to answer later but for now we need to keep this thought in mind. There is no question that it was popular with the kids and parents. The officer's role was to be a friend, a mentor and a role model for the kids. The kids could write secret notes and put it into a shoebox if they had problem at homes. There were a few notes that provide some interesting revelations about the parent's propensity to drug use and sexual abuse. This information was passed on to the assistant principal for follow-up and possible criminal investigation by the police department. The DARE officer did not get directly involved with investigations.

Some other area police departments were getting into DARE. One department in particular, the Dover Police Department was expanding the program into the high school. I have to give them credit where credit was due. They saw a need to educate the kids in the high schools. Matter of fact, DARE America has several curriculums besides the core DARE program in the fifth or sixth grades. They have other programs for the early years in elementary school, a middle school program and a high school program. Each program is designed as a follow up to the core DARE program. I always wondered why more police chiefs or administrators did not expand the DARE program? The real question is whether the department can afford to keep the officers off the street and who is going to pay for it?

Speaking from first hand experience, it is difficult to run the program with little or no funds. You really have to go out to solicit donations to pay for the DARE shirts and other give-aways to the kids. Depending upon the number of kids in the program just the cost of the shirts could wreck havoc in your budget and more so if you are not budgeted for the shirts. It could cost in excess of $500 or more easily. If a follow-up program was planned then you will have to have funds to pay for the shirts and other incentives for the students. Now, I only briefly mentioned the man-hours involved. It is not an easy decision to implement other programs. If you have the luxury of additional manpower then it would be a consideration. In a small department, you have to consider the priority of the patrol division. You actually do need manpower on the street to answer calls for service. If I could have pulled it off I would have implemented the DARE program in the middle and high schools without hesitation. What stopped me was the lack of manpower. I was not worried about the funds because the community was behind me one hundred percent. We could have easily raised the funds. What bothered me was always asking the public for money when it should have come out of the department's operating budget.

When I left the department, I went to Florence, Arizona. The police department already had a DARE program in the fifth grade and was in operation for at least five years. This was no doubt it was a popular program and it was widely supported by the town council, school officials and the community. It was the basic DARE program. The same officer taught the program during this time and it appeared he was doing a good job with it. There were no other follow-up programs at all. The officer had a good rapport with the kids and teachers. When the time came, I was asked to present some remarks and quickly accepted. I think that I caught him by surprise because he did no think that I was going to accept. Little did he know I was not going to miss it for the world? Apparently, the previous police chief did not participate in the culmination ceremony. I wanted to show everyone that I supported what they were doing.

Basically, the DARE graduation followed the same format as my previous department with one exception. The food at the end of the ceremony was very good and it was all funded with donations. This officer approached me and asked if we would consider someone else for the DARE position. He had been involved with it for a number of years and I told him that we would have to train someone else first before the change was made. Other departments in the area for doing the DARE program and it seemed to be the thing to do. There was no evaluation of the program to see if it was effective or not. Everyone like the program but was it keeping kids off drugs? No one was asking the question or perhaps he or she was afraid to ask? As long as the program was popular and the officer was developing a rapport with the kids, it was good enough for me. I was not going to change a thing.

On the other hand, it did cross my mind whether the program was effective or not. If you ask DARE America, they will tell you it is one of the most effective programs ever. I asked the DARE Officer if he thought the program was effective. He said the program was very effective. I thought perhaps he had some data from the previous classes that he ran but no, he was just giving his opinion. By now, the kids that he taught in the fifth grade were now in high school. Other departments that were doing DARE to my knowledge were not keeping any data on the effectiveness of the program. Were the kids keeping away from drugs including alcohol? Alcohol was presented in the program like a drug. I never had the opportunity to study the DARE program further because my two-year contract was not renewed by the town fathers.

My last department in Fort Lupton, Colorado was a different story. The DARE program was in place and there were two officers teaching the basic DARE program to the fifth grade for 17 weeks. When the officers completed this program, they taught an abbreviated four-week program to the third grade. The program was very popular in the community and everyone seemed to support it. There was no reason to change a thing. Matter of fact, I personally visited the classrooms and observed my officers in action. The kids were very well behaved and the officers appeared to have a good relationship with them. The officers did the usual 17 week core DARE program and upon completion had the culmination ceremony. It was the usual fanfares with the DARE shirts, awards and essays and of course the refreshments afterwards. This program was support completely with donations. This program had been in effect for about five years and no doubt, it was a winner.

After this program was completed the officers after a break continued with the mini version for the third grade. After this was completed, the officers taught the GREAT program, a Gang Resistance Education and Training to the sixth grade. The programs were going very well and each was well received by the teachers, parents and kids. There was no formal evaluation of the program.

The Controversy

Nevertheless, a strange phenomenon was taking place. While I was in Colorado, we heard some criticism about the DARE program in other parts of the country. Apparently, some parents did not like to have their child making incriminating statements about their alleged drug abuse. Some of these parents were missing the point. The intent of the program was not to have the kids inform on their parents. The goal was to have the kids resist drugs and violence and not give in to the peer pressure. The parents should have been encouraging their children and be a role model to them. The realities though as we all know many of the parents are certainly no role models. Sometimes the kids were so concerned about their parent's drug use that some did make some revelations. Actually, I have a big problem with any parent smoking dope or doing drugs in front of their kids. The criticism was aimed not so much in Colorado but some editorial from other states were questioning the effectiveness of the DARE program. How could someone challenge a proven program originating in Los Angeles, California that has been around for almost 20 or more years? Who would think that someone was challenging the "sacred cow?" DARE America refuted the editorials and detailed the successes of the program. People were starting to answer questions. Apparently, some other police chiefs wondered about the effectiveness of the program in keeping kids off drugs and they took it one step further. The Boulder Police Department, the famous department that was involved with the controversial investigation of the JonBenet

Ramsey murder, decided to dump their DARE program. They came out and said that it was ineffective and they were going to replace it with another anti-drug program.

Our city administrator in Fort Lupton apparently read the same article in the newspaper because by this time it was making headline news in the Metro area. The news reporters were calling around and asking police chiefs, what they thought. I gave them my patented answers. DARE was the best program that had ever come along.   No one can dispute the popularity of the program.   I told the city administrator the same thing and I sincerely thought it was a worthwhile program for the kids. At the very least, the kids would get to know the officers on a personal level and look to him or her as a role model, friend and mentor. Some no doubt had long lasting relationships through the years. Even though we had no data to prove the effectiveness of the program, I was not planning to dump the program. I would have considered replacing it with another anti-drug program if another program had proven better. Here is a good point. There should be ongoing evaluations of these programs. A police chief and manager should always look to improve or enhance their programs.

Besides, there was no way I was going to dump the DARE program. The community would not support it. A police chief or administrator has to use a little common sense and give it careful thought before a program is removed. Everyone was use to the DARE program and it was well liked. The City Council ranted and raved about it and complimented the police department on the job they were doing. A high percentage of police and sheriff departments were doing the DARE program because it was the thing to do and everyone else was doing the program. The officers established a good rapport with the kids and I certainly did not want to change any of it.

What are the Facts?

What are the facts? Why was everyone so reluctant to survey the kids to see if they would stay away from drugs, alcohol and violence? Personally, I never read any hard data to see if the program actually worked. There I said it! I think that many of us are afraid to admit that the results are saddening. In the three states where I was police chief, there were no DARE studies to my knowledge. If there were then I certainly would have found out about them.

I think we do not ask because we already know the answer. The real truth should not be a big surprise. I suspected right along that the program was not effective in keeping the kids off drugs and alcohol especially in the high schools. Apparently, peer pressure was winning. Whether you agree with me or not after observing the DARE program in three communities, the high schools have a problem with students drinking alcoholic beverages and drug abuse. If the DARE program was so effective then why was the alcohol and drug abuse not minimized? There was no question about it. In each community, we had problems with the high school kids drinking and using drugs. Matter of fact, the town council members in Florence, Arizona criticized me for taking law enforcement action against the kids congregating and drinking alcoholic beverages in the parking lot in the downtown area. They had the nerve to ask me why the police chase them away; the kids would just go into a secluded place in the desert to drink. I said to myself, "Are these guys for real." Sometimes you get some strange individuals as council members. How can anyone selectively enforce the law?

I recall one time it was near the end of a school year and a number of high school students decided to skip school and party out there in the desert. It was "Senior Skip Day." It was an annual tradition that even the student's parents before them partied at the same canal when they were in high school. Officially, it was not an accepted practice but unofficially it took place every year. Even the parents thought it was no big deal. A large number of them partied next to the canal and one female got so intoxicated she fell into the canal and drown. Everyone thought it was a terrible thing and I agreed. How could this tragedy have been avoided? I will tell you how. The culture of the community was such that it was permissible for the minors to drink alcoholic beverages. Even some of the council members did not think it was a big deal. "Leave the kids alone," they say. Anytime someone was injured or killed it is tragic, even more so if the person is young. After this the town council did not question me anymore about stopping kids from drinking alcoholic beverages.

The Pinal Sheriff's Officer conducted the investigation because it was out of my jurisdiction. The case was quickly investigated and forgotten about. The drowning was ruled an accident but what about the real issue? Who supplied the alcoholic beverages for the minors? No one seemed to bother with this question.   The investigation was closed and no one seemed to care enough to ask any questions except for the parents of the deceased. If I were involved in this case, I would have pursued the investigation. There was certainly some liability here.

If the DARE program had been effective like it was supposed to be then perhaps we would not have had the problem with the youths drinking at the canal. I am sure they were all DARE graduates. Just thinking about the kids graduating from the DARE program and remembering how enthusiastic they were impressed me. How soon they forgot their lessons especially one on how to handle peer pressure. The peer pressure is ever so apparent in the high schools. Florence, Arizona was no fluke; there were the same problems in Fort Lupton, Colorado. They had their share of drinking alcoholic beverages and drug abuse. The situation seemed to be the same in all of the schools.

Just to be sure of my suspicions I asked the seniors at two high schools in Harnett County in North Carolina to give their opinion about the DARE program. The kids candidly stated that the DARE program did not do any good. Many of the students freely admitted drinking alcoholic beverages on the weekend, smoking cigarettes and smoking marijuana. They thought that marijuana should be legalized. They did not see anything wrong with it. I try not to be naive, but where have we gone wrong? Now, I know the Sheriff's Department still had an active basic DARE program. A deputy taught the program to the fifth grade for 17 weeks. There were no other follow-up programs taught after DARE. It is frustrating to me to see police officers spend so much time teaching DARE all over the country and not have any impact. In my mind, it is a shame. We could have done better.

Some police chiefs will say if it saves one child then it is worth the effort put into the program. Speaking honestly I can buy this argument to a certain extent but then you have to weigh whether this program is cost effective to implement given the questionable results. It was time to take a second look at the DARE program, the results and controversy.

The Good Points

One of the good things that I liked about DARE and a major benefit is the interaction between the DARE Officers and the kids. If you select the right person, no one can refute this. The DARE Officer is a role model, mentor and friend. Many of the kids do not have anyone. This program accomplished this better than any other program out there with the exception of GREAT, a Gang Resistance Education and Training program, which is a logical follow-up to DARE.

The secondary benefit is the interaction between the school and police department. Before DARE came along the only time police officers were in the schools was when they were called to handle a disturbance and other crimes. No doubt, there was a better interaction between the school administrators and teachers because of the DARE Officer in the school.

The third benefit is not as apparent. Because the officers are in the schools other issues affecting the school were discussed including recommendations for keeping the school safe. I can certainly relate to this and probably you can, too. Before the DARE program the school administrators had very little contact with the police department other than calling for crime related issues. Now, there is open discussion and meetings to discuss issues. Just think of it like this. When you have problems, which do you call, a stranger or someone you know? Of course, you will call someone you know every time.

The fourth benefit is a better rapport with the parents. They have seen the officers on negative contacts being a victim of a crime, stopped for traffic violations or arrested for a criminal offense. Now, they see the officers working with their kids on a positive level and seeing the police officer as a human being. I have seen parents say nice things about police officers and they seem to be more open-minded.

The fifth benefit that I see is the DARE program as a natural extension of Community Policing. I look at it from a prospective of a partnership with the students, school administrators, teachers, and parents. It is definitely a win – win situation.

The sixth benefit is the reputation of the program itself. Everyone in the community and all over the country has heard about the DARE program. If someone had not heard about DARE then they must have been living in a desert with no contact with the outside world. I heard people say, "I like the program because it is good for the kids." People like it because it is a "feel good" type of program. I was not saying this in a negative way. I say this because people generally liked the program and supported it. I have never heard anyone out in the community saying negative things about it. Generally, there is no problem at all in getting donations to support the program.

There are maybe some negative points about the program and it is a concern more students do not keep away from drugs, alcohol and violence. However, the many positive benefits outweigh the negative points. The criticism about the program can be overcome.

What Needs To Be Done?

We all recognize there are many good features about the program but there are definitely some flaws in the program. Now, I am not talking about the content, the individuals modules presented each week for 17 weeks. I am not going into any detail about the specifics of each module because the modules are not the focus of this discussion. The content of the program overall is excellent and if someone wanted to find out more information about it they could check it the DARE America's web page.

What if the program does not achieve the desired results? The bottom line is that the program did not accomplish what it sets out to do and that is to keep kids off drugs as a long term goal. If you do not believe me then do a survey of the high school kids yourself and you will find out. All you have to do is ask the high school kids what they think about the DARE program and they will tell you. They will laugh and tell you as they told me the program does not work. It is an excellent program so why does it not work. What can be done to improve it? These are some key questions that police chiefs thought about and were afraid to ask. It is not the fault of the police officer delivering the program or the lack of support from the school administration. It is just the opposite. The program gets tremendous support from the school administrators and teachers. Many dedicated police officers believe in the program and still do an excellent job.

The following areas are good reasons for the failure of the program:

- Lack of support from Parents
- Lack of follow-up Programs
- Peer Pressure in middle and high schools

Most of the parents do support the program; however, many parents influence their children in a negative way. Take for example some criticism from parents worrying about their child informing on them for being involved in criminal activity including smoking dope. How can the kids learn their lessons from DARE when their parent are at home smoking crack cocaine. Many parents could never be role models and we know it. Some parents do not take an active role in their child's education. They send their children to school to be taught and that is the end of it. There is no active teaching at home. Education does not stop at the school but also important it continues at home. The parents have to be supportive and in many respect it is often lacking. There needs to be more work done with the parents as an additional support mechanism for the DARE program. There should be more emphasis placed on the parents.

The lack of follow-up programs was a major issue that could ultimately spell success or failure of any program. Some police departments implemented a follow-up DARE program with a program specifically for the middle school and the high school. Most of the time after fifth grade the students received no other follow-up program. It is a shame because so many fifth graders were so enthusiastic about the program that it seemed like we cast them adrift to fend for themselves. It would be interesting to find out the success rate for those departments that have a follow-up program in the high school versus the departments that only do the basic DARE program in the fifth grade. I would be willing to bet these departments had better success rates.

The peer pressure in high school is a real issue and more of a problem than we realize. Peer pressure is so strong that very few students would inform on another student even though the activity is a crime including drug activity. More recently, I recall an incident at a high school in North Carolina involving vandalism. Some students spray-painted some signs and the walls of the building. The principal of the school offered a reward for information leading to the arrest of the perpetrators. It was obvious that some of the kids knew who the guilty culprits were but it was clear they were not going to inform on them for a few hundred dollars. I wonder if the principal raised the reward if the results could have been different. Some would inform on their own mother if the price were right. Many of the students will smoke marijuana and drink alcoholic beverages because of peer pressure. Many even think it is acceptable to smoke marijuana and see nothing wrong with it contrary to the lessons taught by the DARE Officer. Some even joked about smoking "weed" over the weekend. Something must be done to break the "cycle of negative peer pressure." It has to be discouraging when these teens will not inform on another teens even though they know it was wrong. We must somehow teach these young people to do the right thing.

The following statement is what I had suspected all along when a critique stated, Drug Abuse Resistance Education, a zero tolerance drug education program admitted what numerous studies have already shown – that it isn't working. Many police departments even Salt Lake City Police Department eliminated the DARE program because of its ineffectiveness. The new revised DARE program would be taught in the seventh grade instead of the fifth grade and would concentrate on social norms among students. Advocates put safety first in much the same way as many parents do around the issue of drinking, which strongly urges teens not to drink. They recognize that if they choose to drink anyway they should know how alcohol affects their body. They should be around people they can trust and call anytime day, or night, rather than drive drunk. Even DARE America admitted the program's ineffectiveness but I have to give them credit for doing something about it. Concentrating more on the safety issues may be a better approach along with recognizing there are many issues that involve the parents. Still the DARE program was still going strong in the majority of school districts and in other countries.

It bothers me that some police departments implemented the DARE program because all the other agencies were doing it. These departments simply become kind of caught up in the tidal wave of DARE. When the program was promoted in New Hampshire and police departments were starting to get involved, the emphasis was keeping kids off drugs and getting them away from violence. No one including me at first thought about the results after four or five years. After all the Los Angeles Police Department implemented it in 1983 and after the rave reviews the program must have been good. After a few years went by I thought about whether the program had any real impact in keeping kids away from drugs.

The police chief should determine if this program is effective or not, like any other program. You can read about other studies that DARE America and other police departments already did in other communities but it will mean more if you do it yourself. It would be important to know some numbers if the program actually did keep kids off drugs. Probably a good place to begin to assess its credibility would be to **conduct a questionnaire** in the high school and *check the official police records* to see if the youth had been picked up for drug activity, alcohol violations and any violence related crimes. I can hear police chiefs saying it now, "we do not have the time or personnel to conduct a questionnaire." I get tired of these excuses; we do not have the manpower or the time. I say, "If there is a will, there is a way." If I had to do it all over again I would have designed a questionnaire with input from DARE America and the school officers. The school administrators could certainly help distribute the survey at the school and assist with the interpretation of the results. DARE America probably already have a survey and if they do, perhaps it could be tailored to the community. Having hard data in hand could certainly benefit and enhance the program in the long run. At least the department will know where they stand and what needs to be done to modify the program. I understand that the program has already been defined and the lesson content established. However, any program can be improved including the DARE program. I am sure if a department had a suggestion that could improve the program, DARE American could then modify the program for everyone to use. Evidently, they did modify the program after hearing negative publicity.

I guess many departments even mine assumed just because the DARE program was implemented in police departments all over the country that it must be good. There is no doubt in my mind that it is an excellent program. After the lessons of DARE were taught the initial impact was tremendous. The kids who were involved very enthusiastic but unfortunately the learning curve set in. As time marches on and the years go by without any sort of follow-up, the lessons of DARE becomes distant in their memory. As the teens bond further in high school the strong peer pressure takes over. I am not saying this is not the case for everyone. I am sure there are a few who do not surrender to the peer pressures but I believe it is more of a stronger family influence than anything else. I am saying that we should not only save just a few but most of them.

Ways to Improve DARE

Even though there are some problems with the DARE program all is not lost. I only wanted to point out some fundamental flaws with the programs but at the same time discuss ways to improve the program. Granted, some police chiefs have already dumped the DARE program and replaced it with some other program. Instead, why not re-evaluate what you are doing and improve upon it. To me this seems to be the more logical choice than outright dumping it. The DARE program is potentially a great program and just like anything else you have to work at it to make it a success. Why should DARE be any different? When the police chief of Boulder, Colorado dumped the DARE program I did not read any specific reasons other than it does not work. Even then, his comments did not receive any fanfare. I think the citizens were entitled to a better response. Anyone can say, "I don't like it, and I'm getting rid of it." This is the easy way out. Before taking action, this program should be evaluated very carefully.

Like any other program there should be a plan of action. Let us not implement DARE at any old time. There must be planning for the inclusion of DARE into the course curriculum in the fall or winter term. Is it better to start the program in the fall or winter? Is it better to teach the program in the morning or afternoon? The school officials will be more interested in taking care of their core courses for the students first instead of worrying about when to include DARE. I agree they need to take care of the primary educational interest of the child first but the timing of DARE is important too. The police chief or his or her representative should meet to discuss the schedule. I believe the schedule can be work out so that DARE would have its maximum impact.

The decision to select the DARE Officer is a critical decision. Just selecting an officer who wants to do DARE is nice; however, he or she has an impact on the children. What kind of job will the officer do? The ideal DARE Officer is one who will be a good role model, mentor and a friend to the children. There should be more interaction with the kids outside the classroom such as field trips, camping or other activities. There should be more interaction with the kid's parents. I do not consider the DARE Officer's function only the classroom. It has to extend beyond it. Gone are the days when the DARE Officer just taught his or her class and then went home. If the DARE program is to be more effective the DARE Officer has to be more interactive and more involved.

The DARE Officer in Somersworth, New Hampshire was excellent. He ate lunch and spent time with kids during the day. He was even involved with them on some outside activities including a camping trip. The DARE Officer put his heart and soul into the program to make it better.

The DARE Officer's performance should be evaluated like a teacher. The officer is given a crash course in being a teacher to present the DARE lesson but it must be done in an effective manner. The classroom teacher should stay and assist the officer. The time for the coffee break is not during the DARE class. The teacher could provide some valuable insight into the officer's teaching technique. The officer should be evaluated at least once during the 17 weeks by the assistant principle one day and a police department command person on another. The evaluations should be compared to see if the officer is presenting the material properly and to see if the message is getting across. It would not hurt to have the students complete a questionnaire about the program.

All too often, the DARE Officer is sent to the school and he or she is not seen again until the program is completed and the police chief is invited to the culmination ceremony. The chief cannot assume everything. He or she must insure that the material is being presented properly. Besides, the officer should get some feedback on his or her performance so the performance can be improved.

In order for the DARE program to be successful and have more meaning the program must be expanded into the middle and high schools. Instead of initiating the program in the fifth grade consider doing it in the seventh grade. However, it is critical that some form of the DARE program or like program be conducted in the high school. One of the reasons why the program has not been successful as it should have been was the lack of a follow-up program. As I had stated earlier, just doing the program in the fifth grade will not have any impact at all. The decision must be made when the program will be conducted and what grade. The freshman year may be too soon and the senior year is too late. Perhaps, ideally it would be better to present a modified DARE program to the sophomore class in the high school. DARE America already have a DARE program tailored for the high school students and it should be considered. The only reason why I did not implement DARE was solely due to manpower considerations. I would have liked the DARE program to be in the high school.

From my perspective the School Resource Officer in the middle and in particular, the high schools could take on a greater role. Rather than just patrol the hallways taking on the role of a security guard why not be more of a friend? There is no reason why the School Resource Officer could not teach the DARE program tailored to the high school student. If they took on this role like some already do then I can say we have taken Community Policing to a new level.

It is unfortunate that many chiefs in small agencies have limited resources. Given a choice it would probably be better to present the basic DARE program in a later grade. Nevertheless, there should be more follow-up programs.

The DARE program should be evaluated. Just like any program, it should be evaluated to see if it is effective or not. Any police administrator would want to know if his or her program is effective and it is reasonable to find out. I would be interested in finding out the ***immediate* and *long-term effects***. Even though the program seems to be successful as the immediate result, I would want to evaluate it anyway. The most important would be the long-term effect. After the program had been in place for at least three years the former students should complete a questionnaire to see if the program still had an impact. This on-going evaluation could only make this program better.

The police chief should get out of his or her office and visit the classroom to see how things are going. Believe me; the DARE Officer will appreciate the visit. It is nice to see that the police chief is interested in the program and it is good for the kids to see the chief too. I enjoyed visiting the classroom.

Keep an open mind about the DARE program. This program may be good but consider ways to improve it and consider other programs. The idea is just not to present a DARE program because of the notoriety of DARE but to present a program that has meaning and a long lasting effect.

The police chief should meet periodically with the school principal to discuss the progress of the course and if there are ways to improve. Keeping the channels of communication is extremely important regardless. Often we just send the DARE Officer to the school and assume everything is moving right along. However, the school administration may have concerns about the program as well so it would be good to get together to discuss the program.

It is good to meet with the police command staff to discuss the DARE program, its immediate impact and long-range effects. In addition, it would be beneficial to discuss ways to improve the program.

The following are some suggestions that the police chief should keep in mind to improve the DARE Program:

- Develop a Plan of Action
- Carefully Select the DARE Officer
- Evaluate the DARE Officer's Performance
- Expand the Program into middle and high schools
- Evaluate the Effectiveness of the Program
- Visit the Classroom
- Keep an Open Mind
- Meet with School Officials
- Meet with Police Command Staff

These suggestions to improve DARE are not inclusive. There may be other ways to improve the DARE program through open dialogue with the DARE Officer, school administration and command staff personnel. The DARE program should not be taken for granted; there is always room for improvement.

Is DARE Worth the Effort?

The question we are afraid to ask, "Is DARE worth the effort." It is my opinion that it is an excellent program and worthwhile to continue. The criticism that we have heard in the past and continue to hear should be a wake up call for action. We should meet the challenge to make the DARE program better.

It saddens me to hear high school kids speaking of attending the party over the weekend and how blitzed they got. They brag about it because it was a cool thing to do. No one thinks about the consequences if something should go wrong like one of their friends becomes involved in a motor vehicle accident because he had too much to drink. Somehow, we must break this vicious cycle of self-destruction. Yes, our children are worth saving. These children must get the message and somehow the DARE Officer must deliver it to them and have it mean something. The DARE program can be a more meaningful program.

After listening to comments about the DARE program from high school age kids, I am more determined than ever to have the program become a success. Through hard work and determination the DARE program can be made to work and I am confident that it can be made to work.

Chapter 19
Special Operations

Police departments have to be ready for any contingency. Years ago, police chiefs thought about protecting the community by providing the basic patrol functions. In small and even medium size police departments no much thought was given to contingencies. Look at what is happening recently with the shootings at high schools across the country, the terrorist attack of the World Trade Center twin towers, the pentagon and another downing of an airliner. There was even an anthrax incident in Florida, which the Federal Bureau of Investigation was investigating. Apparently, the exposure to this deadly anthrax was criminal in nature. The threat of a biological attack on the United States boggles the mind. Generally, police departments are not prepared or equipped to handle this type of emergency. It is not impossible but it will take much planning between agencies and acquire additional resources to handle these types of threats. Who knows the extent of what these evildoers are planning next? Who would have thought this could have happened in the United States? Many challenges lie ahead of police departments and they must meet them. Critical Incident Management is a must for all law enforcement agencies.

Police departments have to be better prepared than ever before. Now, police academies are adding more training programs to deal with specific emergencies such as terrorism and biological threats. Many police departments already have good training but many more lack training. Whatever was done in the past has to be increased to meet these new challenges. The training now was far better than what we had received long ago.

When I was in Bristol, Connecticut, there was no such thing as a specialized unit. Very rarely was there ever an incident worth mentioning. The patrol division handled everything even the occasional barricaded subject with a gun. Back in the 1970s there was no such thing as a Swat team. The SWAT team was reserved for larger departments like the Los Angeles Police Department. Back in the old days, we did the best thing under the circumstances. No doubt if these situations happened today, we would be calling a specialized unit to handle it. Take for example, when I was a street sergeant, my officers and I was sent to a man with a gun threatening suicide sitting at the top of the stairs in a single dwelling house. His mother had called the police and told us exactly where he was located. At the time, we only have about five officers. I went inside to talk to the person, situated myself at the bottom of the stairs behind cover, and engaged him in conversation.

Meanwhile, one of my officers found a ladder and put it up against the house to enter the second floor through the window. This plan was conceived before we even went into the house. While I was keeping him busy by talking to him my officer climbed through the window unnoticed and managed to subdue him. We took him into custody without incident and immediately transported him to the psychiatric unit at the Bristol Hospital. When we checked the shotgun, we were amazed to find it empty. Imagine, we could have easily shot him and be justified in taking this action. If this incident were to happen today, the uniformed officers would have established the parameter and the SWAT team would have taken over this situation. I am glad that he did not want to commit suicide by cop. Looking back, what we did was foolish. He could have easily shot a few cops if his shotgun was loaded. Those were the crazy days. There was little or no training and the officers handled the situations the best they knew how. We "winged it" many times.

Another time we were called to a barricaded subject reported to have a gun in the house. My officers responded to the location and surrounded the house. One officer got impatient and said, "I waited enough" and just walked right up to the house. It is lucky this person did not have a gun because this officer would have been shot. Actually, it was a stupid thing to do. He risked his life unnecessarily along with the other officers. The subject was taken into custody without incident. Again, we dodged another bullet and got lucky. During this time during the 1970s there was no such thing as body armor or special equipment. The officers managed to get the job done and I have to admit many took unnecessary risks and got lucky. Officers could have be easily shot and killed. These situations were handled such as the way I mentioned.

When I went to Somersworth, New Hampshire as police chief this barricaded subject incidents were getting more serious and there was no need to take any more chances. In the early 1990s a subject barricaded himself with a gun and this time it was serious. Our department was called to assist the Berwick Police Department across the river in Maine. Our department had a mutual aid agreement and just because we were in different states, the state line did not stop us from assisting our brother officers in distress. Berwick Police Department has about eight full time officers and they definitely need the help. I sent a number of my officers and I also responded to the scene to assist the police chief. He was clearly in a situation way over his head. The truth being it would have been over my head too. A subject was barricaded in a single-family home with a rifle but this time he was randomly shooting his gun in all directions. A police officer had initially responded in a marked cruiser when he was fired upon. He was lucky that he did not get hit but his cruiser was riddled with bullet holes. The officer did the smart thing and left his cruiser there and headed for cover.

Nothing like this had ever happened before and no one was prepared to handle a situation like this. It sounded like a war zone. You could hear the echo of the gunshot down the now vacant streets and the ricochet of bullets. By the time I had arrived, the uniformed officers had set up a perimeter around the house and had already evacuated the neighbors around the house. No uniformed officers were about to take this guy. It was apparent a specialized unit, a SWAT team had to be called. The Berwick police chief had already called a SWAT team from a nearby community and they had arrived to take up their position around the perimeter. Now this situation had taken place during the winter and this part of the country can be very cold. We could not leave the SWAT team out there for more than two hours at a time. I called the Dover Police Department and they sent their Swat team. By this time, it was well into the night and during the early morning hours; the Maine State Police had been notified earlier and was now set up around the perimeter. They were not in place for one hour when more shooting started. Apparently, the subject shot at one of the troopers and they returned fire. They shot him several times in the chest and he was dead at the scene.

The long ordeal that began in the late afternoon and ended during the early morning hours was now over. The Attorney General of the State of Maine later ruled that the shooting was justified. No kidding! He should have been around when the bullets were zinging through the air. There were questions raised by the media about whether this shooting was a suicide by cop. Who knows for sure? This guy could have been another nut case. At the time this phenomena was just being discussed in other shooting cases around the country but we told the media we did not know. We were no psychiatrist so we could not officially comment but it sure looked like a suicide by cop to me. It was now apparent and clear to me that police departments needed more training in this area. As a rule, with the exceptions of a few small and medium size police departments are not adequately trained nor equipped to handle a situation like this. I thought about what I would do if a similar situation hit Somersworth. We could call the State Police or the Dover Police Department that was located next to Somersworth. In any event we had to keep in mind that the response time for the state police could be one to two hours while the Dover Police Department would have been much less. In any event, we had a plan of action. Our officers understood that their role would be to set up a perimeter and evacuate the residents out of the potential line of fire. We would call for a SWAT team and just wait.

The reality is that I have been saying for years, "anything can happen at any time." After the shooting in a sleepy little town like Berwick, Maine, nothing surprised me anymore but I knew we had to be better prepared and have some sort of game plan during these contingencies. For instance, when I was in Fort Lupton, Colorado I remember making a comment to my lieutenant regarding a shooting incident in a high school in a different part of the country. I told him that we are not immune to violence, it could happen. Sure enough, on April 20, 1999 there was a mass murder at the Columbine High School about 35 five miles from Fort Lupton. After reading all the details about this shooting incident there was a possibility it could have been prevented. It is easy enough to say after the fact and we all know police chiefs sometimes are like Monday morning quarterbacks. However, there were some revealing signs that were ignored. The report of then Governor Bill Owens Columbine Review Commission was critical of the police response and some miscues. With a better response and preparation, perhaps this tragic incident could have been prevented that was discussed in the report. There may be more incidents like Columbine and many others in the future and it is up to police departments to be prepared. I have read recently where police academies are now incorporating training programs to deal with catastrophes associated with terrorism. In the past, we never wanted to think about this possibility but they shocked us with the World Trade Center catastrophe on September 11, 2001. Now police department have to be ready for any emergency.

Being Prepared is the Key

The previous discussions of incidents occurred early in my career is just examples of being reactive. It was not unusual for the police just to react to incident and then develop a plan during the crisis. It is not a good way to function. I told my officers many times do not hesitate to ask for assistance from other police departments if you need it. No one cares where the help comes from as long as you get it, when you need it. Sometimes police chiefs are reluctant to ask for help. I cannot understand it. When I needed help, I did not hesitate to ask.

After I arrived in Florence, Arizona, I wanted to plan for any type of contingency. As stated in an earlier chapter, the Florence Police Department did not have policy and procedures in place regarding responding to any emergencies. I knew that I would not only have to put in place policy and procedures but also plan for any emergency. When you first take over a department, it would be a good idea to meet with the sheriff and other area departments to set up the framework for mutual aid assistance.   The sheriff in Pinal County was very gracious and accommodating.   He said, "Anytime I needed help just ask." There were many times when we had to ask for assistance from the sheriff department and the Arizona Department of Public Safety (DPS).

Each year in February, an interesting event took place. The annual "Prison Run" would take place. Motorcycle enthusiasts from all over the state of Arizona and out of state would come to Florence for their annual bike run to honor their fellow comrades in the Arizona State Prison.   Florence has two large state prison complexes, a private prison, county jail and Immigration and Naturalization Services Detention area. It was like the prison capital of the world. The group who set it up was formerly known as the "Dirty Dozen," an outlaw biker gang that was responsible for serious criminal activity and drug trafficking in methamphetamine. They later changed their colors and joined the Hells Angels. There is no need to identify the Hells Angels. Everyone knows who they are and what they represent. They would want you to believe they are just fun loving bikers who like to ride Harleys. They are heavily involved in drug trafficking and organized crime.

Each year these bikers would make their annual pilgrimage to Florence and have a show of force. About four or five hundred bikers from all over would congregate at one of the local saloons just over the town line to begin their three or four mile run. They would drive in mass on the public road by the state prison and go back to the starting point. Many other communities already have annual biker conventions and usually thousands show up. For example, each year bikers including the Hells Angels from all over the country would go to Laconia, New Hampshire for one weekend of drinking and hell-raising. Usually the trouble was kept to a minimum at these events; however, there was a strong showing of law enforcement.

The annual prison bike run seemed like a simple event. It did not last more than 30 minutes. It required a great deal of pre-planning and coordination with area police department, Pinal County Sheriff's Office, DPS, Correctional Officials and an anti-gang unit out of the Phoenix and Tucson metro area. Altogether, there were about one hundred officers involved in this operation. It all began months prior to the prison run with a meeting of the Dirty Dozen representatives at one of the downtown bars. Five or six would ride into town on their Harley-Davidson motorcycles. Most of them were armed with handguns. In Arizona, it was legal for anyone to carry a firearm, as long it was visible. They knew the law too. They would leave their firearm in the saddlebags on their motorcycles and leave one of their members outside to guard their motorcycles before going into the bar. Now, I do not know about you but I certainly was not use to these events being from the New England States. Being out in the west was a different story. During the meeting, we discussed when the event was going to take place, the time and how many expected participants. They assured me their purpose was to only ride in mass by the prison to show support for their brother bikers locked up. It was an annual event and at this time, it was their thirteenth annual prison run. They stated that they wanted to make this a family event for years to come and there would be no trouble. I had to say that the meeting went very well and they were reasonable. They understood there would be a show of force by law enforcement as in the past. In addition, they would comply with all town and county ordinances. Because they would be on the state highway, they would obtain a parade permit, as they had done in the past, from the Arizona Department of Transportation.

After the meeting, I contacted the sheriff to set up a meeting for law enforcement and we had a meeting with all the law enforcement agencies that would be involved. The sheriff would have his mobile command post van set up next to the county jail to coordinate all communication. My lieutenant would be at the command post. There would be enough uniformed and non-uniform officers to handle any problem. Everyone would have their assignment and would know their role for the day. The planning for this event was excellent. Few problems that had occurred in the past but we were ready for anything. The only problem that I could foresee was the motoring public being inconvenienced for about 30 minutes. They could either take a detour or wait in traffic until the road was clear. In any event, we would have to stop traffic until the prison run had been completed.

It was a remarkable sight. The organizers of the event, the Dirty Dozen, now the Hells Angels would be in the front of the pack. The president was first and his lieutenants next followed by everyone else. It was interesting to see the pecking order of their biker gang. The procession went by the main state prison complex turned around and went back to the saloon. After the event had been completed everyone celebrated at the saloon. Outside there were venders set up with booths to sell food, and merchandise. If someone wanted to get another tattoo, there was a booth set up for that too. Mainly, the participants bought tee-shirts commemorating the annual biker's prison run. These activities ran during the afternoon and when it was about 9:00 p.m., everyone had pretty much dispersed.

All and all, the event went according to plan. There were no problems what so ever. The bikers were very well behaved and polite. Even with the officers walking through the bar area there was no problems. I have to give credit to law enforcement for a show of force. Obviously, Florence Police Department was a small department and would not have been able to handle this activity by themselves. The pre-planning was critical for the successful operation. What is just as important is the debriefing after the event had taken place. The law enforcement agencies met soon after the biker's prison run to discuss the operation, any mistakes or problems and what could be done to improve law enforcement's role for the next year.

In summary, if a law enforcement agency knows about a rally, activity, demonstration or anything else that may require a law enforcement response, then it would be best to consider the following suggestions:

- Contact Law Enforcement Agencies to see if they could assist
- Meet with Department management personnel to discuss the situation and lay out a plan of action.

- Contact and meet with the group's representatives to lay out the ground rules for the activity.
- Arrange a meeting with these Law Enforcement Agencies to plan law enforcement's response to the activity prior to the event.
- Implement the plan during the event.
- Each Law Enforcement Agency should have assigned roles when the event takes place.
- Arrange a post event meeting to debrief Law Enforcement Agencies on what happened, analyze the response and suggest ways to improve.

Some of these events may seem unusual, such as the annual prison run but because law enforcement planned their response and what role they would play there were no problems. Sometimes, it may seem like a waste of manpower and an unnecessary show of force, but law enforcement's presence certainly had something to do with keeping the peace. I would rather have too many officers than not enough. Just think of what could have happened if things got out of control if only the Florence Police would have been involved. I dread what could have happened. You know as well as I do a little incident could certainly escalate into a major confrontation. I keep Murphy's Law in mind; if something can go wrong, it will. You just have to be prepared.

A police chief or manager cannot take things for granted. He or she must keep the lines of communication open and meet with staff to discuss potential problems. Getting everyone involved early on in the planning process will definitely increase the odds for success.

Special Operations Response Team

When I was in Florence, Arizona, I started to put together a Special Operations Response Team (S.O.R.T) for mainly containment and to handle any sort of contingency in the community. Another incident that I recall occurred just outside the town line in the county jurisdiction. Officers were called to a man wanting to commit suicide in front of his house. Here was a prime example for the use of a SWAT team. My officer went to assist and almost ended up getting shot. Apparently, this person was daring the police to shot him. Finally, the Sheriff's deputy shot and killed the subject. This person shot several times at the officer and one of the shots struck the bumper of one of our cruisers. After an investigation by DPS, the shooting was ruled justifiable. The officer did not have a choice but perhaps the outcome would have been different had a Special Operations Response Team been in place. They could have set up a safe perimeter and eventually talk him into surrendering. We will never know because the Sheriff's SWAT team never arrived in time.

I never really completed putting together a team because if you recall the town council did not renew my contract. My personnel were in favor of S.O.R.T. and there was no lack of volunteers. After I went to Fort Lupton, Colorado, I saw a need to establish an S.O.R.T. team and continued the initial planning for it.   This time I wanted to make sure the City Administrator and City Council approved of my plan to implement the S.O.R.T. team. I did not want the council members to think that we had a bunch of ninja warriors dressed in black with helmets and goggles running around with guns. It is best to get their **approval and endorse the plan** upfront so that there are no surprises. In the beginning the council members were cool to the idea. They thought it was not needed and if there was a situation, we could just call the Sheriff's Office to use their SWAT team. Of course, we could always use the Sheriff's team but the problem was the response time. Because Fort Lupton was at the southern end of the county it would take at least two hours or more to assemble a team and have them respond to our community. I knew that there would be another time to bring up this matter again.

I did not have to wait very long when the Columbine shooting took place. Even thought I had mentioned the need for the team and cited other high school shooting incident in other parts of the country, it had no effect until this incident struck close to home. The reality was that these incidents could happen at any time or place. Small communities, such as Fort Lupton were not exempt to mass murder. After the shooting had taken place communities, police department all over the country were rising to a new challenge and had to plan to prevent a repetition of shootings in their community.   In our community, I met with the school officials to provide recommendations and suggestions to make the schools safer. Other communities were doing likewise and in addition, there were new training programs created to help deal with this new problem. Even though Fort Lupton did not have a School Resource Officer, I made sure that our officers had a visible presence. Periodically, during the day the officers would spend some time walking around the high school halls, talking to students, teachers and school administrators.

I used the example of the Columbine shooting to get approval to put together a Special Operations Response Team. It was unfortunate that the Columbine shooting took place anyway but no one wanted to have his or her school be another killing ground.   I told the city council that our S.O.R.T. team would be mainly a containment team. They would only shoot as a last resort to protect their life or someone else.

There was no shortage of volunteers for the S.O.R.T. team. The team consisted of four volunteers and a sergeant and they began training once a week. One member of the team was a former Marine who had been in a specialized unit and he provided a great deal of expertise. You would be surprised with the number of talented individuals you may already have in your police department. We slowly bought equipment and provided training to get the team ready for emergencies.

The following is an excerpt of the Fort Lupton's General Order of the purpose, policy statement and some definitions of the S.O.R.T. team that I had written for this occasion:

PURPOSE:

The purpose of this order is to establish procedures, and responsibilities for a special operations response team consisting of certain designated members of the Fort Lupton Police Department.

POLICY:

Primary responsibilities of the Special Operations Response Team (S.O.R.T.) will be the service of high-risk search and arrest warrants. Members of the Special Response Team shall also be responsible for containing armed individuals who are either holding hostage(s), have barricaded themselves, or are identified as terrorists, until an additional specialized weapons team from another agency (such as SWAT) arrives. They will then assist members of the specialized weapons team. Their primary concern shall be the protection of life. Members of the Special Operations Response Team are authorized to use deadly force pursuant to State Law and the department's General Order on the Use of Force. Members of the Special Operations Response Team will be under the direct supervision of the Chief of Police and/or Operations Lieutenant. In the event that neither the Chief nor Lieutenant is available, the leader or assistant leader of the Special Operations Response Team will assume command of the unit. Members of the Special Operations Response Team will cooperate with any other governmental agency that may have an official interest in the situation; e.g. FBI, State Patrol, and Sheriff's Department, etc

DEFINITIONS

For purposes of this order, the following definitions will be applicable:

HOSTAGE INCIDENT--A situation in which a person/s holds another person/s against his will by force, threat or violence, while law enforcement officials present at the scene are attempting to obtain the release of the person/s being held.

BARRICADED INCIDENT--A situation in which a person, while in a place of cover, who is armed or believed to be armed, resists being taken into custody.

TERRORIST INCIDENT--A situation in which a person commits, or threatens to commit, a serious criminal offense for political or ideological purposes.

HBT-In simple terms, refers to hostage, barricaded gunman, or terrorist.

CONTAINMENT TEAM--A lieutenant and at least three police officers assigned to the Special Response Team who are trained in containment procedures for purposes identified in this order.

HBT PLAN-A predetermined plan of action, which is formally initiated in response to either a hostage, barricaded gunman, or terrorist situation.

INNER PERIMETER--The immediate area of containment as designated by the officer in charge. This area is initially manned by the responding patrol personnel unless relieved by members of the Special Response Team.

OUTER PERIMETER--A peripheral control area surrounding the inner perimeter which provides for a safety zone and which permits access to the inner perimeter by authorized personnel.

COMMAND POST--A secure position within the outer perimeter from which the officer in charge can direct operations.

The policy statement provides the philosophical statement of the police department in how the situation the Special Operations Response Team will be utilized. I included some definitions, not all, just to illustrate some definitions and terms. You will notice that I had already included a definition of a terrorist. I included terrorists because of the ever present threat of terrorism and apparently, I was right. The day America was attacked will live forever in our minds. I specifically stated the team would be used for containment until the more specialized SWAT team arrived at the scene.

The City Administrator and City Council like my approach and endorsed my plan. My philosophy was simple; it was better to be over prepared than not prepared at all. If an incident appeared to be overwhelming, at the very least, we should be able to contain it until more help arrived from other law enforcement agencies. Everyone seemed comfortable with this approach. It may seem monotonous and expensive to train every week. It was not as if we were going to have a barricaded subject with a gun every day. However, the cost is justified because you never know when the team will be need so everyone has to be in a high state of readiness. As stated in the policy, the team could be used for high-risk search and arrest warrant entry team.

Regional Approach

Even small department are not invulnerable to violence anymore in their community. Some police departments can make this concept work by using the regional approach. Several members from each department could form an S.O.R.T team to respond to emergencies. Of course, a mutual aid agreement would have to be approved by their respective municipalities but it could be done. Two communities near Fort Lupton cross sworn their officers to insure their officers were covered legally when they responded out of their jurisdiction. The police chief should always consult with his or her respective town or city attorney to get a legal opinion to establish this concept. Other issues would have to be resolved such as the liability issues, the municipality's insurance carrier and the team leader. Police chiefs are always sensitive about who is going to be in charge of the team. Personally, I do not have a problem with it as long as the right person is in charge.

The **regional approach** does make sense because you can combine resources such as equipment and manpower. The department does not have to commit to a full team just two or three member so the department. Selecting team members is another issue to deal with. How do you select team members without hurting someone's feelings or having someone feel discriminated against? The best way is to have a selection process instead of choosing a friend. It could be a combination oral board panel and a competitive agility testing. Everyone agrees that the team members should be in great shape so the selection process would be easy. If someone has an interest then he or she would have an opportunity to get into condition before the testing. The fact of the matter is that some would be automatically eliminated because of their poor physical conditioning.

Incident Command System

The fire departments have it right. They utilize the "incident command system" when there is a fire, hazardous material incident and any other situation that would require a response by the fire department and if necessary, a mutual aid response from other communities. There is no reason the police departments cannot use the incident command system and many are already using it. If there is a major or critical incident, such as a barricaded subject with a gun, we need to think carefully about the response. There need to be a command post set up a safe distance away from the incident and a staging area for law enforcement and other essential public safety personnel to gather and wait for their assignment.

I first learned about the incident command system after working very closely with the Somersworth Fire Chief. He utilized this system every time the fire department was dispatched to a fire or Hazmat incident. The system worked just fine for the fire department so why not for law enforcement with modifications. Pre-planning law enforcement's response to an incident will no doubt instill confidence in being ready for any kind of contingency. I would strongly urge police departments to train using the incident command system so that everyone understands his or her role. This concept will be explained further in the next section.

Emergency Management

As I stated earlier, I first became associated with the incident command system after working closely with the Somersworth Fire Department. I was part of a team with the fire chief and public works director working on developing the emergency management response plan for the city. The police chief has to wear many hats and one of mine was emergency management. The city had to be prepared for any type of disaster and we had to be prepared for it. Like other cities, Somersworth did not have a plan; it was time to put one together. We worked along with the state to develop a general response plan.

People do not realize what could happen if there was a hazardous materials incident in their community. Generally, people will think, "It will not happen here." It will happen somewhere else but not Somersworth. It was the typical prevailing attitude, even with some of the police officers. What if something did happen? Would it not be better if the emergency services were prepared to handle the crisis, whatever it may be? The crisis is just not limited to Hazmat but winter storms as well.

While we were developing our plan in Somersworth, we had a real Hazmat incident. At a local car dealership, the owner found a good deal and purchased a large quantity of chlorine for swimming pools. No doubt, his intent was to make some extra money but little did he know that it was a violation of the city ordinances and other laws to stockpile chlorine in a small storage building on his property. When someone wishes to store chemicals they have to inform the fire chief so the fire department knows what is on the property and more so that it is stored safely. Somehow, the chlorine ignited and started a fire in the storage building. Fortunately, the fire department did not rush immediately upon the scene because of the color of the smoke. They backed off when they realized it did not appear to be an ordinary fire. If someone had rushed up there to extinguish the fire, we probably would have had a fatality.

The fire chief set up the incident command a safe distance away and set up a safe two-mile perimeter around the car dealership. From the command post, we coordinated an orderly evacuated of residents within the perimeter and the police department established traffic control. Some school children walking to school were exposed to chlorine in the air and were given medical treatment at the hospital. On this particular day, we were quite fortunate. There were virtually no winds so the chlorine did not spread too far and it eventually dissipated into the atmosphere after the fire was extinguished. The fire fighters were properly trained and had the equipment to handle this Hazmat incident. The state's emergency management and Hazmat team arrived to assist. The injuries were kept to a minimum. This was my first exposure to a Hazmat incident and it can be quite scary. However, the fire chief's incident command system worked very well. He made a believer out of me that day.

Conversely, this incident was not concluded. Earlier during the day before the fire broke out a garbage disposal truck emptied the dumpster at the rear of the car dealership and for some reason there was some chlorine in it. As luck would have it, the chlorine caught on fire and there was another Hazmat incident somewhere else on the highway. The occupants of the truck were injured because of the chlorine gas.

I think the owner of the dealership who was well known in the community and a very influential person was quite embarrassed. He was trying to make a quick buck but it turned into a very expensive proposition. He had to pay for the emergency response for the fire and police, the clean up and a hefty fine. I think that he was lucky to get off so easy. Then again, after his dealings with the State Fire Marshall, Fire Chief, and the State Emergency Management officials, I believe he learned a valuable lesson. What started out as an innocent ploy to make some money turned into a potentially serious hazardous materials incident!

Our committee finished the emergency plan for the city and we had to put it into effect several times for winter blizzards and potential hurricanes. We worked hard to keep our plan up to date with some annual exercises. **The key is to keep your plan up to date**. It is not only important to have a plan but also to work the plan. The plan will not be any good if after it is completed you just put it on the shelf to gather dust. The planned exercises, usually a Hazmat related incident was a coordinated effort by the police, fire and ambulance. Now, you have to include school shootings and terrorist incidents. It was good practice for all concerned to evaluate each agency's response and later to discuss mistakes and ways to improve.

One incident involved a collision between a school bus carrying children and a tanker carrying hazardous materials on a bridge over a river. The scenario involved the bus careening into the river and the tanker turning over on the riverbank and its contents flowing into the river. The exercise included a response from the fire department's dive team. All and all, it was a very good exercise and everyone learned something. These drills are good to improve the overall response.

When I went to Florence, Arizona, I developed an emergency response plan for the town. Even though Florence was a rural community, you never know what could happen. I worked with the fire and ambulance to have a practice exercise at the high school. There was a make believe fire in the chemistry lab at the high school. Again, **it is important to have plan and to put it into action**. It is far better to find out your mistakes during a practice exercise than make them during the real thing. Unfortunately, my stay in Florence did not last long. There was much more work that had to be done for emergency management.

Fort Lupton, Colorado was a completely different situation. In Fort Lupton, I was the Public Safety Director that included being the emergency management director. It was an awesome responsibility but I was up to the challenge. Everything that I had learned in Somersworth and Florence I was going to put to good use. One of the first things I did was review the emergency management manual. It was out of date and it was time to rewrite the plan. The City Council would have to give its final approval. I enlisted the help of the Weld County's emergency management director, a deputy sheriff and he was anxious to help. One of his duties was to help communities in Weld County develop an emergency management plan. Fort Lupton had a plan but it was outdated and it stayed on the shelf like many other communities.

It took awhile but the emergency management plan was finally re-written and formally adopted by the City Council. I made sure copies were available for the fire department, school official, public works, ambulance, dispatch center and staff. Why have a plan if you are going to keep it a secret. Little did everyone know that I was planning a practice exercise to work our plan. I was invited along with my lieutenant to participate in an exercise at the airport in Greeley, about 25 miles away. I attended the planning meeting and was there to watch the exercise. The exercise involved a mid-air collision between two planes and both crash-landed in two different locations. The exercise went very well and it was nice to see a coordinate effort by all the agencies involved. Sure, there were some mistakes and everyone learned from them during the debriefing. It is better to make mistakes during practice than during the real event.

After the exercise, I asked for a meeting with the County Emergency Management Director to set up a practice exercise for our community. He was all for it because he wanted to do an exercise in a different part of the county each year so we were going to meet his needs too. It was just a matter of setting the date and deciding on what type of exercise and the exact location. The exercise was planned for June of 2000 and by that time; I had left Fort Lupton so unfortunately I missed it. After a few meetings, we decided to have an incident involving a train versus truck carrying hazardous materials. It was logical because trains were traveling through Fort Lupton during the day and evening all the time. We decided to do the exercise at one of our numerous railroad crossings. It would be a good exercise because you never know what kind of materials are on the trains traveling through the communities. These mishaps could just as easily result from a derailment. It was always a very real possibility because the tracks were in a general state of disrepair. Occasionally, we had some minor derailments.

As I recall, we had a potential Hazmat incident during one of our annual parades. Some minors were fooling around with a crude oil storage tank when all of a sudden it blew up. The storage tanks are used as a collection point for oil that is pumped out of the ground on the oil field. This entire area in Colorado was a huge oil field. One person got the bright idea to light a match and throw it into the tank to see what would happen. It did not take him long to find out. He ignited the extremely volatile fumes that exploded the tank. Fortunately, the tank that caught on fire was not very serious. Potentially, if the oil caught on fire the whole area could have been a fireball. In this particular case, we were lucky again. The youth and his friends just barely escaped with only minor injuries. He and his friends could have easily been killed. This could have been a serious Hazmat incident and you never know what may ensue in your community. There are always surprises and lessons to be learned. The fire department quickly responded to the scene and quickly extinguished the fire. The terrific explosion startled everyone at the parade. This situation could definitely have been worse.

Special Equipment

So far, I have been developing an emergency management plan but had not mentioned anything about obtaining special equipment. **Citing emergency management** was my secret of the trade, so to speak, that enabled me to obtain all the necessary equipment that I needed by using grant money and budgeted money. This strategy worked in all three communities and each time I cited the necessity for emergency management.

You may not be able to get everything you need at once, but you will get it over time. Instead of having the fire department get all the money, I wanted the police department to get its fair share. My philosophy that I always say, "If you do not ask, you will not receive." If I am budgeted money, then I will spend it. Some police chiefs take pride in turning back money at the end of the fiscal year or calendar year whichever budget cycle you are it. Here is the rationale that you hurt you later on. If during the budget requests you ask to purchase a piece of equipment and after being budgeted for it you did not purchase the equipment or waited a long time to purchase it. If I were sitting on the council, I would tell myself the police chief did not need it after all. I think in the end your credibility could be damaged and the council will ask about whether it is needed. I never had this problem because my objective was to purchase these items as quickly as possible. My predecessors always turned back money, but not me. My personnel could hardly believe the budget approvals and were simply amazed at the new equipment that was purchased.

I was always able to relate the department's needs to emergency management. I used the fire department and public works to update our dispatch center in Somersworth including a backup radio system. We were able to purchase a new recording system and dispatch software. Some of my personnel did not like the idea of dispatching for the fire department, namely one of my captains. He thought like many others that the fire department should be dispatching for fire. I did not make a big issue of it but I saw the importance to have public safety dispatch. Why argue about it when we were doing it anyway. There was no point in it. It was like an insurance policy to keep the dispatch center in Somersworth. Periodically, city managers get the bright idea about saving money and have the county dispatch for police and fire. The city could save about $200,000 but look at the diminished service and officer safety issues. Many communities all over the United States did just as I said and transferred dispatch operations to the county.

One strategy that I used was "**show and tell**." The council members in a small community often will try to nickel and dime you to death. They take their job very seriously and try to save every dime they can. It is hard to refuse your request by not only showing the need but inviting the council members to view the need as well. For example, in Fort Lupton I knew that we were in desperate need of an emergency generator. The generator in place was an old engine that had not been operational in years. I knew we were in trouble when no one could remember the last time it ran. I knew the city council was not going to fork over about $12,000 to purchase a new generator so I invited the council members to look at it. They could see for themselves. They knew after I told them it was necessary for emergency management operations. However, I **gave them a deal they could not refuse**. This is how I pulled it off. I sat on the County's Emergency 911 committee as a representative of our community. I convinced the committee to pay half the cost of the emergency generator. The surcharge for telephones were used to help update equipment and the purchase of a replacement generator was an acceptable expenditure. The city council thought it was a great deal and voted to approve the expenditure. In addition, I was able to auction off the old generator at an auction site for trucks and heavy equipment. The city netted about $1,500 hundred dollars so it cost the city less than $5,000 for a new generator that automatically started when the power went out. My personnel were shaking their heads trying to figure out how I pulled that one out of the hat. It is not hard if you have a plan.

In Fort Lupton, I was able to purchase and upgrade equipment in the dispatch center including new E911 dispatch equipment, and new base stations. The base stations were about 20 years old and it was time to replace them. Each time I used the rationale that it was necessary for emergency management.

K-9 Operations

If I had the opportunity, I would have implemented K-9 in each of my departments. As it were, I was able to implement it only in Florence. If I had stayed in Fort Lupton longer then I would have strongly considered it. In Florence, an officer approached me and asked if he could be a K-9 officer. He had recently purchased a German Shepherd dog that he had imported from Germany. He spent about $4,000 to purchase this dog. He was probably looking for me to reimburse him for the expenditure but I was not about to do it. Besides, the town council would never approve the funding after the fact. Frankly, I liked the idea. The dog was supposed to be a very good drug detecting dog and finding people inside buildings.

I know first hand about finding people in buildings. I participated in a training exercise with the K-9 unit. I put on a bite suit and went into the vacant house to find a hiding place. The room was pitch dark but I found a good hiding place, so I thought, in the corner of the room. I heard the officer releasing the dog into the house and before I knew it the dog was on me. I was impressed with the results.

I assigned the officer and his K-9 to the Pinal County Narcotics Task Force. The K-9 unit was going to be used for drug interdiction. It was a good call on my part; it was a two for one deal. I wanted to have an officer assigned to the narcotic task force anyway and they were looking for a K-9 unit so the situation was ideal. One of the Chevy blazers that was confiscated and eventually turned over to the police department as a result of asset forfeiture was converted into a K-9 vehicle. The initial outlay to implement a K-9 unit was minimal. The police department paid for the food, general upkeep, and veterinarian fees. I thought it was funny because one time the dog got angry and bit his handler on the cheek that required a few stitches. Come to find out the reason was that the dog had an abscessed tooth and he had to have a root canal performed by the veterinarian. A root canal on a dog was a first for me. The officer got a great deal of good-natured ribbing from the other officers.

The dog was worth his weight in gold. On two separate occasions, the dog detected a large quantity of marijuana on drug interdictions stops. Coming in from

Mexico on separate occasions one vehicle had about 250 pounds and the other had about 525 pounds of marijuana. The dog had other seizures to his credit but the quantities were much less. In any event, the K-9 unit can work wonders for a police department.

Several times the K-9 unit was used for walk through in the high school and the parking lot. We did not care if we found anything but putting on a show was more important. At least the students were thinking about what we would be showing up next with the dog. Even though I did not have a K-9 unit in Fort Lupton, Colorado, on several occasion I asked the Sheriff's Office to walk their drug dog through the middle and high schools. Again, we did not care if we found anything; it was more of a psychological deterrent. We wanted them to know that we could be back with the dog anytime.

I think that the K-9 unit is a valuable tool for law enforcement. It did not cost much to implement the program because we already had the dog. Any police department that wants a K-9 will find that it will cost about $5,000 for a good one. The warden at Correctional Corporation of America needed a narcotic detecting dog at the private prison. He had a few instances where drugs were smuggled into the prison. In one particular instance, a brick of marijuana tightly wrapped in cellophane to be made waterproof was found in a paint can. The warden asked me to help him get K-9. I found that there was a company in Texas that specialized in training narcotic detecting dogs. The price tag was about $5,000. No problem, the warden sent a correctional officer to be trained and to bring the dog back. It must be nice to be in the private sector and to have a big pot of money. The private prison was experiencing a tremendous growth and they were always adding on to their facility. Now, they have over 3,000 inmates. They needed a narcotic detecting dog. I was glad that I was able to help them.

Having a K-9 unit can be a very expensive proposition as some police departments found out. Take for example; Portsmouth Police Department submitted a grievance that they were owed money for maintenance and training the dog. No one forced the officers to volunteer for the program. The department ended up paying thousands of dollars to these officers for compensation. The United States Supreme Court decision, *Garcia v. the City of San Antonio*, came back to bite them again. The officers argued that they were required by the department to feed and take care of the kennel and train with the dog. The State Labor Board in New Hampshire agreed and the City of Portsmouth as many other cities were required to compensate the officers. They eventually agreed to one-hour pay at time and a half as fair compensation. Now, philosophically I have trouble with this one. In my experience, I find that police officers wanted to volunteer to be K-9 handlers. It was always understood that it was a voluntary assignment and along with it came some benefits. The officer got a dog to keep at home, which he probably would do anyway, and a police marked unit to take home. The officer saved gas money and wear and tear on his own personal vehicle because he did not have to drive it to work.

My officer in Florence never asked for extra pay. If he had submitted a grievance, I know what I would have told him. You can keep the dog, and you can park the vehicle at the police department. I probably would have discontinued the program. Sometimes there has to be a little give and take. Some officers are just too greedy for their own good.

Special Details

A police chief has to be flexible and make adjustments to fit any given situation. Traditionally, the Patrol Division handled all the calls for service and the Investigations Division handled all the serious criminal cases. In a small and even in some medium size police departments it is difficult. Personally, I like to use special details to fit the situation. Now, these special details are designed to augment the patrol activities and fill a need to tackle special problems, as Problem Orientated Policing (POP).

In Fort Lupton, Colorado we had a major problem like any other community with drug trafficking. The police never took action against any of the drug dealers from what I could see and it was suggested many times some police officers were tipping them off. Whether it was true or not I made it a priority to do something about drug trafficking in the community. The City Council mentioned to me early on that we had a problem with drugs in the community. Little did they know that was the feeling in most communities but I did not argue. The reputation of the police department was so bad that the Sheriff's Drug Task Force did not want to share any information. If they were working in the community, they would not tell anyone. Early on, I arranged a meeting with some of the drug task force members and at least got them to let me know when they were actively pursuing drug investigations in our community.

I put together a drug investigation detail, mainly consisted of two officers who reported to the second shift supervisor when he was working or me when he was not. This chain of command cut down on the number of officers who knew what was going on and eliminated the possibility of unintentionally divulging information. Even though the perception was that officers were leaking information, I could never prove it. Other officers were brought in on a need to know basis when an arrest was about to take place. If there were extra officers on a shift, then they would wear plain clothes to facilitate the investigation. Sometimes the officers were brought in on overtime depending upon the workload. The local car dealerships were great. We borrowed different cars so the officers would fit in better. Our plan worked because the officers were able to make a dent in the drug trafficking. They made a number of arrests and seizures and were making so much of an impact that the drug trafficking slowed way down. At least we were making them think that we were just around the corner. The city council was very impressed with the results.

Being prepared for any contingency or emergency is one of necessity for any police chief. A key to the successful conclusion of a contingency is proper planning and coordination along with involving other agencies. Too many police department are ill prepared and this is where the problems occur. Involving key personnel and other agencies is the correct approach to a successful conclusion of an event.

Chapter 20
Accreditation Process: Is it Worth the Effort?

Everyone by now has probably heard about the national accreditation process and wonder whether it is worth the effort. Some police departments say it is worth the effort while some others say it is a waste of time. There is a mixed bag of opinions about the process. I have heard many police chiefs talk negatively about it while others say it is one of the greatest programs ever to come along. I will try to explain the process, give you my views on the program and discuss ways to be successful. My discussion will provide pros and cons on the issue to the extent that you will wonder if I support the program or not. Generally, I fully endorse the accreditation process and admire those agencies that were successful in accomplishing their goal. Simply, I am just stimulating some thought if it is a worthwhile project or not. Is it just busy work? As I go along, I will discuss some the real issues that police chiefs have already thought about and discussed. You probably already have thought about these issues yourself and made up your mind. Perhaps, I am giving you something more to think about. I may not tell you anything new but perhaps, this discussion will bring about a better perspective on whether to pursue accreditation or not.

First, before I go any further, let me tell you up front that none of my agencies was accredited by CALEA, the Commission on Accreditation for Law Enforcement Agencies. Not that I did not want to be accredited, the circumstances were not right. I will go into detail about it later. My last department, Fort Lupton, Colorado was state accredited by the Colorado Association of Chiefs of Police. Many law enforcement agencies opt to go with the State Accreditation instead of CALEA and I will tell you why and will go into detail. However, if I had the opportunity I would definitely have liked to achieve the national accreditation and have my agencies recognized by CALEA.

What is Accreditation?

The national accreditation program for law enforcement agencies recognizing professional excellence is known as CALEA is based out of Fairfax, Virginia. The acronym stands for the Commission on Accreditation for Law Enforcement Agencies. The program is now more than 20 years old. Four organizations, the International Association of Chiefs of Police, National Association of Black Law Enforcement Executives, National Sheriffs' Association and the Police Executive Research Forum developed it in 1979. The purpose of CALEA was to improve the delivery of law enforcement services offering a body of standards, developed by law enforcement practitioners, covering a wide range of up to date law enforcement topics. It recognizes professional achievement by offering an orderly process for addressing and complying with applicable standards. Each agency pays a fee to begin the process, but there is a substantial cost to consider depending upon the size of the department. The benefits according to CALEA are as follows: besides the recognition of obtaining international excellence, the primary benefits of accreditation include controlled liability insurance costs, administrative improvements, greater accountability from supervisors, increased governmental and community support and stronger defense against lawsuits and citizen complaints. I will discuss each benefit as we go along.

Now, you probably have not noticed but police departments are not rushing to obtain accreditation for their department and the question is why? Any police chief looking at the benefits would have to agree. The benefits do look impressive and from a managerial point of view, it could be a police chief's ultimate dream or nightmare. After I finish explaining both sides of the issue, then you can decide. There already has been much published about this process in law enforcement professional journals, such as the Police Chief Magazine. You would think after 20 years most of the law enforcement agencies in the United States would be accredited by now. If you had not noticed, only a small number of departments are accredited or are actively involved in the process. Another observation that I had made through the years is that most of the departments accredited are large agencies. The majority of the small police departments has not gone through the process or even has thought about it. Even if they thought about it, they could not do it. This alone has given me reasons to raise questions.

I was first exposed to the accreditation process during the middle 1980s as a captain of the Support Services Bureau of the Bristol Police Department. Our department was a medium sized agency and we had thought about going through the process. The Board of Police Commissioners had agreed that this was a worthwhile project and the chief appointed me as the accreditation manager. Soon after, I accepted a position to be the police chief in Somersworth, New Hampshire. I had gone to some of the meetings to learn more about the accreditation process itself. At that time, it was still new and there were still many questions left to be answered. In any event, only a few departments made a commitment to get involved. What happened to the project? Well, it was put so far back onto the back burner that the project had been forgotten about until recently. The Police Commission recently approved the project but has not officially begun the process. I am sure they will do it because they are more serious about it now. It was too bad that someone did not pick up where I had left off and guided it through fruition. There were two reasons; the first, the department was not very serious about the accreditation process; and second, the process had not officially begun. The application fee and completed application had not been sent to CALEA. Since no funds were invested into the project, the decision was made to put a hold on it. After I had left the department, I think they realized that it would involve more time and hard work than they wanted to commit. No one said it was going to be an easy process.

One large police department signed up for the accreditation process and blazed through the self-assessment phase of the program. Most departments average about 24 months and this department did it in less than a year. Right away, it should have told you something. They were more interested in the status than what they as a department were about to accomplish. They notified CALEA that they were ready for the on-site inspection. Members of the department and some nice looking women in a limousine met the inspection team at the airport. I still laugh when I think about it. I wish I could have seen the expression on the inspectors' faces. It was too unbelievable to be true, but it happened. The inspection team was not very impressed and by the time the inspection had been concluded they did not recommend this department for accreditation. This should not have been shocking news. I wonder how the inspectors got back to the airport. The audacity of some members of the department trying to make a mockery out of this process created doubts about the program. This incident was the topic of discussion for a long time. The police chief should have thought about it before he turned some of his personnel loose on the on-site inspection team. Police departments spend too much time and effort on the process, even though it was much less than the average 24 months, then to blow it on something foolish. Since this incident, the department that remains nameless never became accredited. It is not known whether they are involved in the self-assessment phase today.

The accreditation process is a voluntary program. It requires a serious commitment from all levels of the organization in order to make it work. Apparently, there is not enough serious commitment and this is a problem with many law enforcement agencies. How can you force a commitment when they are not serious about it to begin with? The police chief should not be the only one to get excited about the accreditation. He or she must first sell it to the staff. If the staff cannot be convinced then it makes no sense to begin the process. The accreditation manager is only one person; he or she cannot do the work alone. Everyone has to do his or her fair share in order to make the project doable. I have seen some expressions on the faces of officers when they were asked what they thought about accreditation. The attitude was portrayed such as:" What, more work?" " Why do we have to do this?" I do not know why the rank and file is always suspicious of management. When I first arrived in Somersworth, New Hampshire, the officers were generally pessimistic about everything. It was doom and gloom. It would have taken time for me to change their attitude about doing police work, never mind trying to convince them about the positives of accreditation. For the time being, I decided to delay the accreditation project.

During my stay in New Hampshire, the Police Standards and Training were getting into the act. They were going to make State Accreditation possible with several levels that would lead into the last phase, Accreditation by CALEA. Many states had adopted this approach and before I could begin the process, I left to become police chief in Florence, Arizona. Again, this program was voluntary and not many departments were rushing to get into the act. I mistakenly thought most of the department would want to get involved. Matter of fact, this subject came up a number of times at the Police Chief Association meetings. I have a theory about it. I believe that many police chiefs did not fully comprehended what the program was all about and not many were recommending it either. The chiefs did not understand what accreditation was all about. Many were asking themselves, "What is accreditation and what does it mean for the department?" If it is only voluntary then some might think that it must not be necessary. From my perspective, everyone knew the program existed but no one from CALEA tried to make a pitch at the various states' Police Chief Association meetings. As long as the program was voluntary, there would only be a limited number of departments doing it, mostly large agencies. Guess what! After 20 years, there still are only a limited number of law enforcement agencies that are accredited.

If you go around the community ask the citizens about accreditation and what it means to them. They may not know or even care. I wonder if the officers in the department have an appreciation for this accomplishment. What about the accreditation logo that you see on the police vehicles? Do people know what it means? Police departments need to remind their community about their commitment. Speaking from experience, I very rarely heard about communities making a big deal about pride in their police department because of this significant accomplishment.

My strategy to at least get ready for the accreditation process was to revamp and add to the policy and procedure manual. I was going to organize the policy and procedure manual according to the chapters on major heading as defined by CALEA. This way, as I was writing the policy and procedures, I had the accreditation standards in mind. The manual outlining the suggested organization along with all the standards for law enforcement is available through CALEA. Even if a police department was not interested in pursuing accreditation, at least they should have a copy of the standards to use as a reference. This was my approach. The standards from what I could see were nothing more than acceptable police practices that should be put into writing anyway. They are not all that difficult to do, but it does take time. You would be surprised with the number of police departments that do not have up to date policy and procedures. In each department where I was police chief, there were either no policy or procedures or many were out-of-date. Even the Fort Lupton Police Department that was State Accredited had many policy and procedures that were outdated.

In Somersworth, New Hampshire, the City Manager was not enthusiastic about the idea. The manager thought I had too many policy and procedures anyway. He said, "What do you need all them for." If I could not convince the boss then it was going to be a losing battle for now. Most everyone was not very excited about the project. I thought it was a great idea but unfortunately, I would have to wait and pick another time. Dover Police Department bordered our community and they were an accredited agency by CALEA. Matter of fact, they got re-accredited for another five years while I still was in New Hampshire. Dover in my view was a very professional and respected police agency in the state. You would think that accreditation would be a much sought after process because accreditation recognizes professional excellence. Everyone wants to be recognized as professionals. The attitude I heard some people say, "Dover has plenty of money." Having money is nice to have but it is not the answer to everything. Even with tight budgets, if the will is there, then the project can be accomplished but it takes a great deal of work. There is no question about it. Anyone who thinks that they can take shortcuts will find they are sadly mistaken. Even though the accreditation process requires a strong commitment from everyone including the personnel and city fathers, it is possible that everyone who begins the project can successfully complete it.

What the Process Involves

By the time you are done the file cabinet will be full. It will require hundred of man-hours and a great deal of paper to complete the process. When you think that you are done, you will find there is more standard to add or modify. The average time it takes to complete the self-assessment phase is at least 24 months and some take longer. This is perhaps one of the most involved processes that I had ever seen. Looking at it from the beginning it appears to be an overwhelming task and for some and it very well be for some.

After you send in your completed application and fee, you are ready to begin. It is best to check out an accredited agency and talk to them about the dos and the don'ts. They have already gone through the process and probably made many mistakes so why repeat them. You will find these departments to be very helpful and will do everything to provide assistance and answer questions. It is nice to have a resource nearby to answer any technical question and there will be many. You still have to do the work. The accreditation manager is the person who organizes all the paperwork work but others have to contribute various pieces.

One problem that I see in the process, there is just too much work for one person to do. In a small department, the task would fall upon the shoulders of the police chief. It is very difficult but not impossible for the chief to do it by himself or herself. Taking into consideration all the other administrative responsibilities and some chiefs and managers actually have to work a shift because of the size of the department, there would be very little time left to work on the accreditation project. However, if the chief and other leaders want his or her agency to be accredited then there is a way. The chief could propose the project to the town or city council to obtain their endorsement to hire a part-time, or better yet a full-time person to be the accreditation manager to help with the re-write of the policy and procedures and organization of the paperwork. I have only known a few small departments that were successful in completing the project all the way to the end.

There are over 400 standards organized into 38 chapters. The mandatory and optional standards are applicable, depending upon the size of the agency. You have to document that it is a policy or procedure or city ordinance. It will probably require a re-write of your entire policy and procedure manual. I found it was best to start over and make sure all the standards are identified somewhere in the policy and procedure. CALEA outlines the process very well and the forms you have to use are available. For an example, I organized my manual according to the following chapters that made the process much easier for the state accreditation in Colorado:

Chapters	Table of Contents
I	Organization
II	General
II	Patrol
IV	Traffic Control and Investigations
V	Investigations
VI	Use of Force
VII	Arrests and Booking
VIII	Juveniles
IX	Court/Summons
X	Property/Evidence
XI	Records/Communications
XII	Training
XIII	Community Relations
XIV	Internal Affairs
XV	Discipline

XVI	Uniforms, Equipment and Appearance
XVII	Personnel Policies
XVIII	Code Enforcement

The titles for each chapter were found to be very useful for a small police department and even a medium agency. Several accreditation chapters in the CALEA manual were condensed into one chapter because it was easier for me. The main point is you need to organize it in such a way that you can easily find the policy and procedure you are looking for when you need it. Another point is that you have to be comfortable with the format. I used this format for three police departments and it worked very well.

I suggest that you use a regular three-ring notebook format. As you go along it will be easier to amend a policy and procedure or a page. All you have to do is replace the pages. In Fort Lupton, they had a small binder that had the pages reproduced at a printer. Doing it this way looks pretty but it is time consuming to make changes and then you have to get the pages reprinted. In addition doing it this way is more costly. Using the regular 8 ½ by 11 sheet of paper is much easier, quicker and less costly for reviewing, revising and adding new policy and procedures then it makes sense to use the regular size notebook. **This task is always a work in progress**. Some departments still make it easier by loading the policy and procedures manual into the computers so that all of their personnel have access to it. At least this way you do not have to print so many copies.

State vs. National Accreditation

Is it better to be State or Nationally Accredited? What it depends upon are the needs of the department, wishes of the town or city council and the real and hidden costs. The fees that you pay CALEA are only one small part of the cost. It is difficult to determine the hidden costs until you do a complete self-assessment. The time and salaries will be considerable. One person will have to devote most of his or her time on the project. This is where the small department has difficulty. The small department does not have the luxury of extra personnel. Another hidden cost is the possible changes to your facility. Some departments would have to make very expensive changes, which is difficult to do with a bare bones budget. Many of the standards zero in on high liability areas such as the booking area and lockup. The police chief may want to first take inventory of the building and compare to the applicable standard to see if they can comply. Some of the buildings are so outdated that police departments would have a difficult time in meeting these standards. The building used by the Somersworth Police Department was a former apartment building built during the early 1930s. The first floor was used as a retail store for years. The town fathers may not be happy about shelling out thousands of dollars to save a few dollars on their liability insurance premium. They may look at it as an unnecessary expense. The city is now planning for a new police department. I congratulate them on their efforts.

Unsurprisingly, you can use the argument that the police department does not meet professional standards and may very well be a liability problem in the end. The town fathers may approve a renovation or a new facility. When I was in Florence, Arizona, the facility was so outdated that it would have been a waste of time to begin the national accreditation process. Just as an example, the evidence room was behind the building in a garage. Two small rooms were part of the garage. If the on-site inspectors ever saw how the police department was set up, they would have died laughing. The building did not meet the existing code. At least there was no police lockup. Prisoners were transported to the Pinal County Jail about two miles away.

The plan was to relocate the police department to the former town hall across the street. The town had been making plans to build a new town hall, senior citizen center and renovate the vacant town hall into an updated police department. This would have been the right time to make the necessary changes with the accreditation standards in mind. After I was replaced, the new chief decided the old town hall was not good enough and he lobbied for a new building, so the town council put the project on hold and nothing was ever done until the current police chief took over the department. The building reminded me of an old sheriff's office right out of the old west. The chief failed to understand the political dynamics. After spending hundreds of thousands of dollars on the new town hall and senior center they were not about to build a new police department, but they would have spent the money to renovate the old town hall. It was a done deal. It would have been suitable for the police department. Anyway, the police chief need not apply for accreditation until they improve their facility. The town now has a new police department. I have to give credit to the current police chief, Bob Ingulli, for seeing the project become a reality.

In Fort Lupton, Colorado, it was an entirely different story. The municipal building was a fairly new facility built around 1985 and the police department was part of it. The State of Colorado has a State Accreditation available for police departments. Like New Hampshire, the state process dovetails into the accreditation for CALEA. When I arrived in Fort Lupton, they were already accredited by the state for five years. During the time I was there, the accreditation expired and I was actively pursuing state re-accreditation. It was still a great deal of work because I had to completely replace the policy and procedure manual, and revise, update it and include many new orders. The process is never complete. If you do it right, you are always reviewing, revising and updating orders as needed.

Once a department becomes comfortable with the process then they can proceed towards the national accreditation. It is a logical progression. I was planning to do just that but then I decided to leave the department.

Everything was all in order and this is where I find some criticism with the state accreditation that should be considered. Once the paperwork was in order, the department was ready for an on-site inspection. Because this was a voluntary program managed by the Colorado Association of Chiefs of Police, there seemed to be a backlog of departments waiting for the on-site team to arrive for the inspection. In all fairness, the on-site inspectors only did this work when they had time. They had their own duties at their police department. It took about six months for the on-site inspection team to make it to Fort Lupton after I had notified the chief's association that the self-assessment phase had been completed. One of the reasons why it took so long was they just forgot about our department. Finally, I was instructed to send the manual to the assessors. I waited and waited and I finally contacted them to get a firm commitment for the inspection date. The inspection occurred just a few weeks before I had left. The entire process was excessively long. I am patient but this was ridiculous. Anyway, they did write a favorable report recommending that the agency be state re-accredited for another five years. The final presentation of the certificate did not take place before the City Council until six months after I had left. If the state accreditation process is to be more meaningful, the inspection has to be done on a timely basis.

The State Accreditation may be the way to go if everything flows smoothly and it is a consideration and far cheaper than the accreditation for CALEA. There are not nearly as many standards but if you decide to go to the next level then it would be a logical approach and less complicated than starting from scratch. If I had known, that the process would have taken so long, I probably would not have bothered. It would be best to check to see if your state has an accreditation program, and many do. It would not hurt to check with a few departments to find out more about the state's process and about how long it would take from start to finish. There is nothing more frustrating than working hard to complete the process as expeditiously as possible, only having to wait for months for the evaluation. My opinion is if a state is going to get into the accreditation business then steps must be taken to avoid unnecessary delays. Colorado has a good process but it simply takes too long. They probably could get more departments involved in the process if they were more serious about it. The accreditation process was available to all police departments, but they did not do a very good job in promoting the program. I knew about it because Fort Lupton was already state accredited and I called the chief's association to find out more details about it. Maybe by now, they have improved their process.

If your state has a good accreditation program, it may be worthwhile to consider. The following are some reasons to consider the state accreditation program first rather than the accreditation by CALEA:

- Cost effective, no large fees
- Develop a comfort zone
- Manageable for small police departments
- User friendly
- Stepping stone to accreditation by CALEA
- State recognized professional excellence
- Not as many standards
- More achievable

These are just some of the things to consider. I am not saying the accreditation by CALEA is bad; it is just the opposite. CALEA has an outstanding accreditation program. The prudent thing to do is to check first with the state's police chief organization for departments in the process of becoming accredited and some that are already accredited. This way you can find out first hand about the process. More information on which departments are accredited can be located at CALEA's website.

If the cost is so prohibitive then it may be better to start with the state's accreditation program until you can get the town or city council to approve renovations to the facility so that it would meet the professional standards. At least you can get some productivity along the way instead of waiting around while nothing is done. Besides, if you can show the town or city council the importance of accreditation then they may buy into the program later on. When looking at almost $5,000 or more in fees depending upon the size of the agency for the accreditation program with nothing to show for it in the beginning, it may be a tough sell. At least CALEA allows an agency to pay in two installments.

What will the state or national accreditation do for the community? Are there good departments that are not accredited and the answer is yes. This is one question that is difficult to answer because I believe people are confused about what it is. People can see the emblem on the marked police vehicles and still not know about the program or what it means. An agency is accredited, but so what. The problem is that you cannot touch, feel or smell accreditation like the one you can with a capital outlay purchase.

Pro or Con

The decision to get involved in the accreditation process will probably be one of your most important decisions. First, you have to determine the pros and cons; evaluate the effectiveness of the program, like any other program, and make an informed decision.

The Pros

The first benefit, controlled liability insurance costs seems to be definitely positive but let us take a closer look. Controlling liability insurance costs would be in everyone's interest but it depends whether you are in the insurance pool or not. Most municipalities are in an insurance pool and this was the case in New Hampshire, Arizona and Colorado. I am sure it is similar in other states. If a department in the insurance pool has a lawsuit and there was a sizeable payout, all the departments will have an increase in their insurance premiums. Essentially all the departments share the potential exposure to a lawsuit. In Somersworth, New Hampshire the liability insurance premium kept increasing every year because other departments were getting sued and large settlements and judgments were paid out. It does not seem fair for the city to continue paying higher insurance premiums because of some bad departments in the insurance pool. It is like a crapshoot, when your insurance premiums are contingent upon the operations of other police departments. Some larger cities are self-insured and being accredited would perhaps lower the cost. If all the departments in the insurance pool were accredited then everyone could benefit in lower premiums. Nevertheless, **it may be better to check the possibility of being self-insured and staying out of the insurance pool**. Find out the potential cost savings if your department became accredited. The point being if your department is accredited and you are in the insurance pool with non-accredited departments, your insurance premium will still depend upon the overall results of all the departments in the pool. If a few bad departments had sizable judgments, then your department will share in the overall increased premiums. The statement about controlled liability insurance costs is questionable and maybe true in departments that are not in the insurance pool. However, the reality is most small and medium size police departments are in the insurance pool and share costs.

The second benefit, administrative improvements seem to be positive as well. It was my goal as well as other chiefs and managers to improve the operations of the police department. Going through the self-assessment phase insures an evaluation of each level of the organization but a police department should be continually evaluating its operations looking for ways to improve it anyway. A department going through the accreditation process will generate a great deal of paperwork and along with it, many checks and balances to insure the department complies with the professional standards. Sure, I agree there has to be administrative improvements with the accreditation process, but there are many departments at the same time that perform very well without it.   It is not critical to be accredited to achieve administrative improvements. It certainly can help but can be done without it. A police chief with **good management skills and a good staff** can accomplish the same thing.

The third benefit, greater accountability for supervisor seems to be a reasonable one too. Here again, if the police chief has good management skills he or she will insure that there is accountability among the supervisors. It should happen anyway with or without accreditation. The more the **supervisors are held accountable for their actions, the better managed the department will be and this in turn will keep liability problems in check.**

The fourth benefit, **increased governmental and community support** is easy enough to say but does it not happen anyway? In each of my three communities, I received tremendous governmental and community support. It was so because I had worked hard at it in each community. Even though Fort Lupton, Colorado was state accredited, there was very little support. This was my perception as well as others. Just because a police department is accredited, support from the community and town or city council may be short lived. The police chief as I had stated earlier must get out of his or her office and get out into the community to find out what it is going on. The initial rush from the department being accredited can quickly change to contempt towards the department. The police chief needs the support from the city council and community. Fortunately, for me I enjoyed both in Fort Lupton, but at the same time, I am a realist too. If there was an unfortunate incident, some police scandals or racial profiling then this support can quickly go away.

The fifth benefit, **stronger defense against lawsuits and citizen complaints is one of the most important benefits.** After all, policy and procedures have been put in place. If the policy and procedures are followed then it should provide good results, less exposure to civil suits and less citizen complaints. On the other hand, if a police chief in a non-accredited department has good policy and procedures to begin with and addresses internal affairs and citizen complaints, then it will accomplish the same thing. One accredited department had a lawsuit go against them because the defense attorney used the policy and procedures against them. Because there are so many policy and procedures, it is almost impossible to memorize each one. It holds true for my former agencies because I also had numerous policy and procedures. I was happy when they were familiar with them, enough to know the philosophy of the department. If there was any doubt about the contents the officer could just look up the applicable policy and procedure in their manual. There was no excuse because everyone was issued a manual for reference and they were expected to keep it up to date. Personally, I would rather have too many orders than not enough to address the everyday issues.

Last, there is **recognition among your peers in obtaining international recognition**.   No doubt, it is a worthy honor to be recognized as one of the best. Since this is such a worthy honor, why do more departments not get involved? There are only a small number of law enforcement agencies from each state that are accredited.   Many police chiefs that I had spoken to over the years have not provided me with an adequate answer or explanation about accreditation. I guess there are many that are just plain indifferent about it.

There are some other benefits to be an accredited agency by CALEA. Each member of the department should have pride in their organization. Many of the accredited departments that I know have higher salaries and they are able to recruit highly qualified individuals. As a chief, it is far easier to argue for a pay increase for your personnel if your department is recognized for its professional excellence. The Marines, a very well respected military organization have no trouble recruiting at all, when they advertise, "Be one of the best."   Everyone wants to associate themselves with the best so **an agency can use accreditation as a recruitment tool.**

I would agree that the community has confidence in their police department and even more so if the department practices Community Policing. The more that the community is involved the better in the end. Just because you are an accredited agency, the work does not stop. You continually have to work hard at it to make it work. A department does not have the luxury of resisting on its laurels. In reality, you can gloat for the moment but you have to continue the process. One of the reasons why the former police chief in Fort Lupton got into trouble was because he maintained the status quo. Everything just seemed to stop. There appeared to be no inclusion of any new policies and procedures after the manual was printed. There was no push to improve existing operations and improve the delivery of service to the community. This police chief was like a "sitting duck" floating in the water waiting for the politicians to do him in. He simply gave the politicians the opportunity to find reasons to terminate him. Though, on the positive side, I would be willing to bet that the longevity of police chiefs in accredited agencies is higher than non-accredited agencies. In addition, a former police chief from an accredited agency has a far easier time getting another police chief's position. Why is this so? The answer is simple, the mere fact that the police agency is accredited by CALEA carries with it professional status.

The Cons

So far, I discussed the benefits and the positives but there must be some criticism. There must be some negatives. The first negative is that the agency has created a **paper monster**. Once you start and finally complete the process, you can never return to the way it use to be. There is simply a ton of paperwork, documenting and supporting all the standards and doing the same for the new policy and procedures. Someone will have to remain as the accreditation manager to keep up with the changing standards and keep everything is up-to-date with the documentation. If you keep everything up the way it should be then the re-accreditation should just be a formality.

Another negative is **false expectations**. Just because a department is accredited, it is not the "Holy Grail" or cure all for all the ills of an organization.   If a department accomplishes its goal then it must continue to work hard to improve. The department's status implies excellence so everyone has to live up to it.

There should be more promotion and advertisement of the program by CALEA and the accredited department itself to entice other agencies to begin accreditation. More agencies would probably be interested in pursuing this program if they had more information. Even though this program is voluntary, there should be some effort by CALEA to get out and explain the program. Some police chiefs do not fully understand the program so why keep it a secret? The state organizations have been very helpful.

The technical support is a serious concern from my perspective. Once you get involved in the self-assessment phase that could take an average of 24 months or longer, you can always call CALEA for advice or visit an accreditation agency but there is no better method than to have personal contact with someone for technical advice.   Other words, contact with a live person would certainly expedite the process.

The small law enforcement agencies are left hanging. If you notice, the greater majority of law enforcement agencies accredited are medium and large departments. Most of them are large departments. They have the staff to assist them with the process.   Small departments do not have the luxury of staff to assist with the process. He or she may want to be involved in the process but simply do not have the time. A small agency can complete the process but it is much more difficult.

The novelty is short lived. Too often, the personnel and town fathers forget about the accreditation status. I think that there must be an on-going effort to keep the pride going. I can relate to this in my own department in Fort Lupton, Colorado.

If you want to know, ask what accreditation means to your personnel, and the citizens. After the initial excitement goes away, everyone seems to forget about it. Just wearing the accreditation pin on the uniform or displaying the emblem on the marked cruiser is not enough. Seems to me, there should be more effort to remind everyone about professional excellence.

In my mind, the positives far outweigh the negatives. The negatives are minor and in itself not enough to not consider the program. They are just something to think about and have thoughts about while considering the program. The difference in reality whether an agency will pursue accreditation or no depends upon what the town or city council will decide. They are the ones you have to convince that the accreditation by CALEA is worthwhile project to justify the expense. What matters is what the council is willing to spend. They may balk when you tell them about CALEA's fee. Some will tell you it is too much money. Nevertheless, the battle will be with the town or city council.

Some Final Thoughts on Accreditation

Is accreditation worth the expense and effort? In my humble opinion, it is worth it. Who would not want to be recognized for professional excellence? If someone said otherwise they would be kidding themselves. It is the essence of being a police chief and good leaders to develop your department to be the best it can be and accreditation is the vehicle. It is too bad more departments are not involved in the process.

When we look at high schools and colleges, we know that they have to go through an accreditation process. It means something to them in the academic world. The same holds true for law enforcement. Recognition as a professional department by CALEA means something. Why do they not make it mandatory for all law enforcement agencies? This is the question that bothered me for a long time. I know about state mandated requirements and the costs involved. Municipalities have to pay out thousands of dollars to meet state mandated requirement all the time and mandating CALEA could be a significant expense. If the state mandates the program then is the state obligated to pay for it? I am sure this is a major consideration in whether the program would be mandated or not.

If I have had the opportunity to seek accreditation by CALEA then I certainly would have pursued it. I would have had a little problem in Florence, Arizona but if there is a will, there was a way. Even if you have a small agency, it is still possible to get accredited. If your willpower is strong and you have a commitment from your staff then it can be done. I think the expense is easily justified. Having a nationally recognized police department is a worthy goal to pursue anytime.

Chapter 21
Risk Taking: When to Gamble

The police chief and top executives periodically has to take a risk. In this world nothing is perfect, so when is it necessary to take the risk and how far do you go is the question? Obviously, if the risk taking is so wild then it may cost the police chief or leader his or her job. On the other hand, if the police chief leader has good information before making a decision then it would be a good gamble. The odds would be on your side. In this chapter, I will discuss some of my good decision along with some of my bad ones too. If I had thought about it more carefully, the risk taking would not have been very critical. If the police chief or manager does not want to take a risk then he or she are in the wrong profession. Risk taking is the very nature of the business. The sign of a good police chief or leader is the willingness to take risks when the situation calls for it.

In the beginning being a new police chief in Somersworth, New Hampshire, it was a feeling out process for everyone including me. I did not know the key players and they did not know me. Here I was as a decision making, which was new for me. In my former department, Bristol, Connecticut I could at least ask the supervisor as I was going up the chain of command. Being second in command is not so bad; at least you can consult with the police chief for advice. I was new in Somersworth and I wanted to do the right thing so I depended upon my staff to give me good information. This was mistake number one. I should have evaluated the information they were giving me very closely. At the same time, I did not want to discourage creativity so I was reluctant to say no on occasion. I use the following analogy to illustrate my point. It was like running an obstacle course at night without a flashlight. Sometimes luck is on your side and other times it is not. After I got burnt a few times on poor advice from staff, namely the patrol commander, I began to rely on good old common sense and asking questions of others. I quickly learned that many of the captain's decisions were spur of the moment without much thought or more important, without facts. This officer was from the old school of policing. Perhaps, you know someone like him. If you did not know the answer, you winged it. Apparently, he did not learn very much from the FBI's National Academy for police executives. I am not trying to be overly critical of one person and to single him out unfairly. This person was a hometown good old boy, if you know what I mean. You may have one or two on your department and you have to be careful. A person with hometown connections can create problems for the police chief coming into a new community. He was a good-hearted person but when it came to making management decisions, he was way out of his league. Any good chief or manager needs to have the best information available before making an important decision. I think most of my decisions were good because I did not rely on any one person and it took me a while to get to this point. I quickly learned that if I relied on one person without checking out the facts, then it would have been a short-lived tenure for me as police chief. If I was going to sink, I did not need help from someone else.

One decision I recall involved a hiring decision. The patrol commander needed some more part time police officers to help out with the shifts. He wanted me to circumvent the hiring process and hire a few people he knew. I told him that we had a process in place and we were going to follow it. Of course, he did not agree with me because these individuals were already certified. Against my better judgment, I agreed to hire two certified officers after having them go through the hiring process. Perhaps, I was just trying to appease him and win him over. Ordinarily, I would have checked further into their background to find out why they would want to leave a higher paying position with an accredited department. This alone has to tell you something. My gut feeling told me this was a bad decision. I asked the patrol captain if he had checked them out and he told me he did. He said, "There were no problems." I gambled with these two individuals and lost. The first officer left after serving almost a year to become a police chief in a one-person department. The other officer I terminated while he was on probation after he was involved in a serious accident with the police cruiser. He had been in route to an alarm and lost control of his marked police cruiser striking a telephone pole. Now we were left with two vacant positions and we had to repeat the testing process and start all over again.

The decision would have been easier to make had we completed a thorough background investigation. On the surface, it looked too good to be true. We were "stealing" from an accredited agency and we felt good about it. They did not mind losing these officers after all; they were replaced in no time. Had we checked further both officers were problems to the agency. The officer who had gotten into a wreck had problems with driving too fast. Well what do you know! It was like the reverse sting. They could not wait to unload these officers. If the truth were known, any police chief or manager would not mind losing the "five per centers." They are the ones who cause grief for the police chief and supervisors. If we had done it right in the beginning, we should never have cut corners. I made up my mind that this fiasco would never happen again. After you learn from your own mistakes, you become more cautious.

Now I do not mind taking a risk but you have to be careful about committing professional suicide. Take for example, when the City of Somersworth hired a new city manager in 1990 I thought I could be clever and try to promote some programs behind his back. I figured the mayor and most of the council members were on my side. It is called doing an "end run" around the manager. By this time, I thought I was pretty well connected and no doubt, this was a risky move on my part. He found out that I was lobbying behind his back to get some additional funding and in no time, he called me into his office. He laid the law down to me and rightly so. We had a nice talk but in no uncertain terms, he stated that it better not happen again. I never tried to pull that stunt again. I had to remember the city council hired this person for a reason and the picture began to get clearer. He was the boss and I was not going to forget it. From then on I always went to see the city manager first and then got his permission to approach the council members. He did not like to have anyone approaching the mayor and council members without his knowledge. He also wanted to know if any had approached me. Some might think he was paranoid but he was just watching his back.

Police chiefs and some managers are in their own right powerful political figures. Do not let anyone tell you otherwise. However, some police chiefs think that they have so much political clout that they do not have to follow orders by the town or city manager. I have seen it happen so often to my fellow chiefs. Their risk taking was fatal to their professional career. In this case, a former police chief who had graduated from the FBI's National Academy and past President of the New Hampshire Association of Chiefs of Police was told by the town manager that he could not charge the maintenance account to fix the police cruiser. Apparently, the account was overspent. He decided that he was the big chief and no one could tell him what to do, so he charged the account anyway without telling the town manager. Guess what? The town manager terminated his employment with the town and there was nothing he could do about it. No one came to his rescue to reverse the termination. All his years with the town, graduating from the prestigious FBI's National Academy and being president of the police chief's association did not matter. He was gone. Sometimes, taking a foolish risk just does not make sense. If I had ignored the warning from the city manager then I would have been gone too. The council's hired gun will win every time and he or she will get the support from the council.

One other risk that I want to discuss involved the former mayor of Somersworth and at the time, he was a state legislator. My sergeant approached me about a complaint involving the person's former wife. She had found a tape recording device in her basement and she suspected her former husband who no longer lived there. I said to myself, "Great I am going to lose my job because we have to arrest a person politically connected." This person knew everyone in the community including most of the department. He was a personal friend with both captains.

After thinking about it, the choice was obvious; I decided that we would conduct a stakeout by hiding an officer in the basement while the complainant was gone for the day. Sure enough, the suspect, the former mayor showed up and he were immediately arrested. Incidentally, I did not tell my management staff about the stakeout until the arrest was made. This was a good gamble because the law was on my side. How can you argue against this? The community, mayor and city council were solidly behind me. One council member told me, "He got what he deserved." The former mayor was mad at me but he should be mad at himself for being stupid. Maybe he thought he was above the law, and he quickly found out he was not.

I found that risk taking and worrying about the politicians when enforcing the law should never be a problem. You can always fall back upon the law that it is your duty to enforce it no matter who it is. The motto, "Justice is Blind" is true. This was my first difficult decision that I had to make regarding the course of action to take without consulting my staff. When they found out about it I told them it was better that they did not know and it was not mentioned anymore.

My time in New Hampshire was a good experience. I felt confident as time went on that I could make the right decision. A police chief or leader has to be a risk taker and know what a good gamble is. If you cannot make a decision then you are in the wrong business. Taking risks is certainly a gamble with your future. It can be physically and emotionally draining and can lead to financial ruin. I knew a few chiefs who were like that. After awhile you develop a sixth sense so eventually you will be increasing your odds in making a good decision.

In my case in Somersworth, New Hampshire, after I had been there for a while I began to get a feel for the position. There were those individuals in my department that you can rely on to get the straight facts. I was one individual who wanted to get the facts, good, bad or indifferent. I did not want to have individuals who only wanted to tell me good news. Some individuals, as in my previous examples, depended upon less for the facts. Unfortunately, this person was in a management position.

Fear in Failing

I do not know any police chief or manager who wanted to fail, but so many do. Why does this happen? I believe it equates to risking taking and making poor choices. Other police chiefs and executives who succeed and have long tenures learned to be crafty in making sound decisions. Do they take risks? Sure, they do but the difference is betting on a sure thing. Other words they are making better decisions with facts from trusted staff. The crafty police chief or leader who has been around for a long time generally has had the luxury of trusted staff in place, so he or she can count on them for good advice. Just surround yourself with good people and turn them to do their jobs. Good things will happen. Just the opposite will happen with a bad one in place. You will have to learn, as I needed to, in how to deal with it. In the private sector, it is fairly easy to hire good management staff. If someone does not fit it then he or she is quickly replaced. The reality is that in law enforcement it is very difficult to get rid of management staff when a new chief comes in from the outside. Usually this management type person has been a fixture in the police department for many years and has strong community ties. If you try to fire him right away, it is just like taking on the community. Finding cause to remove this management person from a responsible position takes time.

In Somersworth, New Hampshire when there was an important matter to be discussed, I liked to involve my management staff to hear their thoughts and ideas. After a while, you will learn which individuals make sense supporting their ideas with facts against those that are winging it. I use to ask them to give me reasons and some use to give me the blank stare like I was challenging their judgment. I suppose it did cross my mind, but I was looking for was facts to support the decision. After I got burnt a few times relying on this captain's advice early in my tenure I still listened but checked with others too. The reality occurs when you first come into the community you are looked upon with suspicion and the individuals who are seeking the police chief's or top executive's position may have ulterior motives for wanting you to fail. The captain who applied for and did not get the police chief's appointment was not going to make me look good. I understood the games that he was playing and I treated him accordingly. If he suggested something, I would not agree until I thought about it more. The truth of the matter was that I wanted to check out the facts first because his judgment was questionable.

You can apply this to any management position. I knew a lieutenant in Bristol, Connecticut who appeared to go into a panic attack every time something happened on his shift. He would walk around, rant and rave about his bad luck working on the shift. He would say, "Why does this happen to me?" I use to think to myself that this ranking officer was falling apart. Where would he be if we had needed his leadership? The personnel can sense this and are reluctant to approach a person like this. It was very difficult for him to make a decision and I truly believed he had a fear of failing. Many times, he would procrastinate before making the decision and I am sure you can relate this fear of failing to others. The point is that **it is acceptable to get input from others before making an important decision**. When I was a street sergeant he could have ask me, but no, he decided to agonize by himself.

If a police chief or leader is reluctant to make a decision sooner or later, he or she will be forced to make one. Hopefully, he or she will have all the facts. Sometimes I wonder about staff intentionally dreaming up problems to present to the police chief or supervisor to take care of it. The days go by and everything seems to be running smoothly when someone from the management staff will present a problem. Most the time these problems could easily be handled by the person after giving it some thought but no, they hold it for the chief and/or leader. When this happens, I usually turn the situation around and ask them what he would do under these circumstances. At this point, I would tell them I would need some more information before making the decision.

In each of my previous departments, I considered myself a cautious risk taker. I did not consider myself reckless. As I got more comfortable with the position, I gained more confidence in myself. In the interest of traffic safety, I decided to have public works put up no u-turn signs in all the intersections in the downtown area in Florence, Arizona. I decided to take on a tradition that lasted for generations. Motorists were cruising up and down Main Street and making u-turns in the middle of the intersections. This maneuver was creating a traffic safety problem. Based upon come close calls with pedestrians almost being hit by cars even though it was tradition, I decided it was time to take action. People thought I was crazy and wondered if it was necessary. Sure, it was a gamble but it was the right thing to do. The law was on my side whether people agreed with me or not. As it turned out, people were starting to joke about it and it was accepted. Matter of fact, even though I have been gone for a while the signs are still there. This little thing turned out to be a big deal after all. Even today, people are still speaking about the no u-turn signs.

Some suggestions to handle the fear of failing would be:

- Trust your instincts
- Make the decision with good information.
- Do rely on trustworthy staff
- If the odds are not good delay the decision
- Avoid Procrastination
- Do the right thing
- Make the decision and move on

Let me say another word about making the decision with good information. After a while, you will be able to depend on certain members of your staff that over time you had developed a mutual trust. Do not try to appease someone who had competed for the police chief's or manager's position and lost like I tried to do. I tried to use some psychology on this person and it did not work. His head was harder than the table so to speak. No matter what you do it will be very difficult to turn around a bitter employee. His or her motivation is waiting until you fail so he or she can get your job. I learned from past experience not to trust the judgment of someone who is a disgruntled employee. After I left the department, the other captain in charge of patrol and investigations became the police chief. One day a few years ago, we had a telephone conversation about this same captain. The new chief could not get him to do anything. Well, what do you know it was finally sinking in? He asked me my advice. I think he understood what I had been going through all those years. I told him that if I had still been there it would have led to termination. It was not too long after our conversation when this captain put in his papers to retire. It was a good choice but a difficult one at the same time because they were once close friends. You have heard the expression, "You can't teach old dog new tricks." In this case, it was very true.

The key is getting the facts. The more information the chief or manager has the easier the decision. Even still, if something does not appear to be right delay the decision. I delayed the decision at times because the timing was not right. Do some of the decisions backfire? Sure, no one is perfect, even the police chief and top executives.

Some communities are different. In Florence, Arizona, it was quite an experience working with the town council. I did not know what to expect at times because the recall council was in place. They had already terminated the town manager who recommended me to be the police chief. Even after the mayor and several council members told the staff everything would remain the same, I did not quite believe them. I took the attitude that if they did not like some of my decisions then they would tell me. However, they did just the opposite, and told me I was doing a great job. They gave me a false sense of security.

One of the most probable reasons why the former town manager was terminated was because he had fired the former police chief. It had turned into an ugly mess. As I had stated early the town manager had no choice but to fire him. During my two years in dealing with the former police chief, my police officers arrested him on three different occasions. This person would not go away or change his ways. Every time we dealt with one of his sons, this person would run around like a lunatic and harass my officers. I do not think you can find any greater risk than taking on a former crazed policy chief. The choice was to ignore him even though he was creating a misdemeanor offense or arrest him. Knowing the political ramifications and the rapport the former chief had with the mayor and current council members, it was a huge risk. However, he left me very little choice but to make sure he was arrested just like anyone else. If I did not than I should not be upholding the oath of office I had sworn to protect and would have lost all credibility in the eyes of my personnel and community.

In each case, the town had to get a special prosecutor and judge because of a conflict of interest. He was found guilty in each case. It was no surprise because we had excellent cases.   After he was found guilty, the judge sentenced him to probation. No one was picking on him as he implied; it was just the opposite. I certainly would have left him alone. Even though the town council did not say anything except that he got what was coming, I knew they did not truly meant it. Besides, he was a friend with everyone on the council. There was no doubt in my mind that he was politicking behind my back to get the council to not renew my contract. If I had to do it all over again, I would have done it the same way. Integrity means a great deal in this profession.

This situation that I just described was a no win situation. There was no way out of it. I did what had to be done and I knew sooner or later there would be some fallout. The general feeling of the community was that the former chief deserved to be arrested for his outrageous actions. When it was time to renew my contract I believe, it was payback. The town council did not renew my contract. In retrospect, I could not have made the decision any different. I have not regrets. Life goes on and you to live with your decisions look forward and not look back.

This community was strange. The former police chief ran for a council seat after I had been gone from the department for a while and to my amazement the people elected him. How quickly do people forget? He was later elected mayor. Even though the people in the community thought he got what he deserved, they still elected him. This former police chief was also a thorn in the side of the police chief who replaced me. This eventually led to his contract being terminated. They did me a big favor in getting me out of that situation.

A police chief or manager in any community, such as Florence or anywhere else cannot worry about losing his or her job. I have known people like this who were so fearful that their decision-making was poor. Sometimes it gets to be ridiculous when a police chief or executive is too overly cautious, but the decision still has to be made.

Take the Leap

How many times have you been in a situation wondering whether to take action or wait. I think we all have been in this situation before. Sometimes you just have to take the leap and not look back. The situation was far easier in Fort Lupton, Colorado. The city council gave me loads of confidence when they told me to do what it takes to straighten out the police department. Having the endorsement up front for me surely helped with the decision-making. One key is to find out from the council what their expectations are and the parameters on taking action. The mayor told me many times to treat everyone the same and there would be no favorites. It was music to my ears. The mayor was a straight shooter. He told you exactly what he was thinking whether you liked it or not. We had a mutual respect for one another and I enjoyed working for him. It was one of those rare situations where we just clicked. Why is this important? I was able to step up my risk taking and not worry about the city administrator or anything else.

Here is an example of what I mean. When I first took over, as the police chief the city council had not hired another city administrator. The interim city administrator was in a situation way over his head and in some cases, he was interfering in the police department's business. Ordinarily either you speak to the city administrator directly about his interference or just not say anything. I did speak to the city administrator about the problem but he did not quite get the picture. His lack of experience in dealing with police departments showed. I went to see the mayor to discuss the situation. Yes, I did the end run around the manager again. You would have thought I had learned my lesson in New Hampshire, but this time the situation was different. What happens is you get a feel for what you can do and get away with.

A woman made an appointment to see me in my office about a problem. She related an incident to me that she was a sexual assault victim by her brother more than 20 years ago in another state. When I asked her more questions I found out her conscious recollection had been repressed regarding this incident until she had gone to see her psychiatrist. During one of her visits, she was hypnotized and that was when she started to recall these events. She wanted the police department to do something about it. I told her that the case was beyond the statute of limitations and the alleged incident occurred in another state. Unfortunately, I told her we would not be able to do anything. Apparently, she did not agree with me and went to see the interim city administrator. Her brother at the time was a volunteer coach helping out in the city's recreation department. She was afraid that he would do harm to the little boys. This individual had been coaching for a while and there had never been any complaints about him. The interim city administrator told her that he would take care of it. He had a conversation with the coach and told him that because of a complaint from his sister he could no longer be alone with the kids. He would have to have another adult there too.

I could not believe my ears when the interim city administrator told me. Not that he had to, but he should have consulted with me first to get my viewpoint. Without any sort of evidence other than the word of a woman and even her information was questionable, the city administrator insinuated that the coach was a suspected child molester. Keep in mind that there was no evidence at all. I believe that the interim city administrator put the city in a severe liability situation. The coach after I spoke to him said that he was very upset and was thinking about suing the city. I told him that I would go to the mayor. I went to see the mayor and laid the whole thing on him. I told him that the interim city administrator overstepped his bounds. He got involved in something that was police business. By this time, the interim city administrator was getting into hot water over some other stupid moves and the city council had just about enough. The city council was close to hiring someone else as the permanent city administrator so they let this person go.

Ordinarily I would have not run interference but in this case, it was necessary because he was hurting the police department and the city. It got back to me that he was saying some uncomplimentary things about the police department. I was part of the selection committee that recommended the current city administrator. He was an accountant or "bean counter" from another community in Colorado and it was his first job as a manager. Everything was going good or so I thought when he announced at a staff meeting that his open door policy was not open anymore. He introduced his secretary as the "Bossette" and instructed us to make an appointment if we wanted to see him. Maybe he did not mean it but he was telling the staff he was too busy to speak to us. There were a few times when he would call me over to his office and ask why he was not informed about an important incident. I politely told him he was busy at the time. This continued on for a while until I spoke to the mayor. Here I was taking a risk again in dealing with the manager. Apparently, the mayor was hearing it from other staff as well and he informed the city administrator that he would have to take the time to meet with his staff during the day. The open door policy was quickly reinstated.

You are probably wondering about my risk taking behavior by this time. Under any other circumstances, I would not have even attempted it but Fort Lupton was different. I had an excellent relationship with the mayor and at the time, he was instrumental in making a great deal of changes for the city. This mayor and four other council members recalled the former city council for mismanagement of city government and they got elected. Let me tell you one thing the mayor was one in a million. He had the common sense and political savvy to bring about changes for the better in Fort Lupton. It was too bad that I did not work for him longer and better yet, what a difference he would have made in my previous two communities. Over the two years that I was police chief, we developed a close relationship. I knew he was an honest man after my first meeting with him. He told it the way it was and even though at times it was crude, it was a pleasant change. How often can you get the truth out of a politician that talks out of both sides of his mouth as we hear so often?

I understood the relationship and knew what I could get away with even to the extent in complaining about the city administrator. It was frustrating for the mayor because he could not understand why good employees were leaving the city. I understood why. Many did not like the new city administrator at first. He was never a city administrator and Fort Lupton was his first attempt. Being new myself, I understood it would take time. I have to say he did make some adjustments to evolve into his own management style. I have to admit that the city administrator was developing into a good manager. The truth of the matter was that I eventually did enjoy working for him. He was very supportive of what I was trying to do after we got to know one another better. Once he got to know me, he depended upon me more often. He even appointed me as acting city administrator during his absence.

When it was getting close for me to leave the department I told him that I did enjoy working for him and the reason for my wanting to leave was for family considerations. I made sure the mayor and council members understood because I did not want to give anyone an excuse to blame the city administrator for my leaving the city. The heat certainly would have been on the manager had I said otherwise.

Taking risks backfired on the court clerk. She was the person who had been promised a police officer position and eventually sued the city. The city settled out of court and she received a sizeable settlement to the tune of over $60,000. Her reputation in how she took the city to the cleaners was all over the city. Now, I know that she did not care about the city administrator and she told me many times. She was an extremely intelligent woman but at the same time, devious. She was trying to get me to join with her in her quest to get rid of the city administrator. I understood her scheme and there was no way I was going to get involved. There is no quicker way in ending a career than to foolishly try to get rid of the city administrator. You have to remember one thing the town or city council hired the manager and before they would let him go, he would really have to screw up badly.

It was getting to a point where the manager could not trust her anymore. Apparently, he heard what she had been trying to do behind his back and since Colorado is a right to work state, she could not hide behind the union. The manager called her into his office one afternoon and fired her. She was always trying to stir up trouble with the other town hall employees playing one against the other and apparently the manager had enough. She was history. She read the city administrator wrong; she did not think that she was going to get fired. I guess she found out that he had the backbone to do it. She did not get any sympathy from the mayor or council members because they remembered the lawsuit. It was now payback. She got an attorney and served the city notice to sue. At this point in time, I do not know the outcome but I can guess that she was not successful. She mistakenly thought that because she successfully sued the city and received a judgment that she could do whatever she wanted. She did get away with some things but eventually it backfired. Being reckless as in her case will eventually spell dome.

Knowing what kind of risk you can take is a guessing game. It depends on how lucky you feel. It is critical for the police chief and other leaders to fully understand his or her relationship with the manager, mayor and council members. If you are not sure then you have to spend the time to find out. While the relationship is good, you can do more and not worry about the consequences. This was what I enjoyed in Fort Lupton, Colorado. The former court clerk understood my relationship with the mayor and city council members so she thought she could use me to gang up on the city administrator. Unfortunately, it did not work.

Looking at Florence, Arizona again, I considered my relationship with the town council good but I did not trust them at all. I knew my relationship with the mayor and town council members were cautious at best, so taking the big leap was not about to happen. However, arresting the former police chief on three separate occasions as I had previously explained was a major risk but there was no other choice.

Challenge the Process

After you understand the players in city government, the police chief and top executives needs to challenge the process in further developing the police department to be the best it can be. There are too many police chiefs and managers alike that maintain the status quo. No one likes to see the chief or leader just sitting back like a "fat cat" and doing nothing. By not paying attention to business morale problem could develop and some police personnel may even be plotting an attempt to undermine the chief or manager.

My philosophy is to stretch the limit and keep my personnel involved. If you are not reaching that ultimately involves some risk taking then you are not doing your best. Every police chief and leaders takes risks, some more than others, but the trick is understanding your limitations.

Let me describe a situation that occurred in Somersworth, New Hampshire. I had been the police chief only for a short time when I wanted to make improvements in the Dispatch Center. The civilian dispatchers wore civilian clothing to work. They looked neat and clean but I wanted to project a professional image. I inquired with the city council to see if it was feasible to put the dispatchers in uniform. Most thought it was a great idea but one said it would never happen as long as he was a council member. This council member was also a member of the Finance Committee so he had a great deal of influence with the others. I was kind of taken by this because I was hired to restore normalcy and at the same time professionalize the department. I did not want to say," I do not work for you, I work for the city manager." I just let the matter drop for the time being until the timing was right. Sure enough, this council member decided not to run for council again and this time I got my budget proposal through for uniforms. It did not take me long and in no time, the dispatchers were wearing uniforms.

One thing you have to remember, **"Never say never."** Just because a council member decides not to run for council it does not mean he or she will not run again. Try not to burn your bridges. I never gloated about my victories. I just went about my business and above all, it was important to stay professional. You never know when this individual might return to the political arena. Sure enough some years later he decided to run for council again and won his seat back. Politicians come and go but sometimes they come back. Perhaps, he eventually found out about the uniforms for my dispatchers. He never asked about it and I did not volunteer any information. It was best to leave it alone. It was a good move taking everything into consideration. The morale among the dispatchers was good and once they were in uniform, they gave an appearance of professionalism.

Timing is everything!

Many times, I waited until the timing was right. The timing is everything when weighing the risks. The odds improve considerably because the situations changes like as I stated in my previous example. Had I been obstinate and tried to do it anyway then I would have been the loser.

One critical example of timing was the time when I decided to reorganize the police department; mainly it was a creative approach, to do something about my ineffective captain. This officer was killing the morale in the patrol division and he complained about everything. I wanted to advance the department further and he was in my way. I needed someone else to direct the operations of the patrol division. It was huge risks for me because this captain was well know in the community and had political connections on the city council. It would have been career suicide for me to try and terminate him because the timing was not right. I did the next best thing and that was to transfer him to be the support services commander. The investigations captain was now the operations commander and his duties included the patrol division too.

Knowing your Limitations

In each of my communities, I challenged myself to make the departments the best it can be. I did not rest on my laurels when a program was put in place. I always kept looking for ways to improve. I think after awhile it becomes second nature to take risks. The more comfortable you are in a particular situation the more confident you will be in making decisions. I was very confident in Fort Lupton. There was nothing I would not try. Failing was not in my vocabulary.

It helps to know your limitations as for example, your authority given by the manager, mayor and city council. In addition, it is important if not one of the key elements in determining the capabilities of your staff. The more trustworthy and reliable the staff, the better choices there will be for risk taking. In Fort Lupton, my staff was experienced and I could rely on them for suggestions to make improvements in the department or even new programs. Many of my staff was enthusiastic in trying out new ideas. They were receptive to new ideas and overall it was an excellent situation for me.

Is Gambling Necessary?

Is gambling necessary in risk taking? The answer is obvious there are certainly degrees in risks. Some risks are good and some are bad. The police chief or manager has to decide for him or herself, which are the good risks. You can increase the odds by basing your decisions on good information and facts.

What happens if you make a bad choice and the situations whatever you are in does not work out? You can do one of two things, you can pack your bags and move on or you can accept responsibility. Admitting when you made a mistake is a big part of risk taking. Take for example; I had a dilemma with a police sergeant in Somersworth, New Hampshire. This person was the acting chief when I got to Somersworth and he was very active in the union. Every time I turned around, he was siding with the union. Was he part of management or union? When there was a grievance or any issue involving the union he would march into my office. This was the same individual who left the antique gun in my desk. The investigations captain probably said it best when he said, "Promote him to lieutenant and get him out of the union." Every time there was a grievance he would be sitting across the table from me at the city manager's grievance hearing and the personnel advisory board hearing. Even though I never lost a grievance or any issue involving a personnel matter, he was getting on my nerves. The men looked to him for advice in personnel issues. This sergeant was a very capable and resourceful person.

I was beginning to exclude him from everything. He was like a cancer that I had to get rid of and I truly believed it. However, after a while I realized what I was doing was not fair to the individual. I was mistakenly looked at it as a personal issue when it was not. They were personnel issues involving management and the person who was stirring up trouble and adding fuel to the fire was the patrol captain. I realized I was making some erroneous decisions on some bad information. My gamble to exclude the sergeant from everything was backfiring. The investigations captain and I spoke about it and he even commented that it was the wrong thing to do. Now, some police chiefs would be stubborn and say, "It is my way or the highway." Some would continue to ostracize an individual and I know it happens. I know it happens because when police chiefs get together one of the favorite topics to discuss is the idiot you have to deal with everyday.

I thought about it and decided to mend the fences. I called him into my office one day and apologized for leaving him out of decisions. He just sat there for a minute and looked at me in disbelieve. I guess he could not believe what I had said. I thought that I had been operating outside my parameters and was starting to take some of these issues personal. It was time to clear the air. We had a very good discussion that seemed to be very beneficial. I guess you might say it was risky to show a sign of weakness but in this case, it was not. Communication was the key. Some chiefs would never show a sign of weakness and they would fall on their sword first. He could have gone out of my office and made a big joke out of it to my personnel, but he never did. I have to respect him for that and the gamble paid off because I never had a bit of trouble from him after that.

After I left the department, the new chief eventually promoted this sergeant to captain and I am sure he did an excellent job. I always said that he had the ability, there was no question about it but his priorities were doubtful.

One thing for sure during my times in three departments I enjoyed the challenge in taking risks. Most of the time my decisions were good and they got better with experience. Taking too many unnecessary risks can take its toll on the police chief and other leaders. Who knows how many police chiefs and managers went out because of heart and hypertension and other physical ailments? Do not be one of those individuals. Make your decision based on good information and increase the odds so the risk is minimal.

Chapter 22
The Ultimatum: Resign or Fired

There is no worse feeling than the dreaded ultimatum. Some do not even have the luxury of the ultimatum. What are the police chiefs and other leaders going to do when the world seems to be crumbling down? Like in a poker game, you have to know when to hold them or fold them. It may sound too simplistic. Is it possible to resurrect your career if suddenly you are given the choice to resign or be fired? Yes, it is possible. Depending upon the circumstances it is possible to rise up after a humiliating ordeal and move on to bigger and greater things. Anything is possible if you do it right. In this chapter, I will describe what happened to me in Florence, Arizona. I know what it is like to find you are without a job. You are the police chief one day and you are mister citizen the next and not by your choice. I will discuss these situations and more and provide some suggestions if you find yourself in this dilemma.

I have known quite a few police chiefs who had received the ultimatum including one was my close friends from Bristol, Connecticut. The average tenure of a police chief is about three years but I think it may be less. In each of my communities, I have seen police chiefs come and go and you start to question yourself about it. They cannot be all bad. How many of them really deserved to be fired? I would venture a guess, very few. As you are going along you think that nothing would happen to you and when it does happen you are devastated.

Florence, Arizona was a nice community or so I thought. Originally, when I was hired the town manager and the town council wanted me to professionalize the department and bring it into the twentieth century. I was up to the challenge like many other police chiefs. They were so far behind that anything I did would have been an improvement. Little did I realize the dynamics would quickly change after the town council was recalled and the town manager was fired? All this happened after I had been there for three months. Nevertheless, I was committed to make the system work and I devoted myself to the task of improving the police department. I had a house built, moved in and felt like a part of the community.

One thing I would think about very seriously is whether to buy a house or not. The council usually requires the police chief to live within the community and I understand it. Matter of fact, I agree the police chief should live in the community he or she works. When the chief buys a home, it usually shows an honest commitment. Even back in Fort Lupton, Colorado the mayor and council were

428 Patrick L. Cote

questioning why it was taking so long for the city administrator to move into the community. Even then, he told them he could not afford to buy a home and found one to rent. Thinking about it now, it was a smart move. If you buy a home, you are just going to have to sell it and sometimes it takes a long time. The important thing is that you want to start clean in your next community without worrying whether or not if you would be able to sell your house. Even though I had sold my house quickly, I still had to make double mortgage payments for about three months.

Fortunately, for me I had a six-month severance clause in my contract that guaranteed my salary in the event the town terminated me or they did not renew my contract even if there was no justification. See Addendum A for details of an Employment Contract. This provision was binding upon the municipality until I found another job. I was not in a hurry to find another one right away. The town council knew about my contract and mentioned that they did not like the severance clause but they had no choice. They had to pay. Many towns and cities do not like it for obvious reasons. In order to get rid of a police chief without cause they have to pay. In addition to the severance pay, the police chief is entitled to unemployment compensation. The former town manager of Florence told me about this one. I was simply amazed. I asked him, "You mean to say they still have to pay unemployment even if I get severance pay?" I went to the unemployment office and filed the claim. There was no problem and I received maximum benefits. I made more money during these six months taking it easy than I would have made if I had been working.

In summary, you have to consider very carefully the following:

- Whether or not to purchase or rent a home
- Insist on a contract or a memorandum of understanding with a severance clause
- Even though you may be terminated even with a contract, you are probably eligible for unemployment benefits

The Shock

There is nothing more disheartening than to be called into the executive session of the council meeting and not know the actual purpose. It was the feeling that I had been experiencing when on a Friday afternoon I found out that I was the topic of discussion for the executive session just before the council was to meet in public session on the following Monday evening. I thought perhaps the council was going to discuss my contract renewal. I never thought they would have terminated me after I have had raving review from the council the previous July and rewarded me with a generous raise. I asked the town manager and the town attorney about the purpose and they stated they did not know the reason. Personally, I think they must have known and did not want to tell me. There was not even a hint of a possible termination. I believed that they were going to renew my contract and give me another raise. There was no other reason to think otherwise. I am sure many other chiefs and top executive experienced similar circumstances, not knowing until the actual meeting.

The dreaded Monday evening came and I was summoned into the executive session. I called this event the "Saint Patrick's Day Massacre." I had gone into detail in an earlier chapter about the discussion that took place so I will be brief. The session turned into a kangaroo court. Each council member took turns and expressed their dissatisfaction about my performance and the morale problem in the department. I was utterly flabbergasted and could not believe my ears. Just the week before one council member was complimenting me about the job I was doing. Therefore, I thought, "What happened to change their minds?" It was apparent to me I could see their direction they were taking. When one council member mentioned morale of the department was low, I could not believe it. I asked them "are you taking about the same department?" I suspected an individual was giving the council incorrect information. I later found out it was one of my sergeant who aspired to be the police chief. I tried to refute this information but the council member said he did not believe me. Another council member wanted to know, "Why did you not fire the lieutenant like we told you." I told them I was not going to terminate someone without justification. After awhile I could see where they were going with this meeting. How can you counter with a defense when their mind was made up? Who were they kidding? They were trying to justify in their own minds why they did not want to renew my contract. I went through the motions in answering their questions and at all times remaining professional. I was resigned to the fact I knew what they were going to do as soon as they got back into public session.

They asked me to wait in the council chambers for them but still not telling me what was going to happen. They did not have to tell me. I already knew. When the council members paraded back into the council chambers and took their seat, the mayor called the meeting to order. The dreaded moment came. One council made a motion to not renew my contract, there was a quick second then vote was taken. It was a unanimous vote. At the beginning of the council meeting, a new council member was sworn in. I did not know this person but she also voted to not renew my contract. My employment with the town was terminated at that moment. I remember the former town manager was very gracious when the council voted his termination. He politely thanked the council for giving him an opportunity to serve. When he said those words, I was blown away. When it was my turn, I could not say anything. You may as well say I was in a state of shock; I got up from my chair and walked out. Later during the evening, they summoned the sergeant to the meeting and swore him in as interim police chief. It was not a big surprise. It was what I had expected. Apparently, everything was prearranged. It did not take him long to scurry to the meeting. One question bothered me. Why did they not have someone accompany me to the police department to retrieve my badge and issued firearm? No one even bothered to check to see if the police chief's assigned vehicle was turned in.

What a blow to my career. I was never terminated from anything before Florence. Later on that evening I cleaned out my office, gathered my personal belongings, said my good byes to the personnel on duty and left. I left everything in order. All the computer files were left alone. I wanted everyone to know that I was leaving as a professional. I did not want to give the mayor and council members any reason to justify their actions. Even then, I wondered what I was going to do. I felt alone and confused. If I had been doing such a great job then why did they terminate me? I asked myself this question repeatedly.

When I finally started thinking clearly I began to put this conspiracy theory back into perspective. The former police chief was working the council members behind the scenes and the sergeant was talking to the mayor and some of the council members. Even though in the beginning after the former town manager was fired they told everyone at a meeting we did not have anything to worry about. It would be business as usual. The mayor sounded convincing to me but the fact remained that the former town manager recommended me had been fired and the former town council appointed me as the police chief was recalled. No matter which way you look at it, I was tainted. I was like damaged goods. They had no ownership in me. They could not get rid of me right away because they needed me to reorganize the police department because it was in dismal shape. They had intended to get rid of me but they probably figured they had to wait. As the police department made major improvements in all areas and people were starting to take notice, this was when I became expendable. The town council knew I had a two-year contract and I believe their intentions all along were not to renew it. They waited until the last possible moment to decide whether to renew my contract or not.

Many police chiefs and other leaders all over the country find themselves in similar situations. Some are not as lucky as me to have not been given a choice. A similar fate waited for my friend in Coolidge, a community about 10 miles from Florence. The police chief from Coolidge and I worked together on many programs including the TRIAD. The TRIAD was a program described earlier where the Sheriff's Office, police departments and senior citizens work together to reduce crime and the fear of crime in the community. After I fell victim to the town council, he probably saw the same thing happening to him. He had several council members that were vocally against him. I do not see why since he was doing a wonderful job in the community. He seemed to be well liked but he was running into the same problem as me. Several members of the department were going directly to the council members and complaining about the chief. When you complain long enough some people start to believe it. Any chief is vulnerable at this point when he or she does not get a chance to refute the misinformation. Unfortunately, my friend did not have a contract with the town. He was an at-will employee like everyone else.

I think that he saw what was coming so he decided to petition to run for a city council seat. The city manager told him he could not run for council because he was a city employee. My friend decided to challenge the system and told him he was going to run for the seat. The city manager placed him on administrative leave without pay. To make matters worse my friend lost the election. After the election was all over with the city manager fired him. He was now out of a job after spending three years in Coolidge and doing many wonderful things. In a short time all the good things were forgotten. The only thing he could do was file a civil suit against the city. To make a long story short, after a few years the civil suit was dismissed. His attorneys dropped the ball when an important deadline was missed filing some paperwork. Another police chief feel victim to the political environment. Personally, I think he made a big mistake in running for a council seat; it was clear he could not do it but he challenged the system anyway. He just gave the city manager cause to fire him but I understand his motivation. Sometimes you can see the termination coming; it is just a matter of time. He just tried to beat it by running for a council seat. Perhaps, it would have been a different story had he won his seat.

However, a police officer who had run for a council seat in the same community had done this before and was not unprecedented. Back in Bristol, Connecticut, a police lieutenant ran and won a council seat and still stayed on as a lieutenant. When the lieutenant ran for mayor and won, he took a leave of absence from the police department that the police commissioners quickly approved. Tell me there was no politics.

Still I have more examples to discuss. Every police chief in the surrounding area was gone for one reason or another. Another police chief from Superior, Arizona about 25 miles from Florence was terminated at about the same time as me. This former chief was selected to go to the FBI's National Academy to attend the police executive training. Before he had gone the chief had gotten into difficulty by allegedly assaulting a motorist and the entire episode was recorded on video. The town had installed a state of the art camera system to watch over the main thoroughfares through Superior. Apparently, one of his own cameras caught him on tape roughing up a young motorist. Whether it was true or not, I do not know because he never had a hearing or was not charged with any offense. In the meantime, the chief went to Quantico, Virginia to complete the three-month program. When he returned, he received a big surprise. The police chief was demoted to patrol officer and the sergeant was appointed as the interim chief.

Apparently, political maneuvering had taken place while the chief was going through the management training. While he was gone, he could not do anything about damage control. The town had to keep the police chief for a while because anyone completing the FBI's management program had to agree to stay in law enforcement a certain number of years. Imagine, one day, as a police chief you are getting your certificate at the graduation ceremony and the next you are a front line patrol officer.   The town fathers showed their gratitude for completing this prestigious program by dismissing him as their police chief.

I was asked why I did not consider applying for the FBI's National Academy in Quantico, Virginia. I had applied for a slot when I was in Connecticut and after leaving to be police chief, I did not give it much thought. It was not that I did not want to, since many chiefs would jump at the opportunity. My reasoning was simple; I did not want to be victimized by the political powers while I was gone. If I had no made some solid political contacts, I could have gone. It was more important for me to stay home and mind the store. What happened to the chief in Superior was not the first time it happened to a police chief.

Another police chief from Eloy about 30 miles from Florence got the boot a second time in the same community. After the first time he was terminated he got a position as a director of the police academy program near Coolidge. One day he approached me and asked if he could get a copy of my contract because he heard that I had a severance clause. He felt that he needed some protection. I did not have a problem with it and immediately faxed a copy to him. He told me the town wanted him to be the police chief again and he was thinking about it. He finally accepted the position as police chief but it only lasted a couple of years. He was terminated from the town a second time. Imagine getting the ax again from the same community?

I could hardly believe it. I use to think the town or city manager position was a highly vulnerable position and has since changed my mind. It appears the police chief is more expendable and more often. Even the states that appear to have protection for the police chief, one should watch their backs. In New Hampshire and Connecticut, a police chief can only be dismissed with cause and a hearing has to be provided when the court is petitioned. I am a firm believer that if the political powers to be want to get rid of a police chief they will find a way. If they try hard, they can find just cause on anyone. I know what you are thinking. Can they do that? Yes, they can. In Florence, Arizona, the mayor asked the town attorney to do something regarding a particular issue. He responded, "I can write it anyway you want." The town attorney was working for the council and he will do anything that they want him to as long as it was ethical. Let me say that many times they are operating in the grey area. Anything is possible if they spend long enough looking for something. Even if the matter goes to court, the town or city has the deep pockets and their attorney in their corner. They can wait as long as it takes to get the judgment in their favor. On the other hand, the now jobless police chief has to hire an attorney and use his or her funds to pay attorney fees at $200-$300 an hour. It does not take long to rack up an attorney fee into the thousands of dollars. The longer the case drags on the more money it will cost and there are no guarantees that the former chief will prevail.

My friend in Newtown, Connecticut was victimized after about three years as police chief. He fell victim like many other chiefs and he had a very good attorney. He finally became a police chief after years of searching. Apparently, some of his personnel did not like the way things were running so they kept complaining to the police commissioners. These police commissioners had the power to hire and fire. Like I said before, if you complain long enough eventually the person will believe it. The Police Commissioners after hearing enough complaints and deciding the chief did not meet the goals they had set for him decided to offer him to resign along with a severance package. He declined to accept the resignation and they placed him on administrative leave with pay. Believe me; I understand why he said no. Considering he had just purchased a home in Newtown probably was a deciding factor and not admitting failure. Obviously, the police commissioners made the move to figure out what they were going to do next.

While he was on administrative leave, he had a provision in his contract to attend the International Association of Chiefs of Police Conference. The police commission had to allow him to go using his assigned vehicle and this time the conference was in Charlotte, North Carolina. It was like, "I am going anyway whether you like it or not and by the way I am going to use the city car and city funds." It was like rubbing their face in it while this episode was taking place. If I was in his shoes, I would not have gone. I would have put my time to better use by negotiating with the commissioners on a one to one basis behind the scenes. Instead, they were probably determined to get rid of him.

In the meantime, the police chief used the copy machine to make copies of documents for his defense. It got to be a little ridiculous because they included as one of the numerous charges unauthorized use of the copy machine. These events led to a hearing before the police commission and they fired him. In the end after all the court battles, the police chief lost in court. He had his day in court and lost. The judge decided there was just cause to dismiss the police chief. At this point, his termination was final. What was he going to do next? His next step would be to file a civil suit against the town for unlawful termination. Whether he will prevail remains to be seen. A once promising future as a police chief was now over. Now he is still out of law enforcement and it is doubtful he will go ever back. Let's face it when you are terminated based upon just cause it would be doubtful if any other municipality would hire him as police chief. Let me add it is doubtful but not impossible.

Many police chiefs as well as administrators find themselves in this situation. They are trying to decide whether to sue a municipality for unlawful termination and at the same time pursue employment possibly as a police chief again or leader. I considered suing the Town of Florence but decided against it for two reasons: the first, my contract prevented me because of the language and being compensated and second, if I wanted to be a police chief again I could not have an active lawsuit. Municipalities get gun shy when they find out that a potential police chief candidate has an active lawsuit against their former community. At some point in time, this question will come up and you have to be prepared to answer it.

One other example that I want to discuss and believe me there are many involved the police chief in Lee, New Hampshire. He had been a police chief for almost 30 years so it was a big surprise when I first heard about it. I had spoken of this case earlier in a previous chapter and it was a case where the chief got involved with a female who was having marital difficulties. The chief allegedly was having an affair with her and was trying to get the husband deported out of the country. This did not work because the judge smelled a rat and wrote a letter regarding his concerns to the Board of Selectman. The selectman initiated an investigated and decided to suspend the chief for one week without pay and placed him on administrative leave with pay until this issued had been resolved. Eventually, after a few court battles in trying to win reinstatement the chief was offered to resign in lieu of termination. If he had been terminated, he could have lost some benefits related to his retirement. The chief opted to retire with over 30 years of law enforcement service. The retirement was tainted by the allegations of his abuse of police power. I guess the handwriting was on the wall.

Let me point out one thing. Whether the charges brought forth by the Board of Selectman are true, I do not know. Apparently, the selectmen were confident that they had a good case. It is not my place to say they had a good case, but it is relevant to mention the outcome. The result was the end of a distinguished career to this point. The chief had been active with the International Association of Chiefs of Police, and the New Hampshire Association of Chief of Police. Like in many other cases, no one remembers the good things he had done just the one incident they focused on. Like many other chiefs and top executives suffering a similar fate, the focus was on the negative.

More recently in Fayetteville, North Carolina, the police chief resigned after about 10 years with the police department. It was a surprise because it appeared he was doing a good job with the department. He brought the department to its national accreditation status. If there were any internal problems in the department, the public was not aware of any. Apparently, the media got wind of the city manager offering a deal to the police chief to resign. After several denials by both, apparently the media was right. There was a deal in the works. The chief accepted a severance package worth over $200,000 paid over five years. The chief would make himself available as a consultant during this time. What a sweet deal. I do not know what was in his contract but he must have had a good one. I thought mine was good but his was great. These deals are rare but if you can negotiate one all the better.

After the initial shock of being fired or place on administrative leave, take into consideration the following:

- Be Professional at all times
- Do not accuse or make threats that you will be sorry for later.
- Ask permission to take your personal belongs out of your office and have a witness to verify what you took. This will overt any suggestion or accusation that you intentionally destroyed, damaged or took any reports, hard copy files, computer files or city owed equipment from your, office, police vehicle or police department.
- At the earliest opportunity, get a transcript, tape and video recording of the council meeting.
- If placed on administrative leave, do not do anything stupid where they will have more ammunition to build a better case.
- Seek advice from an attorney to begin weighing your options for your next course of action.

What is the Next Move?

Each situation is different. What are the police chiefs or managers going to do under the circumstances? It is a good question; hopefully, I can provide some insight. In my situation in Florence, Arizona, the mayor and council members could have saved themselves a bunch of money if they had been honest with me in the first place. If they had told me they were inclined to make a change and had given me notice I would have updated my resume and started looking for another police chief position. No, they did not tell me a thing and waited until the last minute when my contract came up for renewal. I believe it is part of the political gamesmanship not to reveal what they were going to do. Yet they did not take into consideration the commitment I had made to make Florence our home. The reality hit me hard that I was a pawn in the political arena and expendable at the whim of the council.

My next move was to apply for police chief again. I did not know if I was going to be successful but I was going to try. My feeling was that I was still a viable police chief and I was not going to let the Town of Florence's decision sway my decision. During the six months, I had gone to numerous interviews all over the country. I had made the short list many times and I was feeling confident again. I could not help but think that my termination in Florence would hurt me. Much to my amazement, it probably did not hurt me at all. I was offered a police chief position in Montevideo, Minnesota and Fort Lupton, Colorado. I finally accepted the position in Fort Lupton but while I was there other communities were calling for me to interview. It was possible to obtain another police chief's or other leader type position somewhere even if you had been terminated. However, I would like to reiterate one caveat; it would be possible if the circumstances were other than just cause. It is hard to explain how another community had developed just cause but I suppose anything is possible. One thing for sure if the just cause involved the commission of a crime then you might as well forget it.

The police chief from Fayetteville, North Carolina received the best deal that I know about. It was the ultimate "Golden Handshake" that any chief would be envious. If a City manager or council wants a police chief out for any circumstances, the bargaining power rests with the chief. A chief knows that they want him or her out and they are willing to pay. The question is how much are they willing to spend? The more they want you out the more they are willing to pay. If the Town of Florence had offered $200,000 paid over five years, there would have been no doubt as to my decision. I would have been gone in a heartbeat. The decision is much easier if the town or city council is willing to pay.

Weighing the Choices

The dilemma for most police chiefs and likewise top executives is that they are usually caught off guard and are not expecting the ultimatum. Sometimes there is no ultimatum such as in my case. The usual response is "I am going to fight them" or "they won't get me." As I had explained earlier the municipality has all the resources to wait. Time is always on their side. Whatever decision will be made will affect your future and most important your family. You have to give it very careful thought before you decide the best course of action.

Over the course of years, I have seen many police chiefs come and go. The quickest I had seen one go was in a small community in New Hampshire. I do not know what got the town fathers upset but he lasted only one month. It caught my attention because the town had gone through a publicized selection process in hiring the so-called right person. The circumstances surrounding his departure were very suspicious considering it was so quick.

My friend in Connecticut decided to fight the Board of Police Commissioners and hired an attorney to represent him. They had offered a buy-out but he quickly refused. His first reaction was to fight them. How dare they fire the police chief? The chief called me and asked for my opinion. I told him to consider very carefully, what he was doing. Looking back on this situation it was set up before he was ever sworn in as police chief.   He would have been better off to get a police chief's position out of state. Union members from one police department will call union members to another to obtain information, in particular, on someone who was going to be a police chief in their community. This practice is being done all the time. When I interviewed for a police chief's position in a city in Ohio, a union member called my department and spoke to one of my officers to check me out. My officers were surprised to find out that I had been going on interviews. There was no doubt in my mind that someone from the Newtown Police Department called a union member in Bristol, Connecticut to find out about him. I do not think the information provided was very complimentary.

I could easily see how it happened. During the three years, his personnel kept doing an end run to the police commissioners. After a while, they probably had second thoughts about him. No doubt the commissioners were looking for ways to ease out of the situation. Knowing my friend, he was not going away very easily. He was an aggressive and a very knowledgeable police chief and it was a shame he made the wrong choice. Another promising career had been quickly ended. It is not so much how smart you are but **how well you play the game**. Playing the game is finding a comfort level with all the players including the personnel, police commissioners, council members and manager. It is difficult to please everyone but it certainly helps to establish a rapport with your personnel whether they are union or not. It does not matter.

I could see that the police chief was all business and only had the task at hand. He failed to see the telltale signs. Who am I to talk, it happened to me in Florence, Arizona. I failed to heed the warning about the police sergeant and not take preventative action to initiate damage control. As I had already stated in a previous chapter, the police chief has to pay attention to all the signs. Taking action early on may have been effective for damage control.

In any event, the chief after having purchased a home had to make a choice. He did not want to leave and admit failure. Besides every chief has pride. Perhaps, thinking it through and weighing all the options would have prevented the agony in going through the hearing process. The pictures of the hearing were on the Internet.

The pictures told the whole story of the misery he and his wife were experiencing. The picture was worth a "thousand words." What happened to him and countless other chiefs or merely leaders in general occur all over the country.

There is a great deal to consider when you are under pressure. Should the police chief or manager submit his resignation, retire or fight it out and take a chance on being fired. What is going to happen? No one can predict the future. No one can ultimately decide except the police chief or manager. Everyone likes to think they can win the battle and I am sure some can. We all read the famous quote, "You can win some battles but you may lose the war." Unless you have a strong political base sometimes it would be better to think what may happened if you do win the battle. Will the political powers be lying in wait for the next mistake? Take for example; if my friend was successful in beating the charges levied by the police commissioners, what would have been his future? The police commissioners who had not given him a raise in three years would have waited for the next opportunity. No one is perfect; if one waits long enough a police chief along with top executives will make mistakes.

Funny thing, I never have seen a police chief prevail at a termination hearing including those that gone to court. This leads me to believe that the town or city council or police commissioners have their mind made up. Yes, they will go through the motions in having a hearing but the decision had been made long ago.

The issue becomes what is the ultimate goal for the police chief or manager. Does he or she really want to be reinstated in a hostile environment or just move on with his or her life. If the issue is to get on with one's life then the decision is easy, just take your best deal. Had the Town of Florence given me an opportunity to choose, I would have updated my resume and moved on. I would never have wanted to stay where I was not wanted. This is the main issue with me. I always wanted to stay in a place not only where they need me but wanted me. I think it hurts more when they no longer want you even when you are doing a good job or so you are told.

The following are some options to consider very carefully:

- Agree to a Buy-out of your contract or
- Challenge the process and have your day in court or hearing

Best Course of Action

There is no greater decision to be made than one that will certainly affect the future. Weighing all the options, discuss everything with your spouse or significant other. It boils down to one of two decisions: accept the offer and move on with your life or take them to task. Let us analyze each choice very carefully.

Taking them to task is usually the first desired course of action. No one wants to admit failure. Besides, it is simply amazing to me that the police chief can be a hero one day and the goat the next. The fact that the council's opinion can quickly change from one week to the next is a very real issue, such as my case in Florence, Arizona. The reality is at times all it takes is new council members bringing with them an agenda in many cases, getting rid of the police chiefs. It may sound a little crass but it is a fact that when the police chief is doing his or her job eventually someone is going to get upset. A citizen being upset can certainly influence some of the council members. There is always someone on the council who does not like the police chief. I can relate to this very easily in Somersworth, New Hampshire when one citizen tried to get me to bend the law in his favor and when I did not he complained to a city council member. He wanted me to do something unethical and there was no way he was going to get me to do it. I knew if I did not tell him what he wanted to hear that he was going to complaint to the council members. I figure if someone is not complaining about something then you are not doing your job. It is impossible to please everyone.

So now, the town or city manager called you into his office to talk to you about matters that ultimately will lead to a discussion of your resignation or firing. The other scenario is the town or city council calling you into their executive session of their council meeting to discuss personnel matters. It is just a catchall phrase to discuss personnel matters and not tell the public. Before going into executive session, the town or city council has to publish their agenda and post it 24 hours in advance. If you are on the agenda for the executive session, you have time to prepare. Look at it this way; if you go into the meeting unprepared like I did it will be a free for all. Experiencing the town council wrath in executive session made me realize there is a better way. I certainly would have done it differently. Perhaps, the results would not have changed but I would have had my "ducks in order."

Even though the town or city manager may not know the reason, it is a place to start. In my case, I believed the town manager did know and he was holding back on me. Next, I would talk to the mayor and council members who you have developed a rapport with the most and have a mutual respect. Maybe they will tell you or maybe they will not. I would tell them that I was just trying to conduct some research so that I could present accurate facts to their questions. Let me mention rumors again. Rumors are the source of much council inquires. People feast on rumors and even more so with the council members. I found it to be very true in Florence, Arizona and Somersworth, New Hampshire. If certain officers are running to the council members with rumors, the police chief should have a chance to refute them. In my case in Florence, the town council did not give me a chance to refute these allegations. They chose to believe the other individuals and it appeared they had their minds made up.

What happens when you are bombarded with allegations and it is obvious the direction they are taking? You can take one of the following courses of action at this stage:

- Quickly ask if the meeting can go public, so everyone has an opportunity to learn what is going on or
- Request that the council postpone any action until you had a reasonable opportunity to respond to the allegations.

Both scenarios are realistic because the first lets the council know that you are not afraid to have these allegations go public. You might catch the council by surprise because they usually like to discuss these personnel matters in executive session. I look at it this way; if you did not do anything wrong than what is there to hide? If I had been thinking clearly, I would have asked the council to postpone any action until I was able to respond to each allegation in writing or allow an independent party to conduct an investigation. One of the allegations was the morale in the department was low. This would be very easy to check. All you have to do is a survey of all the police department employees to find out the truth. If given a chance, these allegations one by one could be refuted. Asking for time to respond is reasonable. How can they refuse this request? In my case my fate was sealed anyway. It would not have mattered what I had said. They believed the other people and were not interested in the truth. It did not matter to them that they had to pay my severance pay for six months. They could not justify their actions so they terminated me without just cause like many other chiefs. However, this request would give the council something to think about.

What if they decline both requests? They may or may not, it all depend upon how it is presented. While in the executive session, you will find that you will feel alone. The town or city attorney or manager will probably not lend much support because they are the council's hired guns and their jobs could be in jeopardy too. You can be sure they will not stick their necks out very far. If your requests are not granted, then you will have to wait. Your fate rests in their hands and it is not a good feeling to have talking about unproven allegations. If the council gets a majority vote then you are done. At this point all you can do is be professional, take the necessary steps to clean out our office and contact an attorney for advice. It is not just initiating a lawsuit at this point right away but it is good to get an objective point of view or better yet contact one of your peers for advice.

What if the town or city manager has the final say and it is not the council's decision? Obviously, this is a better situation because at least you will have an opportunity to explain yourself. Even though I had worked for the town manager in Florence, the council was the appointing authority so he told the council it was their decision to make regarding evaluations, reporting and other matters. I thought it was absurd for a town manager relinquishing his authority when the decision was clearly his. Supervising the police chief knowing the town's history was not a popular choice for him so he convinced the council into doing it. Nevertheless, any time you have the manager as an insulator between the council and yourself it is the ideal situation. In most cases you will probably get a fair hearing because he or she will base the decision on fact and not rumor. If the manager does not conduct the investigation accordingly and the police chief is terminated, the city is not only on the hook for a lawsuit but the manager's job could be on the line too.

Let me now talk about independent investigations. If the manager decides to hire a private investigator to conduct an investigation, it may be good or bad for the police chief. In my experience these investigation always seemed to go against the police chief. No matter whom it is, if someone looks hard enough, he or she will find something wrong with the department. Often the results of the investigation are used to help expedite the departure of the chief. The manager or council can then say, "See I told you so, this guy was bad news." I do not think the police chief should hinder the investigation in any way. The police chief should cooperate and assist with the investigation. I would rather have the investigator base his investigation on fact so it would be beneficial to provide the information.

When I was in Fort Lupton, Colorado the new city administrator wanted me to read the private investigator's report on the prior chief. As a rule, I do not like to read about the past sins of the former police chief. He thought I could get better insight into the history of the department but mainly the court clerk who was a main player in helping to remove the former police chief. Previously the only thing that I had read was the summary of the investigation. The volumes of the investigation were stored in the city clerk's vault. I set aside some time to read the hundreds of pages of investigation or so called investigation. I think it was luck the city decided to settle with the former police chief instead of a termination. The mayor and recall council settled with the former chief and allowed him to resign and they agreed to a cash settlement. This was the end of the problem.

Conversely, after reading the investigation I think the city was lucky to get away cheap. The statements that I read regarding the allegations of discrimination and abuse of employees were clearly unfounded. Most of the statements were based on hearsay and there was no concrete evidence of any kind. The investigator's opinion was different from mine. He simply told the council what they wanted to hear. If there was a case against the chief I would say so, but it looked to me he was railroaded. The former city council simply believed what they wanted to believe and it seemed to be far from the truth. Therefore, in retrospect a long time police chief in Fort Lupton lost his job based on no evidence and hearsay. Granted, he did make some mistakes. If he had sought the advice of an attorney, I believe the results could have been different. This seems to be a familiar scenario in law enforcement. He could have challenged the council in court but instead he chose to move on with his life.

After the investigator submitted his investigation to the city manager, he or she should request a copy of it or if it is not possible then read it so that a proper response to the criticism or allegations can be made. Oftentimes the investigative report is submitted and some action taken. It is reasonable to request a review of the investigation by a third party to see if an objective investigation was done. Once the investigation had been reviewed, expect the decision. I am not overly optimistic of investigations if the manager or city council hired the investigator. I have not seen one where they ruled in favor of the police chief, but anything is possible, I suppose.

In all fairness if you know they should do an investigation, ask for an investigation by a third party. The third party should be agreeable by both sides, the manager or council and the police chief. At least this way there is a better chance of an impartial investigation. I like to use outside police agencies and you might consider the State's Bureau of Investigation, the Sheriff's Department or the State's Association of Chiefs of Police. Often the city fathers are in a hurry for an investigation and somehow private investigators or consultants contact them. It is not that they will do a bad job and I certainly do not mean to imply all private investigators or consultants are bad, but the police chief should have a say in the selection if at all possible. Let it be a fair and impartial investigation.

Decision Time

Now at this point the manager or council has terminated your employment and/or suggest you submit your resignation. The question is what kind of case do they have against you? I would submit if they have a strong case then they would quickly move towards termination. The discussions after the fact might be changing the termination to accepting a letter of resignation. Attorney involvement at this stage can help in soliciting a letter of resignation. This way they do not have to worry about any civil suit and it is a clean break. Asking for your resignation may be a hint that the town or city has a weak case against you. If you are so bold and are considering another run for police chief ask for a letter of recommendation if you agree to the letter of resignation.

What are you going to do now? Are you thinking about fighting them every inch of the way or are you going to throw in the towel and call it a day. If they are giving you some time to think about it, you need to find out about their case. What are the allegations? Are they criminal, or minor in nature? If the allegations were criminal, they would already have an independent police investigation. If they had a solid case then there would be no negotiations. Fighting the allegations may be the course of action you want to take but is it the smart thing? In every situation, the police chief decided to fight the charges and have a hearing. In my friend's case in Connecticut, he too wanted to fight them. What kind of fairness is it when the police commissioners offered the chief to resign and put him on administrative leave with pay and now are going to have a hearing to decide his fate? How can this body decide a police chief's fate when they had already decided what they were going to do? The hearing was a waste of time. They needed to take formal action before the court review.

If the manager, council or police commission places you on administrative leave, which may ultimately lead to dismissal, you may consider your employment may be ended soon. Rather than wait in agony for months in trying to win your case consider moving on. Some things are not forever, there are better things waiting for you. My friend decided to gamble and hired an excellent attorney. I do not care how good your attorney is if they had already made up their minds, your fate is sealed. He spent thousands of dollars on his attorney to save his job and he lost. Because he was terminated with cause the likelihood of him ever becoming a police chief was very small but not impossible.

Take for instance if somehow you won your case and they reinstated you. You think you won but perhaps you did not. You will still have to work for these same people until such time someone else replaces them on the police commission or council. The working relationship will never be the same again and they will be waiting until you make mistakes. The entire tone will change even with your personnel. They will be wondering how well you will perform. It was something to think about.

As I was watching this scenario unfold in Newtown, Connecticut with my friend, I wondered why he did not accept the offer of resignation with a severance package. He was determined to beat them because he was right. I do not disagree, but you could be right and still lose. The point is they do not want you any longer as their police chief. It is a harsh reality for anyone to accept.

Based upon my experience, it is possible to get another job as police chief after termination. Many police chiefs as well as other top executives who had been terminated were able to obtain other jobs in the same career field. I mistakenly thought it would be harmful in seeking employment. Like town or city managers, there is no stigma if he or she is terminated. It is a fact of life that the council can fire the manager when their welcome has been worn out. The same holds true for police chiefs. If a police chief had been discharged because of just cause then for sure the task will be more difficult.

If the manager or council wants your resignation for other reasons other than just cause, you are actually in a good position to bargain. Most of the time, the reasons are political such as in my case. In the beginning the reasons for my friend were political until they felt challenged and started looking for reasons. If they want you out bad enough they will pay. The question is how much will they pay? There was no question in my mind that if Florence had given me an opportunity we would have entered into negotiations. However, the severance clause was in my favor anyway. Many police chiefs and likely some managers do not have a severance clause in their contract so this could be the starting point. Severance pay will give you time to collect your thoughts; formulate a game plan for the future and an opportunity to sell your home if you bought one. Asking for severance pay is reasonable because if you are not independently wealthy you will need some money to live on. Town or city managers get severance pay most of the time so the police chief should get it too. If you are considering another run for a police chief's position, you can ask for a letter of reference. If the reason for your requested departure was political then they should have not problem in providing a letter. While you are at it, get letters of reference from reputable business people in your community and some of peers. When you do go on interviews, your prospective employer will be checking you out very closely. They will want to know the reasons for your sudden departure. When the City of Fort Lupton, Colorado was doing a background investigation on me they sent a council member who was a retired police officer to do the investigation. They quickly found out after talking to the people in the community that they did not have any reason for termination. The letters of reference from individuals helped.

Many police chiefs negotiated their resignation to their advantage. The police chief from Fayetteville, North Carolina had a great severance package. Many people were upset with the negotiated figure of over $200,000 over five years but if the manager or council wants you to go away they will pay. I thought it was a great settlement. I am sure there are many others who do very well too, but it is the chief in the small and medium size police departments that are abused. Many times they are dismissed out right with very little or not explanation. I have seen too many good police chiefs and other leaders get fired and most leave law enforcement forever.

In summary, if given the choice to resign you would want to consider the following in your negotiations with the town or city:

- Severance Pay for six months or longer
- Continuation of your health benefits for six months or longer
- Letter of Reference from the hiring authority
- Scheduled departure date for an orderly transition
- Assistance in selling your home if they agree
- Agree to pay any attorney fees incurred by you at this point
- Agree to the language for the press release to avoid unfavorable publicity for both parties

Even if the police chief or top executive is fired without an offer to resign all is not lost. It is still possible depending upon the circumstances to get another police chief's or executive position. You have to be determined and persistent that they were not going to beat you. If you choose to go for another chief's or management position and you are willing to move then it should be your decision. Your career is not over unless you want it to be. Some police chiefs and leaders are so frustrated with the political process that they just give up and say the heck with it. I have known many who were in this position. It is very easy to develop a conflict with the town or city council when politics are concerned.

When someone takes a police chief's position there is no real job security. Just look around you and observe carefully. Sometimes you can stay so long that you outwear your welcome. What I mean by this is the political powers can change with the elections. When new council members are sworn in the power of the town or city council may change. Town and city managers pay close attention when this happens. If the wrong people get in then all it would take is a majority vote of the council. It is the harsh reality that a person has to face. The chief or leader who had gone through the ranks to attain the top position has a better chance in staying as opposed to the "carpet bagger," the hired gun that was brought into town to clean up the police department in the first place.

Personally, I think more police chiefs should give more consideration to resigning as opposed to fighting them. If it were my choice, I would resign and move on with my life. Life is too short to hold bitter feelings. However, I can understand why someone might choose to fight his or her termination. My best advice is to weigh what is the best decision one can make under these difficult circumstances. Consider all the options but if you want to become police chief or top executive again then perhaps the resignation is the best choice.

Chapter 23
Success: A Calculated Approach

Why do some police chiefs and top executives succeed and others fail? I do not know about you but I did not know anyone that intentionally failed. Anyone who has been a police chief or leader has gone into the position energized and ready to make all kinds of improvements. Something happens along the way to undermine their plans.

Success can be achieved if there is a plan. Some people might try to wing it but you will not go far. Looking at some police chiefs I know who were considered successful there had to be other reasons for their success other than longevity. There are always multiple factors involved, not just longevity. Many of the chiefs I associated myself with in the State of New Hampshire were some of the finest individuals I had known. They were quick to help someone succeed; all you had to do was ask. When I found myself in New Hampshire for seven years as police chief, I made it a point to become actively involved with the Chiefs of Police Association. I went to every meeting and participated in as much time allowed. While I was participating, I observed how the other chiefs operated. Along the way, they provided some solid advice for me. I eventually became a county representative for the Chiefs of Police Association and thought about running for a higher office if I had stayed in New Hampshire. Many times, I thought about how the police chiefs helped me to resolve some stressful situations. Knowing that I could rely on their years of experience and wisdom was encouraging.

Being part of the chief's association is a good way to network among your peers and to find out about the issues affecting law enforcement. After I became police chief in Florence, Arizona, I became active with the Pinal County Law Enforcement Officer's Association. It was still a good way to network with my peers and other management personnel from other departments. Networking with your peers after they get to know you is a plus. They probably know more about the political environment and the key players than you do. It will certainly save much time and aggravation later on when you are still trying to figure things out. The more you get to know someone the more you can just pick up the telephone to ask a question and seek advice about a situation. I had this type of relationship in all three states where I was police chief. The police chiefs who kept to themselves all the time and never went to any meetings would have succeeded more if they had extended themselves a little. The loners as I called them would never ask anyone for help and sometimes if the loners decided later on to ask, their slow timing would be too late. It is too bad because some of them could have been saved if someone had gotten to them sooner.

One good idea is to have some area police chiefs visit the new chief and welcome him or her and offer assistance. Some State's Association of Chief of Police already does this to some degree but not enough. It is encouraging when police chiefs take time out of their busy schedule to visit a new police chief. A mentoring program for new chiefs should be developed because there are too many chiefs out there that are left floundering especially when they run into difficulty. When the going gets tough and the road ahead looks rocky the chiefs often find themselves alone. Everyone seems to stay away from the individual like he or she has the plague and the disease is contagious. During these trying times occurs when the chief needs help the most. No one wants to admit failure but coming forward at this time to provide assistance may be just enough to help the chief through this ordeal.

Steps to Success

Through the years, I have developed some successful approaches that worked for me. Oftentimes too many chiefs would go into a situation not prepared and not knowing what to expect. The following are some good ways to put you on the success track:

1. Develop a Plan

Developing a plan in particular for those chiefs coming to a new department is essential. There are too many chiefs and top executives out there who are simply not prepared for what is in store for them. This is where you have to find out from the manager and council what are the **immediate priorities** and including **short and long-term goals**. In addition, you have to find out from your personnel what they envision as their priorities and goals. Sometimes it is hard to juggle but there are many issues that have to be tackled at the same time. Where chiefs get into trouble like many that I had know in the past is they have tunnel vision. They seem to tackle one issue at a time while letting others fester. It is easy to forget about these issues and they could come back to haunt you in the long run. I find successful police chiefs and managers are those who can handle multiple tasks at the same time and being able to prioritize.

By **gathering information** from the political powers, police personnel and others is extremely important. The other category includes the other city employees and most important the citizen. Getting information from the citizens was a key factor for me. I was able to get valuable insight into the dynamics of the city politics and their impression of the police department. I was not afraid to ask people what they thought about the police department and at the same time asked them for ways to improve the quality of life in the community.

Getting **small victories** early on is necessary. Just remember how long it took to build Rome. Rome was not built in a day. Small victories show the town manager and council that you are working hard to make improvements. Town managers and councils are results orientated. They want to see results on their investments. Remember, you were brought into the department for a reason and this is why it is important to find out about their agenda as soon as possible.

Developing a **business plan** early on keeps you focused and on target. The private sector does it all the time, where they are now and where they want to be in the future. The plan does not have to be complicated. I like to use the KISS method, "Keep It Simple Stupid." I would suggest writing down in an outline form your short term and long-term plans. This way it will be much easier to review the plan from time to time. As you become more comfortable with the position, you may have to modify your plan because priorities change. The town manager or council may develop another issue that needs to be addressed. When these issues and problems are effectively handled then the results have to be conveyed to them. I like to discuss these issues in monthly reports. In each community that I was associated with, I provided a monthly report. Even in Florence, the town council complimented me on my reports.

Many police chiefs and other leaders do not like to provide any more information than they have to when it comes time to submit a **monthly report**. I am just the opposite. Some will only provide the monthly statistics including the numbers of people arrest, traffic offenses and others. While it is important to convey statistical information, it does not present the entire picture. In addition to the statistical report I like to include a narrative of the month's accomplishments and current programs the department is involved with. Why is this necessary? It is important to keep the town manager and council members informed about what is happening with the police department in particular, the small victories or improvements. The report saves a great deal of time during the council meeting if they had questions about the police department. In Fort Lupton, Colorado, I was on the council agenda for reports from staff. When it was my turn to speak, I spoke briefly about the highlights and sometimes there were questions but generally they like the progress of the department. It was the same situation in Florence, Arizona and Somersworth, New Hampshire. In New Hampshire, I was not on the agenda but was available for any questions. My best advice is to produce a presentable report that just highlights the department's progress. I use to write a brief paragraph about each area. It will be a sure winner if you do it right.

2. Customer Service Attitude

Taking care of the customer, the citizen is one of the most important things if you are going to measure success. It does not matter who they are. Everyone should be treated with respect and dignity and provided the best possible service. In my mind, everyone that I deal with whether they are a city employee or citizen I treat them like a customer. The private sector does it all the time. Their approach is quite simple. If you do not take care of the customer then they will have a hard time turning a profit in their business. In the public sector, our product is service to the people, the customer. A satisfied customer keeps going back to the same store for business. In the public sector, if someone does not like our service he or she can move to another town or city or stay and complain. Usually people express their dissatisfaction to the town manager, mayor or council members.

I recall back in Bristol, Connecticut and other communities' police officers have special derogatory terms to describe the people they do not like to deal with. I heard some of these people called "raggies, dirt bags" and more. Some of the terms are so bad I would not even mention them here. My issue is with the name-calling is there is no place for stereotyping people and using derogatory terms. If you treat people according to the label you give them then they will get less than satisfactory service. I convey to everyone **to** *treat the citizen like the way you would like to be treated.*

How can you check to see if everyone is committed to customer service? I like to refer to it as **quality control**. It is just a simple method to insure that we are treating the customer right and if not what can be done to improve. There has to be a check and balance to see if the delivery of service is the best it can be. Knowing from experience the problem is individual attitudes of your personnel. Someone who has a bad attitude dealing with the public will present a negative image of the police department. I am sure you will agree one person can do a great deal of damage to the department's image. There are several ways to check such as using a questionnaire and telephone surveys. The questionnaires are good but you will only get a small return even if you provide a self-addressed envelope with the postage. People generally do not like to take the time to fill out a questionnaire and include myself in this category. I just do not like to take the time to complete a questionnaire. The better approach in my opinion is the telephone survey. Calling someone is more personal. In Fort Lupton, I had a college student intern who called people regarding their recent police contact. I wanted to know if the officer was polite, provided good service and asked if there was a better way to handle the situation. One chief I knew called people at random each week to see how his officers were treating the citizens. This was a good way to get feedback. All you want is to make sure your officers are doing it right.

Stretch the imagination to see if there are better ways to service the public. Some police departments are so busy that they do not provide an opportunity for the citizen to report their crime if there is little or no investigation. It is not very personal and you do not get to talk with the officer face to face but it is a way to report being a victim without having to wait a long time for an officer to show up. Personally, I do not like the phone in reports because it is so impersonal but if it works for a police department than why not? I always did like the one-to-one contact better. One criticism that I hear all the time is why does it take so long for an officer to respond to a call for service? The phone in report system is only one way to handle this problem. Sometimes it takes more than a few minutes to pick up an enhanced 911 call. There should be no excuse for your call being put on hold when you have only one person answering the phone and all the 911 lines light up at the same time but it does get a little tricky.

Many communities are using the customer service approach and in my view, it is what every community should be doing anyway. This philosophy has to be developed over time and reinforced with **training**. The initial training could be presented in a formal, classroom training session or broken down into modules for roll call.

The mission statement reflects the overall philosophy of the department emphasizing that all citizens will be treated with **courtesy, dignity and respect**. Most of all the citizens' complaints that I hear about are usually about the way they were treated by the officers. Most of the time the person will say the officer was rude. Remember, one discourteous officer can do a great deal of damage to the overall image of the police department.

3. Find out the Needs

What are the needs of the department? You must first find out what is needed so that you can deal with the problems. One specific issue that comes to mind was a need for a new generator that no one thought about. Without a backup generator the police department would be out of business should the power go out. In Fort Lupton, there was a generator but it had not been run in years and no one knew anything about it. It was an old diesel type engine from the 1950s. We were going to rely on a relic that would not start. I knew at this point that we would be in trouble if the power went out. Our immediate need was to obtain a new generator.

With funding from the County's 911 Committee and the city, we were able to purchase a new generator that was fueled by natural gas. No one would ever have to worry about making sure the tank was full. The generator was programmed to run once a week for 20 minutes. The problem was solved. It was not a problem until I had asked questions about the generator and until then no one had given it a thought.

One way to find out about specific need is to **ask your personnel**. As you get to know your personnel, the rank and file will know the real issues in the city. Actually your personnel are your best resource and do not ever forget it. They would be the ones to know. The town manager and council may be able to provide some information but the best source would be the people who work in the department. Early on when I was walking around to see what was going on I would eventually have conversations with everyone. I always include in my conversation the questions about the needs of the department. What are the immediate needs and long range needs? I always asked many questions.

4. Have Your Employees Help

I have known too many police chiefs and managers that tried to do it all alone. One thing for sure, you will be working long hours to get the job done. My friend in Connecticut religiously worked long hours. This person was a workaholic. You probably already know individuals like this. I think that if you worked too many long hours you will burn yourself out in a hurry. Why keep all the "monkeys" yourself? **Put some of the "monkeys" on someone else's shoulders**. It is called **delegation** of authority. Give the task to someone else to complete. The police chief or leader is too busy to be bogged down on major tasks all the time. As I had stated that earlier this was one problem, I found with accreditation by CALEA. It is an excellent program, but the chief cannot do it all by himself or herself. He or she has to find others who are willing to devote time to the project.

My former town manager in Florence, Arizona told me long ago, "I just surround myself with good people and let them do their jobs." He said, "A city manager's job is easy." It was clear to me; it was the approach. Why try to do everything yourself? All you have to do is get your employees to participate. I get them to participate by holding them responsible for different tasks. If you give them a chance to succeed or fail, most of the time you will be pleasantly surprised with the results. However, when they do fail then you cannot be too hard on them. I accept that humans are not perfect and there will be mistakes. I try to impress upon them that I can forgive a mistake but shame on you if he or she repeat the same ones.

I like to include my staff in the discussion of plans to formulate programs. Getting their input and participation is important because then they will have ownership and will do everything in their power to make it work. It is a good strategy to involve them even in controversial programs since no one wants to be associated with losing. You will have a guaranteed winner.

5. Teamwork

Teamwork in my opinion is the best way to get everyone involved in projects and programs. The more you can get them involved the better for you in the end. Generally, people complain more when they feel left out. Maybe they are jealous but we know they can contribute more if they felt part of the team.

6. Energize your Employees

The police chief or leader needs to keep communicating with his or her personnel and be like a cheerleader. Often it is the old thing day in and day out. Often times patrol work is so routine it becomes boring after awhile. When people get bored especially police officers this is when they can get involved in misconduct or make mistakes. Making mistakes can get one seriously injured or killed.

I like to keep everyone **busy**. For reasons hard to explain, the morale level of the department can fluctuate up or down. You have to ask yourself what it means. According to the Merriam-Webster Dictionary the word, morale means the mental and emotional attitudes of an individual to the tasks. Are personnel upbeat all the time? The answer is no. The Florence town council hit me with the morale issue. I suppose if you ask someone how he or she feels if they had a bad day then you can predict what the answer will be. It is a major task to keeping the morale level up all the time. If you do not pay any attention to it then it can work against you.

I found giving someone a pay raise has only a short-term effect. In each of my non-union police departments, I worked hard to convince the council to increase the pay scale for all employees. The starting pay in Florence went from $21K to about $27K a year. Some employees got a big pay increase after their first year. You would think that they would remember but they quickly forgot.

Enthusiasm breeds enthusiasm; it is contagious. There is no better way to energize your personnel than by being excited yourself. Even my personnel would make a remark after awhile by saying, "Why are you upbeat all the time?" I cannot explain it but I try to be optimistic all the time. Just recently, a person told me, "Every time I look at you and see how cheerful you are it makes my day." I was surprised because this person did not know me and I did not think anyone noticed. Everyone is affected by the boss's mood swing so I make it a conscious effort to be positive and upbeat. Do you notice how the mood of the supervisor can affect the other personnel too? It works the other way too; I work hard not to be negative.

Being **creative** helps with the boredom experienced on patrol. Some people will say patrol is boring? In large departments, police officers may run from call to call but in small and medium size police departments there are definitely lulls in the action. In Fort Lupton, I got some patrol officers involved in drug investigations.

Prior to my arrival, the former police chief would not let the officers take any initiative. If there were suspicions of drug activity on a motor vehicle stop the officer had to request a supervisor and often he was not available. I do not know why the former police chief did this. I could only guess that there were some abuses. I quickly changed this practice and turned the officers loose. They did not disappoint me either because they quickly produced results. They were making drug arrests like there was no tomorrow. Of course, I checked the paperwork to make sure no one's rights were violated. It appeared they were doing everything properly and they knew the search and seizure law. I even took it one-step further. We became involved in drug asset forfeitures. The officers did the paperwork and the property was turned over by the court to the police department. The vehicles were sold and the proceeds were deposited into the drug asset forfeiture fund that I had set up. The fund was used to purchase additional police equipment. The officers loved what they were doing.

These officers were so excited that they could hardly wait to report to work. I just added a little diversification to their patrol duties and they responded better than I had anticipated. The trick is to keep your personnel energized. Adding something different to their patrol duties worked. I like to expose their creativity.

7. Take Care of Your Employees

The most important thing that you can do is to show them that you care about them and they are integral part of the team. I emphasized early on that I show concern for my employees. No one likes to feel that they do not belong in an organization. You have heard it all before. If you ask why people leave their place of employment whether it is a police department or another business, they invariably say they did not like the way they were treated.

When I instituted my **open door policy,** I meant it. Some open door policies, as you know, are not open. It was meant more for show. Anyone who wanted to talk to me could at any time. The open door policy worked very well for me because they knew I was concerned about their well-being. This relationship does not happen over night but if you stick with this philosophy, it will evolve into something positive.

Showing them you are a **real person** is a big plus in your favor. You already know the men and woman of the police department will relate if they know the chief is not afraid to be in the trenches with his or her officers. Take for example; General George S. Patton was a great study in leadership during World War II. The men related to him because he was in the trenches with them. They simply loved the man and would go anywhere with him. They knew he cared about them. It is the same principle here. If personnel knew that you are concerned and care about them, they will work hard for you

Some police chiefs and managers have a problem with taking care of their employees. Some may not mean to but they convey a message when he or she only surfaces from the office when it is necessary and only for business. Chiefs often forget that the personnel are people too and you have to relate to them. Being personal and **getting to know them** is just as important as the task. I say this because you need the personnel to accomplish the task. It seems like some police chiefs and leaders' alike have no personality at all. They should realize the work is done through people.

8. Deliver on Your Promise

One thing for sure, if I promise something I will make sure that I deliver. Nothing will destroy morale quicker than broken promises. The police chiefs and top executives are by no means a miracle worker but at times, it seems like it. One area where it can really hurt is a pay raise. If you say words to the effect, "I will try my best or I can't make any promises," it can later haunt you. People seem to remember better, when you cannot do as you promised. They will misconstrue your words to mean I promise. Fortunately, for me I did make good on my promise to get my personnel a pay raise but it was almost a sure thing when I did mention it. I did a great deal of politicking on the side in order to get my personnel much needed pay raises.

Obviously, the broken promise backfired on the former police chief when he allegedly make a promise to a female that she had a police job and later changed his mind. I suspect there was something derogatory on her background investigation that turned up that was probably the reason. I always used written documentation, a conditional offer of employment contingent on successful completion of specific criteria including a background investigation. In any regard, there should have been documentation to support the rejection. Police chiefs and managers need to document more often. It makes sense to me but unfortunately, some police chiefs get sloppy and it costs them in the end. You have to look at the big picture. This person used the broken promise as a means to get an out of court cash settlement and a job as the court clerk. If he had this documentation and the facts to support her rejection as a police officer then the results could have been different.

Did your personnel ever say, "You said?" It is funny how some can easily twist your words into a different meaning. People believe what they want to believe anyway. Actually, you have to be on guard about what you say because your personnel will hold you to it. Even if the statement was said in jest, some will interpret it to their way of thinking. If you promise something, make sure you are clear on exactly what you are promising. Somehow these broken promises always come back to bite you and they will remind you.

456   Patrick L. Cote

9. Do No Give Up

Police chiefs and top executives do not give up. Too many chiefs take rejection personally and give up. They have the defeatist attitude. If this is the type of attitude, you have then you may as well update your resume and start looking for another job. There were many times when I had a notion to quite but I never did.

If one of your programs get rejected or a plan did not go right, keep trying different things until you get it right. When a city council member in Fort Lupton, Colorado tried to cut a new police cruiser out of the budget I could have given up. No, there is always **another angle** you can try. I got support from my police committee and other citizens to lobby the council to get the necessary votes. I always say, **"If there is a will, there is a way."**

Here is a secret. The town manager and council members do not expect you to give up. They will respect you more if you keep pursuing it from a different angle. Their motivation is to save tax dollars and be frugal with the way the taxpayer's money is spent. What I try to do is to convince them of the necessity to spend the funds. It is just a big game and a great percentage of the time I was successful. If I find that there is a roadblock then I will have to take a detour to get to my destination. This is the best analogy that I can give to get my point across.

10. Do Not Listen to the Naysayer

I consider myself an optimist and like to stay upbeat all the time. I do not like to be around the naysayer. Just as I said earlier, enthusiasm breed's enthusiasm, the opposite effect could happen with the naysayer. The captain who once worked for me was always negative. I wonder if anything ever went well in his life. One pet peeve I like to talk about here is the devil's advocate. There is nothing that will turn me off any quicker than someone saying, "Now let me be the devil's advocate." I understand the intent to see both sides of the issues but I do not want to play games with it. If someone has another point of view, let him or her say it. Why play games?

It seems the police departments hire more than their share of cynical people. If someone is complaining all the time and gossiping to others, it will have a negative effect on the police department. The mayor and council members listen to the complainers and rumors all the time and it was especially true in Florence, Arizona and Fort Lupton, Colorado. It was truer in Florence because it eventually cost me my job. It was unfortunate but they chose to listen to the rumors.

Try to **turn the negative into a positive**. When someone is complaining about something, it is easy to turn the tables on him or her. Ask what they would do in a similar situation? Ask what changes they would make to make things better? Instead of this person being part of the problem, turn it around so that he or she is part of the solution. Why not have the complaining employees work on the program or project? Generally, you will find the person will do a good job and the complaining will go away.

Avoid listening and prolonging the conversation by changing to a positive topic. Usually the employees will get the hint. If you do not participate then they will feel uncomfortable and find other things to discuss.

11. Keep Fine Tuning

Never rest on your laurels to maintain the status quo. When one project or program is completed, there are many others to do. I do not see how police chiefs or managers can just sit back and not try to improve what they already have. When chiefs are sitting back and doing little or nothing, they are more vulnerable to criticism leading to personnel problems. Why give someone a chance to criticize - keep everyone busy.

I was constantly looking for ways to improve existing programs and looking for new ones.   I think everyone is energized when they have an opportunity to participate in the planning and implementation of a new program. The key is to continually **review**, evaluate, and when feasible make some changes. In my mind, there is always ways to improve what you are doing. If you do not try then you will never know.

12. Do Not Take Anything for Granted

As a police chief or leader, you cannot take things for granted. When you assume, you know what they say? You make an ass out of you and me. Sometimes we do not need any more help; we just need to follow-up more often. One sign of a good chief is not only delegation but the follow-up is equally important. If you never follow-up, the work will become shabby because it is now acceptable if you do not call them on it. It is human nature to take the path of least resistance. The work has to be challenging but at the same time, it has to be acceptable to the police chief top manager.

If I had delegated a task to a subordinate, I would periodically **check** on the progress to see how things are going and if they need anything. Some individuals work better on deadlines rather than leave it open-ended. It is a fact that many will procrastinate and keep putting the project or assignment off until the chief starts asking about it. There will then be a mad flurry to complete the project. Personally, I think people should be responsible enough to complete projects without being told to hurry up and get it in. One lieutenant would always try to complete the projects as soon as possible but sometimes I would have to tell him to slow down. I would rather have the projects done well than hurried and miss information. One case had to do with a citizen complaint investigation. Some of these investigations can wait for a couple of weeks especially if there needed to be a cooling off period.

The chief still needs to get out of the office and *"put the shoe leather to the road."* There is no better way than to find out what is going on by checking on it yourself. You will probably say that is what I have supervisors for. You are right; I say the same thing. I find it is not only important to check what is going on in the field but also to convey a message that the chief is interested.

If you hear a **rumor,** it would be wise to check it out. Sometimes people are vicious; they will spread rumors intentionally and just sit back to watch the fallout. Even if some people get hurt, it does not matter to them because it is fun. It just simply amazes me how many people not only listen but also believe the rumors. The most important thing is to disseminate the truth to kill a rumor. I knew a chief who published a newsletter every few weeks and he called it the "Rumor Bulletin." I use to do one similar but it was called a newsletter. I only published it when it was needed but I found it was quite successful. It is a good way to promote different programs, recognize individuals and discuss issues. Sometimes I found my time limited so I had to choose when I was going to do it. The best way I found to kill a rumor was to say it in person.

13. Be Innovative

Being the best you can be is not enough sometimes. It is essential to have a **vision** to see where you want to be in the future. Some chiefs stretch the imagination and introduce new programs. You ask yourself sometimes, "Why didn't I think of that?" A police chief or leader cannot be afraid to try out new things to benefit the police department.

A good professional periodical to check out innovative programs to see what other police departments are doing is the Police Chief Magazine. The International Association of Chiefs of Police (IACP) recognized a police department for their innovative approach in dealing with University of New Hampshire students. The police department was always dealing with intoxicated and rowdy students every weekend including special functions. They found a way to be more effective by contacting the parents of the students arrested. Even though the students were adults they still got the parents involved. The arrests were high in the beginning but in time the arrests went down, thus the problem was solved. They probably will not be able to control drinking and rowdiness one hundred percent but at least they had a unique approach to keep it under control.

Police departments need to try different approaches and not be afraid to try something new. People are afraid of failing but one thing for sure you will never know unless you try. Departments all across the country are always trying something new to improve services to the citizens and to reduce the crime rates in their community.

14. Believe in Yourself

The best advice that I can give is to believe in yourself and your abilities to get the job done. There will be times when you will have self-doubt and confusion. I think over time we all experience this wondering if you are doing the right thing. The town manager or council hired the police chief as their expert to do the job and to do wonderful things. Initially they will have confidence in you to further the goals of the community. Even though something may happened where the town manager or council have a change in heart about your ability, so try not to let it affect you. The component introduced into the equation is politics. When it comes right down to it, politics can influence your career. It does not matter what you had accomplished; it is just the fact of life that you can be the hero one day and the goat the next. Sometimes being right does not even matter with the politicians.

The "honeymoon" period could be one of the most effective times for the police chief to get the necessary equipment and programs in place. This period could last six months to a year or last less than a month. It all depends upon the political environment at the time. In my situations in three communities, I experienced extended "honeymoon" periods. Even in Florence, Arizona, the recall town council treated me very well and supported my programs. As I had said earlier, it was a surprise when they did not renew my contract.

Even in this adverse situation, I never doubted my abilities otherwise; I would have sought other means of employment. I was determined to become police chief again and I did. The many initiatives that I began in Florence, I just continued along with more programs in Fort Lupton, Colorado. I thought to myself, "How can I be successful in one community and not another." I do not look at Florence as a failure. No matter how anyone looks at this situation, it was a complete success. Many of the programs that I had put in place are still there and people still remember the professional police department that I had built. When the current police chief asked the town council to embark on a new initiative they told him the former chief already did it, meaning me. He further told me that my name is mentioned often and in a way, it is a tribute to my success. The town council knew they needed my expertise to rebuild the department before they took any action against me. Again, it was politics in action, plain and simple.

You cannot take minor setbacks to heart. I knew one person in Bristol, Connecticut every time he did not get his way he would quit the program or project. There will be a minor setback and you have to overcome it and find another way. If you notice, some police chiefs and top executives seem to get everything they want. They seem to do everything right. The one thing these police chiefs have in common is that they know how to play the political game. The better they are at it the more they will be successful. Some of the long tenured police chiefs that I had known got that way because they knew how to play the politicians. I believe it is not how smart you are but how cunning you can be.

15. Be Yourself

Do not try to emulate someone else's style. Their style may not work in your situation. I found what works best for me is to be myself. Why try to be someone you are not? It is good to see what works for other police chiefs or managers but in reality, you have to develop a style of your own. My style was to be more involved with the community and I did it through the newspapers and television. Every chance I got I was in the news. In Somersworth, New Hampshire, a few people called me a "Ham" in jest. They probably thought I was just a publicity hound stopping at nothing to get my name and picture in the newspaper or television. My public relations ploy was to generate enough publicity about the department so the people would know what we were doing. Some situations may be different but I thought it was necessary to keep generating a great deal of positive publicity. For a long time people read about negative news including the coke machine caper with the former police chief so it was time for the people to learn more about the police department in a positive sense. I felt comfortable with the media. If it involved filming an interesting topic for the community access channel, I was ready. Some police chiefs stayed out of the limelight as much as possible and that is all right. It is what you feel comfortable with in the end.

The most important thing to remember is to develop your own style. The more you are comfortable with it the more confident you will be. Do not worry about what others think.

The Perfect Organization

We like to think that we have the perfect organization, but in the real world, it is not so perfect. There are always some unexpected problems that come up that will challenge you. Some organization may appear to be close but the chief constantly has to work hard to keep it at a high level.

My goal was to develop the police department to be the best it can be. As I had explained, previously it takes a well-organized plan to achieve a high level of proficiency but it can be done. There are many police departments that can serve as a model for your department. It would be beneficial to check out other departments to see how they operate. Believe me there is no shame in asking another police chief or manager if you can view his or her operations. They will take it as a compliment as I did when other chiefs checked out what I was doing. I always liked to highlight my department and besides even when I was looking around, I would borrow their idea in a heartbeat if I could apply it to my department. If the truth were known, many police chiefs "steal" ideas from one another all the time. There is no sense in reinventing the wheel if a program works very well in another police department. Sometimes all that is needed is some tweaking here and there to make it fit your department

I use to get a great deal of ideas from other police department, the State's Association of Chief of Police and the International Association of Chiefs of Police. I strongly recommend joining these associations, as they are an excellent source of information. When you ask for assistance, they will provide it. Another source of information is the IACP NET. When I was in Florence, Arizona and Fort Lupton, Colorado, I found it very beneficial to subscribe to this service. They provide all the information that the police chief could possibly want.

There is no reason a police chief or top executive cannot be successful. I say, "Run it like a business." Forget about the good O'boy system. Taking care of your friends, as the "spoil system" will get the chief into trouble every time. If you stay professional and be consistent with your practices, there is not reason why you could not be close to perfect. In each of my departments, I like to think that they were the best they could be but I always look for ways to improve. Even the so-called close to perfect organizations can be improved.

The following are some recommendations and sure winners to improve the organization:

- Do not be afraid to try something new
- Pay attention to detail
- If it works stick with it
- Emphasize Quality Service to the Citizens
- Fine tune existing programs
- Discuss new ideas with the city or town manager or council
- Surround yourself with good people
- Find out how other successful police chiefs or managers do it
- Always Follow up

Now let us look at the fatal error for a police chief or top leader that ultimately will lead to a termination or resignation:

- Taking for Granted
- Us against Them attitude
- Resting on your laurels and doing nothing
- Let others do all the work
- Sitting back and taking it easy
- Losing the Drive
- Being out of sync with the goals of the city
- Getting into a Rut by staying too long
- No new ideas
- Failure to update—an old dinosaurs

One thing for sure the city or town manager or the council will make a change if needed to add a spark. When a team sport is going bad like a football team, you know what the owner is going to do. He is going to fire the head coach or manager of the team. Maybe there are some bad and unmotivated players but the one that will go first is the head coach or manager. It is much easier to replace one person rather than the entire team. I have seen it happen too often when there is a "vote of no confidence" by the rank and file of the police department. The town or city council or police commissioners will rally around the police chief. However, it will only last just so long. In the case of my friend in Newtown, Connecticut, he received a vote of no confidence and the police commissioners did rally around their chief at first. If the rank and file continues to complain about the police chief eventually, they will stand up and take notice. Eventually my friend was terminated. I have seen one chief survive a vote of no confidence in Portsmouth, New Hampshire. Of course, it made the news but after a while, this issue quietly went away. The police chief was a clever politician who quickly mended some fences with the police union. There was a great deal going on behind the scenes that the public did not know. Many times, it is just a ploy by the police union to get some attention and it usually comes up around collective bargaining time.

If there appears to be on-going problems within the organization and some of the actions of the personnel are embarrassing the city, the city council will eventually make a change. If the current police chief cannot control the problems then the council will find someone who will.

Measure of Success

The question always comes up, "How do you know if you are doing it right?" The answer is simple, you will know. As I stated earlier, I like to establish a pattern of small victories that I can show the town manager and council. The little victories over time will have an accumulative effect. I know it works because I was very successful at it. Obviously, if you are not doing it their way one thing is certain, you will hear about it. Each council member and the mayor have their own pet peeve. All you have to do is find out what it is and take care of it.

In Fort Lupton, Colorado, the council members were interested in straightening out the department and that was only part of the problem. The real agenda many of them had was the code enforcement in the community. Unbelievably they were more interested in people leaving their empty trashcans at the front of the houses too long, trash and junk cars on someone's property or dogs roaming at large. Sometimes I wondered about the priorities of the community when they asked me questions about code enforcement problems and not about serious crime. You would have thought it would have been just the opposite. Now, real cops are not interested in empty trashcans in front of a home. It was a priority with many of the council members so I made it a point to take care of the problem and to make sure my code enforcement officer was taking care of business. In most police department, the code enforcement function was separate but not in Fort Lupton. One thing for sure, if the council members ask you to do something, they will ask later during the council meeting and it would be smart to have your response ready.

If a council member wanted some information or needed something accomplished, I made it a point to take care of their concern as soon as possible. Some might say, "I am not going to kiss up to them." I look at it this way, if I take care of their concerns then hopefully, they will appreciate what I am doing and be supportive of my programs. See, I look at the long term. If I take care of their concerns and make them look good in front of their constituents then at budget time they will take care of my requests. I look at it this way, "One hand washes the other." It certainly worked for me at budget time. My personnel were always amazed at the capital outlay requests, such as police vehicles, radar units, and handguns that were approved by the council. This strategy worked every time.

How can you tell if everything is coming together as planned? There are various indicators such as the town manager and council, the employees and most of all the community. If you are doing it right, you will know and likewise if it is not going exactly as planned, you will know too. There is no big secret and you do not even have to run an approval survey, you just know if all the pieces of the puzzle fit. The only problem when everything is running smooth is the rumors. There is always something or someone who tries to interfere with the smooth operation. Sometimes out of nowhere, an employee will come up with a big issue. You ask yourself this question, "Where did he dream this one up?"

One indicator I always look for are the letters to the editor. Even though they are just opinions many times, it will reflect the attitude towards the police department if a citizen was treated fairly or not. You would be surprised to find out who reads these letters of the editor. I know that the town manager, mayor and council members read them all the time. Fortunately, most of the time people wrote more positive than negative comments. These letters would tell me that the officers were doing a good job in providing service to the community. Were we perfect all the time? No, there were times when mistakes were made but we worked hard to overcome them.

When you get right down to it, there are only two choices, success or failure. There is no middle road. Most of the time, we can predict our own destiny and I chose to succeed. Running a police department can be very rewarding and at the same time very frustrating. It is hard to describe because there are so many intangibles, namely the politicians in power at the time. Everyone knows the complexion and tone of the council can change with a new election.

If you have the determination, mindset and desire to succeed, you will be a successful police chief or top executive. There is no reason to think otherwise. If we tell ourselves things are going badly and there is no hope, then you will fail. If you are enjoying your self and things are going very well just hang on and enjoy the ride.

Chapter 24
After Word

I was quite fortunate to have experienced being police chief in three communities in different states. I did not plan it that way but maybe it was fate. Some police chiefs only do it once; some retire, move on or are terminated. There are so many police chiefs that do not make it for one reason or another, but mainly politics is why I found it necessary to write this book. I wanted to convey my experiences, successes and missteps to help pave the way for others. Unless someone is groomed for the position going up through the ranks, there is very little or no preparation for what is in store for the police chief. Quite frankly, the management 101 courses will not do the trick. What is lacking in many of the police executive type programs is the practical application. We often hear about the theories and they are nice but what is it like to be a police chief. Experience is the best teacher. Unfortunately, some police chiefs do not stick around long enough to get the knowledge and experience.

My insights and experiences that I had gained as police chief are valuable. I would never have dreamed about being police chief three times. Originally, I only wanted to do it once. Circumstances were such that it was time to find another department. There are many police chiefs who have been chief just as many times if not more. They were not afraid to move around and are known as the "Carpet Baggers." I never thought of myself as one but as circumstances dictated, it turned out that way and not by my choice.

If I had to choose which police department was the best, I would have to think long and hard. Even in Florence, Arizona, there were many things I liked about it and even the town fathers were no so bad. The political turmoil and fallout was so bad it would have been difficult for anyone to succeed in that environment but I made the best of it. This community will experience personnel turn over until the town council decides not to interfere. After all the horror stories I wrote about Florence, after analyzing everything, it was not so bad. The council members in the end were not truthful but they did support our programs. I was proud of the many accomplishments even though it was short lived, but apparently, my philosophy still lives on. My approach was to look forward and not look back. This was why I was not very interested in the failures and shortcomings of the other police chiefs. I did not want to be caught up in the political fiasco. A new police chief going into a police department from the outside has its advantages as well as some disadvantages. I think the advantages far outweigh the disadvantages. Coming into the community for the first time is good because you do not know anyone. Some might say this is a disadvantage but it is not. I like to find out for myself what the good and bad points of each organization are.

There was one thing for sure; I was not about to try and save my job in Florence, Arizona at the expense of another employee. The mayor was hinting around why I did not fire my lieutenant. I was shocked when the mayor asked me directly in executive session of the town council meeting, "Why I did not get rid of the lieutenant like I told you." My answer was simple, the man did not do anything wrong and I further told them he was doing an excellent job for me. This statement must have sealed my fate because I told them what they did not want to hear. Do not make the mistake of terminating someone because of political pressure. It is certainly not an ethical thing to do anyway for even the town manager or council members to suggest or imply someone should be terminated without proper justification. I am morally obligated to follow the Law Enforcement Code of Ethics as adopted by the International Association of Chiefs of Police.

If I had listened to some of the personnel and council members in Fort Lupton, Colorado about certain employees reputed to be bad, I would have had problems. I told everyone the slate was wiped clean. I told them I was not going to be influenced by anyone and would find out for myself the positives as well as the negatives. One sergeant turned out to be one of the hardest working employees that I had. He turned out to be a valuable asset in terms of supervision, grant writing, recruitment and selection, computer technician and a host of other duties. You name it he could do the task and do it very well. I was able to rely on him for sound advice. It would have been the worst mistake of my life to terminate him because of rumor.

Another sergeant who I believed was taking and using earned compensatory time without actual earning it. I had talked earlier about the investigation and the only thing he was probably guilty of was bad judgment. The former police chief allowed the practice of accumulating earned compensatory time without the actual documentation. In many cases, the documentation was lacking. After the investigation had been completed by the Weld County Sheriff's Office, I called him into my office to discuss the findings. He asked me straight out, "Chief do you want me to resign?" He caught me by surprise and I did not expect this response. All I had to say was yes and he would have been gone. However, after thinking about it for a second or two, I told him no. I suspended him for one week without pay and took away one-week vacation. In effect, it amounted to a two-week suspension. He had no problem with the discipline at all. He turned out to be a very productive employee. Rumors were also flying around that he was tipping off drug dealers but none could be proven. Actually, I believed that he was not involved after I had gotten to know him. On April 20, 1999 on the same day as the Columbine massacre, the sergeant passed away after being afflicted with cancer. I was truly saddened to hear of his passing and his widow asked me to say a few words at his funeral mass. It was an honor and privilege to do so. In each case, I was glad that they were part of the organization. Privately, a few council members still had misgivings about both of them but they said, "It is your department, you run it the way you see fit."

I had set the tone early on and from the very beginning, I did not get any interference from anyone. Fort Lupton was really an excellent place to be and together we did wonderful things there. Everything fell right into place. So, what was the difference between Florence and Fort Lupton in terms of success? I introduced similar kinds of programs. Each department was successful but the deciding difference was the town council, namely **POLITICS** in Florence. A police chief may have the expertise to operate a police department but if there is no support from the council then there will be problems. You can translate this to anywhere. The town council in Florence chose to succumb to the political pressure by a few including the former police chief in spite of all the wonderful things that we accomplished. They probably thought incorrectly, of course, that everything would be just wonderful and there would be a smooth transition. Man, were they wrong. Perhaps, if the council had hired a professional police town manager then it may have been a different story. I do not know what they were thinking when they hired a cousin of one of the council members who had no experience in police management. It did not take long for everything to unravel and before he realized it, my replacement experienced some serious morale problems. I think the council regretted those words when they told me there were morale problems. In retrospect, the council members had to rationalize why they did not want to renew my contract. Their reasons were insignificant compared to the problems that developed after I had left. However, looking back I was proud of the many things that we had accomplished together. It was a shame that they could not be continued. At the same time, I do not have any regrets for accepting the position in Florence because I did make a difference even though it was short lived.

Many police chiefs will experience something similar or worse. Many will find themselves without a job. There is no worse feeling to have when one day you are the police chief and the next, Mr. Nobody. The council as they often say, "It is necessary to take action in the interest of the City." As I often found out, much of the council's work is done behind the scenes. Sure, when four council members get together they are supposed to give notice 24 hours in advance for their members. This does not happen. In my case in Florence, Arizona, the council members' conspired behind the scenes and did a great deal of communication. They will tell you there is nothing personal about their action; it is just business. When you lose your job, it sure is personal especially since you bought a home and perhaps your children are in school.

My time in Somersworth, New Hampshire was an experience worth cherishing. My fellow peers who were police chiefs were some of the best people I had known. Many of them have since retired, resigned or were fired. There are many new faces and the reality is that many of them will become victims of the political wrath. Often we hear about the "right fit" for the community. What does this mean? I think what it means are the town manager and/or council members being able to work with the individual. Other words, who do they feel comfortable with the most? It is not how smart you are but how politically savvy you can be. Do not get me wrong, being intelligent is a plus but it takes more than just brains to succeed.

I have seen some laid back police chiefs who had been the head of the department for years. After the police chief retired then I saw a turnover of several police chiefs in the same department. When you have been a police chief for 20 years, it is hard to get rid of him or her. Ask yourself this question, "There must be a reason why this old dinosaurs is still there?" Certainly, he was there for so long that he probably gathered information on council members, a black book if you will. They would not dare to go against the chief. Take a look at J. Edgar Hoover as to why he stayed as the FBI's director for so long. It was reputed that he kept files on great many people including Senators and Congressman. Who knows what was contained in the files? I guess that is one way to keep your job. I am not even suggesting or hinting that you consider this because it certainly can backfire on you. I am a proponent for doing the right thing all the time. When you have to rely on your black book to keep your job, I do not think it is ethical nor should it be done this way.

Often I wondered about Somersworth where it all began. I had survived and lasted longer than any of the other police chiefs in the previous 20 years. In reality I could have stayed much longer if I so chose. As I said early, it was the dumping ground for police chiefs. Even in the worst possible conditions, it is possible to survive if you have the mindset to succeed. It was a struggle in the beginning but I believe that in the seven years I was able to make a difference. Sure, there will be problems because no organization is perfect. When you work with people and they all have different personalities anything can happen. It is just the way it is. Some individuals will intentionally gossip and spread rumors just to see what might happen. Unfortunately, people will do it just to test you.

Some people thrive on playing mind games with you and your personnel. Sometimes I cannot understand for the life of me why someone would intentionally upset the apple cart when things are going so well. Some individuals will approach you and hit you with a problem and you ask yourself, "Where did they dream this one up?" If people minded their own business and did exactly what they were supposed to do then there would be no problems. People in organizations make problems; the police chief is just trying to sort thing out. One mistake that police chiefs make is ignoring the little problems. Even though the problems may seem insignificant to you, it is important to the person. These little problems will fester and grow into bigger ones if left unchecked. Before you realize it, there are major personnel problems that should have been dealt with long ago. They always seem to come back to bite the police chief.

The friends that I had made in Somersworth I will never forget. Mayor Jim McLin was the mayor for many years until he decided to not run again. He was the longest running mayor in the city's history. I believe the reason Somersworth is the way it is today is the direct result of the mayor's leadership. He was a straight shooter and above all was honest. Imagine, a politician telling the truth but he did. Even though there were some personnel problems every now and then, I have to say that the city manager, mayor and city council were very supportive. It worked because there was very little or no political interference. Everything had to go through the city town manager and that is the way it should be.

Police chiefs or managers have to persevere to make the organization the best it can be and above all to do the right thing. I always followed this one rule, the decision may be unpopular but above all, **you have to do what is right**. If you **practice what you preach** and **walk the talk**, you will be successful. Failure should not even be a word in the dictionary. If you want to fail or give up, then you will. There is no question about it. If at first you do not succeed, try again. Some of our greatest leaders in our great country had some failures but they overcame them. If each supervisor, middle and upper management and the police chief stressed success look at what could be accomplished.

My purpose in writing this book was to give some valuable insight from the supervisor to police chief in running a police department from a different perspective. Since I was a police chief in three communities, I think I am qualified to speak of all the ins and outs and ramifications in being a police chief. I hope that the police chief candidate, lower level supervisors, middle and upper management and the police chief can pick up some tips, suggestions and recommendations in helping their situation. If I can help you to survive and to make a difference in your community then I will have done my job.

The End or is it The New Beginning

Addendum A

Agreement made on 16th day March, between the Town of Florence, a municipal corporation located at 133 North Main Street, Florence, Arizona 85232, hereinafter referred to as the "Town", and Patrick L. Cote, hereinafter referred to as the "Chief of Police".

Recitals;

WHEREAS, the Town desires to employ a qualified and professional Chief of Police; and

WHEREAS, the Chief of Police is qualified through education, training and experience to provide the professional services sought by the Town and can and will within ninety (90) days, qualify as a professional police officer under the rules and regulations established by the Arizona Peace Officer Standards and Training Board, attached hereto and incorporated herein as if set forth in full; and

WHEREAS, the Town has offered the Chief of Police employment in the capacity of Chief Law Enforcement Officer for the Town, for such compensation, benefits and under the terms and conditions set forth below, and the Chief of Police is willing to accept employment on such terms and commence his employment with the Town on April 10, 19957 and

WHEREAS, the Chief of Police understands and agrees that he will accept said employment with the understanding that he will serve as Chief of Police only so long as a majority of the Town council wish him to serve in said capacity, i.e., at the will of the council without rights of appeal except as herein provided.

In Consideration of the above, it is mutually agreed as follows:

Section 1:   Employment and Duties.

473

A. The Town hereby employs the Chief of Police, and the Chief of Police accepts such employment, for an anticipated. minimum period Of two (2) years, subject to renewal by the written consent of both parties, with the understanding that he will establish and maintain his Arizona Peace Officer Certification and further that he will use his best full time professional effort as Chief of Police for the Town.

B. The Chief of Police agrees to perform said duties on an as needed basis, i.e., in a manner that is customary to the profession, including but not limited to, enforcement of the Town Code and State laws within the Town, budgetary and fiscal responsibility, 'department oversight and supervision, community relations, and at all times to exercise the appropriate degree of professional care, to keep the Mayor and Council informed, and *to* effectively manage the police department and employees,

C. The Chief of Police also understands and agrees that subject to the requirements of his office imposed upon him by State Law and the Town Code, the Town Manager and Town Council shall have the power to determine, from time to time, the specific duties to be performed by the Chief of Police, and the general manner by which those duties shall be performed. The Chief of Police shall report directly to the Town Manager, and only as required to the Town Council, but he shall serve at the pleasure of the Council. In furtherance thereof the Chief of Police understands and agrees that the Town Manager and/or Town Council intend and expect to meet with the Chief of Police at least twice annually to receive the Chief of Police's status report on his administrative accomplishments and recommendations and to candidly discuss and evaluate the same from the standpoint of the Manager's and Council's goals and concerns. Said special meetings shall, at the discretion of the Manager and Council, be held in closed executive session or open work session during the months of January and June or *as* otherwise directed by the Manager or a majority vote of the Council.

D. The Chief of Police shall devote his full working professional time and attention to the management of the Florence Police Department and enforcement of the Town code and State Law within the Town of Florence, and he shall not, without the written consent of the Manager and/or Council, directly or indirectly render services of a professional nature to or for any other person, firm or entity for compensation, or engage in any practice or professional endeavor that compromises the interests of the Town. However, the expenditure of reasonable time and resources for civic, community, political or professional activities shall not be deemed a breach of this provision and is expected.

Section II: Compensation and Benefits.

A.   Salary. For all services rendered by the Chief of Police under this agreement, the Town shall pay the Chief of Police an annual salary of $ 48,000.00 payable **in** the same manner as is customary for other Town employees. Said basic salary may be changed by the Town at any time.

B.   Annual salary adjustment. The parties further agree that on an annual basis, with the date of final adoption of the annual budget serving as an anniversary date, the Chief of Police shall he entitled to a reasonable and appropriate salary adjustment, compatible with the Chief's performance. *The minimum salary adjustment shall be an annual cost—of—living adjustment equal to that provided for other Town employees.*

C.   The Town shall compensate the Chief of Police for all reasonable travel and business expenditures of the Chief of Police in accordance with the general personnel policies of the Town, including but not limited to the payment of professional association dues, membership fees and expenses in a civic organization, one annual out—of—state International Association of Chiefs of Police conference and at least one appropriate in-state professional conference.

D.   The Town shall maintain a comprehensive general liability and errors and omissions policy which protects the Chief of Police from any and all claims associated with the reasonable performance of the Chief's duties.

E.   Vacation, The Chief of Police shall be entitled to a paid vacation on the same basis as other Town employees. Such vacation time shall be effectively coordinated with the Town Manager and Town Council to ensure effective management of the Police Department during the Chief's vacation.

F.   Termination or Suspension,

> 1. <u>Without Cause</u>: If this. contract or the Chief's employment is terminated by the Town, without cause, as hereafter provided, or the Chief or Police is asked to resign by a majority vote of the Town Council, or if a court of competent jurisdiction were to order the reinstatement of the former Chief of Police, Tom Rankin, the Chief of Police shall be given a minimum of six (6) months severance pay/consulting fee end in addition to his regular salary earned during said six (6} month period the Chief of Police and his spouse shall be entitled to an extension of benefits for up to six (6) months, in accordance with the Towns Personnel Rules and Regulations, including health insurance coverage. Provided however, that

during said six (6) month period the Chief shall be required to use hi~ best effort to find and accept new employment and upon beginning the Same said severance pay including benefits shall terminate,

2, Resignation; In the event the Chief voluntarily resigns is position with the Town before the expiration of the anticipated minimum two (2) year term of his employment, then the Chief shall give the Town thirty (30) days notice in advance, unless the parties otherwise agree, and in such event the Chief shall not be entitled to any severance pay or continuation of benefits as provided above.

3. <u>With Cause</u>: If the Chief is terminated with cause, which shall include but not be limited to malfeasance or gross misfeasance in the performance of his duties, failure to acquire or maintain Arizona Law Officer Certification, the commission of any illegal act involving personal gain or of a crime against the Town or State, the Town shall have no obligation to pay or provide severance/consulting pay as stated in paragraph P.1 above, or any other compensation or benefits except

4. <u>Suspension</u>: An affirmative vote of a majority of the Council may suspend the Chief from his duties as Chief of Police with full pay and benefits at any time during the term of this Agreement.

G. Car Allowance. The Town shall. provide the use of a municipal vehicle for official use only. The Town shall be responsible for the cost incurred for liability, property damage and comprehensive general liability insurance and for the purchase, operation, maintenance, repair and replacement of said automobile when deemed necessary,

H. Illness and Disability. The Chief of Polite shall be entitled to accrue stoic leave in the manner customary and routinely extended to other municipal employees.

I. Insurance. Chief of Police shall be entitled to insurance coverage, including health and life, in the same manner and fashion customary to other municipal employees, subject to the provision for continuation stated in paragraph F.l above.

J. Retirement. The Chief will be entitled and required to participate in the Arizona Law Officer's Retirement System in the manner and fashion customary to other police department employees.

K. Moving Allowance:

> 1. <u>Allowance</u>: As an additional inducement for the Chief accepting the offer or employment with the Town, the Town has offered and agrees to pay up to $4,500.00 to assist the Chief In the expense of moving to and relocating his family within the Florence vicinity. Said moving expense to be paid by the Chief and reimbursed upon presentation of receipts.

> 2. Should the Chief for any reason resign Within the first twelve (12) months following his start date, as referenced above, said moving-relocation allowance shall be offset, on a monthly pro-rate basis, against any severance pay that would otherwise be payable to the Chief,

TOWN OF FLORENCE   CHIEF OF POLICE
By: _____   _____

Mayor   **Patrick L. Cote**

ATTEST: APPROVED AS TO FORM:
By: _____
_____

Deputy Town Clerk   Town Attorney

Town Council votes to

dismiss Police Chief Cote

The Florence Town Council dismissed Police Chief Patrick Cote Monday night, effective immediately, after a 90-minute closed-door session.

Cote, who has been chief for two years, said Tuesday, "I had a lot of fun and a feeling of accomplishment doing my job as chief of police. ...I did the best I could, I have no ill feelings and I wish everyone well."

Vice Mayor Wilbur Freeman Jr. made the motion to dismiss Cote, citing "a lack of leadership and a true sense of direction in the police department," and saying he desired to make "a positive change for the town's future." Patsy Williams seconded the motion, and the vote was unanimous.

Freeman declined to elaborate after the meeting, except to say there had been "an ongoing problem, particularly in the last six months." Mayor Marsha Day declined to comment.

The council appointed Sgt. Jim Sherwood interim chief of police, and voted to advertise for a new chief.

Cote disagreed with Freeman's assessment of his work.

"Anyone can say there's a lack of leadership, but I take offense to that. I took the reins of the department at a difficult time, a time of political turmoil. There was a clear direction and a clear mission I set for the department. ... Everyone got a copy of that mission statement."

The mission statement, posted at the police department, says in part: "We will serve and protect all people within our jurisdiction with respect, fairness and compassion, with customer service as our approach. We will investigate problems and incidents, seek resolutions and foster a sense of security and safety in our neighborhoods."

Cote provided some insight into what he believed was behind his firing.

"It's just unfortunate that the council chose to talk to selected employees; rather than me, about problems they felt should have been addressed." He said some employees attributed statements to him that he did not make. He was also aware three weeks ago that "an individual was politicking the council" against him, he said.

He was invited to talk to the council for a portion of the closed-door session, and attempted to present his side. However, "I could tell it was futile," Cote said. "It was obvious they had their minds made up."

After the vote, Florence resident Art Snyder told the council of Cote's work to form the TRIAD, an organization to empower and protect senior citizens against crime.

She said the council's action to dismiss Cote "makes me very sad. ... Please be sure a TRIAD program continues in this town and county."

Cote said the TRIAD was just one of the police department's advances since he took over as chief. He noted he has also instituted "community policing," which gave the town two more officers through a community policing grant; a bicycle patrol; and a police dog or "K-9" patrol.

When Cote came to Florence, he said the police department had no policy manual, and no power to ticket parking violators. Now they do.

He said he has also been chairman of the Pinal County Law Enforcement Association, last year and this year, helping to instill better communications and addressing law enforcement issues. For the Florence police, he said he has fostered better relations with the community and with the sheriff's office and county attorney's office.

Cote further noted he assigned one of his officers to the drug task force, for which the department received 100 percent funding through a grant. The department recently took possession of a special "driving under the influence" enforcement cruiser, with a portable Intoxilyzer and video system. Cote was also chosen to sit on the governor's Drug and Gang Task Force Committee.

Although total reported crimes were up last year, burglaries went down approximately 30 percent, "which is significant," Cote said.

Cote came to Florence from Somersworth, N.H., where he was chief of police. He was with that department about seven years. Previously, he worked for about 18 years with the police department in Bristol, Conn., where he was born and raised. He also taught criminal justice-related courses at a nearby community college.

Cote has an Associate's Degree in criminal justice, and Bachelor's and Master's degrees in criminal justice management.

According to the terms of Cote's contract with the Town of Florence, he has been fired "without cause," meaning he will be given six months severance pay with benefits. If he accepts new employment before the six months are over, his severance pay and benefits will cease.

"I'd like to thank all the citizens of Florence and all the department heads and employees who received my wife and I very well." Cote said. " ... In particular, I'd like to thank Lt. Jerry Williams, whom I consider an outstanding and dedicated employee."

Cote said he had been criticized for promoting Williams to lieutenant, but "as far as I'm concerned, he's a competent employee ... and he's performed very well."

Cote said he will now turn his attention to looking for another job.

"I'll be a chief of police again," he said. "I have no doubt about that. I have the experience and qualifications to be chief of police anywhere."

About the Author

Patrick Cote recently started a private investigator agency called Cote Investigations & Associates, LLC. His website is **www.coteinvestigations.com**. He is a licensed private investigator in Arizona. His specialties are criminal, civil cases and court preparation.

He is currently teaching for the University of Phoenix for over three and a half years. He had taught at the Louisiana Campus in Metairie and online. Now, he is teaching classes in the Phoenix/Tucson metro area. He also developed new courses for the University of Phoenix.

Patrick Cote was the Director of Public Services at Delgado Community College located in New Orleans, Louisiana and had been there for over two years. He was the coordinator of criminal justice at the West Bank Campus and an Assistant Professor. He developed a Homeland Security and Emergency Management Certificate program for the college and was working on an Associate Degree program when Hurricane Katrina changed everything.

He was in law enforcement for thirty years, the last eleven as Police chief in three states. Most recently, he served as the Director of Public Safety for over two years in Fort Lupton, Colorado and retired in 1999. Prior to Fort Lupton, he was Police chief in Florence, Arizona and served in that capacity for two years. He was also Police chief in Somersworth, New Hampshire for seven years. He began his career in Bristol, Connecticut and rose through the ranks and attained the rank of Captain. He was with that department for eighteen years and decided to retire to assume the position of Police chief in New Hampshire.

He has a Masters of Science degree in Criminal Justice Management from the University of New Haven, West Haven, Connecticut; a Bachelors of Science degree in Criminal Justice Administration from Western Connecticut State University, Danbury, Connecticut; and an Associate of Science in Criminal Justice from Tunxis Community College, Farmington, Connecticut.

ISBN 142512069-5